AF361446

The Sutra
of
Perfect
Enlightenment

The Sutra of Perfect Enlightenment

Korean Buddhism's Guide to Meditation

(With Commentary by the Sŏn Monk Kihwa)

Translated and with an Introduction by

A. Charles Muller

State University of New York Press

Published by
State University of New York Press, Albany

For information, address the State University of New York Press,
State University Plaza, Albany, NY 12246

Production by Marilyn P. Semerad
Marketing by Dana E. Yanulavich

Library of Congress Cataloging-in-Publication Data

Ta fang kuang yuan chueh hsiu to-lo liao i ching. English & Chinese
    The Sutra of perfect enlightenment : Korean Buddhism's guide to
  meditation ; with the commentary by the Son Monk Kihwa / A Charles
  Muller.
      p.   cm. — (SUNY series in Korean studies)
    Includes bibliographical references and index.
    ISBN 0–7914–4101–6
    ISBN 0–7914–4102–4 (pbk.)
    I. Muller, A. Charles, 1953–   . II. Kihwa, 1376–1433.   Taebanggwang
  won'gak sudara youi kyong sorui.   English. 1999. III. Title. IV.
  Series.
  BQ2232.E5 M85   1999
  294.3'85—dc21
                                                      98–39738
                                                      CIP

10 9 8 7 6 5 4 3 2 1

Contents

Preface

I first came across the *Sutra of Perfect Enlightenment (SPE)* at the outset of my graduate studies in East Asian Buddhism at the University of Virginia, where, in the course of my reading of late T'ang and Sung Ch'an works, I found the sutra cited with frequency. Some further investigation led me to understand that the *SPE* was one of the most important documents in the history of the Ch'an tradition—that it had long served as a definitive guide to meditation practice, and that it had been studied and extensively commented on by a number of Ch'an luminaries, not least of whom was Tsung-mi, the influential T'ang dynasty scholar-monk. Knowing this, I wondered at the fact that aside from a 1962 translation by Charles Luk, there was almost nothing else to be found on the sutra in the English language. My interest thus aroused, I began to study the text in earnest, along with its various commentaries and its historical background—and began my initial work at the English translation presented here.

In 1988, I began the second stage of my graduate studies career in the program in Korean Studies at SUNY Stony Brook, where I had the opportunity to work in some depth on the *SPE* together with Sung Bae Park, one of the world's foremost authorities on Korean Buddhism. It was in this circumstance that I was introduced to the major Korean commentary on the *SPE*, that by the Koryŏ-Chosŏn monk Kihwa. Reading Kihwa's commentary, I found both its literary style and its religious insight to be exceptional, to the point where reading the commentary was in many places more satisfying than the sutra itself, and so I became newly absorbed in the study of the sutra in conjunction with this commentary. Further investigation revealed that the *SPE* held an even more prominent place in Korean Sŏn than it had in Chinese Ch'an, as from roughly the time of the thirteenth century it had been installed as one of the basic texts used in the Korean monastic educational system, a position from which it would never be displaced. This work also led me to deeper investigation into the oeuvre of Kihwa, one of the most influential scholar-monks in Korean Buddhist history. I ended up doing my dissertation on Kihwa, and presently have other projects in progress concerning his works. Upon completing my dissertation, I was fortunate enough to receive a grant allowing me a period of concentrated and secluded study in Korea, during which time I returned with full attention to the *SPE* and Kihwa's commentary, finally completing my draft translation of the combined text.

It is my hope that this combined translation and commentary will provide a valuable resource for students and scholars of East Asian meditative Buddhism who wish to deepen their understanding of its foundational philosophical and soteriological theories, as well as broaden their understanding of what is implied by the concept of "Ch'an/Sŏn/Zen practice." This work should also help to deepen general scholarly knowledge about Korean Sŏn, especially the role that scriptural study has played in that tradition. And since the situation of the shameful neglect of Korean Buddhist materials has still not changed that much since it first began to be noted in Western scholarship a decade or so ago, I hope that this translation, as well as the introduction, which contains an extensive discussion of certain aspects of Korean Buddhist history, will help in a small way to correct this deficiency.

Finally, this translation should also serve as a useful guide to those who are pursuing Ch'an/Sŏn/Zen practice, as it is packed full of concrete advice on Buddhist philosophy, meditation, monastic conduct, and so forth, presented in a format that simply cannot be found in presently existing works on Zen in Western languages. Up to the present, Zen practitioners in the West have had little other than *kōan* collections or the sermons of their local teachers to serve as their guide, so this work should help to fill in this gap. In studying the *SPE*, such practitioners will have access to the instruction of one of the most authoritative and enduring meditation manuals in the entire tradition.

I have to thank, more than anyone else on the completion of this work, my longtime mentor at SUNY Stony Brook, Sung Bae Park, who from the time of our first meeting during my undergraduate days to the completion of my graduate studies has sparked, energized, and continually helped me to reclarify my interest in, and understanding of, East Asian Buddhism. It is he who led me to the treasure-trove of the field of Korean Buddhism, and I look forward to working with him further in the vitally important task of opening up this area of knowledge to the English-speaking world.

I am also indebted to Robert Siegel, the managing editor of the Korean Studies series at Stony Brook, who in overseeing the early production of the manuscript, offered valuable suggestions for its improvement. I would also like to offer my heartfelt thanks to Jin Young Park, who carefully checked my translation, and saved me from much possible embarrassment. Valuable corrections and suggestions on the introduction were made by my colleague here at Toyo Gakuen, Brian McVeigh. The main part of the translation was completed during my stay in 1994 at the Academy of Korean Studies, with the generous financial support of the Korea Foundation, and I would like to thank both of these organizations for their support. Finally, much thanks are deserved by my wife Maki, who has supported me in countless ways during the long process of finishing this work.

Cover Art: Calligraphy—"Sutra of Perfect Enlightenment" by Masatsugu Miyaji (Osaka, Japan)

Abbreviations and Conventions

AMF — *Treatise on the Awakening of Mahāyāna Faith* (*Ta-sheng ch'i-hsin lun* 大乘起信論)

CYC — *Compilation of Yung-chia of the Ch'an School* (*Ch'an-tsung Yung-chia chi* 禪宗永嘉集)

DS — *Diamond Sutra* (*Chin-kang po-jo po-lo-mi ching* 金剛般若波羅蜜經)

HPC — *Han'guk pulgyo chŏnsŏ* (The Collected Texts of Korean Buddhism 韓國佛教全書)

SHM — *Sutra of the Heroic March Samādhi* (*Śūraṃgama-sūtra, Shou-leng-yen ching* 首楞嚴經)

SPE — *Sutra of Perfect Enlightenment* (*Yüan chüeh ching* 圓覺經)

T — *Taishō shinshū daizōkyō* 大正新脩大藏經

Z — *Dai nihon zokuzōkyō* 大日本續藏經

Terms that are originally of Sanskrit origin but that are now included in English language dictionaries will not normally be diacriticalized, unless the situation calls for it. For example, the term *sutra* will not be diacriticalized in general circumstances, nor will it be diacriticalized in English titles of scriptures, such as *Platform Sutra*. But it will be diacriticalized in the context of the Sanskrit title of a text, such as *Vajrasamādhi-sūtra*.

Chinese readings of Sino-Korean logographs are romanized in the Wade-Giles system and Korean is romanized with McCune-Reischauer. In the case where both readings are given, the Chinese is listed first and Korean second. For example: *chieh/kye*.

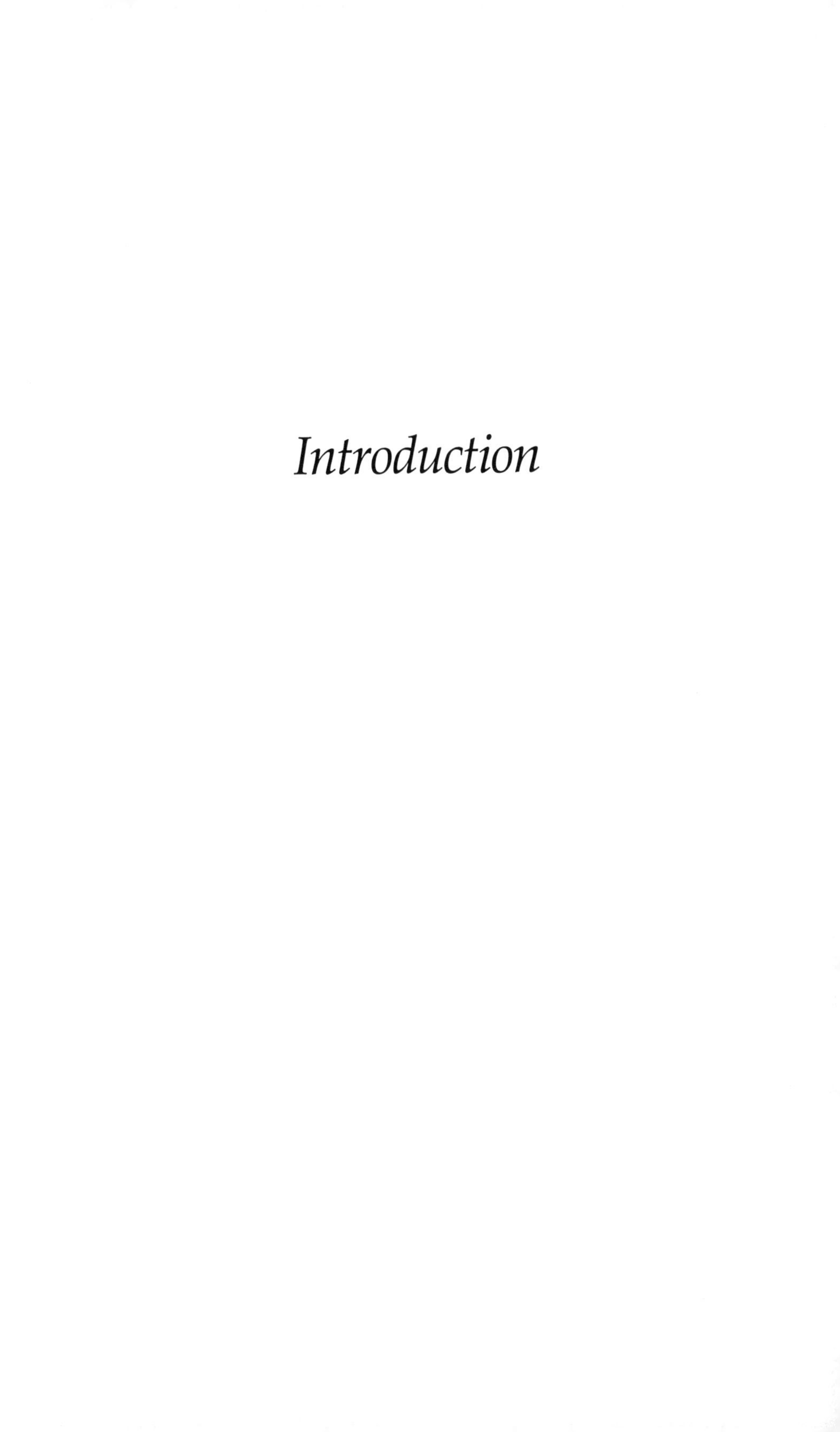

Introduction

Introduction

What Is the *Sutra of Perfect Enlightenment*?

The *Sutra of Perfect Enlightenment* (Ch. *Yüan chüeh ching* 圓覺經 [*SPE*])[1] is a Buddhist scripture that has its origins within the Ch'an and Hua-yen circles of learning, probably composed in China around the beginning of the eighth century. The *SPE* was extremely popular and influential within the meditation-oriented Buddhist schools of East Asia: first in Chinese Ch'an, where its influence was considerable, and then later in Korean Sŏn, where it grew in popularity to the extent that it was made part of the official monastic curriculum of the main Korean school, the Chogye. The *SPE* also had some influence in Japan, although it never received the kind of attention from the Zen schools there that it did in China and Korea.

The high degree of influence and popularity of this scripture can be attributed to two main factors. The first is the distinctly East Asian metaphysical dimension of its soteriology, as the *SPE* contains, in a tightly organized format, focused discussions of the most important theoretical issues concerning the nature of enlightenment that were at the fore of the East Asian Buddhist consciousness at its period of maturation. These are discussed through conceptual frameworks that have their antecedents in East Asian indigenous Buddhist texts such as the *Awakening of Mahāyāna Faith* and *Vajrasamādhi-sūtra*, in indigenous schools such as T'ien-t'ai and Hua-yen, as well as in the pre-Buddhist thought-systems of Confucianism and Taoism.

The second is the *SPE*'s highly practical and concise orientation: much of its content consists of direct instruction on matters of meditation and other related religious issues, such as monastic ritual, confession, the means of selecting a proper teacher, how to maintain a proper relationship with such a teacher, and so on. A large portion of the meditation-related explanations are not merely descriptive, but performative, which means that the reading of such passages is in itself a meditative exercise. The *SPE* does not only explain to its reader the philosophy that grounds the "as-illusion *samādhi*"—it directly leads him/her through an exercise aimed at its attainment in the course of reading.

The introduction to the *SPE* offered in the following pages will serve to frame the background of the scripture, in terms of the circumstances of its production, its doctrinal/practical content, and its seminal role in the development of subsequent East Asian, and especially Korean, Buddhist meditative practice. This introduction will be followed by the main segment of the present work: a translation of the sutra along with the full commentary by the influential Chosŏn Korean monk Kihwa.

Chinese Origins and Effects

The Production of Indigenous Scriptures

Assimilation of Buddhism in East Asia. The period of time that it took for Buddhism to become fully assimilated and stabilized throughout the entire East Asian region was rather long—at least seven centuries. That such a length of time was required is due to two general circumstances: (1) the wide diversity and deep complexity of the Buddhist teachings, and (2) the considerable cultural and linguistic distance that lay between the peoples of the Indian and the East Asian regions.

This long period of assimilation can, for the sake of the present discussion, be roughly divided into three periods of early, middle, and late. The early period, from around the first through third centuries, was the time during which the initial studies and translations of Buddhist texts were being undertaken, but wherein Buddhism was, for the most part, only partially and poorly understood. During the middle period, from approximately the fourth through the sixth centuries, the task of translation of the majority of the important Indian scriptures was completed, with the work of interpretation and categorization of these materials well on its way. This allowed for the formation of distinct sects based on certain Indian scriptural traditions, such as the San-lun, Nirvana (sutra), and Satyasiddhi sects. During the late period, from the middle of the sixth through the ninth centuries, a dramatic new chapter unfolded, with the appearance of new, indigenously originated schools of Buddhism, whose leaders began to articulate new interpretations of the *buddhadharma* that accorded more fully with native East Asian metaphysical and soteriological intuitions.

This third period can again be further subdivided into early and late. The formulators of the East Asian doctrines during the earlier part of this period tended to go to greater lengths to provide an Indian footing for their new ideas. Later thinkers on the other hand, tended to demonstrate greater cultural self-confidence, gradually abandoning the practice of expressing everything through Indian paradigms. Nonetheless, in both the early and late phases of this third period, the general type of Buddhist doctrinal texts that were generated were no longer concerned merely with the transmission of the religion as the perpetuation of its Indian schools and their doctrines. Rather, they paid attention to the articulation of new East Asian interpretations, which in turn were reflected in the formation of new indigenous schools. The major new sects that formed during this period, and that imparted long-term influence on East Asian Buddhist philosophy and practice were the schools of T'ien-t'ai, Pure Land, Hua-yen and Ch'an (Zen).

Indigenous Schools. The first "original school" to appear on East Asian soil was T'ien-t'ai, based primarily on the writings of its de facto founder Chih-i (智顗 538–597). Chih-i was the most successful early figure in terms of his ability to systematically organize the various types of teachings that had been imported from India in such a way that their relationship with each other made sense. Based on his studies of such texts as the *Lotus Sutra, Hua-yen ching,* and *Ta-chih-tu lun,* Chih-i devised his own system of practice utilizing the basic Indian Buddhist meditation exercises of *śamatha* and *vipaśyanā.* Although the T'ien-t'ai school would not continue to hold widespread influence as a distinct entity in later periods of Chinese Buddhism, its doctrinal and practice-related innovations played an important role in the formation of the two later influential schools—Hua-yen and Ch'an.

The seventh century also witnessed the flowering of the Pure Land school, which received its greatest impetus through the works of Shan-tao (善導 613–681), who popularized the practice of chanting the Buddha's name and faith in rebirth in the pure Western paradise. Pure Land became popular in all of the regions of East Asia, especially among the common people, as most of its practices could be followed without needing a deep scholarly understanding of Buddhist philosophy. Many of Pure Land's doctrines, such as that of declining stages of the power of the Buddhist dispensation and the conception of rebirth in the Pure Land, would end up becoming assimilated into the general East Asian Buddhist consciousness, as can be seen by the frequent appearance of Pure Land terminology in the *Sutra of Perfect Enlightenment, Awakening of Faith,* and other influential East Asian Buddhist texts.

The Hua-yen school emerged as the product of a dialectical interaction between a highly developed form of Indian Buddhist dependent-origination based metaphysics and indigenous East Asian metaphysical intuitions of an organically interconnected universe. The early formulators of Hua-yen doctrine, inspired by the miraculous worldview described in the Indian-originated *Avataṃsaka-sūtra* (translated into Chinese as

the *Hua-yen ching*), rearticulated this view, creating a new array of East
Asian metaphysical terminology for its description. At the center of
this new articulation was the language of the relationship of the four
dharmadhātus, or four "realms of reality" (*ssu fa-chieh* 四法界): the realm
of phenomena (*shih* 事); the realm of principle (*li* 理); the realm of nonobstruction between principle and phenomena (*li-shih wu-ai* 理事無
礙); and the realm of nonobstruction between individual phenomena
(*shih-shih wu-ai* 事事無礙). The early Hua-yen thinkers produced a
large corpus of influential philosophical material, and although the
Hua-yen school, like T'ien-t'ai, would also eventually decline as a major
separate and distinct force within the Chinese Buddhist landscape, its
doctrines made a deep impression on the formation of Ch'an thought,
as well as on the orthodox Neo-Confucian metaphysics of the Ch'eng
brothers and Chu Hsi.[2] The Hua-yen school had its deepest and longest-
lasting impact, however, in Korea, where, under the Korean name of
Hwaŏm, it flourished as the leading doctrinal sect for several centuries.
Later, after Hwaŏm's forced assimilation into the Korean meditational
Sŏn school, Sŏn monks remained deeply affected by the Hwaŏm worldview, and many continued to carry out full-scale Hwaŏm scholarship,
a tendency that continues down to the present day.

The Ch'an movement came into being sharing with the Hua-yen
worldview of non-obstruction between phenomena, coupled with a
strong practical orientation that came as a reaction against a perceived
unbalanced stress on scholarly endeavors. This is not to say that prior
forms of East Asian Buddhism had been wholly devoid of the aspects
of meditation and concrete practice toward enlightenment. But the
Ch'an founders came to focus with marked intensity on these aspects
of the religion, developing and fine-tuning them for more comprehensive application in ways that were in accord with the adaptations of
Buddhism to East Asian metaphysical/soteriological intuitions. The
rhetoric derived from this emphasis on concrete practice as opposed to
textual study would later reify, to the extent that the Ch'an movement
came to be caricaturized as "antitextual."

Yet, while many Ch'an writings of the late T'ang and Sung periods
debunked scriptural study, all of the main soteriological positions of
the movement were initially articulated in scriptures. Early Ch'an had
relied on scriptures of Indian origin such as the *Diamond Sutra* and
Laṅkāvatāra-sūtra. But the most significant influences on Ch'an would
end up coming from texts that were composed in East Asia. Among
these East Asian scriptures were texts written by East Asian monks,
whose local origins were plainly indicated in the texts themselves. Such
works include the *Platform Sutra of the Sixth Patriarch* (*Liu-tsu tan ching*),
attributed to a monk named Hui-neng (慧能 638–713),[3] and the *Song
of Enlightenment* (*Ch'eng-tao k'o*), by Hui-neng's student Yung-chia

Hsüan-chüeh (永嘉玄覺 665–713). There were also other texts, produced in the same intellectual circles, whose authors attempted to dissimulate their East Asian provenance. These comprise the Ch'an/Hua-yen/*tathāgatagarbha*-related segment of the East Asian Buddhist *apocrypha*.

Indigenous Texts. The term *apocrypha* is derived from the Greek *apokruphos*, referring to writings that are "secret." The field of English-language Buddhist studies, lacking preexistent technical terminology for the Chinese words *i-ching* (疑經 "scriptures of doubtful authenticity") and *wei-ching* (偽經 "spurious scriptures") borrowed the rubric *apocrypha* from biblical studies, where it had been used to designate a class of literature that, although not necessarily considered heretical, had not, for various reasons, been included into the biblical canon during its formation during the first few centuries after Christ, usually due to doubts regarding authorship or questions of doctrine.[4] Although the term has various shades of meaning, in its most common usage it carries pejorative connotations, as do the original Chinese terms that it is used to translate.

The writing of Chinese scriptures categorized as *i-ching* and *wei-ching* in Chinese Buddhism began at the time of the first introduction of the new religion into East Asia from India and Central Asia, as East Asian Buddhists began to write texts to which they attributed Indian origin and presented as the words of the Buddha. The composition of these "forged" texts in East Asia occurred as a component of the process of assimilation of the new Indian religion into the sinitic cultural sphere. In order to gain full acceptance into East Asia, the Buddhist religion needed to make a wide range of adjustments to new cultural, political, and philosophical sensibilities, and much of the expression of these adjustments came in the form of new compositions.

The new indigenous texts were written on a wide range of themes. A major portion of the earlier East Asian apocryphal texts attempted to overcome problems of initial acceptance. Other scriptures were addressed to issues of the relationship between Buddhism and the rulership, while still others paid attention to the relationship of Buddhism to indigenous religious/philosophical beliefs, and so on. Beyond these, throughout the early and late periods of the assimilation of Buddhism into East Asia, texts were written that were ostensibly the product of divine inspiration, or at least that made claims to be the truly revealed teaching of the Buddha. Among all these categories, there were wide variations in quality.[5]

The apocryphal texts that would end up having the deepest influence, and that would attain the highest level of acceptance, was a group of works produced in connection with the process of Buddhism re-expressing itself as a thoroughly "East Asian-ized" religion with distinctive metaphysical and soteriological underpinnings. Such Buddhist works as the *SPE*, *Treatise on Awakening Mahāyāna Faith* (*Ta-sheng ch'i-hsin lun* [*AMF*]), and *Sutra of the Heroic March Samādhi* (*Śūraṃgama-sūtra, Shou-leng-yen ching* [*SHM*]), despite being East Asian products, were universally recognized as containing profound and enlightening discussions that not only accorded with the most recondite of Buddhist principles, but that also more fully and completely defined these principles for their East Asian audience than had even the most important of the previously translated *bona fide* Indian scriptures. As a result, these works became "more than canonical"—they came to form the core of the corpus of texts upon which the distinctive doctrines of the new East Asian schools of Buddhism were based.

In considering this class of texts in their role as vehicles of the articulation of distinct sinicized metaphysical and soteriological agendas, we must remain aware of their close relationship with the equally instrumental nonapocryphal texts that were produced during the same general period, and within the same religious/philosophical circles—that is, such important works of overt East Asian provenance as the *Platform Sutra*, the *Song of Enlightenment*, and other essays by eminent members of the Ch'an and Hua-yen movements. What we will be discussing henceforth, then, will not merely be texts that are called "apocryphal," but a broader category that I will provisionally label "East Asian Ch'an-Hua-yen definitive texts."

Major Soteriological Issues of the Ch'an-Hua-yen Definitive East Asian Texts

What were the distinctive concerns addressed in these East Asian texts? Many issues were derived from ambiguities inherent in the doctrine received from India—one of the most prominent of which was the problem as to whether the human mind was at its basis originally pure or impure. This matter was one for which well-defined indigenous positions had been articulated in China since the mid-Chou, and which had been openly debated at least since the time of Mencius (371–289? BCE).[6] The question was, if the mind was originally pure (as most forms of the Buddhist doctrine seemed to indicate), how could such a thing as defilement and ignorance occur within it? And if the mind was originally impure or ignorant, then how could such a thing as enlightenment, or nirvana, be attainable?

This problematic issue, firmly implanted in the East Asian religious consciousness several centuries before the assimilation of Buddhism, was replayed in the *ālayavijñāna-tathāgatagarbha* debate in fifth–seventh century China and Korea, wherein adherents of the *ālayavijñāna* viewpoint understood the fundamental human mind to be defiled/ignorant and those of *tathāgatagarbha* influence saw the basic mind as pure/enlightened. The East Asian text that addressed this issue most directly was the *AMF*, whose conclusions on this matter would become the basis for the positions taken in subsequent works such as the *SPE*.[7]

Another of the more important soteriological issues was one that would be pursued with intensity in the *Platform Sutra* during the same approximate era as the writing of the *SPE*: the assertion that the Buddhist enlightenment was not attainable by gradual practice, and could only be met in a sudden flash of insight—an experience of enlightened wisdom. This was a matter of serious concern for East Asian Buddhists, and one that has never died as an issue of contention during the long history of the tradition. On one hand, it is obvious that people can gradually improve themselves by means of serious study and reflection, by living a life based on moral principles, or by meditation on some religious principle. But a thorough understanding of the Buddhist concept of *śūnyatā* seems to undermine the possibility of thoroughgoing awakening based on gradualistic (dualistic) constructs. Why? One who undergoes a penetrating experience of emptiness sees that all things are at bottom devoid of characteristics and that the impediments to enlightenment that are to be removed by gradual practice, such as desire and ignorance, are also inherently empty. From this perspective, the conceptual framework that grounds "gradual practice" is rendered meaningless. Suddenists hold not only that gradual enlightenment is impossible, but also that it is exactly one's attachment to gradualistic/ dualistic perceptions of existence and the Way that prevents direct perception of reality. Thus they recommend that practitioners not be trapped in the confines of gradualistic frameworks, but instead endeavor to see correctly, to view existence in an enlightened way, right here, right now; to eliminate all falsity in one sweep, since falsity does not in fact exist. Gradualists in turn reply to such pronouncements by citing the suddenist tendency to ignore the aspect of moral cultivation, and further ask what is to be done in the case of a practitioner who is simply unable to attain such a sudden insight.[8]

The arguments advocating the positions of sudden enlightenment and innate enlightenment overlap, since both are based in a nondualistic view of existence and the Way. From the standpoint of sudden enlightenment, it can be said that all sentient beings are originally buddhas, and hence nothing special needs to be done in order to make them into buddhas. They merely need to awaken to their own Buddha-nature. The gradualist position, on the other hand, tends to see human beings in terms of their deeply rooted ignorance and desire that keep them trapped in the endless cycle of death and rebirth, enmeshed in a web of alternating pleasure and pain. From this standpoint, the only way out is by continuous practice, through many lifetimes if necessary, of the threefold program of morality, concentration, and wisdom.

In addition to the fundamental metaphysical and soteriological questions such as innate enlightenment/ignorance or sudden/gradual illumination, were a number of other matters of a practical nature concerning which East Asian Buddhists perceived a need for a more thorough treatment in their own parlance. For example, a variety of meditation techniques had been transmitted from India, and these remained alongside newly developing meditative strategies of East Asian origin. But the relationship between these techniques had not been sorted out, nor had their relative value in application. Would-be meditators were therefore confused about what type of meditation was most appropriate for their own situation. They also needed to know concrete details about the proper way to arrange meditation retreats, to practice ritualized penance, and so forth.

Resolving Dualistic Opposition in the East Asian Scriptures: Essence-Function. The authors of these East Asian texts with their special soteriological and metaphysical questions had their own distinctive methods of resolving these issues, of which by far the most pervasive was the hermeneutical tool of essence-function (Ch. *t'i-yung*; Kor. *ch'e-yong* 體用).[9] This metaphysical principle, which has its origins deep in the recesses of early Chou thought in such seminal texts as the *Book of Odes*, *Analects*, *I Ching*, and *Tao Te Ching*, became formally defined and used with regularity in the exegetical writings of Confucian/Neo-Taoist scholars of the Latter Han and afterward.

Scholars of the pre-Buddhist Chinese classics had utilized *t'i-yung* and its earlier equivalents, such as *pen-mo* (本末 "roots and branches") in Confucianism and *hei-pai* (黑白 "black and white") of Taoism, among other things, to explain the relationship of inherent human goodness or spiritual harmony with its not-always-manifest permutations. The Confucian concept of inherent goodness is intimated in the early Chou works, and fully articulated in the *Analects* and the *Mencius*. Of central importance in these texts is the basic human quality of *jen* (Kor. *in*; 仁 "humanity," "benevolence"), which expresses itself in various "functions" such as propriety (*li* 禮) and filial piety (*hsiao* 孝). In the practical application of this relationship, the innate purity of human beings is understood to manifest itself through the effect of a transparent penetration (*t'ung-ta/t'ongdal* 通達) into manifest appearance or active function (*yung/yong* 用).[10]

The process of human perfection then, as it is broadly conceived in the classical East Asian tradition, is one of working toward manifesting one's perfect *t'i* in one's variable *yung*. Or from the other perspective, training one's *yung* to be in harmony with one's *t'i*. Accordingly, methods of spiritual training can also be categorized into two general types: those that are *t'i*-oriented, and have an inner-to-outer focus, and those that are *yung*-oriented, and have an outer-to-inner focus. For example, methods of cultivation that emphasize the training of the social human being through moral practices, such as the Confucian Five Relationships or the Buddhist Ten Precepts, can be seen as *yung*-oriented, and those that concentrate on direct perception of reality through contemplation can be seen as *t'i*-oriented. It is because of this fundamental conceptual view of essence-function in personal transformation that there is such a rich development, in East Asian "study-as-practice"[11] language, of metaphors of "polishing," "training," "smelting," "purification," "accordance," "harmonization" (of, or with the essence), and so on.

In Taoist works such as the *Tao Te Ching* and *Chuang Tzu* there are also implications of the fundamental human capacity for sagehood, but in contrast to Confucian texts such as the *Analects* and *Mencius*, its accomplishment tends to be explained through a more "hands-off" and observant approach, and with a greater emphasis on recognizing and harmonizing with *t'i* (the Tao) rather than external training of and through *yung*. The human mind in its pure nature is alluded to variously in the *Tao Te Ching* as the "uncarved block" (*p'u* 樸), which in improper function ends up becoming fragmented in the form of "utensils" (*ch'i* 器), and the "newborn babe" (*ch'ih-tzu* 赤子), originally soft and pliant but that becomes in improper function rigid and lifeless. The process of attaining sagehood is a "return" (*kuei* 歸, *fan* 反) to this pristine state. Instead of attempting to be transformed by following Confucian norms such as benevolence, filial piety, and respect for one's ruler, the Taoist aspirant is advised to free him/herself from rigid adherence to worldly values such as "loyalty" and "righteousness."

Formally being defined in the *t'i-yung* hermeneutical formula in the Latter Han,[12] *t'i* becomes the ontological ultimate of *pen-t'i* (本體) in Neo-Taoism, and commentarial works from all disciplines begin to rely on *t'i-yung* as an overt hermeneutical principle for analyzing earlier literature. Neo-Taoism and Taoist alchemy become much more systematic in their programs for the refinement of the "embryo of the Tao," explaining their path exclusively through *t'i-yung* language.

The Buddhist religion owed much of its success in East Asia to its affinities with this East Asian conception of the person. In the general Mahāyāna Buddhist view that would come to prevail in East Asia, sentient beings, although varying greatly at the level of *yung*, or manifest activity, possess a pure enlightened Buddha-nature at the level of *t'i*, their essence. This "innate-buddhahood" aspect of the Buddhist dharma, although present in Indian *tathāgatagarbha* doctrine, had not received anything like the attention that it would draw from East Asian interpreters of the religion, who became wholly preoccupied with the articulation of the relationship of the innate (本 *pen=t'i*) and actualized (始 *shih=yung*) aspects of enlightenment.[13] Indeed, we might say that the *AMF* was written almost entirely with the resolution of this issue in mind, and that its author set a precedent for definitive apocryphal texts by casting the entire argument within the framework of essence and function. He did this by declaring that the One Mind has both an essential (true thusness) aspect and a functional (defiled/undefiled) aspect. These two aspects are further subcategorized along essence-function lines.

In its specific East Asian Buddhist hermeneutical applications, essence-function is used as a way of looking at things that attempts to resolve the conflicts brought about by the two opposing tendencies to see things in either (1) a fragmentary/dualistic way, or (2) a simple monistic, undifferentiated way. Thus apparent conflicts between the positions of sudden and gradual, or innate and actualized enlightenment (which arise as a result of dualistic interpretation), are perfect objects for essence-function analysis. We can take the Buddhist soteriological problems mentioned above and say that one is advised to see the human being as pure (empty, enlightened) at the level of *essence*, and that it is at the level of *function* that people differ. Those whose minds are properly functioning, that is, *functioning in accordance with their essence—are* called "buddhas" and "bodhisattvas." Those whose innately enlightened minds are functioning improperly—*whose essence is not properly manifested in their function*, are called "sentient beings" or "worldlings." In terms of suddenly versus gradually attained enlightenment: to see human beings, enlightenment, ignorance, and desire as empty (the sudden view) is to apprehend them in terms of their basic nature, or *essence*. To see human beings, enlightenment, ignorance, and desire as existent (the gradual view), is to grasp them in terms of their *function*.

The *AMF* also adds an intermediate category of "attributes" (*hsiang* 相) to distinguish the marks of enlightenment from its active function. The essence-function construction is also the basis for the suddenistic arguments of the influential nondualistic text, the *Platform Sutra*. The essence-function construction furthermore appears in other analogous forms in the texts of other East Asian Buddhist schools, one of the most prominent being the *li-shih* ("principle-phenomena" 理事) terminology used by the philosophers of Hua-yen.

Texts Most Closely Related to the SPE. We know from catalog records that the *SPE* was a relatively late apocryphal work.[14] Its lateness is also suggested by the degree to which the author shows a mature grasp of three central components of its discourse that were articulated in other late developments: the discussion of original enlightenment in the late *tathāgatagarbha* texts, the assertion of sudden enlightenment in the early

Ch'an writings, and the explication of principle and phenomena (*li* and *shih*) by the Hua-yen patriarchs.[15]

Of all these sources however, it is on the *AMF* that the *SPE* shows the most reliance for metaphysical and soteriological formulations. Of first importance is the primacy in both texts of the discourse on original enlightenment/original ignorance and the similarity in the language with which these positions are articulated. For example, both texts state unequivocally that "all sentient beings are originally perfect Buddhas."[16] Given this position, both texts need to address the problem of how original ignorance and original enlightenment are simultaneously possible (or how they are the same thing in essence). Closely related to this are the discussions in both works of exactly how the transition from the unenlightened to the enlightened states occurs. In the *SPE*, Vajragarbha Bodhisattva asks the Buddha:

> World Honored one; if all sentient beings are originally perfect buddhas, then how is it that they all possess ignorance? If sentient beings are originally ignorant, how can you say that they have always been perfect buddhas? If all the worldlings in the ten directions are originally perfectly enlightened, but later give rise to ignorance, at what point does this happen?[17]

The *AMF* asks:

> [I]f all sentient beings have suchness and all of them are permeated by suchness equally, then why are there differences between those who have faith and those who do not, as well as differences in the various times when faith arises?[18]

Both texts give the same basic answer to the question of the nature of ignorance, denying its substantiality. Ignorance itself can only be perceived through aberrant function. The *SPE* says:

> What is ignorance? Good sons, all sentient beings carry manifold inverted intuitions from the beginningless past, and are just like a person who has lost his sense of direction. These people deludedly take the amalgamation of the Four Elements as their "body" and the cognition of the Six Objects as their "mind." Because of this delusion they repeatedly undergo the suffering of life and death. Therefore, we say there is "ignorance."[19]

The *AMF* says:

> [T]herefore, all sentient beings are not called "enlightened." Since, according to original incessant continuity of thought, they have never been free from thought, we say there is "beginningless ignorance."[20]

Both texts also place strong emphasis on the essence-function relationship of enlightenment and ignorance. The author of the *AMF*, after telling the famous water-waves simile (an essence-function analog), concludes by saying "the characteristics of ignorance are not different from the nature of enlightenment; they are neither destructible nor indestructible."[21] In the *SPE*'s chapter of Samantabhadra, the Buddha says in a similar vein, "Good sons, all sentient beings' various manifestations of illusion are born from the perfectly enlightened marvelous mind of the Tathāgata, just like the sky-flowers come to exist in the sky. Even though the illusory flowers are erased, the nature of the sky is indestructible."[22] The *SPE* and *AMF* also share, together with the *SHM*, the sky-flowers simile, the simile of disorientation of East and West, the discussion of the Two Hindrances, and the presentation of a program for the complementary development of *śamatha* and *vipaśyanā* meditation techniques. The points of thematic and linguistic correspondence between the *SPE* and *AMF* are ubiquitous, with the *SHM* also coming very close in many places.

The major difference between the *SPE* and these other texts is that the *SPE*, having a greater degree of direct Ch'an influence, shows greater reluctance to enter into extended metaphysical discussions than the *AMF* on such matters as the nature of the *ālayavijñāna* and its reception of permeation by suchness and defilement. The author of the *SPE* also does not emulate the lengthy and repetitive contemplations of the nature of the six faculties and six objects in the manner of the *SHM*. While the *SPE* addresses these themes, it does so much more concisely.

Two other texts worthy of mention at this point, which treat the same topics (sudden/gradual and innate/actualized enlightenment) through an essence-function framework, and which are in some ways even closer to the *SPE* than either the *AMF* or *SHM*, are the two works by Yung-chia: the *Compilation of Yung-chia of the Ch'an School (Ch'an-tsung Yung-chia chi* [CYC])[23] and the *Song of Enlightenment*. Said to be a direct disciple of Hui-neng, Yung-chia, like many monks of the period, had extensive background in Ch'an, T'ien-t'ai, and Hua-yen. In both of his texts he deals with the above-mentioned important themes of the period, which are also the topics of the *AMF*, *SPE*, and *SHM*.[24]

Tsung-mi and the SPE*'s Chinese Historical and Commentarial Course*

We find the *SPE* first formally listed in the *K'ai-yüan Catalog of Buddhist Texts* in 726, the putative translator being an obscure monk named Buddhatrāta (佛陀多羅).[25] The *SPE* apparently began to gain some measure of popularity soon after its publication, as at least four commentaries were soon written on it.[26] But the greatest part of the popularization of the text came a century after its writing, at the hands of one of East Asian Buddhism's premier scholar-monks, Tsung-mi (宗密 780–841).

Tsung-mi is one of the most important figures in East Asian Buddhist history, especially valued by modern scholars for his detailed analyses of the development of Ch'an and Hua-yen in the context of the intellectual religious climate of his times. He was both a recipient of, and a great contributor to the development of the new forms of indigenous Buddhism.[27] Tsung-mi had his feet well planted in both the scholastic and meditational streams of Buddhism, to the extent that he would later be counted as a patriarch of both the Hua-yen school and the Ho-tse line of Ch'an. He was, like many later Korean monks whom he influenced, deeply interested in both the practical and doctrinal aspects of Buddhism, and especially concerned about the means for the harmonization of the views of those who tended toward exclusivity in either direction.

Tsung-mi studied all the major texts of the Chinese Buddhist canon of his time, specializing in those works with Hua-yen, *tathāgatagarbha*, and Ch'an affinities, and is especially noted for his work in the area of doctrinal classification (i.e., attempting to account for the apparent disparities in the doctrines of various Buddhist sects by categorizing them according to their specific aims). Although he conducted important studies on other texts such as the *Hua-yen ching*, *Awakening of Faith*, and *Diamond Sutra*, and wrote essays on such issues as the rapprochement of the three teachings and the relationship of various schools of Ch'an, Tsung-mi's work on the *Sutra of Perfect Enlightenment* was the centerpiece of his scholarly career. His major exegesis of the sutra was his *Great Commentary on the Sutra of Perfect Enlightenment* (*Yüan chüeh ching ta shu*), during the course of the composition of which he wrote an extensive series of related abridgments, outlines, and subcommentaries.[28]

Tsung-mi praised the *SPE* as a text that offered both philosophical and practical dimensions: a clear and concise description of the attitudes and mechanics related to meditation practice, along with a solid grounding in *AMF*/Hua-yen metaphysical and soteriological principles. The *SPE* was much shorter and more concise than related works such as the *Śūraṃgama* and *Hua-yen* sutras. It was not as philosophically complex as the *AMF*, yet offered more variety in terms both of philosophy and meditation technique than the *Diamond Sutra*. The fact that Tsung-mi, who would eventually be considered as one of the founding fathers of the Hua-yen school, should have rated the *SPE* to be of greater value than the *Hua-yen ching* is worthy of note. He said, in this regard:

> If you want to propagate the truth, single out its quintessence, and
> thoroughly penetrate the ultimate meaning, do not revere the *Hua-*

yen Sutra above all others. Ancient and modern worthies and masters of the Tripitaka in both the western regions and this land have all classified its as supreme, as fully related in [Ch'eng-kuan's] introduction to his commentary. Yet its principles become so confused within its voluminous size that beginners become distraught and have difficulty entering into it. It is not as good as this scripture (the *SPE*), whose single fascicle can be entered immediately.[29]

Subsequent to Tsung-mi's commentaries on the *SPE*, it continued to be a popular subject of commentary in China down through the Ch'ing period. Among the more famous of these commentaries are those by the Southern Sung Buddhist emperor Hsiao-tsung (孝宗 1127–94)[30] and the Ming scholar-monk Te-ch'ing (德清 1546–1623).[31] An examination of the post–Tsung-mi *SPE* commentaries produced in China reveals the deep influence of Tsung-mi on the subsequent tradition, as the later commentators tended greatly to follow and refer to his works.[32]

The *Sutra of Perfect Enlightenment* in Korea before Kihwa

While the *SPE* became quite popular in Chinese Ch'an Buddhism, it would achieve a decidedly more pronounced influence within the Buddhist culture of the Korean peninsula, where it was gradually popularized through its usage by masters of the Korean Sŏn sect. There are a number of reasons for its eventual attainment of high status in Korean Buddhist circles, which we shall explore below at some length. But first we should gain some background on the history of Buddhist textual assimilation in Korea prior to the *SPE*.

Early Scriptural Influences in Korea

Being geographically attached as it was to the Chinese mainland, the transmission of Chinese cultural developments into the Korean peninsula was always fairly rapid. Once the Korean kings had a sufficient conception of the impact of Buddhism on the mainland, they followed the Chinese emperors quickly in accepting and encouraging the growth of Buddhism as a state religion. Although there were often delays due to internal Korean political conflicts, information about Buddhism, including translated texts, always managed to work its way into the Three Kingdoms of Koguryŏ, Paekche, and Silla. During the fifth and sixth centuries of the Three Kingdoms period, translations of important Indian works from the Mādhyamika tradition, as well as Vinaya works and the *Mahāparinirvāna-sūtra*, held significant influence. Toward the end of the Three Kingdoms and during the early part of the Unified Silla (668–936) however, the Korean Buddhist world received a wide variety of other textual influences, most important of which were the *Hua-yen ching* and its related commentarial works, as well as such "original enlightenment" scriptures such as the *Awakening of Faith* and *Laṅkāvatāra-sūtra*. Beyond these, there was also considerable influence from Consciousness-only (Yusik 唯識) and Pure Land.

While these texts were studied and commented on by a number of energetic Silla scholars, by far the most prolific and influential interpreter of the incoming Chinese Buddhist textual corpus was Wŏnhyo (元曉 617–686), who wrote a commentary for virtually every major Buddhist text available at the time.[33] Wŏnhyo is widely recognized by scholars for having inculcated Korean Buddhism with his applied combination of Hwaŏm-interpenetration and *AMF* essence-function philosophy toward the resolution of sectarian disagreements. In his most influential works, such as the *Harmonization of Doctrinal Controversies in Ten Aspects* (*Simmun hwajaeng non*), his commentaries to the *Awakening of Faith* (*Taesŭng kisillon so* and *pyŏlgi*), the *Sutra of Adamantine Absorption* (*Kŭmgang sammaegyŏng non*) and the *Nirvana Sutra* (*Yŏlban'gyŏng chong'yo*), Wŏnhyo repeatedly demonstrated how the two inseparable themes of interpenetration and essence-function could be universally applied to mitigate the tensions resultant of mutual sectarian exclusivity. The precedent toward sectarian harmonization set by Wŏnhyo tended to be followed with regularity by the leading Korean Buddhist thinkers of successive generations. This tendency is typified in the example of Chinul (the individual most fully responsible for the initiation of the synthetic Hwaŏm-Sŏn character of Korean Buddhism) and is also obvious in the "three-teachings" ecumenical efforts of Kihwa and Hyujŏng during the Chosŏn.

Although Wŏnhyo was not an exclusive adherent of the Hwaŏm school, his high evaluation of Hwaŏm philosophy, along with the influence of the works of his colleague Ŭisang (義湘 625–702), contributed greatly to the initial popularization of Hwaŏm. As it turned out, the Hwaŏm school ended up becoming the most influential stream of scholastic Buddhism on the peninsula from the time of Wŏnhyo down to the present. The majority of teachers throughout the Koryŏ and Chosŏn dynasties were deeply influenced by Hwaŏm, as most of them started their ecclesiastical careers with a strong Hwaŏm background. Beyond this, there were external political and societal pressures that tended to force the meditational and scholastic branches of Korean Buddhism together. The combined result of these various forces was that the mainstream Korean Sŏn school ended up exhibiting a Hwaŏm textual-philosophical character quite distinct from that seen in Chinese Ch'an or Japanese Zen. In this Korean Buddhist environment, such a concise text as the *SPE*—which dealt with the most vital soteriological issues related to meditation practice and offered clear explanations of the process of meditation itself, yet which was permeated with a strong Hua-yen flavor—was especially well suited.

Delayed Arrival of the SPE

Since Wŏnhyo's commentaries included such seminal apocryphal works as the *AMF* and *Vajrasamādhi-sūtra*, the lack of a commentary or even mention of the *SPE* in his writings is another indication that the *SPE* is a relatively late-period apocryphon. If Wŏnhyo would have had access to such a text, which combined Hua-yen, *tathāgatagarbha*, and Consciousness-only philosophy in such an erudite and syncretic manner, at the same time presenting clear guidelines for meditation practice, it would have been so close to his own agenda that there is little doubt that he would have paid it great attention.

As Robert Buswell has noted in *Formation of Ch'an Ideology*, it seems that Wŏnhyo's life was reaching its close just as tidings of the new Ch'an school were arriving in Korea.[34] Knowing this and given the fact that the *SPE* was probably written within a generation of Wŏnhyo's death (686), it has to seem a bit odd that there is little or no reference to the *SPE* in Korean Buddhist literature until the time of Ŭich'ŏn (義天 1055–1101), some four centuries later. Yet if we reflect on the sectarian history of the situation, especially in light of the perceptive analysis provided in *Ch'an Ideology*, the relatively late currency of the *SPE* in Korea can probably be explained.

Although the *Vajrasamādhi-sūtra*, which was apparently written a bit earlier, and quite possibly in Korea, was ostensibly a product of an incipient Ch'an movement, it was still a text that was placing much of its bid for canonicity on its Indian-suggestive attributes, as indicated by the creation of a Sanskritized title and the extensive usage of Indian terminology in its metaphysical discussions on the nature of consciousness. In any case, the *Vajrasamādhi-sūtra* was accepted in Korea along with the array of other scriptures that had received commentaries from Wŏnhyo, which means that it was accepted, to one degree or another, into the corpus of texts studied by the Silla scholastic Buddhist community. But the *SPE*, written only a generation or so later, did not make it in with this group, nor would it gain any noticeable recognition in Korea during the next few centuries.

Why did it take the *SPE* some four centuries to gain recognition on the peninsula? If we pay close attention to the timing, we can note that although the *Vajrasamādhi* was the product of an incipient Ch'an movement, that movement itself, as a distinct entity, had not yet entered into Korea on a large scale at the end of the seventh century. Ch'an finally did arrive in Korea on a widespread basis during the eighth and ninth centuries, through the efforts of Korean monks who had traveled to T'ang China for instruction. These early Korean Sŏn leaders established the "Nine Mountain" schools, taking up, in opposition to Silla scholasticism, a strident line of anti-scriptural rhetoric. A strong anti-scriptural attitude is evident in the sermons of early Sŏn leaders such as Toŭi (道義 d. 825) and Muyŏm (無染 801–888), who sharply criticized the scholastic teachings as inferior to the "direct transmission from mind to mind" and the "tongueless" teaching.[35] Although the mid-T'ang Ch'an masters who were the source of initial instruction for these early Korean Sŏn teachers may not have ever been so vehemently antischolastic, the early transmitters of Korean Sŏn tended to place strong emphasis on this aspect, a major part of the reason being the need to establish for themselves a clear identity in contrast with the firmly entrenched Silla scholastic establishment.

Given this outpouring of antitextual rhetoric, it certainly would not have been efficacious for the founders of the Nine Mountain schools to turn around and introduce a *text*, and especially such a text of such dubious origins as the *SPE*, as a basis of canonical support for their position, or as a guide to their system of practice. The *SPE* was not accepted on a wide scale until the Sŏn school had become firmly enough established on the peninsula such that the criticisms from the scholastic schools no longer carried enough weight to cause serious problems. Therefore, while the slightly later timing of the production of the *SPE* would have the effect of making it into a more fully Ch'an-characteristic text than the *Vajrasamādhi-sūtra*, this lateness seems to have ended up delaying the text's proliferation in Korea by a few centuries.

First Appearances of the SPE *in Korea*

The first significant mention of the *SPE* (known in Korean as the *Wŏn'gakkyŏng*) that I have been able to locate in Korean Buddhist literature is in the writings of Ŭich'ŏn, an important Hua-yen scholar of the early-mid Koryŏ who is known for his popularization of Ch'ŏnt'ae (T'ien-t'ai) Buddhism.[36] In his *Taegak kuksa munjip*, Ŭich'ŏn includes a short essay on the *SPE* (*Kang Wŏn'gakkyŏng palsa*) that is telling in terms of the manner in which the sutra was received and the type of later influence it would carry.

In the first half of the *Palsa*, Ŭich'ŏn identifies the themes of the *SPE* with those of the *AMF*, using an essence-function analysis. The second half of the essay is dedicated to the praise of Tsung-mi's commentaries on the text. Ŭich'ŏn reiterates Tsung-mi's high assessment of the *SPE*, as reflecting the most profound content of the *AMF* and *Hua-yen ching*, and as containing the teaching that equally informs the Sŏn and Kyo schools. This short essay well adumbrates the role of the *SPE* as it would be received in the subsequent Korean tradition: first, the reception and influence of the *SPE* in Korea can never be separated from the personage of Tsung-mi, who, in conjunction with his commentaries on the text, held a commanding influence on the development of orthodox Sŏn doctrine; second, its citation and its influence would invariably come in close conjunction with two other texts whose meaning it is understood as having captured and reflected in condensed form—the *AMF* and *Hua-yen Ching* (*HYC*); and finally, its role as a text that bridged the gap between Sŏn and Kyo. The only other important role of the *SPE* not mentioned here, but which is nonetheless implicit in the invocation of the name of Tsung-mi, is the role of the *SPE* as an arbiter of innate/actualized and sudden/gradual soteriological polarities.

The SPE *in the Works of Chinul*

The individual most responsible for the initial impact of the *SPE* on Korean Sŏn is the same man who introduced an array of related issues in defining the entire future course of Korean Sŏn—Chinul (知訥 1158–1210). Enough has already been published on Chinul that we need not go into extensive detail here regarding his life and thought.[37] It suffices to say that aside from Wŏnhyo, Chinul played the most important role of any figure in Korean Buddhism for determining its future orientation. Besides the basic work of defining and maintaining a pure system of Buddhist study and practice in what was a declining religious environment, Chinul devoted his energies to the effort of reconciling divisive factors that threatened to break down the progress of the solidification of Korean Sŏn, and that threatened to obstruct the course of personal practice. In solving these concerns, Chinul turned to, as two of his most consistent resources, Tsung-mi and the *SPE*.[38] The prominence of the *SPE* in Chinul's writings has much to do with the basic affinity between the text and Chinul's views on innate and actualized enlightenment, the nature of ignorance, and methods of practice.

The most direct way to summarize Chinul's view on practice and enlightenment is to say that his perspective is overwhelmingly essence-function oriented. In virtually all of his writings, Chinul identifies the basic quality of the human mind to be pure enlightenment, which means, at the level of their most basic nature, human beings are equally buddhas. The distinctions between "enlightenment-actualized" and "enlightenment-nonactualized" people are related to the degree to which they are manifesting their basic nature in their function. This, of course, is also the central argument of the *SPE*. Since this is also a seminal position of texts such as the *AMF*, *Hsin hua-yen ching lun*,[39] *Platform Sutra*, and the writings of Yung-chia, these other works are also extensively cited in Chinul's writings.

As might be expected, it is in Chinul's most overtly essence-function–oriented works that he cites the *SPE* with greatest frequency. Most prominent in this regard is his "Direct Explanation of the True Mind" (*Chinsim chiksŏl*). This work is divided into fifteen topical sections, each of which treats the relationship between the true mind and its various phenomenal manifestations in terms of essence-function. For instance, in answer to the question of why, even though all people possess the true (enlightened) mind, there are differences such as that between sage and worldling, Chinul answers by citing one of the *SPE*'s most famous essence-function similes—that of the *maṇi*-pearl, which says:

> Good sons, it is like a pure *maṇi*-pearl which reflects the five colors, depending upon its surroundings. The foolish see that pearl as really having these colors. Good sons, it is the same with the pure nature of Perfect Enlightenment: it appears in people's bodies and minds, according to their individual type. Yet these fools say that pure Perfect Enlightenment really has body and mind.[40]

The *maṇi*-pearl represents the pure (empty) enlightened mind, which varies in manifestation according to its function. In the following section of the same text, Chinul again cites the *SPE* in answer to a question regarding how one may escape the condition of delusion and accomplish sagehood:

> An ancient teacher said, "When there is no place for the deluded mind, that is bodhi. *Saṃsāra* and nirvana are originally equal." The *Sutra of Perfect Enlightenment* says: "Good sons, since the illusory body of this sentient being vanishes, the illusory mind also vanishes. Since the illusory mind vanishes, illusory objects also vanish. Since illusory objects vanish, illusory vanishing also vanishes. Since illusory vanishing vanishes, non-illusion does not vanish. It is like polishing a mirror: when the filth is gone its brightness naturally appears."[41]

Chinul responds to the question of how one may transcend birth and death by saying that they are originally nonexistent, and that they only appear to exist because of false thinking. Chinul accentuates his reply by citing the sky-flower simile and the simile of confusion of direction, which he quotes directly from the *SPE*:

> The *SPE* says: "Good sons, all sentient beings fall into various inverted views without beginning. Just like a disoriented person who confuses the four directions, they mistakenly take the Four

Elements as the attributes of their bodies and the conditioned shadows of the Six Objects as the attributes of their mind. It is just like
when our eyes are diseased and we see flowers in the sky. . . . Similarly, when the sky-flowers disappear from the sky, you cannot say
that there is a definite point of their disappearance. Why? Because
there is no point at which they arise. All sentient beings falsely
perceive arising and ceasing within this condition of non-arising.
Therefore they say that there is transmigration through life-and-
death."[42]

Chinul cites the *SPE* with almost unmatched regularity[43] throughout
his works, and even when not making an exact citation, often alludes to
its themes. This is especially the case in his *Excerpts from the Dharma Collection* (*Pŏpjip pyŏrhaeng nok chŏryo pyŏng ip sagi*), which is a commentary
to an earlier work by Tsung-mi. Since Tsung-mi's main text was the
SPE, the *Dharma Collection* naturally includes much of its imagery and
paraphrase, as when, for example, he distinguishes the various Ch'an
sects by means of the metaphor of the *maṇi*-pearl. The *SPE* also turns
out to be a text well suited for the delivery of flexible interpretations of
sudden and gradual soteriology that were at the heart of the oeuvre of
both Chinul and Tsung-mi. The *Platform Sutra*, the other major East Asian
sutra that most directly addressed the sudden/gradual problematic, took
an exclusively suddenistic stance on the matter, effectively denying the
possibility of gradual practice. The *SPE*, while granting priority to the
sudden view, nonetheless acknowledges the need for the gradual teaching and offers a rationale for its existence along with examples for its
undertaking. The *SPE* was also a suitable text to serve as a canonical
basis for the Tsung-mi/Chinul attempt at reconciliation of extreme views
toward the usage or nonusage of texts in the course of Buddhist religious cultivation, since, although the *SPE* was certainly a sutra, the
positions that it articulated were very clearly of a Ch'an bent. Finally,
with its Hua-yen metaphysical positioning, the *SPE* also accommodated
the Hua-yen proclivities of both these masters. The *SPE* becomes, from
the time of Chinul, an integral part of the Korean meditative tradition,
along with a strong interest in Tsung-mi, a reinvigoration of *AMF*
studies, a lasting concern for the sudden/gradual issue, and reinforce-
ment of the influence of Hua-yen interpenetration metaphysics.

After Chinul

In comparison with pre-Chinul writings, the frequency of direct citation of the *SPE* and the discussion of its prominent themes increases
noticeably in the writings of Chinul's dharma heirs. Chinul's student

Hyesim (慧諶 1178–1234) shows the influence from his teacher by having a keen interest in scriptures, as evidenced in his monumental *Sŏnmun yŏmsongjip*.[44] It is in his teaching record,[45] however, where Hyesim's fondness of the *SPE* is most clearly demonstrated, as he cites the sutra extensively. As with Chinul and other contemporary writers, he tends to cite the profound discussions on the nature of enlightenment and ignorance from the first two chapters of the sutra, along with its popular similes, such as sky-flowers, the *maṇi*-pearl, finger-pointing-to-the-moon, four-directions disorientation, and so on.[46] He also writes a special *gāthā* on the *SPE*, summarizing the sutra's introduction and each of its twelve chapters,[47] an honor that he does not accord to any other work except the *Diamond Sutra*.[48]

Throughout the remainder of the Koryŏ period, the same basic set of texts remained popular in the Sŏn schools: the *SPE, AMF, SHM, HYC, Diamond Sutra*, as well as the works of Yung-chia. The continued regular presence of Yung-chia is worthy of note, since, although it is commonly assumed that the *Platform Sutra*, attributed to Yung-chia's teacher Hui-neng, is one of the most important texts in Korean Sŏn, in terms of quantity of citations and allusions, it is clearly the works of Yung-chia that commanded the greater attention among Koryŏ and Chosŏn Sŏn writers.

Passing down through the next century, Sŏn writings maintain the general character described above—a lot of interest in a reasonably well-defined group of texts, with a gradual increase in attention to *kong'an* literature and Ch'an anthologies. But after this time there is a noticeable change in the writing style of these Sŏn masters, marked by an increase in emphasis on *kong'an/kanhwa*-related lectures, imagistic/nature-influenced poetry, and a new kind of literary terseness. Much of this tendency can be attributed to the second transmission of the Lin-chi (臨濟; Kor. Imje) line of Ch'an, which began to penetrate the peninsula at the end of the Koryŏ.

Three important monks of this period who were instrumental in this Imje revival, and who figured prominently in charting the future course of Korean Sŏn, were contemporaries and friends: Kyŏnghan Paeg'un (景閑白雲 1298–1374), T'aego Pou (太古普愚 1301–82) and Naong Hyegŭn (懶翁慧勤 1320–76). All three went to Yüan China to learn the Imje *kanhwa* teaching that had been popularized by Chinul, and all three returned and established the sharp, confrontational methods of the Imje school in their own teaching. Each of the three also had a large number of disciples, and so this new Imje infusion into Korean Sŏn had considerable impact.

Among the three it was Kyŏnghan who seemed to retain the greatest interest in textual studies. This can be seen in his teaching record,[49] which, although showing a strong *kanhwa* orientation, is permeated with citations from numerous texts, most prominent of which are the *SPE* and the writings of Yung-chia. The works of T'aego and Hyegŭn are even more strongly *kong'an* oriented, with ubiquitous usage of phrases such as "the mind to mind transmission outside of words and letters" and repeated explanations of how to investigate Chao-chou's *mu kong'an*. With this nonscriptural predilection, there is little wonder that these men rarely cited any text at all, much less the *SPE*. But interestingly enough, as we read through T'aego's biography, we come across this passage which describes the early part of his dharma-career:

> During the autumn of 1337 [T'aego] stayed at Pulgaksa occupying a single room alone. Studying the *Sutra of Perfect Enlightenment*, he came across the line that said "The cessation of all illusion is called 'unchanging.'" At this point all that he knew suddenly fell away. Immediately after this, he raised Chao-chou's "*mu*."[50]

Not only did T'aego study the *SPE*, but it also played an instrumental part in his early awakening.

Hyegŭn's writings, like T'aego's, were almost exclusively *kong'an*-oriented sermons and poetry, showing a strong Imje orientation. While their remaining writings are not especially extensive, T'aego, Hyegŭn, and Hyegŭn's famous student Muhak (Chach'o 無學自超; 1327–1405) had large numbers of disciples and their Imje *kong'an*–centered teaching methods, especially the focus on Chao-chou's *mu*, had a deep impact on the later Sŏn tradition.

Kihwa (Hamhŏ Tŭkt'ong)

General Observations

It is Kihwa (己和, Hamhŏ Tŭkt'ong 涵虛得通 1376–1433) to whom we now turn, as the major Korean commentator on the *SPE*, and whose exegesis is translated in full in this work. Kihwa is the inheritor of a Sŏn tradition whose practices were derived mainly from the Imje school, which he received through his teacher Muhak, who was in turn taught by Hyegŭn, both of whom had traveled to Yüan China to receive direct instruction from Chinese Lin-chi masters. The high quality and broad scope of Kihwa's writings would lead him to be later recognized as one of Korean Buddhism's most important scriptural commentators, as well as one of the best poets and essayists of the combined Koryŏ and Chosŏn periods.

Kihwa's Life

Kihwa was born with the name Yu Su-i (劉守伊) into an aristocratic family less than two decades before the demise of the Koryŏ in 1392. His father was a government minister in charge of the reception of foreign emissaries, and Kihwa was educated at the prestigious Sŏnggyun'gwan (成均館) Confucian academy. In the course of his studies at this institution, Kihwa is regarded as having attained to a remarkable level of proficiency in Chinese philosophy and literature, as his biographer goes to unusual lengths to convey the extent to which he was esteemed by his professors.

> Entering the academy as a youth, he was able to memorize more than a thousand phrases daily. As time passed, he deeply penetrated the universality of the single thread, clarifying the meanings of the classics and expounding their content. His reputation was unmatched. Grasping the subtlety of the transmitted teachings, all their meanings were disclosed in his explanations. He possessed a sonorous voice and graceful beauty, like flowers laid upon silk brocade—even such metaphor falls short of description. People said that he would become the minister truly capable of transmitting the heavenly mandate, extending upward to the ruler and bringing blessings down to the people. In his grasp of the correct principles of society he had no need to be ashamed even if he were to face the likes of Chou and Shao.[51]

Admitting the hyperbole that is inevitably seen in the biographical sketches written by disciples of eminent teachers, we must nevertheless pay close attention to what is contained in this passage as (1) there is not, in the entire corpus of Korean Sŏn hagiographies, an appraisal of scholarly (Confucian) acumen comparable to this, and (2) this strong assessment of Kihwa's early abilities is corroborated in the degree to which he, later in his Buddhist career, took such a strong interest in, and showed such unusual ability in literary/philosophical/exegetical pursuits.

According to the same biographical sketch, at the age of twenty-one, Kihwa was so profoundly affected by the death of one of his close friends, that he abandoned his Confucian studies and began a quest for enlightenment through the Buddhist path. After various wanderings and encounters with other teachers, he arrived, in 1397, at Hoeam temple (檜岩寺), where he came under the tutelage of Muhak Chach'o, the National Preceptor of the generation, who instructed him in Imje soteriological methods. His initial training with Muhak was followed by the period of wandering study and practice that was common for

Korean Sŏn monks.[52] In the spring of 1404 he returned to Hoeam-sa, where he entered into a period of isolated, intensive practice in a small hut in the mountains. It is during this period that he had his first major awakening experience. The *Haengjang* says:

> One night, while taking a refreshing walk to conquer the demon of sleep, suddenly, without intention, he blurted out a verse, saying: "Walking, walking, suddenly I turn my head. Lo! The mountain rock pierces the clouds!" Another day, he entered the privy and when he came out, 'dropped the wash bucket'[53] saying: "There is only this single affair of reality—if there is a second, then it cannot be true. These words themselves—how empty!"[54]

After this Kihwa returned to an itinerant life, staying at various monasteries, practicing and teaching. In 1414 he came to Yŏnbong-sa at Mt. Chamo, where he stayed for a time in a small hermitage called "Hamhŏ" (涵虛 lit., "nourishing emptiness"), working unstintingly at the triple practice of morality, meditation, and wisdom. During this stay at Mt. Chamo he also led a number of study sessions on the commentaries of five masters who had expounded the *Diamond Sutra*.[55] After this time, he seems to have passed through another stage of enlightened freedom, as his biographer reports this major change in his lifestyle:

> From this time he never spent a long period of practice stuck in any particular place but allowed his mind to follow its own destiny "wandering free and easy"[56] among the nooks and crannies of the mountains and streams. How could he have a destination at a particular place? Only if strongly invited would he spend the night. He grasped the innermost mind of each person, and his reputation spread throughout the land. Valuing deeply the mind of every person, he responded perfectly to their needs.[57]

In 1420 Kihwa traveled to Mt. Odae in Kangnŭng. This was a dharma-filial pilgrimage for him, since the patriarchs of his lineage were descended from Odae. While in this region, he paid respects to the image of Hyegŭn. Here Kihwa seems to have had a third deepening of his enlightenment. As the biographer reports:

> He stayed at this hermitage for two nights. One night, in a dream, he was approached by the spirit of a monk who addressed him saying, "You will be called Kihwa, styled Tŭkt'ong." Kihwa bowed his head and received this with reverence. Suddenly waking from the dream, his body and spirit were refreshed and calm and he experienced an exalted condition of purity. The next day he went down to Wŏljŏng temple. He threw away his staff, cast off his shoes

and peacefully took up residence in a single room. From this time forth he continuously nurtured the embryo of the Tao. When hungry, he ate. When thirsty he drank, just enjoying the passage of time.[58]

His disciples reported that after this time Kihwa's whole presence and demeanor were transformed such that his influence on those around him became effortlessly powerful. Yet despite his enlightened "freedom and ease," Kihwa was engaged in a series of difficult tasks toward the end of his life, as he was compelled to defend the Buddhist church against the increasingly strident attacks from the Neo-Confucian element that had inexorably moved into the center of political power.

Also, in the early autumn of 1421, he was summoned by the king to teach and perform rituals in the royal temple. While the early Chosŏn rulership had rather strong anti-Buddhist inclinations, it seems that the king T'aejo (r. 1418–50) had softened his personal stance toward Buddhism in his later years. Kihwa spent three years as personal tutor to the king and his family, but in the autumn of 1424, he petitioned the throne to be relieved of this duty. He spent the last several years of his life once again traveling, studying, and teaching at various mountain monasteries in Korea. He ended his wanderings in the autumn of 1431 when he returned to Pongam-sa of Mt. Huiyang in Yongnam, where he supervised the refurbishing of the temple. The repair work done, Kihwa calmly observed the conditions of the times to the end of his life. On the twenty-fifth day of the third month of 1433 he came down with a sickness that lasted to the first day of the fourth month. During the first half hour after 3:00 PM he arose from meditation saying:

How void and empty! Originally there is not a single thing. The spiritual luminosity pervades and penetrates perfectly throughout the ten directions, but there is neither mind nor body to undergo birth and death. Past and future go and return without the slightest hindrance.[59]

A moment later he continued, saying: "About to depart, I raise my gaze to the ten directions of the vast heavens where there is no path to the Western Paradise." Upon this, Kihwa passed away.

Kihwa's Main Works

Kihwa's writings are extensive, including a large collection of poetry, sermons, and short essays on Buddhism and religious cultivation in general. He is best known for his four major works: (1) the *Taebanggwang wŏn'gak sudara youi kyŏng sŏrŭi* (Commentary on the Sutra of Perfect

Enlightenment); (2) his *Kŭmgang panyaparamilgyŏng o ka hae sŏrŭi* (Commentary on the Redacted Edition of Five Commentaries on the Diamond Sutra; usually referred to by the short title of *O ka hae*); (3) the *Sŏn chong yŏnggajip kwaju sŏrŭi* (Sub-commentary on the Compilation of Yung-chia); and (4) a treatise on the intrinsic unity of the "three teachings" of Confucianism, Taoism, and Buddhism, entitled *Hyŏn chŏng non* (Exposition of the Correct).

While Kihwa's renown within Korean Buddhism is largely connected to the first two commentaries, his notoriety in general Korean intellectual history is mainly attributable to the fourth work, a treatise that he wrote during the onset of the purge of Buddhism from its central role in the Korean society during the shift from the Buddhist-influenced Koryŏ to the Neo-Confucian–dominated Chosŏn. Since this dynastic shift occurred right during the middle of Kihwa's life, he, as the leading Buddhist figure at the time, was placed in the position of being the primary Buddhist spokesman in answer to Neo-Confucian anti-Buddhist polemic. In this essay, which is an excellent example of the usage of essence-function thought in the harmonization of the positions of the three traditions, Kihwa elucidates the universality of the concepts of altruism (*jen/in* 仁) and interpenetration (*t'ung/tong* 通) in forming the moral basis for all three teachings.[60]

Looking at his career from *within* the Buddhist tradition, Kihwa is the major successor in the resumption of Chinul's argument against exclusivist positions taken by certain members of the meditational, mind-to-mind-transmission–oriented Sŏn school in opposition to the text-oriented, doctrinal stance of Kyo. While during the late Silla and early Koryŏ the influential Kyo faction had indeed made life uncomfortable for the newly arising Sŏn transmission, by the time of Kihwa's career, it was no longer the case that the Kyo circle (typified by Hwaŏm and Consciousness-only scholars) were making any serious challenge to the Sŏn position, as the Sŏn schools had already held the upper hand for centuries.

Both Chinul and Kihwa were Sŏn monks with a strong meditation-oriented perspective toward religious cultivation, and so Sŏn meditation practice naturally held an undisputed priority within their respective systems. But both men also felt keenly that the continued denigration of Kyo study methods by Sŏn extremists was unnecessary, and even harmful. Thus, both Chinul and Kihwa wrote in such a way as to revalorize scriptural study within the Sŏn camp, supporting their positions with solid examples and rigorous logic, based in essence-function thinking.

Chinul had addressed this matter in a sustained and direct manner, aided by the analysis of the *Hua-yen ching* provided by the T'ang Hua-yen scholar Li T'ung-hsüan (李通玄 635–730),[61] which helped Chinul to utilize Hua-yen philosophy to support Sŏn soteriological and episte-mological views. Chinul in turn composed a lengthy distillation of Li's work, entitled *Hwaŏmnon chŏryo* (Essentials of the *Hua-yen Treatise*). In his famous preface to this work, Chinul utilized the essence-function construction to explain the relationship of the Hua-yen theory of inter-penetration to the Sŏn awakening experience, saying:

> The diligent practitioner who is cultivating his mind should first, by means of the path of the patriarchs, become cognizant of the fact that the fundamental subtlety of his own mind cannot be de-fined in words and letters. Then, using the texts, he should discern that the essence and function of his mind are none other than the nature and characteristics of the realm of reality (*dharmadhātu*). Then the virtuous power of [the actualization of] the interpenetra-tion of phenomena with phenomena, and the efficacious function of the wisdom and compassion [that are gained from an awareness of] the sameness in essence [of all things] will no longer be external concerns (i.e., merely conceptual theories).[62]

Chinul used the same sort of approach in addressing the Sŏn-Kyo relationship throughout his works.[63]

Despite the pronounced attention he paid to the philosophical reso-lution of Sŏn-Kyo tensions, an examination of the writings of major Sŏn figures immediately subsequent to Chinul does not reveal a deep or sustained treatment of this issue as was observable in his writings.[64] It is a long time—over two centuries, before we find the matter of the Sŏn-Kyo relationship again dealt with as a distinct topic in a sustained manner, this time in the works of Kihwa.

Kihwa's Analysis of the Relationship of the Worded and Wordless Teachings

Although Kihwa made a pronounced assessment of the value of scrip-tural study by the mere fact of the writing of his extensive commentary on the *SPE*, it is in his commentary to the *O ka hae* that he really develops his argument for the usefulness of the worded teaching and its basic compatibility with the wordless aspect of the *buddhadharma*. The *Diamond Sutra* is a text that examines the ontological status of language, with the explicit purpose of clarifying the role that linguistic constructs can or cannot play in the individual's efforts toward the attainment of en-lightenment. As students of the sutra well know, its conclusions are paradoxical, first rejecting the reliability of language on ontological grounds, and then reaccepting linguistic constructs on a provisional basis as tools in the effort of salvation, due to the lack of any other alternative. Because of its persistent pursuit of this theme, the *Diamond Sutra* was an especially appropriate object for Kihwa in the expression of his bidirectional approach, which recognized: (1) the necessity of the practice of (nonlinguistic) meditation for a proper actualization of that to which the scriptures refer, and (2) the viability of scriptural study as one means toward the attainment of such actualization. The issue of whether language is a sufficient means for access to the *buddhadharma* was particularly relevant for Kihwa, a monk who understood both approaches.[65] On one hand, he was the descendant of the distinctly antitextual tradition of Lin-chi Ch'an, which had carried with it into Korea many of Ch'an's self-descriptive slogans, such as the school that "transmits directly from mind to mind," or "the special transmission outside of words and letters." The degree of the continued popularity of such slogans at the time of Kihwa is reflected in his frequent quotation of them in his writings. On the other hand, as we have noted above, Kihwa's level of interest and degree of accomplishment in textual/philosophical studies was unusually high, even at a young age. He was furthermore, as a Korean monk, the recipient of a strong textual tradition as was outlined above. Therefore, he was a person who could deeply appreciate both sides of the issue.

When it comes to the bottom line, however, although Kihwa is in favor of an informed usage of scriptural study in Buddhist cultivation, he does not fail to uphold Ch'an's ultimate prioritization of the mind-to-mind transmission. He says early in the *O ka hae*:

> An ancient said: "The Three Vehicles and Twelve Divisions of the Teaching embody the principle and grasp the mystery." This being the case, what is the point of the ancestral teacher's coming from the West? The separately transmitted teaching should also not be found outside of the scriptures. But since that which is contained in the worded teaching has remained concealed, the patriarchs now reveal and spread its truth, so that not only is the meaning of the [scriptural] doctrine made clear, but the "separately transmitted [supralinguistic] teaching" is also fully disclosed. Since there has been something designated as "the transmission of direct pointing," how could this be contained in the doctrinal teaching? If we merely reflect on the story of Ts'ao-chi of Huang-mei,[66] this can readily be seen![67]

He means here that the *Platform Sutra*'s "formless" teaching, which makes strict warnings about the dangers of becoming trapped in language, is something that needs to be kept foremost in one's mind. Although he has first intimated that the Ch'an of the patriarchs and the sermons of the Buddha manifest the same reality, and that one cannot stick to an "antilanguage" position, he subsequently privileges the wordless transmission. Nevertheless, below he offers a view of the issue that is more balanced, pointing out the usefulness of the worded teaching, while at the same time maintaining his warning against attachment to it:

> The dharma that the Buddha has taught is absolute and is relative. Since it is relative, liberation is none other than written language. Since what was taught in the east and taught in the west for forty-nine years[68] is absolute, written language is none other than liberation;[69] yet in over three hundred sermons, Śākyamuni never explained a single word. If you are attached to the words, then you see branches of the stream but miss their source. If you do away with words, you observe the source but are ignorant of its branch streams. When you are confused about neither the source nor its streams, then you enter the ocean of the dharma-nature. Having entered the ocean of the dharma-nature, the no-thought wisdom is directly manifested. The no-thought wisdom being directly manifested, whatever is faced is no impediment, and you penetrate wherever you touch.[70]

Although one should not be attached to words, words also are not to be denied. Here, the essence-function formula can be seen in the source-streams simile. Kihwa first counsels regarding the serious pitfall that had been warned against throughout the Ch'an tradition—namely, that an imbalanced attachment to words (i.e., "function") can lead to an obstruction of the very essence (*ch'e*) of Buddhist practice. Yet to forget words and become absorbed in the wordless is to forget the phenomenal world and be attached to the essence. According to Kihwa neither extreme can be regarded as an acceptable Buddhist position.

Correcting the Scriptures

Having acknowledged as he does, the place of scriptural study within the Sŏn program of religious cultivation, Kihwa goes one step further in the *O ka hae* by making a strong admonishment regarding the need for of gravity in the treatment of scriptures. In considering his point, we may want to remind ourselves of the difficulties involved in the maintenance and dissemination of texts in ancient times before the use of the printing press. Buddhist sutras written in literary Chinese (of which there were often various original versions, with further varying translations) needed to be continually recopied by hand for maintenance and further dissemination. Indeed, this was one of the major activities of Buddhist monks of the pre–printing press era. In the process of copying, the chances of error were high. This is particularly the case in the copying of intricate Chinese logographs, many of which closely resemble each other but which carry variant meanings. Furthermore, in the case of the Mahāyāna Buddhist sutra, the operative logic[71] is profound, and often quite opposite from that seen in a secular argument. If some less-than-qualified copyist were to have a lapse in understanding or concentration, it would be quite easy to omit words or invert their order.

Based on his considerable experience in the handling of scriptural texts, Kihwa had a special sensitivity to this matter, and felt compelled to address it to an extent not seen elsewhere among East Asian Buddhist exegetes. There is also a distinctive Sŏn flavor to Kihwa's admonishment on this topic, since when he encourages proper scholarly discipline in the handling of the Buddhist text, he does not only refer to such academic qualities as technical care or proper philological training. He also prioritizes the development of the commentator's meditative insight, which should inform the scholarly work. Hence, while we can say that Kihwa has, in other places, argued for an inclusion of "Kyo" in "Sŏn," he here integrates the "Sŏn" meditational experience into "Kyo" scholarly activity. The exegete is required not only to read the text deeply enough to penetrate its key themes, but also to engage himself in meditation in order to have the necessary mental purity and "wisdom eye" to carry out the work.

> Written words are the tools for the expression of the Tao and the means for guiding people. The situational themes and the overall theme should support each other, and the overall theme should penetrate the text throughout, being fully reflected down to its minutest details. Only when omissions, superfluous words, inversions and errors do not confuse its points can the text awaken people's understanding and can it become a norm for a thousand generations. If this is not the case, then not only will the text not open people's eyes, it will become a instrument of confusion.[72]

Again, Kihwa's principle of interpenetration and nonobstruction is operating here through the formula of essence and function. In a properly transmitted Buddhist text, its inner meaning, or theme, which is the "essence", should be fully manifest in its outward appearance or "function." Conversely, the external text ("function"), should correctly manifest the internal/invisible essence: they should penetrate (*t'ong*) each other. "Penetration" can again be used as a metaphor to describe the action of the mind of the Buddhist exegete, whose commentarial and editorial work depends upon his meditative preparation.

The task of correcting an error-laden text is not to be carried out lightly, or by a scholar who lacks the proper preparation. Therefore he says, "if you lack the wisdom eye, you cannot but be confounded by arrogance and error."[73] Nevertheless, one who initially lacks the sharpness to overcome these mistakes can still treat a text well with the proper meditative preparation: "Although you may lack the wisdom eye, if you silence your discriminations in order to apprehend the point, then the incongruences between the sentences and the theme can be grasped and straightened out."[74] The responsibility is also great, since the exegete is passing on the dharma for future generations:

> If you have understood that the text's errors are like "gnarled roots and knotted bark," (a metaphor for a state of confusion) and that the meaning is obstructed and not penetrating but, afraid of being criticized, you do not correct them, then how can you reflect the meaning of the compassion of the Buddha? Later generations receiving the transmissions of error-laden texts will in turmoil produce forced interpretations in order to make sense of the text. If it is done in this way, then the uncorrected errors become attached to the words of the Buddhas and the Patriarchs and they will unavoidably be mixed up. This is something which the man of excellence and the thoroughgoing scholar cannot be party to.[75]

This admonishment regarding the treatment of scriptures by Kihwa is of special relevance in connection to his commentary on the *SPE*, since it is there that Kihwa takes the almost unheard of liberty of judging sections of the sutra to be corrupted, and then rewriting them, cutting and pasting passages that are separated by as much as several chapters.

Kihwa's Treatment of the SPE

Kihwa, like Tsung-mi and Chinul before him, perceived the value of the *SPE* as an instructional tool for practitioners of Buddhism who needed a guide for meditation, a guide that included a concise discussion of the tradition's most seminal metaphysical and soteriological issues, such as the relationship of sudden/gradual and enlightenment/ignorance. It was also a text, as Kihwa pointed out, that contained the essentials of Hua-yen's profound interpenetration metaphysics, but in a much more concise form than was found in the *Hua-yen ching*.

Since many of Kihwa's other writings were Ch'an-style imagistic poems, his poetic tone naturally found its way into his commentarial/essay works, and in this regard his commentary to the *SPE* is a remarkably lively piece of literature for an exegetical work. While it is clear Kihwa was conversant with Tsung-mi's work, he made a major departure from his distant T'ang predecessor when he declared that the text of the *SPE*, as it had been received by Tsung-mi, was significantly corrupted by copyist errors. Kihwa identified what he believed to be the corrupted portions, rearranging and filling in the text as necessary.[76] While it would be no easy proposition to convince the publishers of the East Asian Buddhist canonical collections that the current version of the *SPE* should be replaced with Kihwa's amended text, there is no doubt that the document as amended by Kihwa reads more smoothly and makes more sense. This being the case, Kihwa's treatment of the sutra deserves serious attention from those who conduct *SPE* scholarship henceforth.

Since the issues of doctrinal classification and Ch'an sectarian categorization (extensively pursued in Tsung-mi's exegesis) are no longer of concern to Chosŏn Sŏn practitioners who are viewing the *SPE* primarily as a meditation guide, such long, doctrine-related essays as those written by Tsung-mi in connection with his explication of the *SPE* are absent in Kihwa's work, as are the extensive scholarly references made by Tsung-mi that connect the themes of the *SPE* with their appropriate sources in other scriptures. When Kihwa needs to explain the meaning of a difficult passage or concept, he will do so most often not by referring to another Buddhist scripture, but by creating his own new metaphor, or by drawing an image from the *Tao Te Ching*, *Chuang Tzu*, *Analects*, or *I Ching*. The notable exception to this rule is Kihwa's tendency to locate the themes of the *SPE* within the framework of the essence-aspects-function scheme of the *AMF*, or the four *dharmadhātu* of the Hua-yen school, but nonetheless, never with textual references. Alluding references to any text, whether it be Confucian, Taoist, or Buddhist, are almost never identified with a citation.[77] Thus, compared to scholars like Tsung-mi and Chinul, Kihwa is not much of a philologist. He is possessed by a strong poetic streak, valuing the literary balance and flow of the passage more than the identification of its classical sources.

Most instructive for observing Kihwa's metaphysical and soteriological perceptions of Buddhist practice as contained in the *SPE* is his rather substantial introduction, which takes the form of an examination of the words of the title and the implications of their various combinations. He seeks to show the degree to which the *SPE* is a text reflective of the innate enlightenment thought found in the *AMF*, as he starts off directly with an explanation of the implications of the *SPE* in terms of the *AMF*'s triple scheme of essence-aspects-function. He proceeds to praise the balance of the *SPE* as evinced in its skillful simultaneous handling and blending of the absolute (empty, sudden, immanent) aspects of the path with its relative (concrete, corrective, practical) aspects. The *SPE* is a text that has put the Hwaŏm ideals of *ri-sa mu-ae* (理事無礙 mutual nonobstruction between principle and phenomena) and *sa-sa mu-ae* (事事無礙 mutual nonobstruction between individual phenomena) into actualization within its passages. Like Tsung-mi before him, Kihwa extols the merits of the *SPE* by comparing it with the *Hwaŏmgyŏng* (*Hua-yen ching*):

> Outside of the *Hwaŏmgyŏng* only this text exhausts the particulars of, and fully contains the teaching of "phenomena universally pervading and principle completely embracing." This sutra only differs from the *Hwaŏmgyŏng* in terms of length. The phrase "Great Curative Extensive Perfect Enlightenment"[78] is the same as "Great Curative Extensive Buddha."[79] "Buddha" means "enlightenment," especially the full enlightenment of self and others. The term "full enlightenment" (found in the title of the *Hwaŏmgyŏng*) is exactly the same as the term "Perfect Enlightenment." Thus, the two scriptures are basically the same.[80]

Kihwa's blending and reblending of the elements of the title, most importantly the concepts of "practice-awakening-realization and transformation" produces a concise summary of the entire course of Buddhist practice and enlightenment. Kihwa's commentary on the *SPE*, which is studied down to the present day in the Korean monastic educational system, provided a further impetus to the already influential position of the *SPE* in Korean Buddhism. And it is due mainly to this commentary that Kihwa emerges as an important link in the process of the development of Korean Sŏn from the time of Chinul down to the present.

The *SPE* after Kihwa: The Chosŏn Period

Hyujŏng (Sŏsan Taesa)

The next eminent figure in Chosŏn Sŏn to make extensive use of the *SPE* is Hyujŏng (休靜 1520–1604, popularly known in Korea as Sŏsan Taesa 西山大師), who was one of the most influential teachers in Korean Buddhism, second in the Sŏn tradition probably only to Chinul.[81] Following the example of his influential predecessors, Hyujŏng took up the treatment of the divisive religious issues of his day with vigor, insight, and a strong ecumenical bent, solidly based in essence-function metaphysics. He showed a renewed interest in the discussion of the Sŏn-Kyo relationship that was so strongly addressed by Chinul and Kihwa, with his other major scholarly preoccupation being the pursuit of three-teachings syncretism. Hyujŏng compiled and edited an anthology called the *Samga Kwigam* (*Examples from the Masters of the Three Schools*) in which he arranged important excerpts from the teachings of Confucianism and Taoism together with those of Sŏn in a manner that acknowledges all three as simultaneously viable paths. The Sŏn section of this work also includes numerous citations from the *SPE*.

Hyujŏng's most influential work was his *Sŏn'ga Kwigam* (*Examples from the Sŏn Masters*), which is, like the *Samga Kwigam*, an anthology intended as a guide for Sŏn students. The *Kwigam* includes excerpts from a wide variety of Sŏn related works, that fall into two main categories: (1) East Asian scriptures such as the *SPE*, *AMF*, *Platform Sutra*, and so on, and (2) Korean and Chinese later Ch'an literature, especially *kong'an*-related materials. It is in this anthology that we can see the crystallization of the distinctive Korean form of Sŏn that was initiated with Chinul, and that was molded further by the later Koryŏ masters and Kihwa. As we might expect, essence-function related metaphysics and the doctrine of texts such as the *SPE* and *AMF* are foregrounded. In the middle of the *Sŏn'ga Kwigam*, where Hyujŏng elucidates the method of overcoming illusory thought, he cites the *SPE*'s famous line that says: "When you know illusion, you are immediately free, without devising expedient means. Freedom from illusion is in itself enlightenment, and there are no stages."[82] Hyujŏng further comments:

> The mind is the illusory chieftain. The body is the illusory city. The world is the illusory outer-garment. Names and characteristics are the illusory sustenance. Once the mind arises and moves into thought, both words of falsity and words of truth cannot but be illusory. Yet beginningless illusion and ignorance both arise from the enlightened mind. These various illusions are like sky-flowers. The extinction of illusions is called "unmoving." Therefore, a man might, in a dream, see that he has a tumor and seek a doctor. But when he awakes no remedy is needed. "Knowing illusion" should be understood in this way.[83]

Hyujŏng relies on the *SPE* at various places in the *Kwigam* to make similar points. He also cites the *SPE* in his other writings, composing verses and short essays, that offer praise for both the sutra and Kihwa's work on it.[84] The influence of Hyujŏng on subsequent Chosŏn Sŏn was unusually strong, as he had a large number of influential disciples who in turn had their own sizable followings.

Later Chosŏn

Hyujŏng's program, which included the study of scripture combined with *kong'an* meditation, became the norm for the remainder of the Chosŏn. Hyujŏng's descendants wrote mostly poetry and *kong'an*-related material, but there was a renewed interest in Hwaŏm studies, and the *Hwaŏmgyŏng* became the most commonly cited scripture during the post-Hyujŏng period. However, there were still references made to the *SPE* and its commentaries, such as the short poems in T'ae-nŭng's (太 能 1562–1649) *Soyodangjip*,[85] and Ch'ŏnghak's (清 學 1570–1654) *Yŏng-wŏldang taesa munjip*.

The final canonization of the *SPE* as a "required text" in the Chogye tradition occurred during the early eighteenth century when it was included as part of the first generally instituted monastic syllabus. Creation of this set curriculum for the education of Sŏn monks and nuns (which is used in modified formats down to the present) is attributed to the Kŭmsan-sa master Chian (志 安 Hwansŏng 喚醒 1664–1729), who initiated, as part of his program, a set textual study track.[86] The most basic, called the Four Teachings Course (*sagyo-kwa*), included the four seminal scriptures of the Sinitic Mahāyāna doctrinal tradition: the *Sutra of the Heroic March Samādhi*, the *Awakening of Faith*, the *Diamond Sutra*, and the *Sutra of Perfect Enlightenment*.

It seems that Chian's program of textual study gained rapid acceptance, as we can see in the works of succeeding generations a clearly defined interest in this set of texts. Ch'oenul (最 吶 1717–90), in his fascinating *Chegyŏng hoeyo* (Essentials of the Scriptures), includes a detailed chart of the *SPE*'s "twenty-five [meditation] applications." Yuil (有 一 1720–99) and Ŭich'ŏm (義 沾 1746–96) both wrote a series of commentaries that included all of the seminal sinitic doctrinal texts from Chian's curriculum. Yuil's commentaries included the *SPE*, *AMF*, *SHM*, and *Diamond Sutra*, along with other essays and editions of Ch'an-related works.[87] Ŭich'ŏm's commentaries included the *SPE*, *AMF*, *SHM*, *Hua-yen ching*, and *Diamond Sutra*, again, along with other Ch'an-related works.[88] These two sets of commentaries, written during the same time period and including basically the same set of texts, provide a clear indication of the degree of definition that the Korean Buddhist scriptural canon had come to assume. The modern standard scriptural curriculum has certain variations according to the monastery, but the above-listed works remain at the core of the Chogye school's scriptural curriculum.[89]

The *Sutra of Perfect Enlightenment* Today

Scholarship

Although there are a few popular translations of the text in Korea that are used primarily for monastery-style instruction, I have not been able to locate any full-length study of the *SPE*, or of Kihwa's commentary by a modern Korean scholar. The only available English translation at the time of this writing was done in 1962 by Charles Luk, which includes Te-ch'ing's commentary. Luk's work is certainly reliable as translation, but it could have been more useful if he had provided a bit more in the way of his own introduction and commentary. Since his footnotes are used exclusively for the purpose of defining Buddhist technical terms, I suspect that readers without a substantial background in the major issues of the early period of Ch'an have not had an easy time digesting its contents. Nonetheless, being an accurate and faithful translation, it is certainly useful for the study of the *SPE*.[90] [note: Just prior to the publication of my manuscript, a new English translation by Sheng-yen was released by Dharma Drum Publications. I have not had sufficient opportunity to examine this work to be able to offer comment.]

The 1987 translation into modern Japanese by Yanagida Seizan was the first treatment of the text seen in Japanese scholarship for many years. It is a useful contribution in terms of *SPE* scholarship, but as with Luk's work, in view of the fact that the translator seems to consider a nonscholarly audience to be his main target, it may be the case that such an ancient and profound text as the *SPE* needs more thematic introduction, as well as explanatory commentary, to be properly apprehended by the modern-day reader. Another shortcoming of this work is Yanagida's stated decision to translate the text without relying on the traditional commentaries. Because of this, his translation has missed the point in several places where reliance on the commentarial tradition could have resolved issues rather cleanly.

A positive aspect of Yanagida's work, however, is the essay that he adds after the translation, in which he draws on his extensive knowledge of the history of Ch'an to clarify many important issues related to the *SPE*, such as its place within the overall Chinese Ch'an tradition, as well as within Japanese Zen and Tendai. In the course of this essay, Prof. Yanagida explores the position of the *SPE* within the apocryphal tradition and its relationship to other important apocryphal texts such as the *Awakening of Faith* and the *Śūraṃgama-sūtra*, especially laying emphasis on the degree to which, after their appearance, such East Asian texts as the *SPE* and *SHM* began to eclipse traditional Indian Ch'an-favored texts such as the *Vimalakīrti-nirdeśa-sūtra* and *Laṅkāvatāra-sūtras*. He also explains the role and importance of Tsung-mi's scholarship on the *SPE*, showing how the *SPE* and Tsung-mi both had profound effects on each other's future posterity and how Tsung-mi's attention to this text also deeply contributed to the degree of canonicity it attained within the subsequent Chinese Ch'an and Japanese Zen traditions.[91] He makes no note, however, of the far greater role that the sutra played in Korean Buddhism.

An excellent place to look for background on the *SPE*, already cited above, is Peter Gregory's fine book, *Tsung-mi and the Sinification of Buddhism*. Since the *SPE* was Tsung-mi's favorite text, there is discussion of the text in numerous places, as well as a bibliography of Tsung-mi's commentarial works on the sutra.

The Future, the West, the Practitioner

For the same reasons that it achieved its earlier popularity in these distant East Asian cultures, the *SPE* has potential value in modern Western Buddhism as an instructional tool. As the situation currently stands, a great number of modern-day Western Zen practitioners come to the discipline with little or no background in Buddhist doctrine, and thus begin their practice without knowing very much about what they are doing. Approaching a new and foreign tradition such as Zen, they are often lacking in firm criteria by which to judge the accuracy of what they are being taught, or the credentials of their teachers. This situation is often aggravated by the fact that much of what has been initially transmitted to the West under the broad rubric of "Zen" has been a somewhat imbalanced modern transformation of certain narrow aspects of Japanese Zen. For example, in much of modern/Western Zen, it is taught that the study of doctrine, history and philosophy is unnecessary, and even a hindrance, as Zen is a "pure experience" that transcends word, thought, and religion, and that scholarly/academic discussion of Zen is utterly meaningless and inherently wrong. This is a thoroughly mistaken misrepresentation of the actual Ch'an/Sŏn/Zen message.

Anyone who has sufficiently studied the Chinese and Korean historical roots of Zen knows that traditional Ch'an/Sŏn training has always been based deeply in the study of philosophical texts. As evidenced in the biographies of the Koryŏ and Chosŏn masters mentioned earlier in this discussion, it was standard practice to be engaged in a long period of scriptural and philosophical study in conjunction with the deeper aspects of Sŏn contemplation, typified by *kong'an* examination. It is also evident from the biographical material of the Chinese Ch'an and Korean Sŏn masters that a significant percentage of them gave regularly scheduled lectures on the sutras and *śāstras*.

It is precisely due to the cultivation of this deep doctrinal background that once practitioners engaged themselves in the rarefied *kong'an* literature it could have such a powerful impact on their consciousnesses. If a practitioner has been studying the ramifications of Buddha-nature theory for a decade or so in the course of research on the major Mahāyāna sutras, then Chao-chou's pronouncement of the nonexistence of the Buddha-nature in a sentient being is naturally going to have a deeply unsettling effect on his consciousness, and the *"mu" kong'an* can become the "barrier" that Wu-men intended it to be.

Western Zen circles have tended to rely up to this point primarily on English translations of unsystematic and recondite *kōan* collections as the main source of their inspiration. This method of instruction is fine up to a point, but can bring about problems if adhered to exclusively, since these materials contain very little in the way of presentation of

doctrinal background. Such works also do not contain specific explanations of the nuts and bolts of meditation practice, confession, vow-
taking, monastic behavior, and so forth. The *SPE* offers all of these, along
with a discussion of the grounding theories of Zen soteriology, in relatively compact form.

Also important for practitioners is the character of portions of the
SPE as self-contained contemplative exercises. In a manner similar to
such texts as the *Diamond Sutra* and *Platform Sutra*, the *SPE* is composed
of passages that are designed to create a shift in the consciousness of
the reader—to engender awakening (most importantly the first three
chapters, but also in later portions of the text).[92] This is what is meant
by saying that the passages of this scripture are not only descriptive—
they do not only "explain" the doctrine of original enlightenment and
sudden enlightenment. They seek directly, in their very structure, to
force the readers out of their dualistic thinking habits.

Overview of the
Sutra of Perfect Enlightenment

Title

The English title of the text, *Sutra of Perfect Enlightenment*, is a translation of the popular short Chinese title: *Yüan chüeh ching* (圓覺經). The
Chinese ideograph *yüan* 圓 originally means "round," but includes
connotations of "complete," "consummate," or "perfect." Because of this
wide range of meaning, I have seen a multiplicity of tentative translations, including: "Scripture of Consummate Enlightenment," "Book of
Complete Enlightenment," "Sutra of Round Enlightenment," and others.
The reason that I have chosen the term "perfect," instead of "round" or
"consummate," is because of the strong implications within the text
that this enlightenment is not only "complete," "round," or "consummate," but also "correct," "real," or "true." As Kihwa explains in his commentary, it is not only that the doctrine contained within the *SPE* is
"complete" and "all-embracing," but its lectures are "corrective"—they
enable practitioners to fix their mistakes to perfect their practice. With
the impression that it is the word best fit to express all of these aspects,
I have chosen the English word "perfect."

The ideograph *chüeh* 覺 (commonly pronounced by Chinese Buddhist
monks as *chiao*), means to awaken, to realize, or to become enlightened.
Therefore the translation of "enlightenment" is most natural. *Ching* 經
originally means "book," and in the Chinese literary tradition, gradually
came to carry the meaning of "canonical text." With the arrival of Bud-

dhism, it was used to translate the Sanskrit term *sūtra*, the recorded words of a Buddha or other deeply enlightened teacher. With the meaning of "recorded sermons of a great saint," it is quite reasonable to further translate the term into the English "scripture." But this is not absolutely necessary, since the word "sutra" is now considered part of the English language. There are also reasons of convention related to the context of the developing Western Buddhist scholastic tradition, since it has become common practice to say "Platform Sutra," "Diamond Sutra," "Lotus Sutra," and so on, rather than "Platform Scripture," "Diamond Scripture," or "Lotus Scripture." For these reasons, I have rendered *ching* as "sutra."

The term "perfect enlightenment," as it is taught in this text, refers to an enlightenment that is not limited in scope. It is also not an enlightenment that is attained exclusively from any partial aspect of the Buddhist doctrine, such as the so-called "elementary" teachings or *prajñāpāramitā* teachings. It is an enlightenment that can accept and explain all the various aspects of the Buddhist doctrine. This is why the full, formal name of the sutra as listed in the East Asian Buddhist canon is the *Great Corrective Extensive Perfect Enlightenment Sutra of the Complete Doctrine* 大方廣圓覺修多羅了義經. Since Kihwa explains the components of this title in depth in his introduction, we need not treat it further here.

Content Overview

The *Sutra of Perfect Enlightenment* is arranged in twelve chapters, plus a short introductory section. The introductory section describes the scene of the sermon and lists the major participants. The location is a state of deep meditative concentration (*samādhi*) and the participants are the Buddha and one hundred thousand great bodhisattvas, among whom twelve eminent bodhisattvas act as spokesmen. Each one of the twelve gets up one by one and asks the Buddha a set of questions about doctrine, practice, and enlightenment. The structure of the sutra is such that the most "essential" and suddenistic discussions occur in the earlier chapters and the more "functional" and gradualistic dialogues occur later. This kind of structure reflects a motif associated with the doctrine of the Hua-yen school, which affirms that the Buddha delivered the abstruse *Hua-yen ching* as his first sermon, in an effort to directly awaken those whose "roots of virtue" were well matured. The terminology that Tsung-mi and Kihwa use to describe these advanced practitioners is that they possess the capacity for the teaching of "sudden enlightenment"—a direct awakening to the non-dual nature of reality, which necessarily precludes gradualistic, "goal-oriented" practice. In the first two chapters (the chapters of Mañjuśrī and Samantabhadra), the Buddha holds very strictly to the sudden position, denying the possibility of enlightenment through gradual practice. In the third chapter he begins to allow for a bit of a gradual view, and the next several chapters become mixtures of the two. The final few chapters offer a fully gradualistic perspective.

Kihwa's primary means of categorization of the chapters is according to the "three capacities" of practitioners: superior, middling, and inferior. According to Kihwa, the first three chapters are aimed at those of superior capacity, the next seven for those of middling capacity, and the final two for those of inferior capacity. However, this method of categorization does not necessarily mean that the later chapters become gradually easier to read and understand. In fact, some of the most difficult discussions come in the later chapters. Most notable in this regard is the discussion of the "four traces" of self, person, sentient being, and life in chapter 9. Since the distinction between each of these four is extremely subtle, and the wording of the text itself is not that clear, this turns out to be one of the most difficult chapters to digest.

The crux of chapter 1, the chapter of Mañjuśrī, is a discussion of the meaning of the term "ignorance," in which the Buddha warns against perceiving ignorance ontologically—seeing it as a self-existent entity. He describes ignorance using the metaphor of "sky-flowers" (or a "second moon")—flowers one mistakenly perceives in the sky due to an optical malady such as cataracts. This perception of sky-flowers is compared to the perception of cyclic existence—"life and death" (*saṃsāra*) by unenlightened people. When the visual malady is corrected, the sky-flowers disappear spontaneously. There is no point in trying to "gradually" remove the sky-flowers from the sky. The nature of this "ignorance" is also compared to the situation of a person who is temporarily disoriented in terms of the four cardinal directions. There is no entitative blockage to be overcome: it is merely a state of mistaken perception, and all the person has to do is realize that East is East and West is West. In this kind of situation, there is no system of "practice" that needs to be installed. One merely needs to see things as they are.

Since, in his answer to Mañjuśrī, the Buddha has asserted that the human body and mind and all of *saṃsāra* are nothing but illusory sky-flowers, the bodhisattva Samantabhadra, in the second chapter, has to ask how, if all things are illusion, one is supposed to "remedy illusion using illusion." In other words, if everything is illusion, how is it possible to even practice? And if people become discouraged by such a prognosis and do not practice, how can they possibly escape illusion? The Buddha begins his reply by hinting for the first time that there is "something else" besides illusion—that when illusion is erased, the "unchanging mind" does not disappear. He then approves the possibility of "using illusion to remedy illusion" by instructing his listeners how to "separate themselves from illusion," comparing this practice to the rubbing together of two sticks to produce fire. The sticks ("illusion") ignite, and both burn up and disappear. But when they are gone, there is still "awareness." He nonetheless concludes this lesson by clearly stating "there is no such thing as gradual practice."

The third chapter, that of the bodhisattva Universal Vision, is the longest and probably the best known of the chapters, as it is even circulated by itself as a separate text for study in Korean Sŏn monasteries. Universal Vision asks the Buddha to relax his insistence on the sudden view and compassionately offer some expedient methods for the sentient beings to practice. More specifically, he asks "How should we think and abide?" In other words, what sort of mental cultivation or contemplation should be carried out? The Buddha's response is a long, guided meditation starting with an early Indian Buddhist analysis of the body and mind as defiled and baseless, followed by a Consciousness-only/ Hua-yen exercise in the visualization of interpenetration. He finishes with a Ch'an-characteristic exercise in "non-abiding," that is, the development of the ability to remain continually "unstuck" in any sort of paradigmatic framework. The end of this third chapter constitutes, according to Kihwa, the end of the "teaching for those of superior capacities."

The introduction in the prior three chapters of the paradoxical coexistence of the doctrine of original enlightenment and original ignorance causes Vajragarbha Bodhisattva, in the fourth chapter, to question how these seemingly contradictory positions are simultaneously possible. Furthermore, he asks, if ignorance is once quelled, is it possible for it to re-arise? The Buddha begins his answer by once again reiterating his fundamental nondualistic stance. It is by nature impossible for a disturbed, samsaric mind to find its way out of its condition. He provides some metaphors of disorientation caused by relative motion, such as the tendency for a person in a boat to perceive the shore as in motion, or the mistaken feeling of the motion of the moon when clouds are passing by. He also retells the sky-flower simile in terms of the impossibility of the sky to actually be the "cause" of the sky-flowers. But the most important simile in this chapter is that of "purifying gold ore." The gold, a symbol for enlightenment, is already contained in the ore (original enlightenment)—it is not something that is newly created by the smelting. Nonetheless, once the smelting is accomplished (realization of enlightenment), gold (enlightenment) never reverts back to the condition of ore (ignorance). The realization of enlightenment in sentient beings can be understood in the same way. The Buddha concludes the chapter with another admonishment about the impossibility of meeting enlightenment through discursive or samsaric methods.

As in each of the prior chapters, the bodhisattva in the fifth chapter, Maitreya, formulates his first question based on the conclusion of the immediately prior discussion. And since the Buddha admonished Vajragarbha about the impossibility of escaping *saṃsāra* while using samsaric views, Maitreya asks, "How do we sever the root of *saṃsāra*?" He also makes a more direct request for the teaching of expedient (gradual) methods, an indication that we are now well into the midst of the teaching for those of middling capacities. He furthermore queries regarding the types of distinctions that exist between the natures of sentient beings, in terms of their capacity for enlightenment. The Buddha answers the first question by attributing the empowerment of *saṃsāra* to the forces of "attached love" and "desire," which mutually enhance each other. In order to overcome *saṃsāra*, it is necessary to sever these two. The Buddha goes on to distinguish the capacities of sentient beings into "five natures," which are a revision of the five natures theory of Yogācāra. He distinguishes each of these five types of people in terms of their relative degree of freedom from the Two Hindrances, which are called in this text, "the phenomenal hindrance" and "the noetic hindrance," and which correspond to the "hindrance of defilement" and "hindrance by the known" of the Yogācāra school. He concludes this chapter by teaching the vow of the bodhisattvas to save all sentient beings, and explaining that since due to this vow, bodhisattvas must enter the world of desire, it becomes necessary for them to devise expedient methods to help people. The people, on the other hand, need to seek out a teacher who is not himself enmeshed in desire.

As the discussion continues, the questions of the bodhisattvas tend further toward distinctions in discriminated practice. Thus, in chapter 6, the bodhisattva Pure Wisdom asks the question "What differences are there between that which is grasped and actualized by sentient beings, bodhisattvas, and World Honored Tathāgatas?" The Buddha begins his answer by reminding the bodhisattvas once again, that since such things as distinctions in nature are based on illusory views to begin with, such a thing as valuation is ultimately impossible. But he then proceeds to distinguish between levels of attainment in terms of the degree to which practitioners are able to avoid being trapped by the traces of their own enlightenment experiences. These four levels are those of unenlightened worldling, lower-level bodhisattva, higher-level bodhisattva, and buddha. The overriding message of the chapter is that which is given in the passage that summarizes the four stages: What is most important is for the practitioner to learn the practice of "non-abiding"—not to be trapped in one's views or experiences, no matter how sublime they may be.

The bodhisattva of the seventh chapter, Power and Virtue Unhindered, continues to question on the theme of gradations in practice, emphasizing the fact that he and his colleagues, while teaching, find that there are many different paths that one may follow to arrive at the same destination of enlightenment. The Buddha responds by teaching three types of meditation practice, which are defined by the Sanskrit terms *śamatha*, *samāpatti*, and *dhyāna*, understood as techniques applicable to practitioners of varying inclinations. The practice of *śamatha* is defined in a way very close to its original connotation of "mental stabilization" or "calm abiding," referring to a practice of stilling the mind in single-minded concentration on an object. The term *samāpatti*, normally just a general term for concentration or meditation and not so different in meaning from *śamatha*, is here accorded a special interpretation that is equivalent to the concept of *vipaśyanā*, usually translated into English as "observation" or "analytical meditation." This type of meditation is necessary for the bodhisattva's practice of compassion, since through this meditation, he can perceive and properly utilize the phenomenal world of dependent origination. He also gives a special interpretation to the term *dhyāna*, which is also normally used as a general term for meditation. Here it refers to a nondualistic practice that simultaneously subsumes and transcends the prior two forms of meditation.

In the chapter of the bodhisattva Voice of Discernment (the eighth chapter) these three forms of meditation are taught again, this time in terms of various possibilities of application in conjunction with each other, based on more specific distinctions in the inclinations of meditation practitioners. The three are woven together in intricate combinations that result from all the possible variant orderings of these three practices yielding twenty-five formats, called "wheels" (translated in this text as "applications"). Thus, the Buddha has gone from an explanation of three general types of inclinations in practice to twenty-five.

In chapter 9 the discussion moves away from the explication of methods of meditation back to matters of the operation of consciousness, similar to that seen in chapters 5 and 6. As mentioned earlier, the chapter of Purifier of All Karmic Hindrances Bodhisattva is one of the most difficult chapters in the text to grasp because of the subtlety of the distinctions implied in the explanation of the Four Traces of self, person, sentient being, and life. These Four Traces are also discussed in the *Diamond Sutra*, but with different connotations. Here each one is explained on one hand as a level of enlightened awareness, but on the other hand, if any one of them is allowed to reify in the consciousness, it will become an impediment to enlightenment. In the final stage of overcoming these four, the destruction of one's conception of ego is compared to the situation of ice melting away in a bath of hot water.

The centerpiece of the tenth chapter, that of the bodhisattva Universal Enlightenment, is the explanation of the "Four Maladies." These are four viewpoints that are normally associated with religious practice, and to which practitioners often attach as "the Way." These are: (1) "contrivance" or the notion that one can "arrange" his life and practice toward the attainment of enlightenment; (2) "naturalism," a type of "Taoist" view of just letting all things be as they are; (3) "stopping" or "cessation," the view that enlightenment is to be attained by single-minded concentration and stilling of thought; and (4) "annihilation," the view that one should attain enlightenment by observing the emptiness of all things, thereby extinguishing all afflictions. The one who is not constrained by any one of these attitudes, but who holds to the correct Buddhist practice of nonabiding and yet consistently demonstrates a highly moral behavior is fit to be a teacher, and it is this sort of person that students should seek out. However, once they find such a teacher, they should not expect him/her to cater to their egos. The student should keep a steadfast attitude, regardless of whether the Genuine Teacher establishes an intimate or distant relationship. Finally, the Buddha teaches the vow that practitioners should make toward the attainment of enlightenment.

The chapter of Perfect Enlightenment Bodhisattva, which is the eleventh chapter of the sutra, finishes up the main body of the teaching. In this chapter, which is aimed at "sentient beings of the age of the degenerate dharma" of inferior capacity, the Buddha teaches elementary expedients of entry into the three types of meditation for those who are having difficulty getting their practice on track. He advises them to practice long and concentrated confession to help them to overcome the past heavy karma that is currently impeding their practice. This chapter also teaches the mechanics of setting up and entering into a meditation retreat, which can be of three lengths: eighty, one hundred, or one hundred and twenty days.

The sutra concludes with the questions of Most Excellent of Worthies Bodhisattva, who invites the Buddha's enumeration of the inconceivable virtues of the sutra, along with a listing of the names by which it is to be known. This chapter takes the format common to the final chapters of many Mahāyāna texts (called the "dissemination" chapter) wherein numerous types of supernatural beings appear to give their guarantee of protection to the text and those people who embrace it and practice it.

Kihwa's Introduction to the SPE

The Korean pronunciation of the Chinese ideographs in the title of the *Sutra of Perfect Enlightenment* is *tae-pang-kwang-wŏn-kak-su-ta-ra-yo-ŭi-kyŏng* (大方廣圓覺修多羅了義經). *Tae* (大) means "great" or "large." In his introduction, Kihwa will explain "great" through the influential precedent established in the *Awakening of Faith* wherein "great" refers to the greatness of enlightenment in its essence (*ch'e* 體), attributes (*sang* 相), and function (*yong* 用). Kihwa makes a special interpretation of the word "great" to signify the initial experience of entering the path, a kind of initial enlightenment, or transformation in an act of faith. In this usage, the term "great" refers, along with "perfect" (*wŏn*), to a transconceptual experience.

The term *pang* (方) has a wide range of meanings in East Asian literature, the most important being "method," "square," "(de-)limitation," "direction," and "orientation." This ideograph is one of the two comprising the term *pangp'yŏn* (方便), which means "expedient means" or the methods of teaching and practice that are used according to the actual situation in the phenomenal world. Kihwa here interprets *pang* as "the (curative) practices of self-improvement," that is, the concrete methods of religious practice—especially the process of correcting mistaken habituation, of freeing the individual's mind from affliction. The emphasis at the stage of *pang* is on the application of the proper remedies to correct one's own faults. Until one has done this, he or she can do little in the way of awakening others.

Once one has practiced sufficiently to gain a measure of wisdom for oneself, one has the capacity to teach the truth to others. This is Kihwa's interpretation of the meaning of *kwang*, (廣), which literally means "wide," "broad," or "extensive." Kihwa interprets breadth here as compassion in reaching out to save others after one has corrected oneself.

Wŏn (圓) literally means "round." Following Kihwa's interpretation I have translated the term as "perfect." Kihwa explains that this "perfection" indicates the "all-inclusiveness" and "interpenetratedness" of the characteristics of the path of enlightenment. Here Kihwa interprets *wŏn* as "realization and transformation" (*chŭng-hwa* 證化), that is, the activities carried out by a perfect Buddha. At the perfect stage, although one carries out practices, he or she does so from the standpoint of reality, in which there is actually no such thing as distinction between self and other, or ignorance and enlightenment. When each one of the prior three stages of *tae*, *pang*, and *kwang* are seen from the standpoint of perfection, each of their meanings contain each other.

Kak (覺), meaning "awaken," is the logograph most commonly used to signify enlightenment. When Kihwa discusses this term in his introduction, he will show its various aspects by reinterpreting it in terms of *tae* (本覺 original, or innate enlightenment), *pang* (自覺 self-enlightenment), *kwang* (覺他 enlightening others), and *wŏn* (本始不二之覺 the enlightenment that is not distinguished into innate and actualized).

After explaining the meaning of each ideograph individually, with its relationship to each of the other terms, Kihwa also investigates the meaning of the sequence of the terms. He then examines the terms in pairs and in sets of three, to further deepen the sense of their meaning through the contrast of their sequential relationship. The operation of Kihwa's always present understanding of interpenetration is here carried out through the concept of *wŏn* (perfection). Because of *wŏn*, no matter what kinds of distinctions are made in terms of levels of practice, there will always be a single thread that connects the first stage with the final stage. The same fourfold interpretation will be done for each of the words, finally interweaving the meanings of the words to the extent that each single word comes to contain the meanings of all the words in the title, and vice versa. One contains all, all contain one.

The next three ideographs *su-ta-ra* (修多羅) are used for their phonetic value to transliterate the Sanskrit word *sūtra*, normally written with the ideograph *kyŏng* (經). *Yo* (了) means to penetrate, to know, or to actualize fully. Here it combines with the next ideograph *ŭi* (義) which means "meaning" or "doctrine" yielding the compound word *yo-ŭi*, which means "the complete doctrine" or "fully revealed teaching" as contrasted with so-called "partial" teachings such as "Hīnayāna," "Early Mahāyāna," "Sudden," and so on. The final ideograph *kyŏng* (經) is the Chinese translation for the Sanskrit *sūtra*. Both the Chinese and Sanskrit words have etymologies similar to the English word *text*, in that they refer to the weaving, cross-threading, or tying together associated with textile work.

While such titular exegeses are common in East Asian Buddhist commentaries, Kihwa turns this one into a comprehensive, self-enclosed religious discourse. He not only analyzes the meaning of each word to show its great depth of implication, but also shows the deep significance of the precise placement of each word in the title. This is not a mere textual exercise, since he uses the explication of the meaning and juxtaposition of the words to give a comprehensive yet compact explanation of his understanding of the entire process of Mahāyāna Buddhist practice.

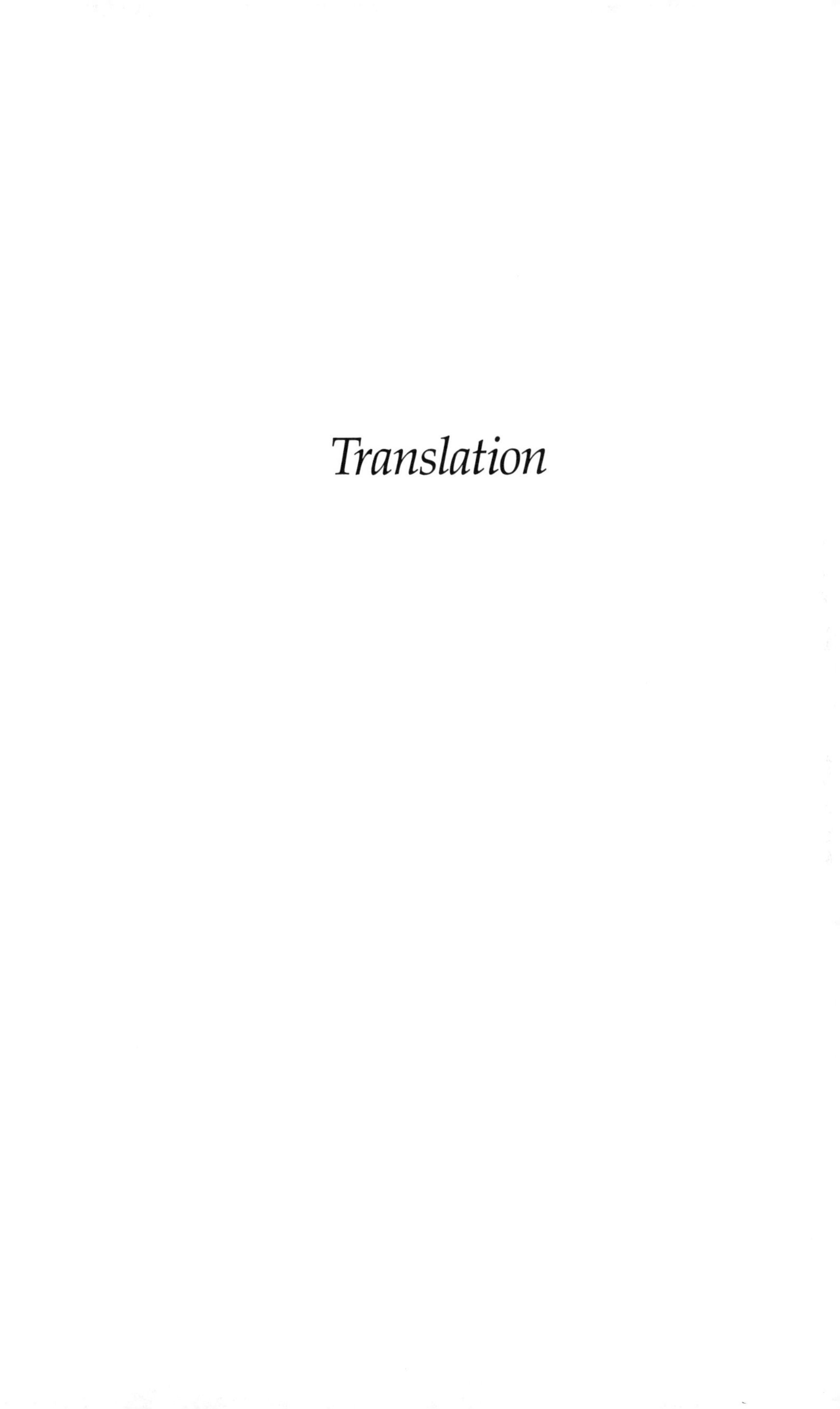

Translation

Notes on Textual Divisions and Markers:

I have used, as the source for this translation, the combined edition
of the sutra and Kiwha's commentary as contained in volume 7 of the
Han'guk pulgyo chŏnsŏ, pages 122 to 169. In order to aid the reader in
following the discussion of the sutra and commentary, textual divisions
have been added that are not contained in the original text. In the chapter
"Kihwa's Introduction" the translated text has been broken into an
outline form of topics and subtopics. The same has been done with the
sutra passages in the main text of the translation, including the addition
of page numbers to the passages of the sutra as they were divided for
exegesis by Kihwa. This is done in order to help the reader follow
Kihwa's commentary, especially in the frequent case where he refers
to a passage in a much earlier or later section of the sutra.

Since Kihwa's corrections to the original text constitute an important
dimension of his commentary, I have placed an inverted black triangle
"▼" as a marker at the beginning of those passages where he has made
an amendment.

Kihwa's Introduction

Clarification of the First Five Words of the Title

The Meaning of Tae ("Great" 大)

[*HPC* 7.123a5]

[Kihwa]

"Great" has three implications: the first is the greatness of [enlightenment's] essence (*ch'e* 體); second is the greatness of its attributes (*sang* 相); third is the greatness of its function (*yong* 用).[1] The essence of Perfect Enlightenment is open. It embraces heaven and earth, it contains the ten spatial directions and is complete without limit. This is the greatness of its essence. [*Interlinear note:* The line in the sutra that says "the *Tathāgatagarbha* is absolute, perfectly complete" refers to this greatness of essence.[2]]

Replete with the three virtues, there is no *dharma*[3] that is not included. Enlightenment originally possesses pure meritorious virtues more than the number of grains of sand in the Ganges River. This is the greatness of its attributes. [*Interlinear note:* This refers to the "*dhāraṇī*-entrance"[4] and the "secret store of the three virtues."]

It is capable of sagely and profane manifestation. It is capable of defilement as well as purity. Involving itself in its entirety in every single situation, it brings every single affair to completion; this is the greatness of its function. [*Interlinear note:* Thus the sutra says: "From it is manifested all purity: suchness, *bodhi*, nirvana, and the *pāramitās* that teach bodhisattvas."[5] The sutra also says: "All sentient beings' various illusions are born from the perfectly enlightened marvelous mind of the *Tathāgata*."[6]]

Taken together, essence, attributes and function pervasively contain the meaning of limitlessness and inexhaustibility. This is why they are called "great." The customary association of "greatness" with the meanings of limitlessness and inexhaustibility as seen in the sutras and *śāstras* is rooted in this.

The Meaning of Pang ("Curative" 方)

[*HPC* 7.123a16]

"Curative (方)"[7] contains the connotation of "stopping (*chi* 止)"; it also has the implication of "correction (*chŏng* 正)." "Stopping" has three further implications: (1) the stopping of restraint (*cheji* 制止); (2) the stopping of repose (*anji* 安止); (3) the stopping of absolute negation (*ssangji* 雙止). The stopping of restraint is also corrective; the stopping of repose is also corrective and so is the stopping of absolute negation. Its opposite is error. Possessing one among these three and lacking the other two is imbalance; possessing two among these three and not the other one is imbalance. Only when the three kinds of stopping are fully practiced is there neither imbalance nor error and can the cure be correct. [*Interlinear note:* Thus the sutra says: "to gain the correct abiding such that they will not fall into erroneous views."[8]]

Correcting mistakes and eliminating errors, you arrive to transcendence of things; this is the correction that is the stopping of restraint. [*Interlinear note:* Thus the sutra says: "[You should] separate from all false realms."[9]] Gathering in what has scattered and returning to the true, and reposing in the principle of justice—this is the correction that is the stopping of repose." [*Interlinear note:* This is the same as the sutra's teaching of the practices of meditation and accordance with the nature of enlightenment.] Sentiments of right and wrong are cleared away; subject and object are both forgotten:[10] this is the correction of the stopping of absolute negation. [*Interlinear note:* Thus the sutra says: "In this realization there is neither subject nor object, and ultimately neither realization nor realizer."[11]] Wherever there is emotional attachment, you completely extinguish it without remainder. One-pointedly according with the enlightened nature, you do not fall again into imbalance and error. This is why it is called "cure." All such teaching themes as the stopping of the adherence to the precepts and the active transgression of them;[12] the active adherence to the precepts and the stopping of their transgression, as well as "not being imbalanced" and "not being in error," are included here.

The Meaning of Kwang ("Extensive" 廣)

[*HPC* 7.123b6]

"Extensive" also has three implications: the first is the extensiveness of the practices that improve oneself (*charihaeng* 自利行); the second is the extensiveness of the practices that improve others (*ritahaeng* 利他行);[13] third is the extensiveness of equalizing self and others, to be perfectly interpenetrated without obstruction.

Completely cultivating a myriad practices, totally extinguishing all hindrances—this is the extensiveness of the practices of self-improvement. [*Interlinear note:* Thus, when the sutra speaks of severing hindrances, it says: "free from all kinds of afflictions"[14] or "separate from all hindrances."[15] When it talks about displaying virtue, it says: "the faculties and objects are universally pure, all is pure, etc."[16]]

Reaching out to the world, extensively bringing about salvation—this is the extensiveness of the practices that are beneficial to others. [*Interlinear note:* Thus, in each chapter of the sutra the Buddha is first asked to teach those present at the assembly (the bodhisattvas), and then he is asked to teach for the sentient beings of the degenerate age. This is the case until we get up to the two chapters of Universal Enlightenment and Perfect Enlightenment. There the focus is on the sentient beings of the degenerate age, so the Buddha is asked about expedient means.]

In severing evil, there is severing, yet nothing is actually severed;[17] in cultivating goodness, there is cultivation, yet nothing is actually cultivated; transforming the world, there is transformation, but nothing is actually transformed. Both adherence to and transgression of moral discipline are forgotten, self and other are equalized: this is the extensiveness of unlimited perfect interpenetration. [*Interlinear note:* Thus the sutra says: "(Bodhisattvas) are not attached to the *dharma* and do not seek liberation from the *dharma.*"[18]]

Wherever there is something to be eliminated, there is nothing that is not eliminated. Wherever there is something to be cultivated, there is nothing not cultivated. Wherever there is someone to be perfected, there is no one not perfected. This is so up until not hating *saṃsāra* and not loving nirvana; one stays and goes without obstruction. It is because of this that it is called "extensive." Such doctrinal themes as "reaching out to the world," and "perfect interpenetration without any obstruction," can be understood in this same context.

The Meaning of Wŏn *("Perfect"* 圓*)*

"Perfect" also has three implications: the first is the perfection of self-enlightenment; the second is the perfection of enlightening others; and the third is absolute perfection. Severing delusion and consummating virtue, washing away hindrances, and fulfilling enlightenment: this is the perfection of enlightening oneself. Universally gathering those of the three capacities[19] to return as one to Perfect Enlightenment; this is the perfection of enlightening others. Realizing even though there is nothing to be realized and transforming even though there is nothing to be transformed, realization and transformation are carried out to the utmost, and there is no being to which they do not reach. This is absolute perfection. Reality is mastered and sentiments are forgotten; immersed in sagehood, yet the same as worldling, you keep not even the most subtle partiality in view. It is for this reason that it is called "perfect." The ordinary understanding of "perfection" as well as the meaning of "total fulfillment" is also included here.

The Meaning of Kak ("Enlightenment" 覺)

"Enlightenment" also has three implications: the first is innate enlightenment;[20] the second is actualized enlightenment; the third is the enlightenment of the nonduality of innate and actualized enlightenment. Innate enlightenment is called "greatness," enlightening oneself is called "curative," and enlightening others is called "extensive." When the enlightenment of self and other are fulfilled, they return to the sameness of innate enlightenment; this is called "Perfect Enlightenment."

Why is innate enlightenment called "great"? If we discuss enlightenment in terms of its essence, then it is all-embracing without limit. If we discuss it in terms of its attributes, then it includes a myriad virtuous characteristics. If we discuss it in terms of its function, then it manifests itself without limit. It is flows out in purity with transparent penetration and spiritual permeation. In the sage it becomes *bodhi* and becomes nirvana, yet nothing is added. In worldlings it becomes affliction and becomes *saṃsāra*, yet nothing is subtracted. It is like the bright moon in the sky that does not distinguish between the pure and the impure or the beautiful and the ugly, and that does not care about poverty and wealth, elevation, or debasement. It equally enlightens all those who approach it. In this way its mysterious essence embraces the entire cosmos, yet it is not large. It rests on the tip of a hair, yet it is not small. It includes both past and future, yet is beginningless and endless. It pervades countless worlds without missing the slightest area. It is neither existent nor nonexistent, and there is no time that it is not "just-so." This is why innate enlightenment is called "great."

Why is self-enlightenment called "curative"? When all those who are trapped in bondage suddenly rely upon a teacher and spontaneously return to their innate abilities, reflecting on their own pure and fully endowed attributes, they will arise faith and understanding; they will cast off error and return to the correct, resist evil and follow the good. They will return defilement to *bodhi*, return ignorance into *prajñā*, transform *saṃsāra* into nirvana. This is why self-enlightenment is called "curative."

Why is enlightening others called "extensive"? Since one is already able to enlighten oneself, he ends delusion and consummates virtue;

he thoroughly perceives that although sentient beings are of the same basic nature, they are deluded. At this point, one spreads out compassionate teachings like clouds in the sky. Like waves arising and crossing the ocean, he manifests various forms, teaches various dharmas, and is extensively able to benefit all sentient beings. This is why enlightening others is called "extensive."

However, while self-enlightenment is called "curative," it also includes the meaning of "extensive." And while enlightening others is called "extensive" it also includes the meaning of "curative." In quelling evil, there is no evil not dispelled. In practicing goodness, there is no goodness not upheld. In one's capacity to be free, there is nothing from which one is not free. In one's capacity to create, there is nothing that one does not create. This is why self-enlightenment can be called "curative" and yet at the same time be called "extensive." Universally causing all [others] to cease [evil] just as I have, there are none who do not cease it. In doing goodness as I have, there are none who do not do it. This is why improving others is called "extensive," but at the same time has the meaning of "curative."

The enlightenment of self and others is fulfilled, and you return to innate enlightenment. Why is this called "Perfect Enlightenment?" Even though you have self-realization, if you grasp to the idea of "realization," you still abide in the view of subject and object, and have not let it go. How could you possibly call this a thoroughgoing realization? Even though you transform others, if within yourself you have not let go of the idea of a transforming subject, and outside of yourself there is still a realm of things to be transformed, how could you possibly call this "great transformation?" Only after forgetting the idea of obtaining realization can there be thoroughgoing realization. Only after you stop giving rise to views of buddhahood can there be great transformation. The states of thoroughgoing realization and great transformation coalesce with innate enlightenment, arising dependently without obstruction. Wrong and right, good and evil, pollution and purity, yes and no, holy and profane, delusion and awakening—all merge into one realm. *Bodhi* and defilement do not interfere with each other, *saṃsāra* and nirvana are also not contradictory. Wisdom and foolishness merge as *prajñā*; hell and heaven are the same Pure Land. Selecting and rejecting are both in your hand; pleasure and pain are according to the situation. This is why the fulfillment of the enlightenment of self and other, which is the return to innate enlightenment, is called "Perfect Enlightenment."

The Semantic Relationship between
Tae-pang-kwang-wŏn-kak 大方廣圓覺 and
Anuttarā-samyak-saṃbodhi
(*Mu-sang-chŏng-pyŏn-chŏng-kak* 無上正徧正覺)

[*HPC* 7.124a24]

The Sanskrit word *anuttarā-samyak-saṃbodhi* means "unsurpassed correct(ive) universal true enlightenment." This "unsurpassed correct(ive) universal true enlightenment" means the same thing as "great curative extensive Perfect Enlightenment." "Unsurpassed" (*musang* 無上) is the same as "great" (*tae* 大). "Correct(ive)-universal" (*chŏngp'yŏn* 正徧) is the same as "curative-extensive" (*panggwang* 方廣). "Correct enlightenment" (*chŏnggak* 正覺) is the same as "Perfect Enlightenment (*wŏn'gak* 圓覺)." Correct(ive) wisdom is self-enlightenment; universal wisdom is enlightening others. Since neither self-enlightenment nor enlightening others is biased or wrong, they are called "correct(ive) universal true enlightenment." The meaning of "cure" as the forgetting of both subject and object, the meaning of "extension" as the equality of self and other, the meaning of "perfect" as absolute, complete inclusion, and the meaning of "enlightenment" as the nonduality of innate enlightenment and initial enlightenment all contain the same meaning of "correct enlightenment." Therefore we know that what is called "correct enlightenment," is the same as what is called "Perfect Enlightenment."

The Meaning of the Relative Placement of
the Words of the Title and
the Importance of their Distinction

[*HPC* 7.124b8]

Why is it that the title says "great (大)" before "curative (方)" and says "curative (方)" before "extensive (廣)" and says "perfect (圓)" after "curative-extensive (方廣)"? "Great" refers to faith and understanding; "curative" refers to self-improvement; "extensive" refers to improving others. "Perfect" refers to realization and transformation. Why are faith and understanding called "great"? It is because that which is believed and understood is great. Why is self-improvement called "cure"? Because the practices one performs are corrective. Why is improvement of others called "extensive"? Because in the act of improving others, one extends oneself. Why is realization-transformation "perfect"? Because what is realized and transformed is perfection.

Thus, "great" being first and "cure" being next means that one completes one's understanding and then engages in correction. Why do I say "complete understanding"? Because complete understanding is the principle by which we thoroughly penetrate good and evil, defilement and purity, death and life, darkness and illumination. It is the same as "the wisdom reaching to all the myriad phenomena" and "in the phenomenal nothing not known" and "in the principle nothing not penetrated."[21]

[*Translator's note*: "Principle" is one English translation for the ideograph *li/ri* 理, a concept that has a long history of development in classical East Asian thought. In certain contexts it can be correlated roughly to the Western concepts of *logos* or *theos*, but it lacks the linguistic connotations of the former and the personal or anthropomorphic implications of the latter. Nonetheless, *li* refers to an inner and preponderant patterning/governing law (synonymous in some contexts with the Chinese term *tao* 道, and the Sanskrit term *dharma* 法), which should be followed, and in the case of the sages, be fully realized.

When doctrinal Buddhism developed in China, *li* received more specific definition, becoming associated with the Buddhist concept of *paramārtha-satya*, the higher, or absolute truth. The basic non-entitative character of the term is further defined in Buddhism, as *li* becomes identified with *śūnyatā* ("emptiness" 空). In the Hua-yen school, the concept *li* is set up in contrast to the concept of individual concrete phenomena (*shih/sa* 事) in the establishment of the teaching of the "four *dharmadhātus*," or four levels of religious awareness. Taking advantage of the philosophical development of the term *li* through Hua-yen, Neo-Confucian thinkers such as the Ch'eng brothers and Chu Hsi used the term once again with a related meaning, referring to higher moral order contained within the human psyche, which was contrasted with "material force" (*ch'i/ki* 氣). By the time Kihwa writes this commentary, the concept of *li* has many connotations attached to it.]

[Kihwa]

Why do I say "practice of curing"? Because in practice there is stopping and going, apprehension and discarding and scrupulous correction without error. It is like the saying "extending everywhere without error."[22] It is also like the saying "reverence corrects from the inside, righteousness aligns on the outside."[23] Well-known concepts such as "stopping evil and developing goodness" and "casting off evil and returning to the correct" are the same as this. Why is cure first and extension next? Once you have virtue in abundance you can reach out to the world and can give of yourself without any reservations. This is like the saying: "abiding at peace and valuing benevolence, you can love people."[24] It is also like the saying: "Only when you have goodness within yourself can you stimulate the goodness of others. Only when there is no evil within yourself can you correct the evil of others." It also means "possessing goodness and possessing discipline you improve sentient beings."

Why do "cure" and "extension" come before "perfection"? You have already established the practices of self-improvement and improvement of others relying on your "selecting and rejecting."[25] Now, after being able to forget the idea of selecting and rejecting, and after wiping out the views of subject and object, you are able to attain to the realm of thoroughgoing realization and great transformation. Even though the Tao lacks definite shape, it is attainable. It is like the saying: "spirit has no shape and change has no essence."[26] [Such well-known Buddhist phrases as] "Neither practice nor realization" and "nothing arising in transformation" and "no-arising of non-transformation" and so on, are the same as this. These are the reasons that "great" comes before "cure," "cure" comes before "extension," and "cure-extension" comes before "perfection."

Though "great" and "perfect" are different words, they have the same meaning. An example is the phrase "great perfect complete enlightenment." Faith-understanding and realization-transformation are penetrated by one thread from beginning to end.[27] The phrases "according with the wisdom of Mañjuśrī is none other than beginner's mind," and "when you enter the stage of the practices of Samantabhadra there is already no separate essence" express this same meaning.

[*Translator's note*: The stage of *faith-understanding* 信解 is the level of entry into Buddhist practice while "realization-transformation" 證化 is the highest stage, equivalent to Buddhahood. At the stage of faith-understanding one is gaining confidence in, and gaining a conceptual grasp of the Buddhist teachings. At the stage of realization-transformation, one fully confirms (證) one's own Buddha-nature and also teaches (化) other sentient beings. Throughout this translation, the Buddhist technical term *cheng/chŭng* 證 will be rendered as "realization" and should be understood as denoting this *highest* stage of attainment. The same is true for the word "transformation" (*hua/hwa* 化), which often appears linked to this term.

Mañjuśrī Bodhisattva is a Mahāyāna symbol representing the Wisdom aspect of the Buddhist path, and thus in many Mahāyāna scriptures, the sections connected with his name are the most profound. In the *SPE* the chapter of Mañjuśrī contains the sudden teaching that admits of no gradualism whatsoever. Samantabhadra (in contrast to Mañjuśrī) represents the "gradual practice" aspect of the Buddhist path, in which practices are carried out in reliance upon a phenomenal understanding of cause and effect. "Faith-understanding" is the initial stage of Buddhist practice, while "realization-transformation" is equivalent to Buddhahood. Yet Kihwa says here that both of these are "penetrated by one thread from beginning to end" (信解與證化始終而一貫). Here Kihwa is elucidating a position articulated in the Hwaŏm school, that since all things are interpenetrated and contain each other, there can ultimately be no such thing as a separation between the early stages of so-called nonenlightenment and the final stage of enlightenment. The same message is expressed in the two following quotations, which identify the highest stage of wisdom with the very beginning of practice. For an explication of this important Hua-yen interpretation of mutual containment of the stages of the path toward enlightenment, see Sung Bae Park's *Buddhist Faith and Sudden Enlightenment*, pages 118–22.]

The Semantic Relation of the
Individual Words to Each Other

[*HPC* 7.124c14]

Furthermore, "great" and "extensive" have related meaning, and "cure" and "perfect" mutually respond. Already, the enlightenment that knows the sameness of essence is "great" without border or limit; that self and other are not distinguished. You are now able to extend yourself to the world and "extensively" awaken others. This is the mutual connection of "great" and "extensive." "Perfecting the 'great' king of enlightenment and 'extensively' saving all kinds of sentient beings," can be understood in the same way. It is like when the *I Ching* says: "we match greatness with heaven and extensiveness with earth. With wisdom we speak of [heaven's] greatness; with goodness we speak of [the earth's] extensiveness."[28] Only after you are able to combine the virtues of wisdom and goodness and unify the Tao of heaven and earth, can you embrace the imperfect and the perfect, fully contain the "extensive" and the "great" and assume the title of "sage." Therefore it is said: "The *changes* are that by which the sage elevates his wisdom and extensively acts."[29] "Elevating wisdom" means that wisdom penetrates all things and illuminates them from above like heaven. It is the same as *samyak-saṃbodhi*. "Acting extensively" means that the Way gives succor to all those in the world while being as broad as the earth itself. It is like the "great compassion that saves the world." The meanings of "great" and "extensive" are the same as this.

Since you are able to cast off evil and return to the correct, cut off delusion and perfect virtue, and blend with the worldly while keeping unity with the sagely, you respond perfectly without any limitation. This is the "complementarity of cure and perfection" This means that if you desire to gain this perfection, you must have the cure first. In the sutra the Buddha first sets up the stages of worldling, worthy and sage[30] and then concludes by saying "all hindrances are none other than ultimate enlightenment."[31] This is like in the Confucian classics where they first mention the various worthies and summarize the discussion with Confucius' words, "there are none who are capable and none who are incapable."[32] This is why the title says "cure" first and "perfect" after. The *I Ching* says: "Knowledge exalts and propriety makes humble. The exalted imitate heaven and the humble pattern themselves after the earth; perfecting one's nature and maintaining it: this is the gate of righteousness and the Tao."[33] Heaven envelops the exterior of the earth, completely containing it without boundary: this is high, this is great, this is "perfect." The earth stays within heaven and is heavy, unmoving. This is the humble, the extensive, the "cure." The interdependence of the three powers[34] and myriad things is called the Way. The sage embodies it and universally responds without any partiality—this is "perfection." Practicing with goodness as the basis and attaining the Way accurately— this is "righteousness." The sage uses this and holds to the correct without error: this is called "cure." Only when you have become a sage do you unite with heaven and earth and blend the sacred and profane. Then you are able to practice the curative and the perfect and there is nothing to which you cannot apply yourself. This is like the phrase: "There is no place where the sagely nature does not penetrate." Once a great sage has been born into this world, he cannot avoid taking on limited views and the affliction of delusions. Therefore [the *I Ching*] says: "The benevolent see it and call it benevolence; the wise see it and call it wisdom; the common people use it daily without awareness."[35] Because of this they do not see the great completeness of the Way and are unable to practice the curative and practice the perfect. This is the meaning of "cure-perfection."

The Explanation of the Relationship between the Triplet Compounds of the Title

[*HPC* 7.125a22]

"Great-curative-extensive" (大方廣) refers to the disclosure of cause and effect from within no-cause-and-effect. "Curative-extensive-perfect" (方廣圓) takes cause and effect and returns it to no-cause-and-effect. The phrases "no not following the flow of this reality-realm and no non-returning to this reality-realm" reflect the same message. Already awakened and then practicing; practicing for oneself and transforming others: this is "great-curative-extensive." Already having practiced and reaching to realization, you realize even though there is nothing to be realized. Having already realized, you disclose [reality] and transform [others] even though in this transformation there is nothing that is transformed. Since realization and transformation are both perfected, you function freely without obstruction: this is "curative-extensive-perfect." It is because of all of these that the magnificently adorned path of enlightenment is the adornment of no-adornment. Even though the words of the lofty and luminous teaching speak of the enlightened nature of the sage, it is necessary to first have this cause and effect of practice and realization. How true these words are!

Categorization of the Twelve Chapters

Categorization by the Words of the Title

[*HPC* 7.125b6]

If we match the words of the title to the twelve chapters of the sutra then the single chapter of Mañjuśrī[36] clarifies "greatness" relying on the [initial] practice of [the path] of faith-understanding. The eight chapters[37] from Samantabhadra up to Purifier of Karmic Hindrances clarify "cure" depending upon the practices of self-improvement. The single chapter of Universal Enlightenment clarifies "extensiveness" depending on the practice of improving others. The single chapter of Perfect Enlightenment clarifies "perfection" depending on the final practice of realization and transformation.

How is it that the chapter of Mañjuśrī Bodhisattva is guided by the practice of faith and understanding in clarifying greatness? The text says: "possesses the great *dhāraṇī*-entrance, which is called Perfect Enlightenment. From it is manifested all purity: suchness, *bodhi*, nirvana, and the *pāramitās* that teach bodhisattvas."[38] This is how it clarifies "greatness" It also says: "All *tathāgatas* rely on the attributes of perfectly luminous pure enlightenment to sever ignorance and directly accomplish the Buddha-way."[39] The term "perfect illumination" is a synonym for "faith-understanding" This is why the chapter of Mañjuśrī Bodhisattva clarifies greatness relying on the practice of faith-understanding.

Why do the eight chapters from Samantabhadra Bodhisattva to Purifier of All Karmic Hindrances Bodhisattva explain "cure" relying on the practices of self-improvement? Each chapter teaches how to destroy delusion and manifest virtue, to clearly distinguish between true and false, between the correct and the mistaken. The course of practice is clearly analyzed and contains the doctrine of "restraint-stopping," "repose-stopping," and "stopping by absolute-negation." This is why we can say that the eight chapters from Samantabhadra clarify the cure based on the aspect of self-improvement. These chapters also contain the doctrine of "extension" but this is supplementary, and is not the main point.

How is it that the chapter of Universal Enlightenment Bodhisattva clarifies "extensiveness" based on the practices of improving others? The words "universal enlightenment" mean "universally using my own enlightenment to enlighten those who are to be enlightened after." The text says: "What kind of person should we have the sentient beings seek? On what kind of teachings should they rely?" and so on up to: "prevent the blind multitude from falling into mistaken views"[40] and "completely embracing all types of people, extensively making them awaken." This is how the chapter of Universal Enlightenment clarifies "extensiveness" depending on the aspect of improving others. Within this doctrine the meaning of cure is not absent, but it is supplementary and not the main point.

How does the chapter of Perfect Enlightenment Bodhisattva clarify "perfection" depending on the aspect of the final practice of realization and transformation? The term "Perfect Enlightenment" means "the fulfillment of the enlightenment of self and other" and "ultimate, complete inclusion." When the text says: "[we] have already attained awakening,"[41] this is the perfection of self-realization. "Completely embracing all kinds of people and returning them together to Perfect Enlightenment,"[42] is the perfection of transforming others. The phrase "already enlightened" and the concept of "completely embracing" have not been expressed in earlier chapters—they are only found here. This is why I say that the chapter of Perfect Enlightenment Bodhisattva clarifies perfection based on the final practice of realization and transformation.

Categorization by the Three Levels of Capacity

[*HPC* 7.125c14]

Among the twelve chapters, the two chapters of Samantabhadra Bodhisattva and Universal Vision Bodhisattva teach the practice and realization of those of superior capacity, since these chapters contain the doctrine of realization.

[*Translator's note*: In this categorization of the chapters according to the three capacities, Kihwa has omitted the first, the chapter of Mañjuśrī. According to his discussion of the chapter of Mañjuśrī in the main body of the commentary, it should certainly be classified as aimed at those of superior capacity (this is how Tsung-mi categorizes it; see Tsung-mi's *Great Commentary* Z 243.9.334c17). It also may be that because of its radically suddenistic content, Kihwa considers the chapter to be completely apart from the realm of practice.]

[Kihwa]

[*Interlinear note:* Thus in the chapter of Samantabhadra Bodhisattva it says: "Separation from illusion is itself enlightenment."[43] The chapter of Universal Vision Bodhisattva says: "When the filth is gone, [the mirror's] brightness naturally appears."[44] It also says: "In the one who realizes, there is no 'contrivance,' 'stopping,' 'naturalism,' or 'annihilation'."][45]

The six chapters from the chapter of Vajragarbha Bodhisattva are the [teaching of] practice and realization for those of middling capacity. The chapter of the Bodhisattva Purifier of All Karmic Hindrances especially focuses on the fact that the subtle mark of cause quickly reaching effect needs to be eliminated, since once these defilements are eliminated, one is able to realize and enter [into enlightenment]. The two chapters of Universal Enlightenment Bodhisattva and Perfect Enlightenment Bodhisattva operate in the sphere of complete, ultimate realization and transformation and are aimed at aiding those of inferior capacity. Therefore they embody the teaching of the practice and realization of those of inferior faculties. At this point, the Correct Doctrine[46] is complete and is fit to be transmitted as a norm for later generations. Therefore it is followed by the chapter of Most Excellent of Worthies Bodhisattva. This chapter is the Dissemination chapter[47] that summarizes the general import of all the chapters.

Categorization by Interpenetration

[*HPC* 7.125c23]

It can now be seen with great clarity, as if one were examining a jeweled mirror, that the five words "Great Curative Extensive Perfect Enlightenment" completely summarize all the chapters, and that the twelve chapters as a whole articulate the marvelous point of the title. The dharma [objective principle] that is realized is called Great Enlightenment, is called Perfect Enlightenment, is called Marvelous Enlightenment. The subjectively actualizing person, and the subjectively actualizing wisdom are also called Great Enlightenment, are also called Perfect Enlightenment, and are also called Marvelous Enlightenment. How is it that the subjective and objective aspects of enlightenment have the same name? It is because in the realm of ultimate realization "person" and "dharma" are both forgotten. Since "forgetting both" is also nihilated, principle and wisdom are both complete. Since they are both complete, the completion of both also vanishes; both are complete and both vanish. Since subject and object lack duality, subjective and objective realization have the same name.

What is the textual basis for the objectively realized dharma being called "Great Enlightenment," "Perfect Enlightenment," and "Marvelous Enlightenment"? These are expressed in the sayings: "Space arising from the midst of Great Enlightenment";[48] "Possesses the great *dhāraṇī*-entrance, which is called Perfect Enlightenment;"[49] and "Unsurpassed marvelous enlightenment pervades the ten directions;"[50] and so on.

What is the textual basis for the subjectively actualizing person and the subjectively actualizing wisdom also being called "Great Enlightenment," "Perfect Enlightenment," and "Marvelous Enlightenment"? These are expressed in the sutra when it says: "Greatly Enlightened World-Honored One," "Perfectly Enlightened Bodhisattvas," "Marvelously Enlightened Bodhisattvas," and so on.

"Awakening-cultivation[51]-realization-transformation" (*wu-hsiu-cheng-hua/osu-chŏnghwa* 悟修證化) is the main teaching of this particular text, and it is also the doctrinal theme of many scriptures. Yet some schools discuss it in the context of "innate enlightenment" and "actualized enlightenment," while others discuss it in the context of "enlightening oneself" and "enlightening others." In either method of explication, "awakening-practice-realization-transformation" is reflected limitlessly.

Comparison with the *Hwaŏmgyŏng*

[*HPC* 7.126a18]

Outside of the *Hwaŏmgyŏng* only this text exhausts the particulars of, and fully contains the teaching of "phenomena universally pervading and principle completely embracing." This sutra only differs from the *Hwaŏmgyŏng* in terms of length. The phrase "Great Curative Extensive Perfect Enlightenment" is the same as "Great Curative Extensive Buddha."[52] "Buddha" means "enlightenment," especially the full enlightenment of self and others. The term "full enlightenment" (found in the title of the *Hwaŏmgyŏng*) is exactly the same as the term "Perfect Enlightenment." Thus, the two scriptures are generally the same. Since this sutra takes "awakening-practice-realization-transformation," discharges them and gives them their full expression, magnificently adorning the *dharmadhātu*, it is "hwaŏm."[53] Therefore it is said: "taking an inexhaustible amount of *dhāraṇī*-jewels and magnificently adorning the true jewel palace of the *dharmadhātu*."[54] When it says "inexhaustible," the meanings of great and small, partial and complete, expedient and true, sudden and gradual, incomplete and complete doctrines are completely dissolved without remainder. It is like the lack of border between a river and the ocean into which it flows. This is why the *Hwaŏmgyŏng* is praised as "great teaching," and is also called "perfect."

The Meaning of
"*Sūtra*-Fully-Revealed-Doctrine-Scripture
(修多羅了義經)"

[*HPC* 7.126b5]

What is the meaning of the phrase "*sūtra*-fully-revealed-doctrine-scripture"? Among the many sutras, those that are distinguished by the term "fully revealed doctrine" (*liao-i/youi* 了義) are those sutras that adapt to people's capacities. Thus this sutra is called "complete doctrine" and is also called "sudden" (*tun/ton* 頓). This is a minor difference between the two.[55]

"*Sūtra*" (*ching/kyŏng* 經) means "warp and woof." "Warp and woof" means "vertical and horizontal."[56] This is like the marvelous instruction discussed above: it explains horizontally and vertically, sometimes refuting, sometimes establishing—taking words, phrases, and sentences, putting them together to form a teaching that becomes the norm for ten thousand ages; opening up the understanding of living beings and causing them to reach the other shore. This is what is called a "*sūtra*." To express my understanding of the meaning of the title "Great Curative Extensive Perfect Enlightenment Sutra Complete Doctrine Scripture," I offer the following verse:

> The exceedingly deep, marvelous dharma is subtle and difficult
>   to expound,
> Yet when we lift our eyes to see it, it is already present before us.
>
> If we fully know that the title has not a single word,
> Then in reading the scriptures, how can we follow verbal
>   explanations?

[Here Kihwa ends his explication of the title and begins to treat the first line of the actual sutra, which is the testament by the Buddha's assistant, Ānanda, that what follows below is "what he has heard."]

[*HPC* 7.126b16]

The Buddha continually extended himself to vast numbers of people—more than a thousand bodhisattva "ocean assemblies," and each of these crowds numbered a hundred thousand people. How is it that only Ānanda said "I have heard" and his statement has appeared at the beginning of all sutras down through the ages? How is this? Among the ten great disciples Ānanda had heard the greatest number of the Buddha's sermons.

[*Translator's note*: According to Buddhist tradition, Ānanda was the Buddha's administrative assistant during most of his teaching career, and was present at almost every sermon. He was supposed to be possessed of great intelligence and a powerful memory, and could therefore recount the content of the Buddha's sermons. However, when he appeared at the first convocation after the Buddha's death to offer his versions of the sermons, the council chairman, Mahākāśyapa, rejected them on the grounds that Ānanda had not yet attained enlightenment, and therefore his understanding and rendition of the Buddha's sermons could be flawed. Ānanda subsequently endeavored with all his strength to attain enlightenment, and once he succeeded, the council accepted his accounts. Therefore, all Buddhist sutras that propose to be an actual account of the teachings of Śākyamuni start off with the phrase, "Thus I have heard . . ."]

[Kihwa]

And Ānanda's merit was due to the fact that he had long ago sown the roots of virtue; his sharpness exceeded that of others, and he always cherished the opportunity of being the Buddha's assistant. Thus, he kept in his memory every single phrase and every single verse of the Buddha's words without recording anything in writing. At the time of the Buddha's *parinirvāṇa*, his only question to the Buddha was what kind of phrase should be placed at the beginning of all the sutras, and the Buddha told him to say "Thus I have heard." Now after the Buddha's passing away, Kāśyapa was the first to attain the condition of "extinction of outflow,"[57] and therefore he served as chairperson at the first convocation. But when the assembly raised the three doubts,[58] Ānanda clarified them with this single phrase. Therefore we know that this phrase is something that was personally recommended by the Buddha, and the means by which Ānanda was able to overcome their doubts. And this same phrase starts off every one of the scriptures that appear as the result of forty-nine years of the Buddha's teaching. According to the content of his sermons, Ānanda transmitted it through an eternity up to the present. Subjected to each person's examination, everyone has praised it as "excellent." Is this not wonderful? The oceanic teaching that poured directly from the Golden Mouth, overflowed from India and poured out in East Asia, permeating people's eyes and ears and arousing the goodness of their minds. The wheel of the Dharma eternally abides and transmits, while wisdom and life continue without lapse. Whose merit is this? He earned the prediction to become the King Mountain Sea Wisdom Omnipotent Penetration—can this be without reason?![59]

Generally the format of the sutras outside of the main body of the text itself is first an introduction of the time and place, the Buddha and his followers. After a proper ritual is performed for asking a question, the listeners receive the teaching with faith and sincerely practice. All sutra writers follow this order. So now comes the introduction of time and place, Buddha and followers. My verse:

> The Womb of Radiance alloys worldling and sage within;
> In the assembly of equality, ritual clearly occurs.
> Without dropping a single word, his voice shakes the earth.
> After finishing the speech, he has not enlightened all of the
>   people.

[Sutra (#1)] [*T* 842.17.913a27; *HPC* 7.126c18]

如是我聞。一時婆伽婆

Thus I have heard. One time, the Bhagavan . . .

[Kihwa] [*HPC* 7.126c19]

"Thus" ["like this" 如是] refers to the subsequently expounded dharma. "I have heard" means that "I have heard this dharma from the Buddha." Why does he say "One time"? If we recorded the dates for the preaching, then each sutra would be different. By simply saying "one time," he covers all of them. Therefore he merely says "one (time)." Bhagavan is another name for the Buddha. Since this word has such an extensive range of meaning, I leave it untranslated in the Sanskrit.[60]

[Sutra (#2)] [*T* 842.17.913a27; *HPC* 7.126c24]

入於神通大光明藏三昧正受。一切如來光嚴住持。是諸衆生清淨覺地。身心寂滅平等本際。圓滿十方不二隨順。於不二境、現諸淨土。與大菩薩摩訶薩十萬人俱。其名曰文殊師利菩薩、普賢菩薩、普眼菩薩、金剛藏菩薩、彌勒菩薩、清淨慧菩薩、威德自在菩薩、辨音菩薩、淨諸業障菩薩、普覺菩薩、圓覺菩薩、賢善首菩薩等、而爲上首。與諸眷屬、皆入三昧、同住如來平等法會。

. . . entered the supramundane great radiant bright *garbha*, in the exactly attained *samādhi*, where all tathāgatas abide in radiant splendor. This is the ground of pure enlightenment of sentient beings, the equal original reality where body and mind are completely erased. He completely filled the ten directions with the accordance with nonduality, and in this nondual state manifested all pure lands.

He was with one hundred thousand great bodhisattva-mahāsattvas. Those who served as leaders of the assembly were: Mañjuśrī Bodhisattva, Samantabhadra Bodhisattva, Universal Vision Bodhisattva, Vajragarbha Bodhisattva, Maitreya Bodhisattva, Pure Wisdom Bodhisattva, Power and Virtue Unhindered Bodhisattva, Voice of

Discernment Bodhisattva, Purifier of All Karmic Hindrances
Bodhisattva, Universal Enlightenment Bodhisattva, Perfect Enlightenment Bodhisattva, and Most Excellent of Worthies
Bodhisattva. With their retinues, all entered into the same *samādhi*
as the Tathāgata at this assembly of the equal dharma.

[Kihwa] [*HPC* 7.127a11]

That in which things are stored is called *garbha*; it has the meaning of
"containing"; it also has the meaning of "producing." It refers directly
to the essence of enlightenment. The reason that the essence of enlightenment is indicated with this word is because it is where myriad virtues
are gathered, and it is the place from which the supramundane radiance
emanates. As for the phrase "the exactly attained *samādhi*," this is the
situation where the essence of enlightenment is clear and self-luminous
and is not affected by external conditions. "Enter" means "to accord
with and stably abide in" this clear and self-luminous body. Yet within
this clear and self-luminous *garbha*, it is not only the Tathāgata who
accords and stably abides—it is the place where all tathāgatas abide
together and mutually illumine and adorn each other. And it is not a
place where only buddhas abide—no sentient being is excluded. It is
only because of the impediments of body and mind that they are unable
to accord and stably abide within. The body and mind that are within
this *garbha* are originally quiescent. It is because we see from the perspective of the traces of body and mind that there seems to be a difference
between sage and worldling. If we see from the perspective of the quiescent essence, then sentient being and Buddha are equal, and this equal,
original reality is the universally pervading, fully containing, perfectly
interfused realm of nonduality. The Buddha accords with it and stably
abides in it. Without leaving quiescence, he manifests worlds in response
to conditions. The bodhisattvas, 100,000 in number, comprise the audience. These 100,000 bodhisattvas, along with their retinues, all enter
samādhi in the same subtle state as the Buddha.

[*Translator's note: Samādhi* is a Sanskrit term that refers to the state of
pure concentration experienced in the deepest of meditations. *Tathāgata*
is a Sanskrit epithet of the Buddha, usually translated into English as
"thus-come." The Buddha is not a transcendant god, but a human being
who has had to pass through the course of suffering and practice. The
naturally enlightened condition that the Tathāgata "abides" in is described as "adorned with light." The above-mentioned "supernatural"
samādhi, which has been described as a spiritual state of the Tathāgata
is identified as the "ground" (or "stage" 地) of pure enlightenment" of
sentient beings, that is, ordinary people. Here ground refers to that

which is in itself pure enlightenment—the human mind. Thus the equality of Buddha and sentient being is posited in the first passage of the sutra. In this text, as well as in many other Mahāyāna texts, the term "equal" (*tŭng* 等) should not be understood as "social equality" or equality in any worldly sense. The "equality" of all things is due to their emptiness, or their unity or interrelationship in the perspective of marvelous existence. The *ten directions* 十方 are the four cardinal points, the four intermediate directions, the zenith and the nadir. The term means "everywhere throughout the universe."]

1

Mañjuśrī Bodhisattva

[Kihwa] [*HPC* 7.127b6]

[*Interlinear note*: "Mañjuśrī" means "most profound."] The unfathomable is called "profound" (*mañju*). The first among many is called "most" (*śrī*). The reason he is called "most profound" is because he gathers a myriad virtues without showing them, such that even the gods cannot fathom him. Though he carries out a myriad transformations, he is never depleted; though he is high, he cannot be looked up to. The reason one hundred thousand bodhisattvas select Mañjuśrī to initiate the teaching is because of his level of wisdom. "Wisdom" is the spearhead of a myriad practices and at the same time their marvelous final product. If the myriad practices lack wisdom then they will all develop flaws.

[*Translator's note*: The word being translated here as "flaws" is the Buddhist technical term *yu-lou/yuru* 有漏 (Sanskrit *āsrava*) which literally means "having outflow" or "leaking." The concept of *āsrava* is instructive in regard to the Buddhist understanding of the human consciousness in its unenlightened and enlightened conditions. *Āsrava* refers to the uncontrolled "flowing-out" or "leaking out" of consciousness to the six objects of desire, thus it means "defiled," or "impure." The possibility for this leakage is directly associated with the condition of ignorance, which allows the consciousnesses to be tricked by the illusions of subject and object, like and dislike. But the enlightened mind, on the other hand, is able to operate without outflow (*wu-lou/muru*; 無漏 *anāsrava*), and therefore whatever is created by it can be pure and perfect.]

[Kihwa]

If wisdom is lacking in the final product, then that final product will be nothing but evil seeds. Therefore it is said: "Among the myriad practices, there is not a single one that can lack this ruler [wisdom]." It is also said: "Not devising these [ignorant] understandings is called 'the excellent state.' If you devise these understandings, you invite countless errors." The way to avoid "devising understandings" is through the power of wisdom.

It is because the Buddha wants to make all practitioners of Perfect Enlightenment first rely on wisdom and then practice, that he has Mañjuśrī ask the question, first explaining the dharma-practice of the Tathāgata's causal stage. This "dharma-practice of the causal stage" is none other than the above mentioned "faith-understanding." First you must have "faith-understanding" and then you can begin to practice and reach to realization. This is why Mañjuśrī is first to raise a question. My verse:

> If you want to understand the practices of the Tathāgata's causal
>   stage,
> Read and understand the questions put forth by Mañjuśrī.
> When you fully realize the emptiness of dharmas, emptiness is
>   also forgotten;
> From this a fool is transformed into a king of enlightenment.

Mañjuśrī's Question on the Dharma-Practice of the Causal Stage

[Sutra (#3)] [*T* 842.17.913b15; *HPC* 7.127b23]

於是文殊師利菩薩在大衆中即從座起。頂禮佛足右繞三
匝。長跪叉手而白佛言：

Mañjuśrī Bodhisattva arose from his seat in the great assembly. He bowed his head to the Buddha's feet and circumambulated him three times to the right. He then knelt down with his hands clasped and addressed the Buddha, saying:

[Kihwa] [*HPC* 7.127c2]

He gets up from meditation and fixes his hair and clothing. First he bows to the Buddha's feet with clasped hands, then he uses words to transmit his message. This is the ultimate in revering the Buddha and revering the dharma.

[Sutra (#4)] [*T* 842.17.913b8; *HPC* 7.127c4]

大悲世尊...

Greatly Compassionate World-Honored One . . .

[Kihwa] [*HPC* 7.127c5]

The fundamental reason that all buddhas appear in the world is to save sentient beings. Since the vast desire to save sentient beings is originally from his great compassion, whenever someone wants to ask him to teach the essentials of the dharma, they should first address him as "greatly compassionate."

[Sutra (#5)] [*T* 842.17.913b9; *HPC* 7.127c7]

願爲此會諸來法衆、說於如來本起清淨因地法行。及說菩
薩於大乘中發清淨心遠離諸病、能使未來末世衆生求大乘
者不墮邪見。作是語已、五體投地。如是三請終而復始。

Please, for all members of this assembly who have come for your dharma, teach us about the dharma practice of the Tathāgata's originally arisen pure causal stage. Also, please teach the bodhisattvas to arouse pure mind in the great vehicle and become distantly removed from all afflictions, such that they can prevent the future sentient beings of the degenerate age who seek the great vehicle from falling into mistaken views." Having said this, he prostrated to the ground. He asked this question three times in succession.

[*Translator's note*: The term translated here as "degenerate age" is *mo-shih/malse* (末世), which could also be translated as "latter age" or "final age." The concept comes from the doctrines of Pure Land Buddhism, in which it was taught that there were three ages of the Buddhist dharma. The first age is the age of the "true dharma," during which it is relatively easy to meet a good teacher and attain enlightenment. The next age is that of the "semblance dharma," when there is greater delusion in the world and it is more difficult to attain enlightenment. The final age is that of the "degenerate dharma," which is the period of greatest delusion, during which there are few enlightened teachers, and during which (in Pure Land thought) it is impossible to attain enlightenment through one's own efforts. The writer of the sutra is not intending strict Pure Land interpretations, but nonetheless, it is to be understood that during the degenerate age there are few reliable teachers, and since most sentient beings are deeply immersed in ignorance, it is extremely difficult for them to attain enlightenment. Throughout the sutra the Buddha and the eminent bodhisattvas who participate in the discussion will regularly distinguish between teachings that are aimed at the present audience (the "great assembly") and those that are aimed at sentient beings of the "degenerate age."]

[Kihwa] [*HPC* 7.127c12]

In contrast to final product we say "originally arisen." In contrast to defiled habituation we say "purity." In relation to the anticipated goal we say "causal stage." In contrast to dirty and painful karmic activity we say "dharma practice." Now if perfect illumination also has "faith-understanding," this means that the fundamental cause is already perfected. In the "final stage," which normally refers to "perfect realization," there must also be practice against defiled habituation and work toward further purification. There must be transformation of karmic activity into dharma practice—the practice of accordance with reality.

What is the meaning of "arouse pure mind?" Originally-existent enlightenment is not different from Buddha. It is only because of deluded thought that we are not fully enlightened. Knowing this, you should think: "The only reason there is a difference between the Buddha and I is because of the stain of false thinking. First I must correct my habits and eradicate defilement by changing the old and actualizing the new in order to return to the fount of purity." Thinking in this way is called "the arousal of pure mind (*bodhicitta*)."

What is the meaning of "distantly removed from all afflictions"? The afflictions that cripple the dharma-body are not of a single type; therefore he says "all." Since the various cures are effective and one is completely freed with no affliction remaining, he says "free." Why does he say "able to prevent"? If you want to save others, you must first save yourself. If you have not attained salvation yourself, how can you save others? Therefore Mañjuśrī asks on behalf of the bodhisattvas for the Buddha to teach the dharma-practice of the causal stage. Then he asks for the way to save oneself and save others. As for "Having said this . . . three times in succession": Having stated his point, he uses the technique of repetition.

> The water is clear,
> The moon reflects;
> With sensitivity total,
> His response is immediate.

[*Translator's note*: The Buddha is said to have a few different types of bodies, each of which represents a different way of perceiving his existence. The most basic division of the bodies of the Buddha is into three, in Sanskrit *trikāya*. These are the *dharmakāya* (法身), *sambhogakāya* (報身), and *nirmānakāya* (應身, 化身). (1) The *dharmakāya* is a reference to the transcendence of form and realization of true suchness; (2) the *sambhogakāya* is the buddha-body that is called "reward body" or "body of enjoyment of the merits attained as a bodhisattva"; (3) the *nirmānakāya* is the body manifested in response to the need to teach sentient beings. Of these, the dharma-body is the most profound, in that the Buddha is here seen as the ultimate truth, or principle of all of existence. One might also understand the term to mean "the original, enlightened nature of all of existence." The term is very close in connotation to that of "reality-realm" (*dharmadhātu* 法界).]

[Sutra (#6)] [*T* 842.17.913b14; *HPC* 7.128a7] ▼

爾時世尊、告文殊師利菩薩言：善哉、善哉。善男子、汝
等乃能爲諸菩薩諮詢如來因地法行。乃爲末世一切衆生求
大乘者得正住持、不墮邪見。汝今諦聽、當爲汝説。 時文
殊師利菩薩奉教歡喜、及諸大衆默然而聽。

Then the World-Honored One, speaking to Mañjuśrī Bodhisattva, said: "Excellent! Excellent! Good son, you have skillfully asked on behalf of the bodhisattvas about the dharma-practice of the Tathāgata's causal stage. You have also enabled the sentient beings of the degenerate age who seek the great vehicle to gain the correct abiding such that they will not fall into erroneous views. Now listen well, and I shall explain for you."

Mañjuśrī Bodhisattva received the teaching with reverence and joy; all those in the great assembly became silent and listened.

[*Translator's note: Correct abiding* is a central topic in this scripture, since its definition and methods of attainment are a major problem in the practices of all Buddhist schools, whether they be Theravāda, Mahā-yāna, Zen, Hua-yen, and so on. Practitioners of meditation are hampered by the movement of their mind, which operates according to deeply ingrained habits developed through ignorance, attachment, and desire. If practitioners are to stop their minds from "abiding" in these conditions, they need to know exactly where they are supposed to place their attention.]

[Kihwa] [*HPC* 7.128a13]

In between "dharma-practice of the causal stage (因地法行)" and "also enable sentient beings of the degenerate age (乃爲末世一切衆生)," the text seems to be missing a line which should say: "cause all bodhisattvas to arouse pure mind in the great vehicle (令諸菩薩於大乘中、發清淨心)." Also the *wei* ("for," "on behalf of" 爲) of *chi wei* (乃爲) is probably mistaken for *ling* ("cause" 令). The sentence should say:

汝等乃能爲諸菩薩諮詢如來因地法行令諸菩薩於大乘中發
清淨心。 乃令末世一切衆生求大乘者得正住持不墮邪見。

You have been able to ask for the bodhisattvas about the dharma-practice of the causal stage of the Tathāgata, and have caused all the bodhisattvas to arouse the pure mind in the great vehicle. You have also caused all sentient beings of the degenerate age who seek the great vehicle to gain correct abiding such that they do not fall into erroneous views.

At the conclusion of this chapter, the text says: "Bodhisattvas, depending on this, arouse pure mind in the great vehicle. Sentient beings of the degenerate age, depending upon it (this practice), will not fall into erroneous views."[1] The agreement between this later sentence and the above one is it thus quite obvious.

What is the meaning of "gain correct abiding"? In the essence of Perfect Enlightenment, nature and characteristics are both submerged, and all mistakes are cut off. One does not generate the hindrances that come from the views of "nature and characteristics" or "being and nonbeing" and so on, but single-mindedly actualizes the enlightened nature. It is by means of this that you attain correct abiding. If you do not do this, you will not avoid falling into the pit of mistaken views.

Why does he say, "Now listen well and I shall explain for you"? In the present for those at the assembly, and extending to future ages, he discloses the causal practice, letting this become the basis for their activities. First he shows the seriousness of his intentions and then he responds according to their capacities. Therefore he praises the question as "excellent" and agrees to explain. Although the moon does not withhold any of its luminosity, only still water can reflect it, and although the Buddha's voice is perfectly impartial, it cannot enter a scattered mind. Therefore he admonishes them to "listen well." "Joy," refers to the joy of the dharma. "Silently," refers to the bliss of meditation. This implies embracing the enjoyment of the dharma and the bliss of meditation within while listening for the Buddha's subtle voice. Therefore he says "[receive with] joy" and "[became] silent [and listened]."

The Buddha's Answer

[Sutra (#7)] [*T* 842.17.913b18; *HPC* 7.128b9]

善男子、無上法王有大陀羅尼門。名爲圓覺。流出一切清
淨：眞如、菩提、涅槃及波羅蜜、教授菩薩。

Good sons, the unsurpassed King of the Dharma possesses the great *dhāraṇī*-entrance. It is called "Perfect Enlightenment." From it is manifested all purity: suchness, *bodhi*, nirvana and the *pāramitās* with which he teaches bodhisattvas.

[Kihwa] [*HPC* 7.128b12]

"Great" refers to the three Greatnesses of essence, attributes and function. *Dhāraṇī* denotes the greatness of attributes, but it also includes the meaning of "curative." "is manifested all purity: suchness, *bodhi*, nirvana, and the *pāramitās* with which he teaches bodhisattvas" is what I have referred to as the greatness of function; but it also includes the meaning of "extensive." Why is *dhāraṇī* defined as "attributes" and "curative?" Since the word *dhāraṇī* has such a wide range of meanings, I leave in the Sanskrit untranslated.[2] If we must translate it, then I would say "completely retaining (總 持)," since an unimaginable amount of virtuous functions are fully preserved without being lost. Yet it also means "able to maintain (能 持)," as well as "able to dispel (能 遮)." In maintaining, all good dharmas are maintained, and in dispelling, all evil dharmas are dispelled. It completely retains an unimaginable amount of virtuous functions: this is the greatness of attributes. It keeps the good and dispels the evil: therefore it has the meaning of "curative."

Why is it that "manifested all purity: [. . .] suchness with which he teaches bodhisattvas" is called "function" and is called "extensive?" The opposite of falsity is called "truth." The opposite of change is called "suchness." "True suchness" is the teaching that dispels falsity and dissolves distinctions. The opposite of defilement is called *bodhi;* the opposite of *saṃsāra* is called *nirvana. Bodhi* and nirvana are the dharmas resultant of transforming defilement and separating from *saṃsāra.*

The sufferings which develop from defilement number more than 84,000. The *pāramitās* are the marvelous method by which those defilements are transformed, yet none of them lie outside the process of "stopping evil, keeping goodness, getting rid of mistakes, and returning to the correct." Therefore, generating these kinds of innumerable marvelous functions is called the "greatness of function." These are used to teach bodhisattvas without excluding any sort of person whatsoever— this is why I have also called them "extensive." Since these kinds of innumerable virtuous attributes and these kinds of innumerable marvelous functions all depend upon the same essence for their existence, I have also said "greatness of essence." If enlightenment is *really* going to be enlightenment, it must include these three greatnesses. Then it can be called Perfect Enlightenment. Since this is the most pure enlightenment in which one escapes bondage, the term is only appropriate to the Buddha. Therefore the text says "the unsurpassed king of the dharma." Since it says "possesses the great *dhāraṇī*-entrance that is called Perfect Enlightenment," we know that which totally permeates awakening, practice, realization, and transformation without lapse is the Perfect Enlightenment possessed by the Buddha.

The concept of "entrance" includes the two basic meanings of: (1) entering upon a journey, or (2) entering into a room. "Entering into a room" has the meaning of "going from shallow to deep." Entering upon a journey has the meaning of "going from the beginning to the end." The waves over a vast expanse all originate on the same great ocean. A thousand different paths have their origin at the same gate. Therefore the present meaning of "entrance" is that of "going from beginning to end." In metaphorical terms, Perfect Enlightenment is the "root" of the myriad virtues and the "origin" of ten thousand practices. Therefore none of the expedient means of practice and realization and the teaching of the doctrine can be initiated without it. This is why Perfect Enlightenment is called an "entrance." This entrance is innumerable, infinite; thus it is called "great." It is replete with the three Greatnesses, therefore it is called Perfect. It is clearly bright, silently luminous; thus it is called Enlightenment.

[Sutra (#8)] [*T* 842.17.913b21; *HPC* 7.129a2]

一切如來本起因地皆依圓照清淨覺相、永斷無明方成佛道。

All tathāgatas in their originally arisen causal stage rely on the perfect illumination of the attributes of pure enlightenment to permanently sever ignorance and directly accomplish the Buddha-Way.

[Kihwa] [*HPC* 7.129a4]
The enlightened illumination experienced by beginners cannot but include essence and function. But [in the case of beginners] the essence generates deluded conceptualization and in its function it is covered over by the everyday mind. Since the consciousness of the beginner is covered over, his illumination does not reach to the essence and his function is incomplete. Only the Buddha thoroughly actualizes his essence and completely unfolds his function. The enlightenment illuminated by the beginner is nothing more than being trapped in the attributes of the purity of the enlightened nature. Therefore, saying, "illumination of the attributes of pure enlightenment" is like the so-called "realm of objective faith." This is the same as being bound to the realm of the purity of the nature.
Yet since these attributes are also limitless, including all virtues, "illumination" in this text is said to be "complete illumination." And since merely being able to "completely illuminate all attributes of enlightenment" is sufficient to overturn ignorance and accomplish correct enlightenment, all tathāgatas, because of their ability to completely illumine, sever affliction and accomplish the Way. Therefore we know that developing myriads of practices and reaching realization, realizing great enlightenment and saving sentient beings, all depend upon the power of complete illumination. Accordingly, what has been taught is called "the dharma-practice of the causal stage of all tathāgatas."

The Definition of Ignorance

[Sutra (#9)] [*T* 842.17.913b22; *HPC* 7.129a17]

云何無明。善男子、一切眾生從無始來種種顛倒。猶如迷
人四方易處、妄認四大爲自身相、六塵緣影爲自心相。譬

彼病目見空中華、及第二月。善男子、空實無華、病者妄
執。由妄執故、非唯惑此虛空自性。亦復迷彼實華生處。
由此妄有輪轉生死。故名無明。

What is ignorance? Good sons, all sentient beings fall into various inverted views without beginning. Just like a person who is disoriented and confuses the four directions,[3] they mistakenly take the Four Elements as the attributes of their bodies and the conditioned shadows of the Six Objects as the attributes of their mind. It is just like when our eyes are diseased and we see flowers in the sky, or a second moon. Good sons, the sky actually has no flowers—they are the false attachment of the diseased person. Because of this false attachment, not only are we confused about the self-nature of the sky; we are also mixed up about the place where real flowers come from. From this there is falsely existent transmigration through life and death. Therefore it is called "ignorance."

[*Translator's note*: The *Four Elements* that represent the range of sensory experience are Earth, Air, Fire, and Water. In some schools of early Indian metaphysics, the elements were conceived as being inherently existent. In later Mahāyāna philosophy, however, these four sensible tendencies that exist in the material world are not self-existent properties, but only appear in relation to other things.

The *Six Objects* are the objects of vision, hearing, taste, touch, smell and conceptualization. The relation of these factors to the construction of a false idea of self is discussed in detail in chapter 3 and it is also a predominant theme of the *SHM*.]

[Kihwa] [*HPC* 7.129a23]

Awareness (Skt. *vidyā*) has the meanings of "marvelous illumination" and "illumination of the correct." Ignorance (Skt. *avidyā*) means "to turn away from illumination and face the darkness," or "lose the true and abandon oneself to error." Abandoning the true and falling into error is generally called "inversion." Since the types of error are not limited to one kind, the text says "various."

If the nature is originally clear and bright, how can there be ignorance? Beyond the clear and bright essence, delusion suddenly arises, and one loses the true brightness and correct wisdom, turns to darkness and falls into error. It is like a person who suddenly becomes confused, mistaking North for South and East for West. The marvelously bright true mind is still and luminous at the same time. Being luminous yet still, it is called the dharma body. Being still yet luminous, it is called true wisdom. True wisdom ends thought; the dharma-body lacks attributes. Yet even though the attributeless dharma-body is the true body, we take the material body as our own body; and while the thought-ending wisdom is the true mind, we take conditioned thought as our own mind. Since we take conditioned thought to be our mind, we confuse true wisdom. Since we take the material body to be our body, we confuse the dharma-body. Because of this, not only are we confused about the dharma-body and true wisdom, we also don't know that the material body and conditioned thought are both unreal. All of this is brought about by the most primary manifestation of nonenlightenment.

It is like looking into the sky with impaired vision and seeing flowers there; or pressing on the eyeball while looking at the moon and seeing a second moon at the edge of the moon. The "vast sky" refers to the dharma-body; the "sky-flowers" refer to the material body; the "real moon" refers to true wisdom; the "second moon" refers to conditioned thought. Even though the true body lacks attributes, we take the material body as [our own] body. Even though the true mind severs thought, we take conditioned thought to be [our own] mind. This is just like seeing flowers in the sky or a second moon at the edge of the moon. The material body has attributes, yet in the end they again dissolve into extinction. The conditioned mind is false; it arises and ceases according to the environment. Because of our attachment to the body of arising and ceasing and taking it to be real, we falsely perceive transmigration through life and death. This is the error of nonenlightenment, which is exactly the characteristic of ignorance.

If we hold to the marvelously luminous essence and constantly awaken, and take the dharma-body as our body and take true wisdom as our mind, then, since the dharma-body and true wisdom originally lack the marks of arising and ceasing, we will definitely not perceive transmigration through life and death. The Tathāgata's originally arisen practice of his causal stage, which is the complete illumination of the attributes of pure enlightenment, is none other than this.

[*Translator's note*: Ignorance is none other than the mistaken view regarding our own existence. Not only do we create an illusory person where there is none, but we also do not understand the way in which we truly exist, much less the nature of absolute reality. We have the habit of reifying concepts and attaching to them. Therefore, when we are told that the obstruction to enlightenment is our ignorance, and that ignorance is the basis for desire and suffering, "ignorance" immediately becomes an "it"—an objective "something," separate from our real consciousness.

Here the Buddha explains that ignorance is *not* "something," that "ignorance" is a term used to describe the mistaken perception of the mode of our being. Thus, if we can call ignorance anything, it is our continuing false perception of our own selves. This incorrect mental function results in: (1) the formulation of things that really do not exist at all (sky-flowers; a false self); (2) the misunderstanding of the correct way to perceive phenomenal existence (the place where a real flower has its being; the true way of existence); and (3) the misunderstanding of the nature of the real, or the absolute (the sky; *śūnyatā*). These three can be correlated with the "three natures" of Consciousness-only: (1) "sky-flowers" represent the nature of (mistaken) discriminating conception (*parikalpitaḥ-svabhāva*); (2) the true mode of the existence of flowers is the nature of dependent origination (*paratantra-svabhāva*) and (3) the quality of the sky is comparable to the nature of perfectly accomplished reality (*parinispanna-svabhāva*).]

Ignorance Lacks Substance

[Sutra (#10)] [*T* 842.17.913b28; *HPC* 7.129c5]

善男子、此無明者非實有體。如夢中人。夢時非無、及至
於醒了無所得。如衆空華滅於虛空、不可說言有定滅處。
何以故？無生處故。一切衆生於無生中妄見生滅。是故說
名輪轉生死。

Good sons, this "ignorance" actually lacks substance. It is like a man who is dreaming. At the time of the dream, there is no non-existence, until he awakens and finds that there is nothing for him to hold on to. Similarly, when the sky-flowers disappear from the sky, you cannot say that there is a definite point of their disappearance. Why? Because there is no point at which they arise. All sentient beings falsely perceive arising and ceasing within this condition of non-arising. Therefore they say that there is "transmigration through life-and-death."

[Kihwa] [*HPC* 7.129c10]

Because of our confusion, we perceive the existence of transmigration through life and death as well as the perfect illumination of the marks of enlightenment. Yet on the other hand, if we investigate how it is that there *is* life and death, and how delusion arises, then we will find out not only that life and death cannot be confirmed, but that delusion itself lacks any essence. It is just like the case of a man who sees various things in a dream. When he awakens, those things cannot be held and the contents of the dream cannot be confirmed. This is because the dream *and* its phenomena all lack a point of arising. It is also like looking at the sky with impaired vision and seeing flowers: if the impairment can be corrected, you will see the flowers return to nothingness. Still, although the sky-flowers are seen to arise and seen to disappear, these flowers in the sky originally have no point at which they arise, nor have they a place in which they disappear. Transmigration through life and death is just like the dream realm, and just like the sky-flowers. If we investigate to the source, there is really no point where they arise. It is only because of false conceptualization that we perceive arising and ceasing. Therefore there it is called "transmigration through life-and-death."

[Sutra (#11)] [*T* 842.17.913c3; *HPC* 7.129c21]

善男子、如來因地修圓覺者知是空華即無輪轉、亦無身心受彼生死。非作故無。本性無故。

Good sons, the practice of Perfect Enlightenment in the causal stage of the Tathāgata is to know that these are "sky-flowers,"[4] which is the same as knowing that there is no transmigration, and that there is no body/mind to undergo life-and-death. But they are not caused to be nonexistent. They are nonexistent because they lack original nature.

[Kihwa] [*HPC* 7.129c24]

When we completely illuminate the marks of enlightenment, we know that the real is originally existent. And since, when we observe ignorance, we find it to be false, lacking an essence, there is no objective delusion such as "*saṃsāra*," nor any subjective delusions such as "body and mind." These are not made nonexistent by any activity (i.e., such as conceptual analysis), rather, their original nature is perfectly empty.

The Dharma-Practice

[Sutra (#12)] [*T* 842.17.913c5; *HPC* 7.130a4]

彼知覺者猶如虛空。知虛空者即空華相。亦不可說無知覺性。有無俱遣。是則名爲淨覺隨順。

Now, this [prior] awareness is just like empty space. Yet since the knowledge that it is like empty space is none other than the appearance sky-flowers, you also cannot say that there is no nature of awareness. When existence and nonexistence are both dispelled, it is called "according with pure enlightenment."

[Kihwa] [*HPC* 7.130a7]

Even though you know the real originally exists, and realize that the false originally does not exist, the awareness that knows this [existence and nonexistence] is also originally non-arisen. Also, even though you know of the non-arisenness of this awareness, this knowing is also the same as the non-arisenness of body and mind and life and death, which is again, the same as the sky-flowers. If you will just not discriminate between existence and nonexistence, you will experience unity with the fount of the real. How could there be no awareness whatsoever? If we say there is no awareness, it is the same as the view of nihilism. This is because the marvelously luminous originally existent true nature is not the same as the present counteractive awareness.[5] When the counteractive awareness exhausts itself, then original luminosity is ever present. Therefore it is called "according with the nature of enlightenment."

[Sutra (#13)] [*T* 842.17.913c7; *HPC* 7.130a15]

何 以 故 。 虛 空 性 故 常 不 動 故 如 來 藏 中 無 起 滅 故 、 無 知 見 故 。 如 法 界 性 、 究 竟 圓 滿 徧 十 方 故 。 是 則 名 爲 因 地 法 行 。 菩 薩 因 此 於 大 乘 中 發 清 淨 心 。 末 世 衆 生 依 此 修 行 、 不 墮 邪 見 。

Why? Because its nature is completely empty; because it is eternally changeless; because there is neither arising nor ceasing within the Matrix of the Tathāgata, and because there are no fixed points of view. Like the nature of the reality-realm it is totally complete and perfect, pervading the ten directions. Therefore it is called the "dharma practice of the causal stage." Bodhisattvas, relying upon it, arouse their pure mind within the Mahāyāna. Sentient beings of the degenerate age who practice relying on this will not fall into erroneous views.

[*Translator's note*: Matrix of the Tathāgata (如來藏; *tathāgatagarbha*) is a term that signifies the sentient being as the circumstance of future buddhahood. The concept arose in Buddhist thought as an explanation of how original buddhahood can exist in the state of delusion called "sentient being." Thus *tathāgatagarbha* expresses the already perfect aspect of the original nature of the mind that is clear and pure without arising or cessation.]

[Kihwa] [*HPC* 7.130a20]

The body and mind exist. Life and death change. Even though the sky-flowers seem to exist, they do not exist; even though they seem to change, they do not change. So how can the Buddha say that the body and mind and life and death are the same as sky-flowers?

Furthermore, the view that sees the disappearance of flowers is not the same as the view that sees the appearance of flowers. The knowledge of the non-arisenness of body/mind, life/death is not the same as the false knowledge that authorizes body/mind or the false view that sees birth and death. Why then, does he go on to say "this awareness is just like empty space"?

Furthermore, the nature's own spiritual understanding originally has awareness. Since he has already said that this awareness is the same as space, why does he go on to say that it is the same as the appearance of sky-flowers?

Furthermore, since all views are repeatedly cleared away until they are utterly extinguished, why does he go on to say: "you can't say there is no essence of awareness"?

[The answers to these questions are as follows:]

Why does he point to body and mind, life and death and call them "the same as sky-flowers"? Even though body and mind seem to exist, it is only by mistaken conceptualization that they appear to exist. In terms of their essence they are like the sky; their existence is exactly their nonexistence. Even though life and death seem to change, it is only through mistaken conceptualization that they appear to change. In their change there is no change in their nature; their change is eternally changeless. Therefore he says that body and mind, life and death "are the same as sky-flowers."

Why is it that even though body and mind, life and death are known to be like sky-flowers, this knowledge is again said to be like "the sky"? And this knowledge that knows knowing to be like "the sky" is further said to be "the same as the appearance of sky-flowers"? Well, it is only by mistaken conceptualization that we see body and mind, life and death, which is like the impaired eyes' seeing the appearance of sky-flowers. Once you are free from mistaken conceptualization you do not perceive the existence of sky-flowers. Once the impairment is corrected you do not perceive the disappearance of sky-flowers. Since this perception that sees arising and sees cessation is originally based on and fully effected by [the view of] body and mind, life and death, so is the perception that knows knowledge to be like space dependent on the view of arising and ceasing for its own existence. None of these can avoid turning into the stain of views. In the Matrix of the Tathāgata there is originally no arising and ceasing of body and mind, or life and death. There is also no perception that sees arising or sees cessation, and there is no perception which knows knowing to be like space. Therefore the text says: "this (prior) awareness is just like empty space. Yet since the knowledge that it is empty space is none other than the appearance of sky-flowers . . ."

If all views have been utterly extinguished, how can he say "you cannot say that there is no nature of awareness"? This awareness that understands the sky-flowers exists based upon body and mind, life and death. The awareness that knows knowing to be like space in turn exists in dependence on this awareness that understands the sky-flowers. Both exist in their relation to conditions. This "counteractive awareness" is not "originally existent awareness." If it were an originally existent awareness, it would not exist in dependence upon counteractive awareness, and also would not be attained from conditions. This is the marvelous completely real and eternally real awareness of the Tathāgatagarbha. Its scope is vast. Just like the nature of reality-realm, it is perfectly complete, it pervades and penetrates the ten directions, yet it is not attained subjectively or objectively by corrective views. Therefore the text says: "you cannot say there is no nature of awareness."

When this awareness that recognizes body and mind and life and death, and the corrective awareness that follows conditions are both dispelled, then the originally existent attributes of pure enlightenment appear before you, and this is called "the dharma-practice of the originally arisen causal stage." Because of this, bodhisattvas conceive themselves to be originally the same as the Buddha, different only in terms of conditioning. First quelling conditioning, then actualizing purity—this will arouse *bodhicitta*. Sentient beings can also cultivate pure practices based on this *bodhicitta*, and so doing, will not fall into the pit of error.

The *Gāthā*

[Sutra (#14)] [*T* 842.17.913c11; *HPC* 7.130c15]

爾時世尊欲重宣此義而説偈言：

文殊汝當知　一切諸如來
從於本因地　皆以智慧覺
了達於無明　知彼如空華
即能免流轉　又如夢中人
醒時不可得　覺者如虛空
平等不動轉　覺徧十方界
即得成佛道　衆幻滅無處
成道亦無得　本性圓滿故
菩薩於此中　能發菩提心
末世諸衆生　修此免邪見

Then, the World-Honored One, wanting to restate the gist of this, spoke a verse. He said:

Mañjuśrī, you should know
All Tathāgatas
From their originally arisen causal stage
Penetrate ignorance
With enlightened wisdom.
Knowing it to be like sky-flowers
They are able to escape transmigration.

It is like the man in the dream
Who has nothing to grasp upon awakening.
Awareness is like space,
Equal, changeless.
Enlightenment pervading the worlds of the ten directions
Is none other than the attainment of the Buddha-way.
All illusions cease at no-place
And in accomplishing the Way there is nothing attained.
That's because the original nature is complete, perfect.
In it, bodhisattvas
Are able to produce *bodhicitta*.
All sentient beings of the degenerate age
Practicing this, will avoid erroneous views.

[Kihwa] [*HPC* 7.130c23]

Know the real to be originally existent. Understand that falsehood is originally empty. From this you avoid the view of *saṃsāra*. Then you are able to realize that the views of "knowing the real" and "understanding falsehood" are both sky-flowers—both lack anything whatsoever. Yet this mind that is cleared of views also does not exist. From the realm of neither delusion nor enlightenment, you abide still, without change. Here, you coalesce self and things without gap, you unite the reality-realm with the essential nature. It is through this that the Buddha-way is accomplished. The "accomplished way" removes the defilement of illusion. When the defilement of illusion is gone, "counteractive awareness" also vanishes. Therefore he says: "in accomplishing the Way, nothing is attained."

2

Samantabhadra Bodhisattva

The word *samanta* (普) means "universally extending." *Bhadra* (賢) means "great virtue." The word *samantabhadra* means to extend great compassion such that no type of sentient being is not improved, and to practice myriads of practices such that no virtue is not perfected.

Why does Samantabhadra ask the Buddha another question after Mañjuśrī? Mañjuśrī emphasizes the aspect of faith, while Samantabhadra emphasizes the aspect of practice. Since Mañjuśrī emphasizes the aspect of faith, he asked the Buddha to reveal the dharma-practice of the causal stage, first causing everyone to awaken pure Perfect Enlightenment. Since Samantabhadra emphasizes the aspect of practice, he asks the Buddha to teach the stages of practice and make everyone begin their practice relying on their awakening.

In a lamp, oil and flame are both necessary. In a person, eyes and legs both help each other. If the flame lacks oil, it will certainly go out. If legs cannot be guided by eyes, one's advance will certainly be halted. The flame, depending on the oil, gets brighter without going out. The legs, depending on the eyes, can further advance without having to stop. The relationship of practice to understanding is just like that of oil and flame. The relationship of understanding to practice is just like that of the eyes to the legs. An understanding that does not have practice is empty. A practice that does not have understanding will be obstructed. Therefore: if you desire to practice, you must first activate your understanding. If you have activated your understanding then you must begin to practice. It is for this reason that Mañjuśrī first awakens pure Perfect Enlightenment. Samantabhadra then, will cause the listeners to rely on their awakening and begin to practice. My verse:

> Right understanding already accomplished,
>   you must begin to practice.

Therefore Samantabhadra asks for the method.
When freedom from illusion is complete,
   there is nothing from which to separate.
That from which one cannot separate is the true constant.

Samantabhadra's Questions on the Possibility of Practice

[Sutra (#15)] [*T* 842.17.9c23; *HPC* 7.131b5] ▼

於是普賢菩薩在大眾中即從座起。頂禮佛足右繞三匝。長
跪叉手而白佛言：
　大悲世尊。願爲此會諸菩薩眾及爲末世一切眾生修大乘
者。聞此圓覺清淨境界。云何修行？

Then Samantabhadra Bodhisattva rose from his seat in the great assembly. He bowed to the Buddha's feet and circumambulated him three times to the right. He knelt down with his hands clasped, and said to the Buddha:

"Greatly Compassionate World-Honored One. I would like to ask for all the Bodhisattvas at this assembly, and for sentient beings of the degenerate age who are practicing Mahāyāna: let them hear this teaching of the pure realm of perfect enlightenment. How should we practice?"

[Kihwa] [*HPC* 7.131b10]

Between the two phrases "practicing Mahāyāna (修大乘者)" and "hear this teaching of perfect enlightenment (聞此圓覺)" there is probably a line missing, saying "reveal the expedient stages of practice (開示修行方便漸次)." The text should read:

大悲世尊。願爲此會諸菩薩眾及爲末世一切眾生修大乘者：
開示修行方便漸次，聞此圓覺清淨境界。云何修行？

"Greatly Compassionate World-Honored One. I would like to ask for all the bodhisattvas at this assembly and for the sentient beings of the degenerate age who are practicing Mahāyāna: Please reveal the expedient stages of practice and let them hear of this pure realm of perfect enlightenment. How should we practice?"

This means that since they have been able to awaken pure Perfect Enlightenment they must also initiate practice. If they want to initiate practice, upon what kind of expedient means of gradual practice should they depend?

[Sutra (#16)] [*T* 842.17.913c26; *HPC* 7.131b17]

世尊、若彼衆生知如幻者、身心亦幻、云何以幻還修於幻？

World-Honored One, if these sentient beings know about "illusion," and that body and mind are also illusion, how can they remedy illusion using illusion?

[Kihwa] [*HPC* 7.131b19]

The myriad practices of the bodhisattvas depend upon body and mind. In the realization of the myriad practices, *wisdom* is the cutting edge. But the sutra has already said: "This awareness is just like empty space. Yet since the knowledge that it is like empty space is none other than the appearance of sky-flowers."[1] This being the case, then the wisdom that guides practice is illusory and not real. Again, the sutra has said: "know that these are 'sky-flowers,'[2] which is the same as knowing that there is no transmigration, and that there is no body/mind to undergo life-and-death."[3] This being the case, the realm of practice is also illusory and not real. Since subjective and objective practice are both totally illusory, then in the one body of "[subjective] illusion and [objective] illusion" there is no place from which to practice. Where does the so-called practice have its referent?

[Sutra (#17)] [*T* 842.17.913c28; *HPC* 7.131c3]

若諸幻性一切盡滅則無有心。誰爲修行？云何復説修行如幻？

If all illusory natures are completely annihilated, then there is no mind. Who is going to carry out the practice? Moreover, [based on this,] how can you teach the practice of "illusion?"

[Kihwa] [*HPC* 7.131c5]

It has already been said that all views of body and mind are illusion. Therefore illusion is empty without substance and also returns to extinction. If this is the case then there is no one who is able to practice. Who can carry out the myriad practices? It has already been said that all illusory practices are also to be called illusion. Yet the fact that practice leads to Buddhahood is well established. So how can we say practice is "illusory"?

[Sutra (#18)] [*T* 842.17.913c29; *HPC* 7.131c10]

若諸衆生本不修行於生死中常居幻化。曾不了知如幻境界令妄想心、云何解脱？

If all sentient beings originally do not practice, then they will remain forever trapped within the illusion of life and death. Not having penetrated the realm of the illusory, how will they liberate the mind that is trapped in false conceptualization?

[Kihwa] [*HPC* 7.131c13]

If you say that practice is illusory, and fundamentally lacks any principle, then the present sentient beings will remain in illusion forever without ever completely realizing the "illusory realm," and their falsely conceptualizing floating mind will haphazardly arise and cease. If they do not remedy their illusory conceptualization, how can they be liberated?

[Sutra (#19)] [*T* 842.17.914a2; *HPC* 7.131c17] ▼

願爲末世一切衆生作何方便漸次修習令諸衆生永離諸幻。

I implore you on behalf of all sentient beings of the degenerate age: What kind of expedient means of gradual practice should we introduce to cause sentient beings to be permanently free from all illusions?

[Kihwa] [*HPC* 7.131c19]

There is probably text missing both before and after the phrase "all sentient beings of the degenerate age (末世一切衆生)." Before, it should say: "all the bodhisattvas at this assembly (此會諸菩薩衆)," and "as well as for (及爲)" After, it should say "teach the gradual expedient means of practice (開示修行方便漸次)." Thus, the text should read like this:

願爲此會諸菩薩衆及爲末世一切衆生開示修行方便漸次作何方便漸次修習令諸衆生永離諸幻？

I implore you on behalf of all the bodhisattvas at this assembly, as well as for all sentient beings of the degenerate age, to teach the gradual practice of expedient means: What kind of expedient means of gradual practice should we introduce to cause sentient beings to be permanently free from all illusions?

Starting from the top, the question points out three problems:

1. If subjective and objective illusion form one body, is there no standpoint from which to initiate practice?

2. Even though the Buddha has said everything is illusory, can practice be said to be in vain?

3. Even though the Buddha has said that practice is originally empty and fundamentally lacks any principle, the present sentient beings have fallen into false views and are bound up in their false conceptualization. If they do not practice, how can they be liberated?

Having posed these questions, Samantabhadra makes a request that we may paraphrase by saying: "If we desire to reach Buddhahood, we must first be freed from false conceptualization; if we desire to be free from false conceptualization, we must provisionally practice; if it is necessary to practice, we must know the stages. The Buddha has already revealed the perfectly enlightened pure realm, universally causing us to awaken and enter, and has made practice the basis. I hope that he will also teach the stages of practice to cause the multitude at this assembly, as well as all the sentient beings of the degenerate age to be free from false conceptualization and be able to reach realization."

[*Translator's note:* "*Provisional explanation,*" or "*expedient means,*" is a vitally important aspect of the Buddhist teaching, and is directly related to the concept of "two truths." The real or "absolute" Buddhist teaching is the immediate apprehension of the true nature of existence, which has no duality, is perfect in itself and inconceivable. The content of the chapter of Mañjuśrī is emblematic of this kind of teaching. But the fact is, as Samantabhadra states here, that almost all sentient beings are completely bound in their illusory perceptions and conceptions, and when they hear the "truth," it goes over their heads, and makes no sense. Therefore the Buddha, adapting to the various capacities of his followers, provisionally gives them a teaching that they can grasp, which includes physical and mental techniques that purify body and mind. But since these methods are provisional, and practitioners are apt to hold to them as "reality," in this sutra and others like it, the Buddha will often undermine the substantiality of the provisional teaching soon after giving it.]

[Sutra (#20)] [*T* 842.17.914a4; *HPC* 7.132a13] ▼

作是語已、五體投地。如是三請、終而復始。
　爾時世尊告普賢菩薩言：善哉、善哉。善男子、汝等乃
能爲諸菩薩及末世衆生修習菩薩如幻三昧方便漸次。令諸
衆生得離諸幻。汝今諦聽、當爲汝説。時普賢菩薩奉教歡
喜、及諸大衆默然而聽。

Having said this, he prostrated fully to the ground. He asked this question three times in succession.

Then the World-Honored One, speaking to Samantabhadra Bodhisattva, said: "Excellent, excellent! Good son, you have practiced well the bodhisattva's expedient gradient, 'as-illusion' *samādhi* for all the bodhisattvas as well as for the sentient beings of the degenerate age. This practice enables all the sentient beings to gain freedom from illusion. Now listen well, and I shall explain it for you."

Samantabhadra received this teaching with great joy and reverence; all in the great assembly became silent and listened.

[Kihwa] [*HPC* 7.132a20]
Having caused them to awaken, he also wants to teach them how to practice. Since the bodhisattva has requested appropriately, the Buddha gives his emphatic approval.

Between the phrases "sentient beings of the degenerate age (末世衆生)" and "practiced [well] the bodhisattva's (修習菩薩)" the text should probably include the phrase "ask the Tathāgata (諮問如來)."[4] It should say:

汝等乃能爲諸菩薩及末世衆生諮問如來修習菩薩如幻三昧方便漸次。

You have well asked the Tathāgata on behalf of the bodhisattvas and the sentient beings of the degenerate age about the expedient stages of the practice of the bodhisattva's "as-illusion-*samādhi*".

The word *cha* (諮) means "to ask about goodness." It means that he asks the Tathāgata about the provisional stages in the practice of the bodhisattvas' "illusion-*samādhi*," requesting him to teach about them. The words "ask the Tathāgata" can be found in each chapter in this place.

"Bodhisattvas' *samādhi*" is the bodhisattvas' excellent performance of myriad practices, with every single practice being pure without any conceptualization or attachment. Once every single practice is done without attachment, even the most fervent activity is nothing but illusion, and ultimately does not exist. Therefore he says "illusion-practice." When this practice is done by those of superior faculties, there are definitely no stages. Yet since there are people of both dull and sharp faculties and in actual practice there is difficult and easy, provisional stages must be taught. This is why the bodhisattva asks the Buddha to teach; and this is why the Buddha gives him "emphatic approval."

The Buddha's Answer

Illusion Is Baseless

[Sutra (#21)] [*T* 842.17.914a10; *HPC* 7.132b12]

善男子、一切衆生種種幻化皆生如來圓覺妙心、猶如空華從空而有。幻華雖滅、空性不壞。衆生幻心還依幻滅、諸幻盡滅、覺心不動。依幻說覺亦名爲幻。若說有覺、猶未離幻。說無覺者、亦復如是。是故幻滅名爲不動。

Good sons, all sentient beings' various illusions are born from the perfectly enlightened marvelous mind of the Tathāgata, just like the sky-flowers come to exist in the sky. Even though the illusory flowers vanish, the nature of the sky is indestructible. The illusory mind of sentient beings also vanishes based on illusion, and while all illusions are utterly erased, the enlightened mind is unchanged. The use of illusion to speak of enlightenment is also called illusion. If you say there is enlightenment, you are not yet free from illusion. If you say there is no enlightenment, this is the same thing. There-fore, the cessation of illusion is called "unchanging."

[Kihwa] [*HPC* 7.132b18]

The word "sentient being" contrasts with "Tathāgata." Aside from one person—the Buddha—everyone is called "sentient being." Hence "inner worldlings" and "outer worldlings" are both called "sentient being." Therefore it is said: "Both inner and outer worldlings are sentient beings." Thus, the body and mind and life and death that they experience are still the same in that they are illusion. They only differ in being "fragmentary *saṃsāra*" and "miraculous *saṃsāra*." Therefore the text says "various." Yet since this differentiation has no place as its basis besides Perfect Enlightenment, the text says: "all [sentient beings' various illusions] are born from the perfectly enlightened marvelous mind of the Tathāgata." Such doctrines as "apart from Perfect Enlighten-ment there are no Six Destinies" and "without Perfect Enlightenment there are no Three Vehicles" are the same as this. The reason every-thing is called "illusion" is because the mind of enlightenment is origi-nally pure, and has never had arising or cessation. Whenever there is arising mind and movement of thought, there is illusion.

[*Translator's note*: Sentient beings remain trapped in *saṃsāra* until they attain Buddhahood. Thus bodhisattvas, or beings who are enlightened in some measure, are still in *saṃsāra*. But the *saṃsāra* of the bodhisattvas is experienced in a different way from the discriminated, fragmentary *saṃsāra* (分段生死) of regular unenlightened people. Because they are aware of the miraculous nature of transformation, the bodhisattvas' *saṃsāra* is called the "*saṃsāra* of miraculous transformation (變易生死)." The message in this passage however, is that both kinds of *saṃsāra* are still illusion. "Inner worldlings (內凡)" are sentient beings who have advanced to the bodhisattva level, who have had some experience of emptiness. "Outer worldlings (外凡)" are totally unenlightened people. In Mahāyāna Buddhism, "inner" usually refers to the Three Stages of the Worthies (三賢位), and "outer" refers to the Stage of Ten Faiths (十信).

The *Three Vehicles* are the two "Hīnayāna" vehicles of *śrāvaka* (聲聞 literally, "hearer" who awakens by listening to the sermons of the Bud-dha) and *pratyekabuddha* (緣覺, 獨覺 "solitary realizer" who awakens by practicing isolated meditation), plus the Mahāyāna vehicle of the bodhi-sattva. In Mahāyāna texts such as the *Śrīmālā-sūtra*, the enlightenment of *śrāvakas* and *pratyekabuddhas* is explained as being inferior to that of the bodhisattva, who understands emptiness and bases his practice in compassion. The *Lotus Sutra* teaches that all three vehicles are merely provisional, and there is in reality only one true Buddha-vehicle.

The term *Two Vehicles* refers to the practices of the *śrāvakas* and *pratye-kabuddhas*. These two kinds of practitioners are presented as foils in Mahāyāna texts such as this, as being representative of the best possible result of the practices of the earlier Indian (so-called "Hīnayāna") forms of Buddhism. These practitioners are regarded as being limited to the teachings of early Buddhism, specifically the Four Noble Truths and the Twelve Limbs of Conditioned Origination. In Mahāyāna texts such as the *SPE*, the practitioners of the Two Vehicles are understood to be far superior to nonpractitioners, but due to an incomplete understanding of emptiness, and a lack of compassion for other sentient beings, their level of insight is considered to be inferior to that of practitioners of the Third Vehicle—the bodhisattva vehicle.]

[Kihwa]

The wisdom of the Two Vehicles is capable of curing the sickness of the Six Worldly Destinies. The wisdom of the bodhisattva is able to cure the mistakes of the Two Vehicles. Even though these two kinds of wisdom are different from each other in terms of superiority, from the point of view of the mind of pure enlightenment neither can avoid becoming illusory appearances—ultimately there is nothing there. Therefore, they are both called illusion. Hence the text says: "just like the sky-flowers come to exist from the sky." The sky-flowers arise from the sky and also cease from the sky. Yet even though the sky-flowers cease, the nature of the sky is indestructible. Illusion is born from en-lightenment and also ceases from enlightenment. Yet even though illu-sion ceases, the nature of enlightenment is unchanged.

As for the phrase "The illusory mind of sentient beings also vanishes based on illusion": Even though the wisdom of the practitioners of the Two Vehicles cannot avoid becoming illusion, if it is not used to over-come the afflictions of the Six Worldly Destinies, then those who are within the Six Destinies will be trapped there forever. Hence, it is nec-essary to use the wisdom of the practitioners of the Two Vehicles to overcome the afflictions of the Six Worldly Destinies. The wisdom of the bodhisattvas corrects the mistakes of the Two Vehicles, and the Bud-dha-view corrects that of the bodhisattvas. When, through this sort of correction, all illusions are completely erased, the great wisdom of Perfect Enlightenment alone luminously remains. This is the meaning of the sentence "The illusory mind of sentient beings also vanishes based on illusion, and while all illusions are utterly erased, the enlightened mind is unchanged."

The Three Poisons[5] and the Ten Fetters[6] of the Six Worldly Destinies, and the Four Noble Truths, the Twelve-fold Conditioned Origination, and the Six Perfections of the practitioners of all three vehicles are all illusion. All fall under dependent origination. It is like an ocean giving rise to waves due to the wind. Though a difference may be found in the water in terms of cloudy and clear, all are nonetheless called "waves."[7] When conditions are exhausted, illusion vanishes, yet the mind of enlightenment eternally remains. It is like the ocean: when the wind stops, the waves cease, yet they rely upon the primordial stillness. In the place where illusion is exhausted and enlightenment is actualized, there is never again arising mind and movement of thought. How wonderful!

Yet people have difficulty in attaining this state. A great worldling who expounds enlightenment depending on illusion has not yet let go of fixed views. He regards illusion as something that ceases and regards enlightenment as something that manifests, and still retains the sentiments of loss and attainment, like and dislike. These are called fixed views; they are also "illusion." If, at the point where illusion is extinguished and enlightenment is actualized, you again produce mentation and move thought, and believe that illusion has indeed been completely extinguished and that the mind of enlightenment eternally remains, then you have not let go of "enlightenment" and have fallen into the view of eternalism. Because of this, you do not let go of fixed views and do not free yourself from illusion.

Again, if you hear this and again produce mentation and set thought into motion, imagining that you have indeed extinguished illusion, and that enlightenment is also nonexistent, then you are following the nihilistic view and are not free from illusion. But if you maintain awareness at the point of the cessation of all illusions and you do not again produce mentation and set thought into motion, the mind of enlightenment will be self-apparent. It is like polishing a mirror. When the filth is gone, the brightness appears. This brightening does not come from the outside, nor is it produced from within. The primordial stillness, which is clear and self-luminous, is called "unchanging."

Separation from Illusion

[Sutra (#22)] [*T* 842.17.914a15; *HPC* 7.133a15]

善男子、一切菩薩及末世眾生應當遠離一切幻化虛妄境界。
由堅執持遠離心故、心如幻者亦復遠離。遠離爲幻亦復遠
離。離遠離幻亦復遠離。得無所離即除諸幻。比如鑽火兩

木相因。火出木盡灰飛烟滅。以幻修幻亦復如是。諸幻雖
盡不入斷滅。
　善男子、知幻即離、不作方便。離幻即覺亦無漸次。

Good sons, all bodhisattvas and sentient beings of the degenerate age should separate[8] from all illusory and false realms. By firmly abiding in separation from thought, you also separate from the thought of "illusion." As this separation becomes illusion, you again separate from it. You again separate from this separation from separation from illusion, until you reach "nothing to be separated from," which is the removal of all illusion. It is like making a fire with two sticks. The fire blazes and the wood is consumed; the ashes fly away and the smoke vanishes. Using illusion to remedy illusion is exactly like this. Yet even though all illusions are extinguished, you do not enter into nothingness.

Good sons, when you know illusion, you are immediately free, without devising expedient means. Freedom from illusion is in itself enlightenment, and there are no stages.

[Kihwa] [*HPC* 7.133a24]

The teaching of "illusion-practice" has been explained completely. Now he wants to clarify the matter of the "stain of views," as well as the idea of provisional stages. He also wants to make it clear that if we are only able to separate [from illusion] without arising discriminations, then there are no provisional gradual stages. It is only to perfect the person of the capacity for the Perfect and Sudden teaching of the Great Vehicle that he says: "Good sons, all bodhisattvas and sentient beings of the degenerate age should separate from all illusory and false realms [and so forth up to] when you know illusion, you will immediately be free, without devising expedient means. Freedom from illusion is itself enlightenment and there are no stages."

As for the phrase "should separate from all illusory false realms": Except for the Buddha's own accordance with of the nature of enlightenment, peoples' bodies and minds and peoples' views are all called "illusory and false realms." Therefore he says "all." People who want to actualize the nature of enlightenment must be free from all these illusory realms. If they can just free themselves and not again produce their discriminations, then there will be no more illusion, and they can be said to be "*according with the nature of enlightenment.*" Then why should they carry out provisional gradual cultivation? It is because they are unable to carry out the above accordance, and are hopelessly stuck in the arising of discriminations. Only after not being able to attain accordance is there the teaching of provisional stages.

As for the sentence "By firmly abiding in separation from thought,

you also separate from the thought of 'illusion.' As this separation becomes illusion, you again separate from it. You again separate from
this separation from separation from illusion": The defilement of views
is shown here, and the provisional teaching is explained in detail to
gradually cause them to practice. Using this provisional method of
gradual practice, purity consumes all without remainder. Because of
this, one attains "'nothing to be separated from,' which is the removal
of all illusion." One gradually practices and purifies oneself completely
without remainder.

Why is "purity consuming all without remainder by gradual practice"
characterized with the simile of "making a fire with two sticks of wood,
the wood being consumed and the fire vanishing"? The *Sutra of the Heroic
March Samādhi* says: "Space arising from the midst of Great Enlightenment is like the ocean producing a single bubble; a myriad defiled lands
are born from space."[9] The earth exists in dependence upon space; wood
exists in dependence upon the earth; fire exists in dependence upon
wood. Now, even though wood and fire both depend upon the earth
for their existence, if we trace them back to their origin, then they actually exist in dependence upon space. Therefore it is said: "The nature of
fire is actually that of space; the nature of space is actually that of fire;
penetrating everywhere in the ten directions, purity is the original condition."[10] Apart from space there is no earth; apart from earth there is
no wood; apart from wood there is no fire.

Space, then, is a metaphor for Great Enlightenment. Earth is a metaphor for all the worlds of sentient beings. The two sticks are metaphors for the ability to cure and that which is cured. That which is
cured is like original wood—it represents the personality that is transformed. The ability to cure is like the ignition of the wood—it represents the remedy that is able to transform. The "remedy" is actually
"compassion and wisdom." The fire is the enlightenment that is actualized—this is "actualized enlightenment." The emergence of actualized
enlightenment depends on compassion and wisdom. The arousal of
compassion and wisdom depends on being sensitive to the actual circumstances of individual people. That which the actual circumstances
of individual people follow is the karma of all sentient beings. That
which all sentient beings follow depends upon Great Enlightenment.
Apart from Great Enlightenment there are no sentient beings; apart
from sentient beings there is no application to the actual circumstances
of individual people; apart from application to the actual circumstances
of individual people there is neither compassion nor wisdom; and apart
from compassion and wisdom there is no actualized enlightenment.
Therefore it is said: "Apart from Perfect Enlightenment there are no Six
Destinies; apart from Perfect Enlightenment there are no Three Vehicles." It is also said: "Depending upon sentient beings he manifests his

Great Compassion; depending on Great Compassion he produces *bodhi-citta;* depending on *bodhicitta* he accomplishes Equal Correct Enlightenment." This is like the earth existing in dependence upon space, wood existing in dependence upon earth, and fire existing in dependence upon wood. "The wood being consumed and the fire vanishing" is a simile for pulling out nails, removing the wedges, dissolving the glue, and unloosing the bonds. This is emancipating completely down to the last detail, purifying all without exception.

As for equating the fire with actualized enlightenment: The sayings, "Only waiting for the appearance of (the planet) Venus" and, "Upon returning home, you reach your goal for the first time," contain the same meaning. "The appearance of Venus" refers to the manifestation of actualized enlightenment and the fire is a symbol for actualized enlightenment, yet it is said to "vanish." Actualized (initial) enlightenment exists only from today; it does not refer to the absoluteness of innate (originally existent) enlightenment. The relationship between actualized enlightenment and innate enlightenment can be compared to the clear skies of a single day and the sky that has existed forever. It is also like blurry vision suddenly seeing the clear sky, which also cannot avoid becoming illusion. Illusion arising from enlightenment, and also ceasing from enlightenment, is like fire arising from space and also ceasing from space. Though the fire ceases from space, the nature of space keeps its primordial stillness. Though illusions cease from enlightenment, the nature of enlightenment has not changed from antiquity. Hence the text says: "using illusion to remedy illusion is exactly like this."

As for the phrase "Yet even though all illusions are extinguished, you do not enter into nothingness": This is like the above teaching of gradual provisional stages, which exist only when one is not able to attain Buddhahood. If you do not again produce discrimination at the point of the very first separation from illusion, then "when you know illusion, you will immediately be free, without devising expedient means. Freedom from illusion is in itself enlightenment, and there are no stages." This is the correct path of the bodhisattvas and the most direct course of practice. Sentient beings only create the quagmire of fixed views. They are unable to stably abide in this state [of freedom from illusion], and thus force the Tathāgata to have no recourse but to teach expedient means and stages of practice.

[Sutra (#23)] [*T* 842.17.914a21; *HPC* 7.134a14]

一切菩薩及末世衆生依此修行如是乃能永離諸幻。

All bodhisattvas and sentient beings of the degenerate age who depend upon this practice will accordingly be able to free themselves from all illusion.

[Kihwa] [*HPC* 7.134a16]

The meaning of sudden and gradual has been fully explained. Thus it is said: "Those of sharp faculties practice using the sudden; those of dull faculties practice using the gradual." The application of this is to practice according to the various teachings as appropriate. Then you will be able to be free from all illusions, and actualize the nature of enlightenment.

The *Gāthā*

[Sutra (#24)] [*T* 842.17.914a23; *HPC* 7.134a20]

爾時世尊、欲重宣此義而説偈言：

普賢汝當知　一切諸衆生
無始幻無明　皆從諸如來
圓覺心建立　猶如虛空華
依空而有相　空華若復滅
虛空本不動　幻從諸覺生
幻滅覺圓滿　覺心不動故
若彼諸菩薩　及末世衆生
常應遠離幻　諸幻悉皆離
如木中生火　木盡火還滅
覺則無漸次　方便亦如是

Then the World-Honored One, wanting to restate the gist of this, spoke a verse. He said:

> Samantabhadra, you should know
> The beginningless illusory ignorance
> Of all sentient beings
> Is all created from
> The perfectly enlightened mind of all Tathāgatas.
> It is just like the sky-flowers
> That appear in relation to the sky;
> Though the sky-flowers vanish
> The sky has never changed.
> Illusion is born from enlightenment;
> In the cessation of illusion, enlightenment remains perfectly
>   complete.
> This is because the enlightened mind is changeless.
> If these bodhisattvas
> And sentient beings of the degenerate age
> Always appropriately separate from illusion,
> They will completely free themselves from it.

Like the flame that springs from wood:
The wood is consumed and the flame again disappears.
If you are enlightened, then there are no stages of practice
Nor is there such a thing as expedient means.

[Kihwa] [*HPC* 7.134b4]

Illusion arises from enlightenment, like the flowers that appear in the sky. This is the aspect of "creating characteristics because of confusion regarding reality." When illusion ceases the nature of enlightenment is self-so. When the flowers vanish the nature of the sky remains as it always was. This is the aspect of "going against the flow and returning to one's nature." The Buddha has taught these two aspects to encourage sentient beings to separate themselves from illusion. Thus, the culmination of both of these teachings, the "disclosure of the partial" and "going against the flow" is the encouragement to separate from illusion. Yet it is also said: "in separating from illusion there are differences of gradual and sudden." "Gradual" is like the fire coming from the wood, and the wood disappearing because of the fire; the wood and the fire both vanish, leaving the sky remaining. Although people of dull faculties are able to separate from illusion, they are not able to avoid again producing discriminations, and so they must repeatedly separate from illusion. Then they can return to Perfect Enlightenment. If you can separate from illusion and not again produce discriminations, then enlightenment will appear before you without any mental strain. The way that is used is: "when you know illusion, you will immediately be free, without devising expedient means. Freedom from illusion is in itself enlightenment, and there are no stages." This is like cutting through a roll of thread—in one slice all threads are cut. This is called the "sudden." It is used by those of sharp faculties.

3

Universal Vision
Bodhisattva

[*Translator's note*: this is the longest chapter of the sutra, a guided meditation that analyzes various facets of existence from the viewpoints of progressively subtler contemplative approaches. This chapter is considered to be so valuable for its contemplative content that it is often circulated for study as a separate document in Korean monasteries. At the end of the prior chapter, the Buddha has again denied the validity of the concept of "gradual practice," but Universal Eyes begins immediately with this topic, pressing the Buddha for a provisional explanation. Kihwa, as in the other chapters, begins with an explanation of the meaning of the bodhisattva's name.]

[Kihwa] [*HPC* 7.134b19]

The sun's pervasive illumination is called "universal"; the faculty of sight is called "vision." The term "universal vision" means that in the same way that the shining sun leaves no darkness unilluminated, compassion and wisdom operate universally, having no place where they do not function. Why does Universal Vision ask another question after Samantabhadra? Mañjuśrī has demonstrated awakening and Samantabhadra has elucidated practice, so the principles of awakening and practice have already been clarified. But since the method of initiating practice is difficult to elucidate, this bodhisattva wants to take the content of his own penetrating vision and use it as the method for initiating practice, thus causing everyone to engage themselves in the as-illusion *samādhi*,[1] to realize and enter the Tathāgata's great quiescent ocean. Therefore he asks the Buddha to reveal the method of initiating practice.

Self and other, body and mind, are illusory and originally empty. Worldling and sage, who differ only in terms of their correctness, are interpenetrated in one realm; there is only a singular purity that pervades the reality-realm; this is the content of the penetrating insight of

100

Universal Vision Bodhisattva. Using this as the method and creating this kind of penetrating view, people will not wander off on other paths. Since they truly tread the correct path of *bodhi*, the method is called "the correct expedient method," and this view is called "correct thought." If you initiate your practice based on this, how could it not be effective? And how could you not be free from illusion? Actually, practice is already accomplished and you are already free from illusion. How could you be in Perfect Enlightenment, yet be afflicted and not awaken and enter? This is why Universal Vision asks another question after Samantabhadra. My verse:

> If you want to know the most fundamental method for being
>   free from illusion,
> Then fully grasp the chapter of Universal Vision.
> With right contemplation, the illusion of body and mind
>   vanishes.
> With purity, and perfect clarity, the Buddha-realm is
>   illuminated.

Universal Vision's Question on Expedient Means

[Sutra (#25)] [*T* 842.17.914b6; *HPC* 7.134c15]

於是普眼菩薩在大眾中、即從座起。頂禮佛足右繞三匝。
長跪叉手而白佛言：大悲世尊。願爲此會諸菩薩眾及爲末
世一切眾生、演說菩薩修行漸次。云何思惟？云何住持？
眾生未悟、作何方便普令開悟？世尊、若彼眾生無正方便
及正思惟、聞佛如來説此三昧、心生迷悶、則於圓覺不能
悟入。願興慈悲爲我等輩及末世眾生、假説方便。作是語
已、五體投地。如是三請終而復始。

Then the bodhisattva Universal Vision arose from his seat in the great assembly. He bowed to the Buddha's feet and circumambulated him three times to the right. He then knelt down with his hands clasped and addressed the Buddha, saying: "Greatly Compassionate World-Honored One. I beg of you on behalf of the bodhisattvas of this assembly and the sentient beings of the degenerate age, to expound on the bodhisattvas' stages and practice. How should they think? How should they abide? For sentient beings who have not yet awakened, what kinds of expedient means should be devised to cause them all to awaken?"

"World-Honored One, if these sentient beings lack the correct expedients and correct thought, then, when they hear you explain this *samādhi*, confusion will arise in their minds and they will be unable to awaken and enter. Please arouse your compassion for us and for the sentient beings of the degenerate age, and provisionally explain these expedient methods." Having said this, he prostrated himself to the ground. He made this request three times in succession.

[Kihwa] [*HPC* 7.135a2]

A journey of a thousand miles starts with one step.[2] The myriad practices of the bodhisattvas begin with meditation. If the first step is incorrect, then each subsequent step will wander off onto other paths. How can you proceed directly to the realm for which you are aiming? If the object of meditation is incorrect, then every step will be off of the correct path. How will it be possible for you to straightforwardly actualize the result you are seeking? Therefore he must teach the correct view to the deluded aspirants, so that they will not wander off on different paths, and be prevented from reaching the treasure trove. This is why Universal Vision Bodhisattva discloses what has not been disclosed and asks his question. The terms "correct expedient means" and "correct thought" refer to "correct contemplation." If you do not have the correct contemplation, then even if you hear the Buddha's teaching of the practice of the bodhisattvas' illusory *samādhi*, and of the stages of expedient means, you will still be confused and will be unable to awaken and enter.

The Buddha's Answer

[Sutra (#26)] [*T* 842.17.914b14; *HPC* 7.135a12]

爾時世尊、告普眼菩薩言：善哉、善哉。善男子、汝等乃
能爲諸菩薩及末世衆生問於如來修行漸次、思惟、住持、
乃至假説種種方便。汝今諦聽、當爲汝説。時普眼菩薩奉
教歡喜、及諸大衆默然而聽。

Then the World-Honored One, addressing the bodhisattva Universal Vision, said: "Excellent, excellent! Good son, you have asked well for the bodhisattvas and sentient beings of the degenerate age about the stages of the Tathāgata's practice; about his thought and abiding, and about the explanation of all the various expedient means. Now listen well, and I shall explain for you." Universal Vision Bodhisattva received this instruction with great joy. The great assembly became silent and listened.

[Kihwa] [*HPC* 7.135a18]

Since it is also the Buddha's original intention to cause all sentient beings to first create the correct view and then perform the myriad practices, he gladly gives his approval and admonishes them to listen well.

The Meditation on No-Self

[Sutra (#27)] [*T* 842.17.914b19; *HPC* 7.135a20]

善男子、彼新學菩薩及末世衆生欲求如來淨圓覺心、應當
正念遠離諸幻、先依如來奢摩他行。堅持禁戒安處徒衆、
宴坐靜室恒作是念：我今此身四大和合。所謂髮毛爪齒皮
肉筋骨髓腦垢色皆歸於地。唾涕膿血津液涎沫淡淚精氣大
小便利、皆歸於水。煖氣歸火、動轉歸風。四大各離、今
者妄身當在何處？即知此身畢竟無體。和合爲相、實同幻
化。四緣假合、妄有六根。六根四大中外合成、妄有緣氣
。於中積聚、似有緣相假名爲心。善男子、此虛妄心若
無六塵則不能有。四大分解無塵可得。於中緣塵各歸散滅
、畢竟無有緣心可見。

Good sons, these newly awakened bodhisattvas and sentient beings
of the degenerate age who yearn for the pure enlightened mind of
the Tathāgata must correct their thoughts and rid themselves of
all illusions, first relying on the Tathāgata's practice of *śamatha*.

[*Translator's note*: Śamatha is the first type of meditation normally taught
in Buddhist meditational traditions, and is translated into English as
"concentration," "cessation of thought," or "calm abiding." It is a form
of meditation where the practitioner focuses his mind on one thing
(the breath, a certain phenomenon, etc.) to develop one-pointedness.
In most schools of Buddhism, the practice of *śamatha* by itself is not
considered sufficient for the apprehension of reality, but the concentration power developed from *śamatha* is used in conjunction with other
types of meditation. At this point in the sutra, *śamatha* is to be practiced
before one carries out the upcoming analytical exercise.]

[Sutra]
Firmly established in moral discipline and living in harmony with
like-minded students, then practicing silent sitting in a quiet room,
they should uninterruptedly be mindful of the following:

This present body is a synthesis of the Four Elements. Hair, nails,
teeth, skin, flesh, bones, marrow, brains, and pigment all return to
Earth. Saliva, mucus, pus, blood, sputum, scum, phlegm, tears,
semen, urine, and feces all return to Water. Heat returns to Fire,
and movement returns to Wind. When the Four Elements have
been separated, where can the false body exist? Now you know
that this body ultimately has no substance. As a synthesis it appears,
but in reality it is like an illusion conjured by a magician.

When these four factors temporarily combine, the Six Faculties[3]
falsely appear; through the internal and external matching of the
Six Faculties and Four Elements, there is the deluded apprehension

of conditioned energy. Within this conglomeration, there seem to
be marks of this conditioned energy, which is provisionally called
"mind." Good sons, if this false mind does not have its Six Objects,
it cannot exist. If the Four Elements are separated, there are no
objects to be experienced. At this point, the cognized objects each
disperse and vanish, and ultimately there is no dependently arisen
mind to be seen.

[Kihwa] [*HPC* 7.135b11]

The distant traveler who desires to return to his homeland must find
the correct route. Mistakenly conditioned aspirants who wish to actualize Perfect Enlightenment need to know the essential technique of
returning to the origin. The meaning of "correcting thought," then, is
the subtle aspect of religious cultivation. It is the correct method of
separating from illusion; it is the essential technique of returning to
the origin. Without it, there is nowhere from whence to initiate practice,
and no final result of separation from illusion and attainment of realization. Therefore he says: "who yearn for the pure enlightened mind of
the Tathāgata must correct their thoughts and rid themselves of all illusions." The meaning of "correct thought" is the same as that of "correct
contemplation."

Regarding the line: "first relying on the Tathāgata's practice of *śamatha*."
The religious cultivation of a great worldling does not go beyond the
three practices.[4] Concentration is produced depending upon moral discipline; wisdom is produced depending upon concentration—this is
the order of practice. Concentration cannot be complete without moral
discipline; wisdom cannot be manifested without concentration. The
meaning of "correct [their] thought[s]" is "*prajñā*." The concept of "setting up proper observation" is the same as this. The meaning of "firmly
established in moral discipline" is "*śīla*." "Silently sitting" refers to the
practice of *samādhi*; it is also the same as the practice of *śamatha*. If you
enter into contemplation without concentration, wisdom will not be
correct. If you enter into concentration without moral discipline, concentration will not be correct. If you want correct contemplation, you
must first enter concentration; if you want to enter concentration, you
must first maintain moral discipline. If you enter concentration after
being well established in moral discipline, then this is *śamatha* in the
real sense of the word. Depending on this (*śamatha*) practice, you set
up your contemplation. Therefore it is called "correct thought." Having
this correct contemplation, you are aware that body and mind ultimately lack substance and you are able to separate from all illusions.
Thus the line "must correct their thoughts and rid themselves of all
illusions" refers generally to the fact that you must first correct your
thinking and then you can separate from all illusion. The passage "first

relying on *śamatha,* uninterruptedly be mindful of the following": shows how to think correctly. The passage from "Now you know that this body ultimately has no substance" up to "and ultimately there is no dependently arisen mind to be seen" shows how to separate from illusion.

"First using" means that you first must keep the precepts and then begin the practice of concentration. Only after you have truly practiced *śamatha* can you set up contemplation. How could the Buddha possibly say "first practice *śamatha* and then keep the precepts"? There is no such thing as first practicing wisdom and then concentration, or first practicing concentration and then keeping the precepts. Thus the phrase "Firmly established in the guidelines of moral discipline and living in harmony with like-minded students, then practicing silent sitting in a quiet room" refers to "keeping the precepts and then starting concentration practice," that is, "practicing *śamatha.*" In the chapter of Voice of Discernment Bodhisattva it says: "you must maintain practices of purity, quiescence and contemplation."[5] Here, the "practices of purity" means keeping the precepts. "Quiescence" means "practicing concentration" and "contemplation" means "wisdom." This, then, is the line of reasoning for "Firmly established in the precepts, silently sitting in a quiet room and being mindful."

Body and Mind are Illusory Filth

[Sutra (#28)] [*T* 842.17.914c2; *HPC* 7.135c20]

善男子、彼之衆生幻身滅故、幻心亦滅。幻心滅故、幻塵
亦滅。幻塵滅故、幻滅亦滅。幻滅滅故、非幻不滅。比如
磨鏡、垢盡明現。善男子、當知身心皆爲幻垢。垢相永滅
十方清淨。

"Good sons, since the illusory body of this sentient being vanishes, the illusory mind also vanishes. Since the illusory mind vanishes, illusory objects also vanish. Since illusory objects vanish, illusory vanishing also vanishes. Since illusory vanishing vanishes, non-illusion does not vanish. It is like polishing a mirror: when the filth is gone its brightness naturally appears. Good sons, you should understand both body and mind to be illusory filth. When the defiled aspects are permanently extinguished, the entire universe becomes pure."[6]

[Kihwa] [*HPC* 7.136a1]

One who strives to actualize Perfect Enlightenment realizes that body and mind are illusory filth. The same happens with illusory objects and thus all of them vanish. This vanishing also vanishes and there is nothing else to dispel. Since the nonillusory nature of enlightenment originally does not arise based on illusion, it also does not vanish based on illusion. Hence the text says: "Since illusory vanishing vanishes, nonillusion does not vanish. It is like polishing a mirror . . ."

Now "every single realm in the ten directions," "the distinction between worldling and sage based on correctness" and "self and other," "body and mind" are all in Perfect Enlightenment and yet are illusory filth. This is just like dust hiding the brightness of a mirror and preventing it from reflecting. Since in the correct contemplation, "knowing illusion is exactly freedom," the characteristics of filth permanently vanish, and everything in the ten directions becomes pure, it is like that old mirror: its dirt is cleared away and it reflects clearly without obstruction. Therefore the text says "you should know both body and mind as illusory filth. When the defiled aspects are eternally extinguished, the entire universe becomes pure."

Perfect Enlightenment Is Like a Maṇi-Pearl

[Sutra (#29)] [*T* 842.17.914c6; *HPC* 7.136a12]

> 善男子、比如清淨摩尼寶珠、映於五色隨方各現。諸愚癡
> 者見彼摩尼實有五色。善男子、圓覺淨性現於身心、隨類
> 各應。彼愚癡者説淨圓覺實有如是身心自相、亦復如是。
> 由此不能遠於幻化。是故我説身心幻垢。對離幻垢説名菩
> 薩。垢盡對除、即無對垢及説名者。

Good sons, it is like a pure *maṇi*-pearl that reflects the five colors,[7] depending upon its surroundings. The foolish see that pearl as really having these colors. Good sons, it is the same with the pure nature of Perfect Enlightenment: it appears in people's bodies and minds, according to their individual type. Yet these fools say that pure Perfect Enlightenment really has body and mind.

It is only because these people are unable to free themselves from illusory appearances that I call body and mind "illusory filth." The one who opposes and removes illusory filth is called the "bodhisattva." When filth is gone, its opposition is removed; then there is no opposition, no filth, nor anything to be named.

[*Translator's note*: A "*maṇi*-pearl" is a gem in Indian mythology that is completely pure and possesses various occult powers. The first sentence here describes the experience one has when, with one-pointed concentration, he follows the meditation of negation to its end. The illusory, defiled world suddenly vanishes and everywhere one looks, one sees purity. In the next part, the simile of the *maṇi*-pearl, the ignorant do not see that the pearl ("body and mind") and Perfect Enlightenment have no real existence. In the way that it is the *emptiness* of the *maṇi*-pearl (its lack of own color) that allows it to reflect whatever color meets it, it is the emptiness of Perfect Enlightenment that allows all things such as the appearances of body and mind, to occur. This teaching of *śūnyatā* is similar to that taught in the *prajñāpāramitā* literature, which explains things to be empty not because they can be analytically subdivided ad infinitum, but because emptiness itself is the nature of all things.]

[Kihwa] [*HPC 7.136a20*]

The Buddha has already established that body and mind are illusory filth. But now he wants to clarify *how it is* that body and mind are illusory filth. He uses the example of the *maṇi*-pearl in order to show that Perfect Enlightenment is pure, originally lacking body and mind. This body and mind that come to exist only obtain their attributes from external conditions. Ignorant people are not aware of this, and attach to them as if they are real. Because of body and mind, they do not distinguish impurity and purity, and though both body and mind are in Perfect Enlightenment, body and mind become illusory filth, which prevents people from directly awakening and entering. Though he has already caused them to be aware of illusion and thus separate from it, it seems that at the point of separation from illusion, they have not forgotten subjectivity/objectivity, and despite the fact that their basic nature is Perfect Enlightenment, they reestablish their own obstructions. They should also wipe out the views of an apparent subject and object and forget both self and things. Only after all images are completely erased are they able to intimately realize the state of Perfect Enlightenment.

The reason he uses the *maṇi*-pearl as a metaphor is to show that enlightenment is originally pure and that it is body and mind which are illusory filth. After he causes them to be free from defilement, he also causes them to be completely free from any sentiment of freedom from defilement. Therefore, he says: "When filth is gone, its opposition is removed . . ." and so forth.

[Sutra (#30)] [*T 842.17.914c12; HPC 7.136b10*]

善男子、此菩薩及末世眾生證得諸幻、滅影像故、爾時便得無方清淨。

Good sons, because these bodhisattvas and sentient beings of the degenerate age fully realize [the nature of] all illusion and dispel all [illusory] images, they directly experience limitless purity.

[Kihwa] [*HPC 7.136b12*]

The defiled and pure bodies and minds of the ten directions, despite their being in Perfect Enlightenment, are all manifesting as illusory filth. Their inability to be pure is merely because sentient beings attach to [body and mind] as real and are unable to separate themselves. Now, since the awareness of illusion directly results in separation from illusion, all attachment-based perceptions are thoroughly erased. Since you do not again give rise to sentiments, the ten directions are pure, leaving no obstructions whatsoever.

The Permeation of the Senses by Purity

[Sutra (#31)] [*T* 842.17.914c13; *HPC* 7.136b17] ▼

無邊虛空覺所顯發。覺圓明故顯心清淨。心清淨故、見塵
清淨。見清淨故、眼根清淨。根清淨故、眼識清淨。識清
淨故、聞塵清淨。聞清淨故、耳根清淨。根清淨故、耳識
清淨。識清淨故、覺塵清淨。如是乃至鼻舌身意亦復如是
。善男子、根清淨故、色塵清淨。色清淨故、聲塵清淨。
香味觸法亦復如是。
　善男子、六塵清淨故、地大清淨。地清淨故、水大清淨
。火大風大亦復如是。善男子、四大清淨故、十二處、十
八界、二十五有清淨。彼清淨故、十力、四無所畏、四無
礙智、佛十八不共法、三十七助道品清淨。如是乃至八萬
四千陀羅尼門一切清淨。

Enlightenment reveals limitless space. Since enlightenment is perfectly clear, the manifest mind is pure. Since the mind is pure, the objects of vision are pure. Since vision is pure, the eye faculty is pure. Since the eye faculty is pure, the visual consciousness is pure. Since this consciousness is pure, hearing is pure. Since hearing is pure, the ear faculty is pure. Since the faculty is pure, the auditory consciousness is pure. Since the consciousness is pure, all perception is pure, and so it is true for smell, taste, touch and conceptualization as well.

[*Translator's note*: *Space* is a translation of the Chinese *hsü-k'ung* 虛空, which, as an East Asian rendering of the Indian Buddhist concept of *ākāśa*, goes beyond the simple meaning of "space." It possesses a distinct connotation of "that which has the nature of nonobstruction." There is also the meaning of "the place that form can occupy" as well as the meanings of limitlessness, pervasiveness, and "unconditioned (無 爲)." The connotations of this term are close to that of emptiness (*śūnyatā*), rendered in Chinese as *k'ung* 空.]

[Sutra]

Good sons, since the eye faculty is pure, the color spectrum is pure. Since color is pure, the field of sound is also pure. The same is true of the fields of smell, taste, touch, and conceptualization.

Good sons, since the six objects are pure, the Earth element is pure. Since Earth is pure, Water is pure, and so are Fire and Wind. Good sons, since the Four Elements are pure, the Twelve Loci,[8] the

Table 1: The Cognitive Operations and the Eighteen Realms

Cognitive Operation	Faculty (subjective)	Object (objective)	Consciousness (subject to object)
Sight	Eye	Color	Visual consciousness
Hearing	Ear	Field of Sound	Auditory consciousness
Smell	Nose	Odors	Olfactory consciousness
Taste	Tongue	Taste objects	Gustatory consciousness
Touch	Nerves	Physical Objects	Tactile consciousness
Thought	Mind	Concepts, symbols	Mental consciousness

Eighteen Realms and the Twenty-Five Kinds of Existence[9] are pure. Since these are pure, the Ten Powers,[10] the Four Kinds of Fearlessness,[11] the Four Types of Unobstructed Wisdom,[12] the Buddha's Eighteen Distinctive Characteristics,[13] and the Thirty-Seven Aids to Enlightenment[14] are pure, and so on up to the eighty-four thousand *dhāraṇī*-entrances,[15] everything is pure.

[*Translator's note*: In this passage the author shows how the initial experience of purity (brought about by the contemplation of insubstantiality) has a purifying effect on all of one's perception and cognitive faculties, as well as their objects and the consciousnesses that connect them. This purification is made through the structure of an early Indian theory of consciousness and perception that would serve as a template for Buddhist epistemology throughout the later spread of Buddhist thought. In this theory, all cognition that occurs in the world happens through the six organs of eye, ear, nose, tongue, body (as a tactile organ), and mind (which has concepts and symbols as its objects). Each "organ" represents the subjective capacity to perceive an object. In order for the organ to perceive its object, to connect with it, a specific consciousness is necessary. This is schematized as in Table 1.

In Buddhist terminology, the first five, without the mind, are usually referred to as the five consciousnesses, five organs, and five objects. When the category of mind is included, they are called the six organs, etc. The six organs (or "faculties"), together with their objects are called the *Twelve Loci* and these twelve, when combined with the six consciousnesses, are called the *Eighteen Realms*.]

[Kihwa] [*HPC* 7.136c7]

Before the phrase "Limitless space … (無邊虛空)" the text is probably missing the words "Good sons (善男子) …" This phrase always marks the new discussion, so why wouldn't it be the same here? "Purity" is the opposite of "illusory filth." When enlightenment is not yet disclosed, the faculties and their objects are nothing but illusory filth. When the nature of enlightenment is apparent, the faculties and their objects return to purity. Why is this so? Limitless space, along with these faculties and their objects, the Four Elements, the sage and worldling's "distinction by correctness," mundane and transmundane mental states, all return to their origin. All are manifestations of the nature of enlightenment. It is like one hundred thousand lamps that all get their initial light from one lamp. Because the original light is pure, the light from one hundred thousand lamps is pure. All things in existence are just like this. Since they are originally manifestations of pure enlightenment, all are completely pure. Before, it was just because of mistaken attachment that all things became illusory filth. Now that mistaken attachment has been removed, the nature of enlightenment is suddenly apparent. Therefore, all things in existence are again pure. It is like the light from a lamp, which is unclear due to a person's cataracts. Once the cataracts are removed, every single light is clear, with no obstruction whatsoever.

If you single-mindedly concentrate on body and mind as illusory filth but do not further illumine the purity of everything, then individual things will not be properly established and the marks of reality will also not be discernible. Since the Buddha wants to disclose the true marks of all things, he first shows where all things come from and says: "Enlightenment reveals limitless space." And since space is revealed by enlightenment, can we not say that all the things that exist in space, such as the faculties, the objects, the Four Elements, and the mundane and transmundane dharmas can be understood as manifestations of enlightenment? Since he has revealed the source of all things, he then shows the real marks of all things and says: "Since enlightenment is perfectly clear, the manifest mind is pure. Since the mind is pure, the objects of vision are pure. Since vision is pure, the eye organ is pure, and so on up to the eighty-four thousand *dhāraṇī*-entrances, everything is pure."

Now the purity and defilement of all things is conditioned by the presence or absence of mistaken attachment, in the same way that the brightness or dullness of the lamp's light depends upon the clarity of one's eyes. Therefore "purity" means that at the point of the erasure of illusion and appearance of enlightenment, the true marks of all things can be seen clearly.

The Permeation of the Universe by Purity

[Sutra (#32)] [*T* 842.17.914c25; *HPC* 7.137a11]

善男子、一切實相性清淨故、一身清淨。一身清淨故、多
身清淨。多身清淨故、如是乃至十方眾生圓覺清淨。善男

子、一世界清淨故、多世界清淨。多世界清淨故、如是乃
至盡於虛空、圓裏三世、一切平等清淨不動。

Good sons, since all true marks are pure in their nature, one body
is pure. Since one body is pure, many bodies are pure. Since many
bodies are pure, the same is true of all sentient beings in the ten
directions, who are perfectly enlightened and pure. Good sons,
since one world is pure, many worlds are pure. Since many worlds
arc pure, we can see that throughout all of space, completely including the three times, all things are equal, pure, and changeless.

[Kihwa] [*HPC 7.137a17*]

Above it was said that when we are in illusory filth, every single thing
is defiled, incapable of purity. We were also told that when we are free
from illusory filth every single thing is in motion and cannot be properly
established. Now, with the disclosure of all their true marks, every
single thing, such as "self and other," "body and mind," "distinction of
sage and worldling based on correctness," everything in the whole
universe, including all the three time periods, is equal, pure, and changeless. Why is this so? Since the purity of the nature of enlightenment is
originally changeless, the purity of every single thing is also changeless.

[*Translator's note*: Earlier, it was shown that impurity only appears as a
characteristic in the realm of duality. In nonduality, where there is no
distinction of good or bad, and so on, all things are clear, just as they
are. This is the meaning of purity here, which should not be understood
as a dichotomous opposite of impurity, but as a state of clarity, where
there is neither purity nor impurity. From here, this purity pervades
throughout the universe.]

All Things are Equal and Changeless

[Sutra (#33)] [*T 842.17.915a2; HPC 7.137b1*]

善男子、虛空如是平等不動、當知覺性平等不動。四大不
動故、當知覺性平等不動。如是乃至八萬四千陀羅尼門平
等不動。當知覺性平等不動。

Good sons, since space is equal and changeless, you should know
that the nature of enlightenment is equal and changeless. Since
the Four Elements are changeless, you should know that the nature
of enlightenment is equal and changeless. The same holds true all
the way up through the eighty-four thousand *dhāraṇī*-entrances
that are equal and changeless. Therefore you should know that
the nature of enlightenment is equal and changeless.

[Kihwa] [*HPC* 7.137b5]

This explains that all mundane and transmundane dharmas are manifestations of enlightenment and are already pure and changeless.
Because of this we can know inductively that the nature of enlightenment is originally pure and changeless. For example, knowing the purity
and nonobstruction between one hundred thousand lamps, we can
inductively know the purity and changelessness of one lamp.

Perfect Mutual Interpenetration

[Sutra (#34)] [*T* 842.17.915a5; *HPC* 7.137b9]

善男子、覺性徧滿清淨不動圓無際故、當知六根徧滿法界
。根徧滿故、當知六塵徧滿法界。塵徧滿故、當知四大徧
滿法界。如是乃至陀羅尼門徧滿法界。善男子、由彼妙覺
性徧滿故、根性塵性無壞無雜。根塵無壞故、如是乃至陀
羅尼門無壞無雜。如百千燈光照一室。其光徧滿無壞無
雜。

Good sons, the unchanging purity of the nature of enlightenment
completely pervades—it includes everything without restriction.
Therefore you should know that the six faculties completely pervade the reality-realm. Since the faculties completely pervade, you
should know that the six sensory fields completely pervade the
reality-realm. Since the sensory fields completely pervade, you
should know that the Four Elements completely pervade the reality-
realm. It is the same way with all things, including the *dhāraṇī*-
entrances, which completely pervade the reality-realm.

Good sons, since this marvelous nature of enlightenment completely pervades, there is neither conflict nor confusion between
the natures of the faculties and their objects. Since the faculties and
objects have no conflict, it is like this through all of existence, including in the *dhāraṇī*-entrances, which have neither conflict nor confusion. It is like one hundred thousand lamps shining in one room.
Their light completely pervades without conflict or confusion.

[Kihwa] [*HPC* 7.137b17]

The teaching in this section explains that since the nature of enlightenment is originally pure and completely pervades the reality-realm,
all mundane and transmundane dharmas that are revealed by enlightenment are also identical in essence and function universally. Pervading
the reality-realm again and again without exhaustion, they contain and
enter each other without obstruction. It is like the light from one lamp
that has already filled one room. The light from one hundred thousand

lamps, which were ignited from this one lamp, also fill the same room again and again without exhaustion, containing and entering each other without obstruction. Yet the light rays do not damage the other individual lights, nor are the lights confused with each other. The individual characteristics of each lamp are not damaged—each characteristic remains just as it is. The separate rays of light interpenetrate to form one realm, together lighting the one room. All dharmas being the same in essence yet functioning universally is just like this.

The part above, from "This present body is a synthesis of the Four Elements . . ." up to "immediately experience limitless purity" clarifies separation from illusion and manifestation of enlightenment—that is, "going against the flow and returning to the source." The part from "Infinite space is the manifestation of enlightenment" up to "throughout all of space, completely including the three times, all are equal, pure and changeless" shows that the faculties and the body, the container world,[16] mundane and transmundane dharmas are already the manifestation of pure enlightenment; therefore, they are identical with purity of the essence. Like the five colors that reflect from the *maṇi*-pearl—each one is pure. It is also like the hundred thousand lights which have been derived from the light of one lamp—each one is also pure. This aspect is like that expressed in the saying: "there is nothing that does not flow out from this reality-realm."

The part from "space is equal and changeless" up to ". . . the eighty-four thousand *dhāraṇī*-gates that are equal and changeless. Therefore you should know that the nature of enlightenment is equal and changeless" can be characterized by such sayings as "by seeing the shoots you can know what kind of roots there are" and "by seeing the branches you can know what kind of roots there are." This teaching is expressed by the saying: "there is nothing that does not return to this reality-realm." The format of the earlier teaching was going from the one to the many; this one is "starting with many, yet being one." Or: "the same yet different; different yet the same."

The passage from "the unchanging purity of the nature of enlightenment completely pervades—it includes everything without restriction. Therefore you should know that the six faculties completely pervade the reality-realm" up to "Their light completely pervades without conflict or confusion" is an expression of the mutual inclusion of one and many and the nonobstruction between individual phenomena. This is also like the saying: "one atom contains all the atoms of the universe." The Tathāgata has clarified defilement and purity in great detail; he has fully expounded the hidden and the manifest; selecting and rejecting, killing and giving life, rolling up and extending out freely. This is the realm perceived by Universal Vision Bodhisattva.

Detachment in Nonduality

[Sutra (#35)] [*T* 842.17.915a11; *HPC* 7.137c22]

善男子、覺成就故、當知菩薩不與法縛、不求法脫。不厭
生死、不愛涅槃。不敬持戒、不憎毀禁。不重久習、不輕
初學。何以故？一切覺故。譬如眼光曉了前境。其光圓滿
得無憎愛。何以故？光體無二、無憎愛故。

"Good sons, since their enlightenment is fully perfected, you
should know that bodhisattvas are not attached to dharmas, and
do not seek liberation from dharmas. They do not hate *saṃsāra*
and do not love nirvana. They do not venerate one for keeping the
precepts, nor despise the person who breaks them. They are not in
awe of the long-time practitioner and do not look down on the
beginner. Why? Because they are all enlightened. It is like vision
seeing an object. The vision completely pervades without experiencing attraction or aversion. Why? Vision, in essence, has no
duality, therefore it has neither attraction nor aversion.

[Kihwa] [*HPC* 7.138a5]

From the perspective of disclosure of Perfect Enlightenment the Buddha has already shown the purity of all existences. From the perspective
of purity he has shown that everything is changeless. From the perspective of changelessness he has also shown that each faculty and each object
and all kinds of things each pervade the reality-realm, containing each
other without obstruction. By clarifying the meaning of nonduality, he
shows reality to be like this. At this point he also clarifies that "entering
and attaining" is like this, and that "acting in accordance" is like this.

The clause "their enlightenment is fully perfected" means that they
have already gained complete awareness of the marvelous nature of
Perfect Enlightenment—that sage and worldling are of the same nature,
defilement and purity have the same source and they are able to act
according to this awareness. This clarifies "entering and attaining in
this way." The phrase "not attached to dharmas" means that since they
are already aware of the nonduality of the nature of Perfect Enlightenment and are able to act according to it, they do not give rise to discriminative and selective views in regard to such dichotomies as sage
and worldling, binding and liberation, *saṃsāra* and nirvana, keeping
the precepts and breaking the precepts, longtime practitioner and beginner. Having attained this state, they are able to appear in the world and
experience it as it is.

The question "Why?" means "Why is it that they have this kind of
awareness and this kind of perception and function?" When the marvelous nature of Perfect Enlightenment exists in the sage, nothing has been

added; when it exists in the worldling, nothing has been subtracted; it is bound yet unbound, it is liberated yet not liberated. With *saṃsāra* and nirvana, keeping the precepts and breaking the precepts, the long-term practitioner and the beginner, there is also neither addition nor subtraction. This is because there is neither duality nor discrimination. This shows the basis for acting in accordance with nonduality, yet neither selecting nor rejecting.

The clause "It is like vision seeing an object" refers to the time when vision meets its objects but sentiments regarding the object have not yet arisen. This is the meaning of the saying "aware of only the single step in front of one." In the vision of a great worldling it is only at the first instant of his perception of form that there is no discrimination. Immediately after that, he manifests affected views and produces like and dislike. Therefore it is said: "When first abiding in perfect direct perception, floating dust has not yet arisen; subsequently you fall into the perception of the stage of the *mano*-consciousness,[17] and the concealment and disclosure of the external world takes place." At the time of no-discrimination, even though you meet beautiful and ugly, you do not know them as beautiful and ugly; therefore there are no views of attraction and aversion or grasping and releasing. The participation in the world of differences by the practitioner of enlightenment, without having the view of difference, is like this.

The line "Why? Vision, in essence, has no duality" asks why vision is perfect and has neither attracting nor aversion. The direct perception of the visual faculty is what is referred to by "the essence of vision." This "essence of vision" is the same as "nondiscriminated illumination." Since the illumination lacks discrimination, there are no views of attraction and aversion or grasping and releasing. The earlier eight negations ("is not bound to the dharma, does not seek freedom from the dharma, etc.") express the one "no-mind." "No-mind" means the mind of no duality or choosing. "Vision, in essence, has no duality" is another way of saying "no-mind."

Sentient Beings are Originally Perfect Buddhas

[Sutra (#36)] [*T* 842.17.915a16; *HPC* 7.138b16]

善男子、此菩薩及末世衆生修習此心得成就者、於此無修
亦無成就。圓覺普照寂滅無二。於中百千萬億阿僧祇不可
說恒河沙諸佛世界猶如空華、亂起亂滅。不即不離無縛無
脫。始知衆生本來成佛、生死涅槃猶如昨夢。善男子、如昨
夢故、當知生死及與涅槃無起無滅無來無去。其所證者、
無得無失、無取無捨。其能證者、無作無止、無任無滅。
於此證中無能無所畢竟無證亦無證者。一切法性平等不壞。

Good sons, these bodhisattvas and sentient beings of the degenerate age who cultivate this mind and are able to fully consummate it, have neither cultivation nor consummation. Their Perfect Enlightenment illuminates everywhere, and is perfectly still, without duality. Here, Buddha-worlds a quintillion times as many as the incalculable amount of grains of sand in the Ganges River haphazardly arise and cease like flowers in the sky. There is neither sameness nor difference, neither bondage nor freedom. Now you know for the first time that all sentient beings are originally perfect buddhas; that *saṃsāra* and nirvana are like last night's dream.

Good sons, since they are like last night's dream, you should know that *saṃsāra* and nirvana have neither arising nor ceasing, neither coming nor going. In the realization of this there is neither gain nor loss, neither selecting nor rejecting. In the one who realizes, there is no "contrivance," "stopping," "naturalism," or "annihilation." In this realization there is neither subject nor object, and ultimately neither realization nor realized one. The nature of all dharmas is equal and indestructible.

[Kihwa] [*HPC* 7.138c4]

"this mind" is the above-mentioned mind of neither grasping nor releasing. For the person who cultivates this mind and is really able to consummate it, there is no thought of practice or realization—there is only the originally existent nature of enlightenment, which is perfectly luminous and shining everywhere. In this universal illumination, which is equanimous and quiescent, there are no longer marks of difference.

The phrases "Buddha-worlds like sky-flowers," "sentient beings are originally perfect buddhas," and "*saṃsāra* and nirvana are like last night's dream," and so on, all show the aspect of nonduality from total nihilation. If you see through diseased eyes, then the sky-flowers are not nonexistent. If you see through clear eyes, then the sky-flowers are not existent. The world is also like this. From the perspective of deluded consciousness, it is not nonexistent. From the perspective of the nature of reality, it is not existent. Neither existent nor nonexistent is the same as "neither the same nor different; neither bound nor free."

What is the meaning of the clause "all sentient beings are originally perfect buddhas"? Since Suchness is involved as an entirety in every single situation, according to conditions and consummating all kinds of false and defiled existences, Buddha is a sentient being. Since deluded existences are fundamentally empty and all are exactly Suchness, sentient beings are Buddha. Since Buddha is a sentient being, nirvana does not obstruct *saṃsāra*. Since sentient beings are Buddha, *saṃsāra* does not obstruct nirvana. Since *saṃsāra* is nirvana, *saṃsāra* is like last night's dream. Since nirvana is *saṃsāra*, nirvana is like last night's dream.

What is the meaning of the clause "*saṃsāra* and nirvana have neither arising nor ceasing"? *Saṃsāra* and nirvana are like Mercury and Orion: when one is visible the other is always invisible. When *saṃsāra* is disclosed, nirvana is concealed; when nirvana is disclosed, *saṃsāra* is concealed. "Disclosure" here is equivalent to "arising" and "coming." "Concealment" is equivalent to "cessation" and "going." In this way, nirvana and *saṃsāra* are like Mercury and Orion, but they have different traces. Now, since *saṃsāra* and nirvana are like last night's dream, their disclosure is not true disclosure; there is no "arising"; there is no "coming." Their concealment is not true concealment: there is no "cessation"; there is no "going." This is why he says that *saṃsāra* and nirvana are just like last night's dream, but are actually the same as illusory flowers.

What is the meaning of the clause "In the realization of this there is neither gain nor loss." When one is awakened, it is called "attainment" or "selecting." When one is deluded, it is called "losing" or "rejecting." Seen from the viewpoint of reality, at the time of awakening there is neither attainment nor selecting, and at the time of delusion there is neither losing nor rejecting. When one is awakened, it is just because of the original existence of awakening. It is not that you formerly lost it and now you have first attained it, or that you had rejected it before and now you have first selected it. When you are deluded, it is just because delusion is originally present. It is not that you had formerly attained it and now you have for the first time lost it. Nor is it that before you had selected it and now you have rejected it. Attaining and losing, selecting and rejecting are nothing but the deluded projections of sentient beings. The nature of enlightenment is originally present: its existence or nonexistence does not depend upon delusion and awakening.

What is the meaning of "In the one who actualizes, there is no 'contrivance' 'stopping,' 'naturalism,' or 'annihilation'?"[18] "Contrivance," "stopping," "naturalism," and "annihilation" are distinctions made by the practitioner. When it has been said above "that which is to be actualized," that was in reference to the consummation of dharmas (objective events). Here, the phrase "the one who actualizes" refers to the person. This phrase means that in terms of dharma (objective event) there is no such thing as distinction between attaining and losing, selecting and rejecting; from the position of the person there are no discriminations of contrivance, stopping, naturalism, and annihilation. In the nonduality of total nihilation the subjective realizer and the objective realization are erased together without a trace.

As for the meaning of the phrase "The nature of all dharmas is equal and indestructible," what is the meaning of "indestructible?" It has already been said that the dharma-nature includes the meanings of both one and many. The singular is not destroyed in the accomplishment of all things, and all things are not destroyed when they merge into singular reality. One does not change the singular reality in order to accomplish all things, and one does not change all things in order to merge with singular reality. You also do not destroy one characteristic in order to include all characteristics, or destroy all characteristics in order to enter into one characteristic. You do not change one characteristic so that it can include all characteristics; you do not change all characteristics so that they can be contained and enter into one characteristic. It is one and yet many, it is many and yet one. The nature of one and many is equal. Originally they are not two.

[Sutra (#37)] [*T* 842.17.915a25; *HPC* 7.139b5]

善男子、彼諸菩薩如是修行、如是漸次、如是思惟、如是住持、如是方便、如是開悟。求如是法、亦不迷悶。

Good sons, these bodhisattvas use this kind of practice, gradually advance like this, think in this way, abide in this way, use these kinds of expedient means and awaken in this way. If you seek this kind of dharma, you will not again be vexed.

[Kihwa] [*HPC* 7.139b8]

In the original question he said: "I beg of you on behalf of the bodhisattvas of this assembly and the sentient beings of the degenerate age, to expound on the bodhisattvas' stages and practice. How should they think? How should they abide? For sentient beings who have not yet awakened, what kinds of expedient methods should be devised to cause them all to awaken?" He also said: "if these sentient beings lack the correct expedients and correct thought, then, when they hear you explain this *samādhi*, confusion will arise in their minds." The Buddha, in his answer, said: "[those] who yearn for the pure enlightened mind of the Tathāgata must correct their thoughts and rid themselves of all illusions." Now, when he says "use this kind of practice," he is referring to the whole discussion about "correct thought" and "separation from illusion." This is the summary answer to the questions about practice.

Also, in the first set of questions the Buddha had said: "first relying on the Tathāgata's practice of *śamatha*. Firmly established in moral discipline and living in harmony with like-minded students, then practicing silent sitting in a quiet room, they should uninterruptedly be mindful of the following." Now, when he says "these stages" he is referring to the passage that says "first moral discipline, then *samādhi* and then practice analysis" This answers the question about stages. Next, he teaches the contemplation of "body and mind as illusion," which corresponds to the line in this part of the text that says: "think in this way, abide in this way." This corresponds to the lines that explain the contemplation of body and mind as illusion, etc., and it answers the question "how should we think, how should we abide?"

He has already shown that body and mind are illusory filth. He has also said "The one who opposes and removes illusory filth is called the 'bodhisattva.' When filth is gone, its opposition is removed; then there is no opposition, no filth, nor anything to be named." Now, [at this point] when he says "these kind of expedient means" he is referring to the passage that talks about opposing and separating from filth, the exhaustion of filth and removal of opposition. The next part of the Buddha's answer says: "[because these bodhisattvas and sentient beings of the degenerate age] fully realize [the nature of] all illusion and dispel all images, they directly experience limitless purity." The present line saying "awaken like this" refers to that passage that said "fully realize [the nature of] all illusion." This answers the question that says: "For sentient beings who have not yet awakened, what kinds of expedient means should be devised, to cause them all to awaken?"

The words "this kind of dharma" refer to all the teachings of practice, stages, thought, abiding, expedient means, and awakening. When he says "seek this kind of dharma, and not again be vexed" it means that it is not only the bodhisattvas of this assembly who can practice like this and awaken like this. Sentient beings of the degenerate age who seek this kind of dharma will also gain enlightenment and not again be deluded. Since in his question the bodhisattva said "If these sentient beings lack the correct expedient means and correct thought, if they hear the Buddha teach this *samādhi*, they will arise delusion" the Buddha concludes his answer in this way.

The *Gāthā*

[Sutra (#38)] [*T* 842.17.915a28; *HPC* 7.139c14]

爾時世尊、欲重宣此義而説偈言:

普眼汝當知　一切諸衆生
身心皆如幻　身相屬四大
心性歸六塵　四大體各離
誰爲和合者　如是漸修行
一切悉清淨　不動徧法界
無作止任滅　亦無能證者
一切佛世界　猶如虛空華
三世悉平等　畢竟無來去
初發心菩薩　及末世衆生
欲求入佛道　應如是修習

Then the World-Honored One, wanting to restate the gist of this, spoke a verse. He said:

Universal Vision, you should know
The bodies and minds of all sentient beings
Are only illusion.
The body is composed of the Four Elements;
The mind depends upon the Six Objects.
When the Four Elements disperse,
Who will be there as a synthesis?
In this kind of gradual practice
All is completely pure,
Unchanging, pervading the reality-realm.
Without contrivance, stopping, naturalism, or annihilation
And also without any subjective "realizer,"
All Buddha-worlds are
Just like sky-flowers.
The three times are all the same
Ultimately without coming or going.
Bodhisattvas who have recently arisen their minds
And sentient beings of the degenerate age
Who want to enter the Buddha Way
Should practice like this.

[Kihwa] [*HPC* 7.139c22]

The body is composed of the Four Elements; the mind depends upon the Six Objects. If you reflect in this way, the nature is empty, just clear. All things are pure, unchanging, equal and nihilated. There is also neither practice nor realization; there is also neither coming nor going. The Way of practice and realization is culminated here. Those of sharp faculties have already been awakened. But since those of middling and dull faculties have not yet awakened, after this the Buddha will accept many more questions and give many more answers. The sentence "Bodhisattvas who have recently arisen their minds and sentient beings of the degenerate age who want to enter the Buddha Way should practice like this" closes the prior section and adumbrates the next section.

4

Vajragarbha Bodhisattva

[*Translator's note*: The name Vajragarbha is composed of the two Sanskrit words *vajra* and *garbha*. *Vajra*, in Indian religious literature, is the hardest substance in existence—the essence of diamond or metal. It also means "thunderbolt" as wielded by the god Indra, or mythical vajra-warriors. *Garbha* is the Sanskrit term for "storage place" or "container" but simultaneously contains the meaning of "womb" or "matrix"—a fertile environment where things are nourished in a prenatal state. In his treatment of the term *vajra* below, Kihwa focuses on the meaning of the two Sino-Korean logographs that are used to translate the term, which are *chin/kŭm* (金), which means "metal," "gold," "hard," or "valuable," and *kang/kang* (剛), which means "hard" or "strong." When he explains the connotations of *garbha*, however, he will pursue the Sanskrit etymology.]

[Kihwa] [*HPC* 7.140b6]

The reason *vajra* is called "strong" is because it is so hard that it is impervious, and so sharp that it can cut anything. In its use as a metaphor for the subtlety of wisdom, it is that which demons cannot enter, and that which doubt cannot confuse; it is able to destroy the net of doubt, to cut away the cords of restriction. "Store" refers to the "radiant, bright *garbha*."[1] This store-mind contains the subtle wisdom that is difficult to conceive, and contains the virtuous functions of hardness and sharpness. Bodhisattvas, actualizing this, are able to sever their own hindrances and are also able to sever the net of doubt that restricts sentient beings. This is why he is called Vajragarbha ("Store of the Adamantine").

Why does Vajragarbha question further after Universal Vision Bodhisattva? Mañjuśrī has revealed "awakening;" Samantabhadra has disclosed "practice;" Universal Vision has shown "the correct contemplation that results in realization." Certainly the instructions for awakening, practice and realization have been well clarified. However, while those of superior capacity who are sharp in their discernment get the whole point in a single hearing, those of middling and inferior capacities whose power of discernment is weak, cannot avoid arising doubt.

Why? The chapter of Mañjuśrī says: "permanently sever ignorance, and directly accomplish the Buddha-Way."[2] The chapter of Samantabhadra says: "beginningless illusory ignorance/Is all created from/The perfectly enlightened mind"[3] thus completely revealing ignorance, faults, and afflictions, causing them to be completely severed. But then in the chapter of Universal Vision it says: "you know for the first time that all sentient beings are originally perfect buddhas; that *saṃsāra* and nirvana are like last night's dream."[4] This is done in order to show the doctrine of "neither-practice-nor-realization." Since what was said before and after seem to be contradictory, doubt arises.

Now contemplation is the correct path of practice, which reaches to the sublime state of the Buddha. Doubt is a heavy obstacle to the practice of contemplation and it impedes correct cultivation. If you want to do the "correct contemplation that results in realization," you cannot be hindered by doubt. If there is doubt in your mind, contemplation cannot be brought to fruition, and in the end there will be no achievement of realization. Therefore Vajragarbha follows Universal Vision with another question, asking the Buddha to resolve doubts. My verse:

> The transformation and nontransformation of both sentient
>   Being and Buddha are doubted:
> If there were no great enlightenment, who could tell?
> The gold, the flowers: with one cry you are awakened from your
>   dream.
> The clouds dissipate: the sky and moon are perfectly revealed.

Vajragarbha's Questions on the Paradox of the Coexistence of Enlightenment and Ignorance

[Sutra (#39)] [*T* 842.17.915b10; *HPC* 7.140c6]

於是金剛藏菩薩在大眾中、即從座起。頂禮佛足右繞三匝
、長跪叉手而白佛言：大悲世尊。善爲一切諸菩薩眾宣揚
如來圓覺清淨大陀羅尼因地法行漸次方便。與諸眾生開發
蒙昧、在會法眾承佛慈誨、幻翳朗然、慧目清淨。世尊、
若諸眾生本來成佛、何故復有一切無明？若諸無明眾生本

有、何因緣故如來復説本來成佛？十方異生本成佛道、後
起無明、一切如來何時復生一切煩惱？

The bodhisattva Vajragarbha rose from his seat in the great assembly and bowed his head to the Buddha's feet. He circumambulated him three times to the right, and then he knelt down with his hands clasped and said to the Buddha:

"Greatly Compassionate World-Honored One, you have lectured superbly for all these bodhisattvas about the purity of Perfect Enlightenment, the great *dhāraṇī*, the dharma practice of the causal stage and gradual practices according to provisional explanations. You have cleared away the sentient beings' clouds of darkness; all those at this dharma assembly, having received your compassionate instruction, have clarified their optical illusions and purified their wisdom eye.

World-Honored One; if all sentient beings are originally perfect buddhas, then how can they also possess ignorance? If sentient beings are originally ignorant, how can you say that they have always been perfect buddhas? If all the worldlings in the ten directions are originally perfectly enlightened, but later give rise to ignorance, at what point do all these tathāgatas regenerate these afflictions?

[Kihwa] [*HPC* 7.140c17]

"Dharma practice of the causal stage" refers to the teaching of the chapter of Mañjuśrī. "Gradient practices according to provisional explanations" refers to the teaching of the chapter of Samantabhadra. The sentence "If all sentient beings are originally perfect buddhas, then how can they also possess ignorance?" doubts the teaching of the chapters of Mañjuśrī and Samantabhadra based on the teaching of the chapter of Universal Vision. The sentence "If sentient beings are originally ignorant, how can you say that they have always been perfect buddhas?" doubts the teaching of the chapter of Universal Vision based on the teachings of the chapters of Mañjuśrī and Samantabhadra. The sentence "If all the worldlings in the ten directions are originally perfectly enlightened, but later give rise to ignorance, at what point do all these tathāgatas regenerate these afflictions?" doubts actualized enlightenment based on the idea of innate enlightenment. The doubt, then, is threefold. The first doubt says that if we are originally buddhas, then delusion should not arise. The second doubt says that if delusion is originally present, then we cannot originally be buddhas. The third doubt says that if sentient beings are originally enlightened yet now deluded, even though the Tathāgata has actualized enlightenment, he should also be deluded, and still need to do "the correct contemplation

that results in realization." These three doubts function as great impediments at a deep level. You must first get rid of these doubts, and then
you can develop and master correct contemplation and penetrate to
the sublime state of the Buddha.

[Sutra (#40)] [*T* 842.17.915b18; *HPC* 7.141a9] ▼

惟願不捨無遮大慈、爲諸菩薩開秘密藏、及爲末世一切衆
生得聞如是修多羅教了義法門、永斷疑悔。

My only request is that you not discard your limitless great compassion and that you reveal the concealed treasure to the bodhisattvas,
and that you, for all sentient beings of the degenerate age, gain
access to this kind of sutra teaching, the teaching of the complete
doctrine, so that they can permanently sever doubt and regret.

[*Translator's note*: This sentence does not make sense as it is. If Kihwa
did not correct it directly below, I would have to make an interpretive
decision to make the translation sensible. But since Kihwa does treat it,
I leave it as is, in order to make clear the point of his correction.]

[Kihwa] [*HPC* 7.141a12]

This is another passage that does not read smoothly. There may be
an error of omission, or there might have been a lot of text skipped
over in reflexive abbreviation. After "the bodhisattvas (諸菩薩)," there
should also be the phrase "and sentient beings of the degenerate age
(及末世衆生)." After "concealed treasure (秘密藏)" it should also say
"cause bodhisattvas to gain unshakable faith (令諸菩薩得決定心)."
Also *chi wei* (及爲—"for all sentient beings") should be *chi ling* (及令—
"cause sentient beings"). The text should say:

爲諸菩薩及末世衆生開秘密藏。令諸菩薩得決定心、及令
末世一切衆生得聞如是修多羅教了義法門永斷疑悔。

My only request is that you not discard your limitless great compassion and that you reveal the concealed treasure to the bodhisattvas
and sentient beings of the degenerate age. This will cause
bodhisattvas to gain unshakable faith, and allow all sentient beings
of the degenerate age to gain access to this teaching, which is a
sutra instruction of the complete doctrine, such that they can permanently sever doubt and regret.

[Sutra (#41)] [*T* 842.17.915b21; *HPC* 7.141a20]

作是語已、五體投地。如是三請終而復始。

Having said this, he prostrated himself to the ground. He asked
this question three times in succession.

The Buddha's Answer

爾 時 世 尊 告 金 剛 藏 菩 薩 言 ： 善 哉 、 善 哉 。 善 男 子 、 汝 等 乃
能 爲 諸 菩 薩 及 末 世 衆 生 問 於 如 來 甚 深 秘 密 究 竟 方 便 。 是 諸
菩 薩 最 上 教 誨 了 義 大 乘 、 能 使 十 方 修 學 菩 薩 及 諸 末 世 一 切
衆 生 得 決 定 信 、 永 斷 疑 悔 。 汝 今 諦 聽 、 當 爲 汝 説 。 時 金 剛
藏 菩 薩 奉 教 歡 喜 、 及 諸 大 衆 黙 然 而 聽 。

Then the World-Honored One, speaking to the bodhisattva Vajragarbha, said: "Excellent, excellent! Good son, you have asked well
for the bodhisattvas and sentient beings of the degenerate age about
the Tathāgata's extremely deep and recondite final expedient
means. This is the highest teaching given by the bodhisattvas, the
fully revealed doctrine of the Great Vehicle, which is able to cause
the enlightening bodhisattvas of the ten directions, as well as the
sentient beings of the degenerate age to gain unshakable faith and
permanently sever doubt and remorse. Now listen well, and I shall
explain this for you."

Vajragarbha Bodhisattva received this instruction with reverence
and great joy and those in the great assembly became silent and
listened.

[Kihwa] [*HPC* 7.141b5]

Faith is the origin of enlightenment and is the mother of the accumulated power of virtuous actions. It fosters and develops all good
dharmas.[5] Doubt is its opposite. It is the thief who steals accumulated
virtue-power and brings the enmity that destroys the roots of goodness. If doubt is not removed, faith cannot be produced. How will you
be able to use correct contemplation to penetrate to the sublime state
of the Buddha? First you must destroy doubt, then you can arouse faith
and correctly contemplate, bringing about realization. In order to resolve
this doubt, Vajragarbha asks the Buddha to teach the extremely deep
and recondite final expedient means, and [the bodhisattvas'] highest
teaching of the fully revealed doctrine of the Great Vehicle. He is thus
able to cause everybody to attain unshakable faith, severing doubt and
remorse. Since causing everyone to enter the "contemplation that results
in realization" is also the Buddha's heartfelt wish, he gladly teaches.

Saṃsāra's *Disorienting Power*

[Sutra (#42)] [*T* 842.17.915c1; *HPC* 7.141b14] ▼

善 男 子 、 一 切 世 界 始 終 生 滅 、 前 後 有 無 、 聚 散 起 止 、 念 念
相 續 、 循 環 往 復 、 種 種 取 捨 、 皆 是 輪 廻 。 未 出 輪 廻 而 辨 圓

覺、彼圓覺性即同流轉。若免輪廻無有是處。譬如動目能
搖湛水。亦如定眼由廻轉火。雲駛月運、舟行岸移、亦復
如是。善男子、諸旋未息。彼物先住尚不可得。何況輪轉
生死垢心、曾未清淨、觀佛圓覺而不旋復？是故汝等便生
三惑。

Good sons, all worlds begin and end, are born and die, have prior
and after, exist and do not exist, gather and scatter, arise and cease.
Continuing without a moment's lapse, the circular motion of going
and returning, of variously selecting and rejecting—this is all cyclic
existence. The nature of the Perfect Enlightenment that is discerned
without having left cyclic existence is simply transmigratory. If
you think you can escape cyclic existence in this way, you are completely off the mark.

[*Translator's note*: For conveying the sense of *saṃsāra*, the *SPE* uses four
different terms, three of which appear here in this passage. Although
their implications are basically the same in this text, I have translated
them systematically (and perhaps arbitrarily) in order not to blur their
distinction in the original text. These terms are: *lun-hui* 輪廻, which I
have rendered as "cyclic" and "cyclic existence," *lun-chuan* 輪轉, and
liu-chuan 流轉, rendered as "transmigration" and "transmigratory," and
sheng-ssu 生死, translated as "life-and-death" and "samsaric." *Sheng-
ssu* could have been rendered throughout as "life-and-death" if not for
the difficulty of using such a phrase adjectivally and adverbially.]

[Sutra]
It is comparable to the way in which shaking the eyes can make
still water appear to move, or the way that a transfixed gaze can
enable the appearance of a fire-wheel.[6] In the same way, clouds
flying past the moon make it seem to move, and when you are in a
moving boat, the shore appears to move.[7] Good sons, all these
things are in motion without cease, and even though the objects
are already still, you can't get a fix on them. How can you possibly
expect to get a glimpse of the Buddha's Perfect Enlightenment with
the transmigratory, samsaric, stained mind that has never been
clear? Because of this, you are prone to give rise to these three
doubts.

[Kihwa] [*HPC 7.141b24*]
The two phrases "Continuing without a moment's lapse (念念相
續)" and "the cyclical motion of going and returning (循環往復)" are
probably inverted. The text should say: "this cyclical motion of going
and returning without a moment's lapse, variously selecting and reject-

ing, is all cyclic existence (聚散起止循環往復念念相續種種取捨皆是輪廻)."

As for the phrase "all worlds": though the word "world" names a single thing, it contains the distinction of inner and outer. Therefore the text says "all."[8] *Kye* (*chieh* 界) has the meaning of "division" and has transformation as its way of being. It is the faculties, body and container world. *Se* (*shih* 世) has such meanings as "before and after," and has the characteristic of temporality. The birth, aging, sickness, and death of the organs and body, and the formation, abiding, disintegration, and disappearance of the container world are referred to by this term. So "beginning and end, birth and death, prior and after" are indicated by *se*. "Existence and nonexistence, gathering and scattering, arising and cessation" are indicated by *kye*. The phrase "cyclical motion of going and returning" speaks in reference to the merging of space and time. The part up to here is all said in reference to the faculties and body, and the container world.

"Without a moment's lapse, variously selecting and rejecting" refers specifically to the arising, abiding, changing, and ceasing of the mind. With the faculties and the body, once there is birth there is death, and once there is death there is again birth. With the container world, once there is formation there is disintegration, and once there is disintegration there is again formation. These are precisely the characteristics of *saṃsāra*. In the mind, the cessation of the prior thought brings subsequent awareness, and the subsequent thought arises in continuity with the prior cessation. In the world, selecting and rejecting are not the same. These are also the characteristics of *saṃsāra*. Therefore, the text says: "this is all *saṃsāra*. The Perfect Enlightenment that is discerned without having left *saṃsāra*." The earlier part shows how life and death and the defiled mind are *saṃsāra*. This part shows how the assumptions made through deluded conceptualization are such a heavy obstacle.

The pure nature of Perfect Enlightenment originally has neither arising nor ceasing. If you contemplate this pure nature with the defiled, samsaric mind, the nature, which actually never changes, seems to be the same as *saṃsāra*. It is like fluttering eyes looking at still water. Though the water actually never moves, it seems to move. When, with a rigid stare you look at a twirling fire-rope, the fire is actually not a wheel, but it appears to be a wheel. Or when you look at the moon through flying clouds; the moon is actually not moving—it only appears to move. When you look at the shore from a moving boat, the shore is actually not moving, but it appears to move. If fluttering eyes do not rest, the water cannot but appear to move. If eyes engaged in a fixed stare do not rest, the spinning fire cannot but appear as a wheel.

If the passing clouds do not stop, the moon cannot but appear to move.
If the boat does not stop, the shore cannot but appear to move.

Thus, if the subjectively observing mind is not settled, the objectively
observed realm cannot stop being impure or stop vacillating. In the
state of Perfect Enlightenment, there is originally nothing to be in doubt
about. Now you are using your defiled mind to observe the realm of
Buddha. Therefore you have produced these three doubts. Yet if you
merely observe with a clear mind, enlightenment will naturally appear
before you. Why must you conjecture in ignorance about arising and
non-arising and the accomplishment of buddhahood and non-accomplishment of buddhahood, and thereby keep yourself from the correct
contemplation?

The Simile of Illusion and Sky-Flowers

[Sutra (#43)] [*T* 842.17.915c9; *HPC* 7.142a10]

善男子、譬如幻翳妄見空華。幻翳若除、不可説言：此翳
已滅、何時更起一切諸翳？何以故？翳華二法非相待故。
亦如空華滅於空時、不可説言：虛空何時更起空華？何以
故？空本無華、非起滅故。生死涅槃同於起滅。妙覺圓照
離於華翳。

Good sons, it is like an illusory eye-disease falsely engendering a
vision of sky-flowers. If the illusory eye disease is removed, you
cannot ask: "Now that this eye-disease is cleared away, when will
other eye-diseases reappear?" Why? Because these two things—
flowers and eye-disease—are not interdependent.

It is also like when the sky-flowers vanish from the sky. You can't
ask: "When will the sky again produce sky-flowers?" Why? Since
the sky originally has no flowers, they do not arise and cease.
Saṃsāra and nirvana are the same as arising and ceasing; marvelous
enlightenment illuminates perfectly, and is free from flowers or
eye-disease.

[Kihwa] [*HPC* 7.142a17]
Since doubt is now fully manifest, it must be removed. Therefore he
gives the two similes of gold[9] and flowers in order to destroy the three
kinds of nets of doubt. He is saying that sentient beings are originally
Buddha, and they originally have no ignorance. Only when confusion
is originally present and you develop ignorance do you mistakenly see
saṃsāra and nirvana. The deluded mind, once restored, never again
becomes deluded. Delusion has been erased! Since body and mind and
life and death are also erased, there is no more delusion to depend
upon, and there is also nothing that illusory falsehood can depend upon.

As in the example, the sky originally has no flowers. It is only because of eye-disease that one mistakenly sees sky-flowers. If the illusory eye-disease is removed, there will never again be eye-disease. Indeed, once the eye-disease is gone, in that, the flowers are also gone. There is no further eye-disease to depend upon, and also no flowers to depend upon. This being the case, there is no principle by which these two things—the flowers and the eye-disease, should re-arise once they are erased. Delusion, along with body and mind and life and death should be understood in the same way. In the pure nature of Perfect Enlightenment there is originally neither body and mind nor life and death, just as in the sky there are originally no flowers. This is because in essence there is no arising or cessation. *Saṃsāra* is the same as the flowers appearing in the sky. Nirvana is like the flowers' vanishing from the sky. In the perfect illumination of marvelous enlightenment, there is originally neither delusion nor enlightenment, neither *saṃsāra* nor nirvana. It is like the eyes that originally have no disease and the sky that originally has no flowers. Therefore the text says: "*Saṃsāra* and nirvana are the same as arising and ceasing; marvelous enlightenment illuminates perfectly, and is free from flowers or eye-disease." This answers the first question.

[Sutra (#44)] [*T* 842.17.915c14; *HPC* 7.142b11] ▼

善男子、當知虛空非是暫有、亦非暫無。況復如來圓覺隨
順、而爲虛空平等本性？

Good sons, you should know that the sky does not exist for an instant nor does it not exist for an instant. How much more so it is in the Tathāgata's Perfect Enlightenment closely according (*sic*) and becoming the sky's equal original nature.

[Kihwa] [*HPC* 7.142b14]
The phrases "closely according (隨 順)" and "Perfect Enlightenment (圓 覺)" are probably transposed in the text. It should say "closely according with Perfect Enlightenment (隨 順 圓 覺)." It also could say: "How much more so with the Tathāgata's perfectly enlightened *marvelous mind*[10] and becoming the equal original nature of the sky (況復 如來圓覺妙心而爲虛空平等本性)?"
The premise that sentient beings are originally buddhas and originally lack ignorance has been firmly established. This being so, there should be no doubt about either the existence or nonexistence of the originally present marvelous nature of Perfect Enlightenment in sentient beings and buddhas. Why? Space is something that is manifested from enlightenment. If even this space is not for an instant either existent or nonexistent, how could we possibly debate about the existence or nonexistence

of the subtle nature of Perfect Enlightenment that space depends upon? This answers the second question.

The Simile of Purifying Gold

[Sutra (#45)] [*T* 842.17.915c17; *HPC* 7.142b22]

善男子、如銷金鑛。金非銷有。既已成金、不重爲鑛。經無窮時、金性不壞。不應說言本非成就。如來圓覺亦復如是。

Good sons, it is like smelting gold ore. The gold does not come into being because of smelting; once it is perfected, it will never again become ore.[11] Even though it passes through endless time, the nature of the gold is never corrupted. It is wrong to say that it is not originally perfect. The Perfect Enlightenment of the Tathāgata is also like this.

[Kihwa] [*HPC* 7.142c1]

Even though the gold is originally pure, it needs provisional refinement to become true gold for the first time. Once true gold is perfected, its essence cannot again become ore. Even though we are originally buddhas, we become obstructed by our afflictions. We must receive new perfumation and then accomplish correct enlightenment. Once we accomplish correct enlightenment, we will not again suffer affliction. You cannot say that we are not originally buddhas. You also cannot say that there will be a return of delusion. This is the answer to the third question.

[Sutra (#46)] [*T* 842.17.915c19; *HPC* 7.142c7]

善男子、一切如來妙圓覺心本無菩提與於涅槃、亦無成佛及不成佛、無妄輪廻及非輪廻。

Good sons, the marvelous perfectly enlightened mind of the tathāgatas originally has neither *bodhi* nor nirvana; it has neither accomplishment of buddhahood nor non-accomplishment of buddhahood; no false cyclic existence and no noncyclic existence.

[Kihwa] [*HPC* 7.142c10]

Having solved the third problem, he discloses Perfect Enlightenment, which cuts off the path of thought and speech and cannot be fathomed by discrimination. He first reveals that originally there is neither truth nor falsity, thus erasing all relativity. The term *bodhi* is established in contrast to *affliction*; the term *nirvana* gets its meaning [in its contradistinction to] saṃsāra. In the marvelous mind of Perfect Enlightenment there is originally neither truth nor falsity, neither delusion nor awakening, neither buddhahood nor nonbuddhahood, neither *saṃsāra* nor non-*saṃsāra*. How could relative concepts possibly function in debate about this?

The Futility of the Use of Discrimination

[Sutra (#47)] [*T* 842.17.915c22; *HPC* 7.142c16]

善男子、但諸聲聞所圓境界、身心語言皆悉斷滅。終不能至彼之親證所現涅槃。何況能以有思惟心、測度如來圓覺境界？如取螢火燒須彌山、終不能著。以輪廻心、生輪廻見、入於如來大寂滅海、終不能至。是故我說一切菩薩及末世衆生先斷無始輪廻根本。

Good sons, in the final stage of the *śrāvakas* path, there is complete severance of the karmic activities of word, thought, and action. Yet they are still incapable of attaining their own actualized and manifest nirvana. How can you possibly expect to fathom the Tathāgata's state of Perfect Enlightenment using discursive thought? It is like trying to burn Mt. Sumeru with the fire from a firefly—it is impossible! Using the cyclic mind, you produce cyclic views and you will never be able to enter the Tathāgata's ocean of perfect tranquillity. Therefore, I say that all bodhisattvas and sentient beings of the degenerate age should first sever the beginningless root of cyclic existence.

[*Translator's note*: The *śrāvaka* was introduced as one of the practitioners of the Two Vehicles in the second chapter. The difference between the *śrāvaka-pratyekabuddha* enlightenment and that of the bodhisattva was sometimes articulated in Consciousness-only literature in terms of the so-called "two hindrances" (*erh-chang* 二障). The first of the two hindrances, the more crude of the two, is called the "hindrance of defilement" (*fan-nao chang* 煩惱障). This hindrance includes all the various karmic limitations to our being that are developed from the twin forces of attraction and aversion. Thus included are all forms of love, hatred, jealousy, envy, anger, desire, and so on. The *śrāvakas* and *pratyekabuddhas*, through their practices of morality and meditation, are eventually able to eradicate these (no mean task!). The second, more subtle and qualitatively different hindrance is called the "hindrance by the known" (*so chih chang* 所知障). This hindrance refers to the fact that it is precisely our current perception of reality that we are clinging to that prevents us from properly actualizing our originally enlightened nature. This hindrance can be equated with the "ignorance" defined in the chapter of Mañjuśrī, and can only be overcome through the use of the proper

Mahāyāna meditations taught in this and other Mahāyāna texts. The Two Hindrances are discussed further in chapter 5, sutra passage 57.]

[Kihwa] [*HPC* 7.142c23]

Above he has disclosed the erasure of all relativity. Here he shows that it cannot be attained through discursive thought. The *śrāvaka* is the lowest level among the four sages.[12] Yet even he severs views of love[13] and extricates himself from birth-and-death. Though he has not reached the level of bodhisattvas and buddhas, he has gone far beyond the birth and death of regular people. This is the meaning of the phrase "above, incomplete; below, there is remainder." Even in the final stage of the *śrāvakas*, the marks of speech and thought are annihilated. How much more so in the state of the Tathāgata's Perfect Enlightenment? And do you think you can completely realize [through conceptualization] the final stage of the *śrāvaka*, where thought and speech are extinguished, and also penetrate to this?! If the worldling's mind cannot even conceptualize the final stage of the *śrāvakas*, how could it so easily conceptualize of the state of the tathāgatas? Compare this to Mt. Sumeru, which is the king among mountains. A firefly could not even come close to burning up any regular mountain. How could it possibly scorch Mt. Sumeru? Discursive thought is cyclic mind. Conceptualization is cyclic view. The state of Perfect Enlightenment is no-mind and no-views— the great quiescent ocean. How could you possibly use this kind of thought and views to enter such a state? Therefore, if you desire to actualize Perfect Enlightenment, you must first learn "no-thought." No-thought merges with enlightenment. The mind of thought has difficulty in following.

[Sutra (#48)] [*T* 842.17.915c27; *HPC* 7.143a15]

善男子、有作思惟從有心起。皆是六塵妄想緣氣非實心體、已如空華。用此思惟辨於佛境猶如空華復結空果。展轉妄想無有是處。

Good sons, habituated discursive thought arises from the conditioned mind. The six data-fields, false conceptualization, and conditioned energies are not the true essence of mind—indeed, they are like sky-flowers. But using discursive thought to discern the Buddha-state is like the sky-flowers further producing "sky-fruits." Circular false thoughts are useless here.

[Kihwa] [*HPC* 7.143a19]

The reason discursive thought cannot actualize Perfect Enlightenment is because discursive thought is falsity, and the nature of enlightenment is truth. Truth and falsity cannot meet. It is like the difference between light and darkness. If you use falsity to discern truth, truth will not be discerned and one's effort will be wasted in aimless wandering. Therefore falsity augments and enhances falsity, just like sky-flowers further producing sky-fruits.

[Sutra (#49)] [*T* 842.17.916a2; *HPC* 7.143a24]

善男子、虛妄浮心多諸巧見不能成就圓覺方便。如是分別
非爲正問。

Good sons, false floating thoughts and numerous clever views are incapable of perfecting the expedient means of Perfect Enlightenment. Using this kind of discrimination, you cannot even formulate a proper question.

[Kihwa] [*HPC* 7.143b2]
Discursive thought has already been adjudged a hindrance, useless in the realization of enlightenment. The Buddha concludes by showing that the question has also come from discursive thought, and is therefore flawed and incorrect. He has said that discursive thought is "floating thought" and that clever views are not the correct expedient means. If you straighten your mind and correct your views, then you can personally actualize the expedient means of Perfect Enlightenment. When he first addressed the question, he called it "the highest teaching of the fully revealed doctrine of the Great Vehicle."[14] Now he disparages it, calling it "floating thoughts and clever views," taking this as an opportunity to sever doubt. Therefore, that which is questioned can be called "the highest teaching of the fully revealed doctrine of the Great Vehicle," but in its use [in attaining] Perfect Enlightenment, it cannot avoid becoming floating thoughts and clever views.

This chapter first shows that when you use falsity to discern truth, truth is transformed according to falsity. Then he uses reality to directly sever the three doubts. Then he reveals Perfect Enlightenment, erasing all relativity. He next shows that it is not something that thought can conceptualize, in order to encourage "no-thought." Next he shows discursive thought to be circular and false. Finally he returns to assail the original question as being "floating thoughts and clever views," teaching instead "no discursive thought or discrimination" as the correct expedient means.

This chapter concentrates on cutting off doubt and inducing faith. The reason he criticizes discursive thought and discrimination so harshly is because they are the mental states that contain doubt. Those mental states that darken and cover the true nature and enhance ignorance are the Five Obscurations.[15] The Five Obscurations are the source of false defilement and are the hindrances to the practice of contemplation. Doubt is one of the Five Obscurations, and is the deepest hindrance to the practice of contemplation. Faith is the basis for the initiation of practice; if there is doubt, then faith cannot arise and there will be no basis for the initiation of practice. Therefore it must be cast off. Hence, Vajragarbha says in his request: "cause bodhisattvas and sentient beings of the degenerate age to attain unshakable faith, and sever doubt and remorse." From here to the chapter of Voice of Discernment, each of the Five Obscurations are removed, one by one.

Though Mañjuśrī has already induced faith and understanding, the reason why doubt is again severed and faith is encouraged here is because although those of sharp faculties have already attained faith and understanding, and have initiated the practice leading to realization, those of middling and inferior faculties have not only not arisen faith, but have also begun to waver, and this wavering has now become a hindrance. Therefore in this chapter Vajragarbha again raised the question, to sever doubt and bring forth faith. In this way, this chapter has been a teaching of faith and understanding aimed at those of middling and inferior capacities. In the following chapters, they will be taught how to commence their practice.

The *Gāthā*

[Sutra (#50)] [*T* 842.17.916a3; *HPC* 7.143c6]

爾時世尊、欲重宣此義而説偈言：

金剛藏當知　如來寂滅性
未曾有終始　若以輪廻心
思惟即旋復　但至輪廻際
不能入佛海　譬如銷金鑛
金非銷故有　雖復本來金
終以銷成就　一成眞金體
不復重爲鑛　生死與涅槃
凡夫及諸佛　同爲空華相
思惟猶幻化　何況詰虚妄
若能了此心　然後求圓覺

Then the World-Honored One, desiring to restate the gist of this, spoke a verse, saying:

> Vajragarbha, you should know
> The Tathāgata's perfectly tranquil nature
> Has never had a beginning or end.
> If you use the cyclic mind
> Discursive thought just revolves,
> At most, reaching the limits of cyclic existence,

And you are unable to enter the Buddha-ocean.
It is like smelting gold ore:
The gold does not exist because of smelting,
Yet crude gold, from smelting
Once subsequently perfected,
Never returns to the state of ore.
Saṃsāra and nirvana,
Worldlings and buddhas
Like sky-flowers, are appearances.
Discursive thought is just an illusory phenomenon:
How can it penetrate falsity?
Only after you fully know this mind
Can you seek Perfect Enlightenment.

[Kihwa] [*HPC* 7.143c14]

The Way originally has no thought. Thought goes against the real. Because of this, the three doubts can only produce clever views, which in turn induces the Tathāgata to create the similes to destroy them. If thought is at odds with reality, how can words possibly embrace it? If you want to actualize Perfect Enlightenment, you must first know the mind. The mind is originally no-mind. No-mind is the Way.

5

Maitreya
Bodhisattva

[*Translator's note*: "Maitreya," means "benevolent" or "compassionate." According to Buddhist tradition, he is the bodhisattva who will appear in this world to become the next Buddha after 5,670,000,000 years, when he ends his life in the Tuṣita Heaven. He is said to preside over the spread of the *sangha*, and to protect its members. The Sanskrit name "Maitreya" is translated into Chinese with the ideograph *tz'u/cha* (慈), which is generally rendered into English as "compassion." I would have done the same here, except that in his commentary Kihwa breaks the Chinese compound word commonly translated into English as compassion, (*tz'u-pei/chabi* 慈悲), into two words for the sake of analysis. In order to make a consistent presentation of this argument by keeping unity of word usage, there is no recourse but to make the word "compassion" a compound of two words, which I have attempted with "kindness" and "pity." Fortunately, this word choice does not have to achieve perfect success to communicate Kihwa's main point, which is to show how this chapter of the sutra distinguishes selfless forms of caring, such as "kindness," "compassion" and "pity" from defiled forms such as "attached love" (*ai/ae* 愛), "craving" (*t'an/t'am* 貪), and "desire" (*yü/yok* 欲).]

[Kihwa] [*HPC* 7.143c19]

  "Kindness (慈)" is comparable to "pity (悲)," and is also close to "attached love (愛)." Attached love generates life-and-death; kindness develops merit and wisdom. Pity can remove suffering; kindness can enhance happiness. Sentient beings transmigrate through various destinies based on desire and attachment: this is why attached love generates life-and-death. All buddhas, because of their "kindness-and-pity" ("compassion") marvelously adorn the path of enlightenment: this is why kindness develops merit and wisdom. This is how Maitreya transforms

136

attached love into kindness and fulfills the role of successor to Śākyamuni. The hallmark of Śākyamuni's teaching is the use of pity to remove suffering. The hallmark of Maitreya's teaching is the use of kindness to enhance happiness. This is why Maitreya appears in the world as a successor to Śākyamuni. But the "pity of Śākyamuni" and the "kindness of Maitreya" are only phrases used to express a special tendency of the teachings of these two buddhas. In fact, how could Śākyamuni possibly possess "pity" and lack "kindness"? And how could Maitreya possess "kindness" and lack "pity"? Generally speaking, pity and kindness fit with each other to refer to one thing. [That is, "compassion."]

Why does Maitreya raise another question following Vajragarbha? Vajragarbha transformed doubt into faith and thus imparted the wisdom that the listeners could use for themselves. Maitreya transforms attached love into kindness and makes them feel pity for other beings. The questions raised by Vajragarbha concentrated on severing doubt. The questions raised by Maitreya concentrate on severing attached love. Yet although the "wisdom of Vajragarbha" and the "kindness of Maitreya" lead one to focus on their distinctive attributes, there is no doubt that they enhance each other and contribute together to the metamorphosis of great enlightenment. How could Vajragarbha possibly possess wisdom and lack kindness? And how could Maitreya possibly possess kindness and lack wisdom? Since Vajragarbha has already fully disclosed the [meaning] of wisdom, Maitreya will now do the same for kindness. This is certainly the proper order of the teaching. My verse:

> With the root of attached love destroyed, the sprouts of suffering are also burnt away.
> Great and small enter the forest of sagehood by the same road.
> The moon of wisdom—the flower of compassion—the triple world is radiant.
> Living spirits, following this, will avoid floating and sinking.

[Sutra (#51)] [*T* 842.17.916a15; *HPC* 7.144a20]

於是彌勒菩薩在大眾中、即從座起。頂禮佛足右繞三匝。
長跪叉手而白佛言：大悲世尊。廣爲菩薩開秘密藏、令諸
大眾深悟輪廻、分別邪正。能施末世一切眾生無畏道眼於
大涅槃生決定信。無復重隨輪轉境界、起循環見。

The bodhisattva Maitreya arose from his seat in the great assembly and bowed his head to the Buddha's feet. He circumambulated him three times to the right, and then knelt down with his hands clasped. He addressed the Buddha, saying:

"Greatly Compassionate World-Honored One, you have opened wide the secret treasure for the bodhisattvas and have made all in the great assembly deeply awaken to [the marks of] transmigration and distinguish between the correct and mistaken. You have been able to impart the Fearless Eye of the Way and unshakable faith in Great Nirvana to the sentient beings of the degenerate age; they will not again chase after cyclic existence or give rise to cyclic views."

[Kihwa] [*HPC* 7.144b3]

What was not explained before is now disclosed. Therefore he says, "opened the secret treasure . . . and have made them awaken." It has been made clear that clever views and floating thoughts are incapable of actualizing enlightenment. But if you have the correct mind and right view, then you can intimately actualize expedient means. This is why he says, "distinguish between correct and mistaken" and "impart to them the Eye of the Way." The "Eye of the Way" is an eye that is obstructed neither by emptiness nor existence, that cancels and illuminates simultaneously and penetrates to perceive the Middle Path. Sometimes it is called "great Perfect Enlightenment;" sometimes it is called "Great Nirvana." "Perfect Enlightenment" is a term that is used to point directly to the essence of enlightenment. "Nirvana" is a term that is used to point directly to the awareness of no-arising-and-ceasing beyond the essence. Within this meaning there is perfect faith without a bit of doubt, such that one does not again produce confusion. This is why the text says, "unshakable faith in Great Nirvana" and "they will not again give rise to cyclic views."

Maitreya's Questions on
the Severance of the Root of Transmigration

[Sutra (#52)] [*T* 842.17.916a20; *HPC* 7.144b14]

世尊、若諸菩薩及末世眾生欲遊如來大寂滅海、云何當斷
輪廻根本？於諸輪廻有幾種性？修佛菩提幾等差別？廻入
塵勞當設幾種教化方便度諸眾生？惟願不捨救世大悲令諸
修行一切菩薩及末世眾生慧目肅清、照耀心鏡、圓悟如來
無上知見。作是語已、五體投地。如是三請、終而復始。

World-Honored One; if the bodhisattvas and sentient beings of the degenerate age aspire to float on the Tathāgata's great tranquil ocean, how should they sever the root of cyclic existence? In the various kinds of cyclic existence, how many types of beings are there? How many differences are there in types of practice of the Buddha's *bodhi*? When we re-enter the dirty and difficult world, what kinds of teaching devices should we establish to save all sentient beings? I implore you not to relax in your world-saving great compassion—that you clarify the wisdom eye of all practicing bodhisattvas and sentient beings of the degenerate age, illuminate their mind-mirror, and completely awaken them to the Tathāgata's unsurpassed insight." After saying this, he prostrated fully to the ground. He asked this question three times in succession.

[Kihwa] [*HPC* 7.144b22]

"Great tranquil ocean" refers to "great nirvana." It also implies the cessation of the awareness and views of body and mind, and the deep, vast, and difficult-to-perceive subtle entry of *samādhi*. Since this is not something that you can enter using the views of the cyclic mind, he asks, "How should they sever the root of cyclic existence?" Vajragarbha had asked his questions based on the clause in the chapter of Universal Vision that says "[all sentient beings are] originally perfect buddhas."[1] Maitreya now asks his question because of the clause in the chapter of Vajragarbha that says "first sever [the beginningless root of] cyclic existence."[2] But that sentence only says "first sever the root of cyclic existence," and does not clarify exactly what the root *is*. Therefore Maitreya expresses this doubt in the form of a question and asks the Buddha to dispel it. Since the distinction of the two kinds of doctrines concerning arousal [of faith] and practice [to sever defilement], as well as the attainment of realization and the bringing about of transformation also have not yet been clarified, he asks these questions one after the other to initiate the instruction.

"Wisdom eye" refers to the subjectively observing wisdom. "Mind-mirror" refers to the objectively perceived principle. "Insight" is the meritorious function beyond the principle. The Wisdom Eye of sentient beings is originally completely pure. The Mind Mirror is originally perfectly bright. Insight is originally replete. It is only because of the obscurations of craving and attachment that the Wisdom Eye suffers impairment, that the Mind Mirror becomes blemished and that insight is incomplete. If we sever craving and attachment, then the eye lacks impairment and is clear; the mirror lacks blemish and is perfectly bright and one's insight is replete, lacking nothing. Therefore Maitreya requests the Buddha to remove these obstructions and the Buddha, out of his great compassion, expounds the teaching.

The Buddha's Answer

[Sutra (#53)] [*T* 842.17.916a27; *HPC* 7.144c17]

爾時世尊告彌勒菩薩言：善哉、善哉。善男子、汝等乃能為諸菩薩及末世眾生請問如來深奧秘密微妙之義、令諸菩薩潔清慧目、及令一切末世眾生永斷輪廻。心悟實相具無

生忍。汝今諦聽、當爲汝説。時彌勒菩薩奉教歡喜、及諸
大衆默然而聽。

Then the World-Honored One, addressing the bodhisattva Maitreya, said: "Excellent, excellent! Good son, you have questioned well on behalf of the bodhisattvas and sentient beings of the degenerate age about the Tathāgata's mysterious, secret, subtle doctrine. You have enabled the bodhisattvas to purify their wisdom eye, and allowed all sentient beings of the degenerate age to permanently sever themselves from cyclic existence. Their minds will awaken to their true characteristic and they will possess the equipoise that comes with the awareness of the non-arising characteristic of existence. Now listen well, and I shall explain this for you." Maitreya received this instruction with joy and great reverence. All those in the great assembly became silent and listened.

[Kihwa] [*HPC* 7.145a1]

Since severing attachment and creating compassion, completing realization and bringing about metamorphosis is also the Buddha's own heartfelt intention, he naturally gives his approval to this request. "Mysterious" is like a small room inside of another room, which is hidden behind many doors, and into which outsiders never come. "Secret" is like an extremely valuable gem in a room that is kept hidden in a secret repository, and that people never see. "Subtle" is like the most delicate of young maidens, who is perfectly exquisite and who does not allow herself to be touched. The Buddha has explained the nature of existence as cycling through birth-and-death, and so the processes of practice and transformation are now known to everybody. But if they are unaware of the variations in the bases of transmigration, the distinctions in the basic types of practice and the variety of expedient methods of transforming others, then they will be obstructed by their attachment and their wisdom eye will be impaired. Through the falsely conceptualizing mind, the principle of true marks will be confused; through samsaric views, the principle of unarisenness will be obscured.

Maitreya raises these questions for the sentient beings to make them understand attached love to be the root of transmigration and to permanently sever it. By further explaining the distinctions in practice and the expedient means for teaching and transforming, all can be completely clarified without remainder, so that the deludedly conceptualizing mind is stopped and samsaric views are extinguished. The impairments of the wisdom eye can once again be cleared away; the confusions about the principle of true marks can once again be illuminated; the obscurations of the principle of non-arising can once again be suddenly removed. This is why the questions of Maitreya are called "excellent."

Attached Love/Desire as the Root of Transmigration

[Sutra (#54)] [*T* 842.17.916b4; *HPC* 7.145a20]

善男子、一切衆生、從無始際、由有種種恩愛貪欲、故有
輪廻。若諸世界一切種性、卵生、胎生、濕生、化生、皆
因淫欲而正性命、當知輪廻愛爲根本。由有諸欲助發愛性
、是故能令生死相續。欲因愛生、命因欲有。衆生愛命還
依欲本。愛欲爲因愛命爲果。

Good sons, all sentient beings are in cyclical existence because of
their possession, from beginningless time, of affection, attached
love, craving, and desire. Since all the different types of beings—
those born from eggs, those born from wombs, those born from
moisture and those born by transformation—all receive their birth
and life from sexual desire, you should realize that cyclic existence
has attached love as its basis. This tendency to be gripped by
attached love is abetted by the existence of all desires, and therefore it is able to empower the continuity of *saṃsāra.* Desire arises
depending upon attached love; life power exists depending upon
desire. Furthermore, the attached love and life of sentient beings
have desire as their root. Attached love and desire are causes;
attached love and life are results.

[Kihwa] [*HPC* 7.145b2]
Attached love is the basis of being and becoming[3]—the root of cyclic
existence. With attached love at the root, you are bound to produce
craving and desire. With desire as an aid, you are bound to produce the
nature of attached love. With attachment and desire working together,
you naturally undergo rebirth. Having been caused by attachment and
desire, you receive the empowerment of life. Again, caused by attachment and life power, you again produce craving and desire. In this way
you complete the circle of the continuity of cause and effect. Hence the
sutra says, "attached love and desire are the causes; attached love and
life-power are the results." This answers Maitreya's question about the
root of cyclic existence.

But "attachment" has distinctions of pure and impure, and rising and
falling are not the same. The objects of desire are not one—among those
things that are desired there are a thousand differences. Since the types
of attachment are not the same, and since there are a thousand differences between the objects of desire, there are also differences in the
type of birth one receives. From this we know that these three "attached
love," "desire," and "life-power" are the cords that keep sentient beings
in bondage.

The Causes of the Various Rebirths

[Sutra (#55)] [*T* 842.17.916b9; *HPC* 7.145b12]

由 於 欲 境 起 諸 違 順。 境 背 愛 心 而 生 憎 嫉、 造 種 種 業。 是 故
復 生 地 獄 餓 鬼。 知 欲 可 厭、 愛 厭 業 道、 捨 惡 樂 善 復 現 天 人
。 又 知 諸 愛 可 厭 惡 故、 棄 愛 樂 捨。 還 滋 愛 本、 便 現 有 爲 增
上 善 果。 皆 輪 廻 故 不 成 聖 道。 是 故 衆 生 欲 脫 生 死 免 諸 輪 廻
、 先 斷 貪 欲 及 除 愛 渴。

It is in reference to the objects of desire that you produce varieties of comfort and discomfort. When the object is contrary to the attached mind, you give rise to aversion and jealousy, creating all sorts of karma. It is because of this that you are reborn as a hell-being or a hungry ghost. But then, knowing that desire should be abandoned and adhering to the path of abandonment of karmic activity, you cast off evil and enjoy goodness; hence, you are reborn as a god or human. Again, knowing that you should dislike all forms of attachment, you let go of attachment and enjoy detachment. This greatly nourishes the root of attachment and you automatically produce conditionally enhanced positive states. But since all of this is cyclic existence, you still do not attain to the sagely Way. Therefore, sentient beings who desire to be free from life and death and want to escape cyclic existence, first have to sever desire and rid themselves of attached love.

[Kihwa] [*HPC* 7.145b19]

Placed in contact with agreeable and disagreeable objects, your mind gives rise to attachment and aversion, and based upon this attachment and aversion, you create all sorts of karma. When your karma is evil, you are reborn in the Three Evil Destinies.[4] When you detach from evil and follow the good, you are reborn as a god or human. Casting off attachment and enjoying detachment, you naturally produce conditionally enhanced positive states. Karma has good and bad, attachment has purity and defilement. Even though there are differences between good and bad and distinctions between purity and defilement, since none of these are free from discrimination, none can avoid cyclic existence. Since cyclic existence cannot be avoided, through what means is the sagely Way to be realized? Therefore, if you desire to accomplish the sagely Way, you must avoid cyclic existence. If you want to avoid cyclic existence, you must first sever craving and attachment. Therefore the sutra says, "If you want to avoid cyclic existence, first sever craving and desire and be rid of attached love." This section answers the questions on the distinctions in nature.

The Nonattached Compassion of the Bodhisattva

[Sutra (#56)] [*T* 842.17.916b15; *HPC* 7.145c5]

善男子、菩薩變化示現世間、非愛爲本。但以慈悲令彼捨
愛假諸貪欲而入生死。若諸末世一切衆生能捨諸欲及除憎
愛、永斷輪廻。勤求如來圓覺境界於清淨心、便得開悟。

Good sons, when bodhisattvas appear in the world to teach, it is
not based on attachment. It is only because of their compassionate
intention to have the sentient beings discard attachment that they
provisionally take on all kinds of desire and enter life-and-death.
If all sentient beings of the degenerate age can cast off their desires
and remove love and hate, they will permanently end their cyclic
existence. Seeking the perfectly enlightened state of the Tathāgata
in their pure minds, they will directly attain awakening.

[Kihwa] [*HPC* 7.145c10]

It has already been settled that attached love is the root of cyclic existence and that it is to be severed. Now, the Buddha is fearful of people
mixing up attached love and compassion—that they might become
muddled, bringing harm to the compassion that they possess. Hence
he reclarifies the distinction between purity and impurity, to make it
understood exactly how compassion differs from attached love. If
attached love is mistaken for compassion, it can corrupt the meaning
of compassion. Since compassion is similar to attached love, it can easily
be spoiled by attached love.

Now a bodhisattva, motivated by his great pity in order to save sentient beings from their intense suffering, is born into the secular world
and adapts to its customs. He takes a wife and has a baby with her. In
advancing in the world and making his living, there is nothing that he
cannot accomplish. But if he lacks the wisdom to regulate this pursuit,
then it will turn into craving and be defiled by attachment and he will
be unable to avoid the trap of cyclic existence. This is the meaning of
"attached love spoiling compassion because of their similarity."

On the other hand, it is possible for this bodhisattva to go from one
bar to another and from one brothel to another, living with people and
transforming them and maintaining a constantly pure mind: in this case
wisdom and compassion work together without falling into attached
views. Even though desire and compassion are similar in appearance,
they differ in terms of purity and defilement. It is like comparing heaven
with the earth: Can you ever say that they are the same?

Therefore the Buddha discusses craving and attachment—to provide
a means for practitioners to discriminate purity and impurity. Craving
is of the nature of *saṃsāra*; compassion is of the nature of enlighten-

ment, and the distinction between purity and impurity is as clear as the difference between heaven and earth. The lack of manifestation of the enlightened nature is due solely to the obscuration by craving. When the stain of attachment and desire is wiped out, the mind is pure and the great wisdom of Perfect Enlightenment shines brightly. Therefore he says "attain awakening."

The Five Natures and the Two Hindrances

[Sutra (#57)] [*T* 842.17.916b20; *HPC* 7.146a8]

善男子、一切衆生由本貪欲發揮無明、顯出五性差別不等
。依二種障而現深淺。云何二障？一者理障、礙正知見。
二者事障、續諸生死。云何五性？善男子、若此二障未得
斷滅、名未成佛。若諸衆生永捨貪欲、先除事障、未斷理
障、但能悟入聲聞緣覺、未能顯住菩薩境界。
　善男子、若諸末世一切衆生欲汎如來大圓覺海、先當發
願勤斷二障。二障已伏即能悟入菩薩境界。若事理障已永
斷滅、即入如來微妙圓覺、滿足菩提及大涅槃。善男子、
一切衆生皆證圓覺。逢善知識、依彼所作因地法行。爾時
修習便有頓漸。若遇如來無上菩提正修行路、根無大小。
皆成佛果。若諸衆生雖求善友遇邪見者、未得正悟。是則
名爲外道種性。邪師過謬非衆生咎。是名衆生五性差別。

Good sons, due to their inherent desire, sentient beings generate ignorance and manifest the distinctions and inequalities of the Five Natures. Due to the Two Hindrances they manifest deep and shallow [afflictions]. What are the Two Hindrances? The first is the noetic hindrance, which obstructs correct awareness; the second is the phenomenal hindrance, which enables the continuation of *saṃsāra*.

What are the 'Five Natures?'

[*Translator's note*: The writer from here introduces a combination of three different doctrines as a way of distinguishing between differences in level of practice, yet at the same time making a characteristic "Mahāyāna" universalistic argument. First he brings into play a concept which held much influence, and was at the same time cause for much controversy, that is, the doctrine of the "Five Natures" of the Yogācāra school. The exponents of this late Indian school had articulated a scheme in which the religious capacities of human beings were divided into five categories, according to a predetermined level of attainment an individual practitioner might reach. This determination was according to the "seeds" (*bījas* 種子) contained in ones *ālayavijñāna* or "store consciousness." The Five Natures were: the nature predetermined for *śrāvaka*; the nature predetermined for *pratyekabuddha*; the nature predetermined for *bodhisattva*, the indeterminate nature (meaning that any of the prior three were possible) and the so-called *icchantika* (an exceedingly evil person, considerd devoid of seeds of buddhahood) nature.

This doctrine was imported into East Asia primarily through the translations of Yogācāra texts done by Hsüan-tsang and his school. While many aspects of Yogācāra doctrine became influential in East Asia, East Asian Buddhists were on the whole rather unreceptive to this rigid doctrine of Five Natures. They were especially doubtful of the proposition that any person could be completely devoid of the Buddha-nature, as *icchantikas* were supposed to be. So here the sutra writer reinterprets this doctrine to make his own point. He has already stated clearly above that "all sentient beings actualize buddhahood." For him, the Five Natures will represent different levels of penetration into truth, or different degrees of the removal of the hindrances of enlightenment.

The doctrine of the *Two Hindrances* (already introduced in the prior chapter) is another important Buddhist concept that comes from Yogācāra and was incorporated to some degree in Hua-yen and Ch'an doctrine. This doctrine teaches that the inability of sentient beings to attain enlightenment was due to two general types of obstructions. The first was called "the hindrance of defilement (煩惱障)." This means that people are prevented from attaining liberation because of their desire, craving, fear, hope, attachment, dislike, anxieties—all the afflictions that engender suffering. In the Mahāyāna view, this hindrance may be overcome by so-called *hīnayāna* practices—the practices of the Two Vehicles. This hindrance is expressed in the above passage of the *SPE* as the "phenomenal hindrance" (事障). The second, more subtle hindrance, is called the "hindrance by the known" (所知障), referring to the fact that it is exactly our attachment to our present level of knowledge, awareness, or wisdom (no matter how deep or subtle) that prevents us from attaining enlightenment. This is expressed in the above passage as the "noetic hindrance" (理障). Other possible translations of this term might be "hindrance in regard to principle" or "hindrance of attachment to understanding."

In Yogācāra soteriological theory it is believed that one may only overcome the hindrance by the known ("noetic hindrance") through the development of the emptiness-based wisdom of the bodhisattva. Thus, while *śrāvakas* and *pratyekabuddhas* may only overcome the hindrance of defilements, bodhisattvas may overcome both. The Chinese terms being translated here as "phenomenal" and "noetic" represent the two important categories of discourse seen in Hua-yen Buddhism: *shih/sa*

(事 "phenomena," "events") and *li/ri* (理 "principle," here, "noetic"). In this scheme, to be hindered at the *phenomenal* level would mean that one is obstructed in terms of the activity of one's desires and aversions, that one has not yet penetrated to a truly deep and transformative religious experience.

To be hindered at the *noetic* level would mean that one is obstructed precisely by the religious insight he or she has attained. Here, some distinction needs to be made in contrast to renderings of the term as "hindrance of rationalization" or "hindrance of intellectuality" (seen in some other scholarly works) as these two attribute a distinctively discursive character to this hindrance. In the *SPE*, one's deepest and most profound experiential realizations may be considered as "noetic hindrances"—as long as they fall short of the perfect realization of the Buddha. As the sutra says, "this awareness of enlightenment again becomes an obstruction." The sutra will define the Five Natures in terms of the practitioner's ability to deal with these two hindrances.]

[Sutra]

Good sons, if sentient beings have not yet been able to destroy the Two Hindrances, this is called "nonconsummation of one's Buddhahood." If sentient beings permanently discard desire, then they have succeeded in removing the phenomenal hindrance, but have not yet severed the noetic hindrance. They are able to awaken in the way of *śrāvakas* and *pratyekabuddhas* but are not able to manifest and dwell in the state of the bodhisattva.

Good sons, if all sentient beings of the degenerate age desire to float on the great ocean of the Tathāgata's Perfect Enlightenment, they should first arouse the determination to do away with the Two Hindrances. Once the Two Hindrances are subdued, one can awaken and enter the state of the bodhisattva. After permanently destroying the noetic and phenomenal hindrances, one is able to enter the sublime Perfect Enlightenment of the Tathāgata, and able to fully accomplish *bodhi* and great nirvana.

Good sons, all sentient beings without exception actualize Perfect Enlightenment.[5] When you meet a Genuine Teacher, rely on the dharma-practice of the causal stage that he sets up for you. When you follow this practice, both sudden and gradual will be contained. If you come upon the correct path of practice of the unsurpassed *bodhi* of the Tathāgatas, then there are no "superior" or "inferior" abilities of people: all accomplish buddhahood.

If, while seeking a Genuine Teacher, sentient beings meet one with mistaken views, they will not gain the correct awakening. Although this is called the "heterodox nature," the fault lies with the teacher, not with the sentient beings. This is the "distinction of the Five Natures" of sentient beings.

[Kihwa] [*HPC* 7.146b2]

Above he has answered the question about the various natures, and in explaining the various natures, has identified attachment as their basis. Next he explains that attachment and compassion, while having similarities, are actually quite different. He lastly explains that when the dross of attachment and desire are burnt away, you awaken to the enlightened nature. Also, wanting to answer the question about variations in practice, he first refers to the Five Natures so that he can explain how it is that there happen to be five.

The reason that there are both dense and light hindrances is because in their creation there is both shallow and deep. No-mind penetrating to the principle: this is correct insight. But although one perceives the principle, the discriminated awareness of perceiving the principle remains, and changes to become a hindrance—the noetic hindrance. The mind is originally unarisen and deluded karmas are all quiescent. But the arousal of one single thought brings the whole of *saṃsāra* into activity. This is the phenomenal hindrance.

Originally arisen ignorance is activated by desire. Due to ignorance, the Two Hindrances exist. Based on the Two Hindrances we can distinguish the Five Natures. He has said that when the Two Hindrances are not severed it is called "noncompletion of Buddhahood." It is when you first know the cessation of the Two Hindrances that you perfect your Buddhahood. Sick of suffering, you sever its arising; although you are freed from *saṃsāra*, the perception of the principle remains in your mind and you cannot prevent it from turning into a hindrance. This is the meaning of the "nature of the Two Vehicles."

Having gotten free from the phenomenal hindrance, you now subdue the noetic hindrance, but have not permanently severed it. This is the so-called "bodhisattva nature." With the Two Hindrances permanently extinguished, you fulfill your *bodhi* as well as great nirvana. This is the so-called "nature of Buddhahood." In relying on the dharma practices devised by a Genuine Teacher, practice has both sudden and gradual. When you encounter the Buddha's unsurpassed correct path of practice, everyone perfects the Buddha-fruit. This is the so-called "indeterminate nature." Despite a determination to find a Genuine Teacher, your activities depart from your intention, and the teacher you meet is not a genuine one; you are influenced to form mistaken views and do not attain the correct awakening. This is the so-called "heterodox nature."

Now you are aware for the first time that the natures of all sentient beings have no lack of goodness—all are capable of intimately actualizing Perfect Enlightenment. However, depending on [what kind of teacher]

Table 2: The Distinction of the Five Natures

Type of Practitioner	Accomplishment
[Nonconsummation of Buddahood (Worldling)]	[Both hindrances intact]
1. The Nature of the Two Vehicles	Phenomenal hindrance subdued
2. The Nature of the Bodhisattva	Both hindrances subdued
3. The Nature of the Buddhahood	Both hindrances extinguished
4. Indeterminate Nature	All attain Buddhahood
5. Heterodox Nature	Misleads Students

they meet, [the sentient being's] practices will bring about error or correctness. The responsibility for this error or correctness lies with the teacher—it is not the an affliction originating from the sentient beings. Having explained the Five Natures, he concludes by saying "this is called the distinction of the Five Natures of sentient beings." This answers the question about the variations in practice.

[*Translator's note*: Although only Five Natures are clearly distinguished as such, we can actually outline the components of the above section into six parts. That is, prior to the definition of the Five Natures per se, the Buddha mentions the initial condition of "nonconsummation of Buddhahood (未成佛)." The Five Natures, along with this condition of nonconsummation, are schematized in table 2.]

[Sutra (#58)] [*T* 842.17.916c7; *HPC* 7.146c4]

善男子、菩薩唯以大悲方便入諸世間、開發未悟、乃至示
現種種形相、逆順境界。與其同事化令成佛。皆依無始清
淨願力。

Good sons, it is only through their greatly compassionate expedient means that bodhisattvas enter the secular world, awakening the unenlightened, manifesting various forms and shapes, functioning in agreeable and disagreeable circumstances. It is only relying on the beginningless pure power of their vow to save all beings that they physically work together with these people and cause them to accomplish buddhahood.

[Kihwa] [*HPC* 7.146c8]

Earlier he explained the distinctions in practice; here he explains the expedient methods for saving sentient beings. Bodhisattvas, out of their great compassion, adapt to the world and awaken the unenlightened. According to the differences in the sentient beings, the characteristics they manifest are various—sometimes pleasing and sometimes not.

They work together with the beings in their worldly tasks, and by creating many expedient methods they transform them into Buddhas. Here at the causal stage they have already made the vow to save all beings. Relying on the power of that vow, they have reached to the transformations of the present circumstance. Therefore it says: "all rely on the beginningless pure power of their vow." This answers the question on the expedient means that save sentient beings.

The Vow of the Bodhisattva

[Sutra (#59)] [*T* 842.17.916c9; *HPC* 7.146c15]

若諸末世一切眾生於大圓覺起增上心當發菩薩清淨大願。
應作是言：願我今者住佛圓覺求善知識、莫值外道及與二
乘。依願修行漸斷諸障。障盡、願滿、便登解脫清淨法殿
、證大圓覺妙莊嚴域。

Any sentient being of the degenerate age who would arouse the mind intensified toward great Perfect Enlightenment must arouse the pure great determination of the bodhisattvas. He should say, "I hereby vow to dwell in the Perfect Enlightenment of the Buddha, to seek Genuine Teachers and not to plant roots with heterodox paths or practitioners of the Two Vehicles." Practicing based on this vow, you sever the hindrances one by one. When the hindrances are gone, the vow is fulfilled. You will automatically ascend to the Pure Dharma Palace of Liberation, and actualize the marvelously adorned realm of Great Perfect Enlightenment.

[Kihwa] [*HPC* 7.146c21]

In the prior passage he taught the bodhisattvas' reliance upon their vow to save sentient beings. Here he encourages sentient beings to arouse the vow to practice. "Intensified mind" is the mind that is intensified in compassion and wisdom toward the highest fruit. Intensified in wisdom, it severs doubts and actualizes the real; intensified in compassion, it awakens and transforms sentient beings. Arousing this kind of mind, you produce the pure vow. This is the "one leg raised by the crane in the deep marsh,"[6] and the "first step of a thousand-*li* journey."[7] The purpose of the Buddha's encouragement is exactly this. You should produce the vow, saying: "In the past I turned my back on enlightenment and became immersed in the sensory realm. I passed through destinies of suffering—unspeakable suffering. The past is gone and can never be retrieved, but the future can be dealt with. I vow that henceforth I will abide in the Perfect Enlightenment of the Buddha without moving from it, and will not take rebirth in the three worlds." Once you have completed this vow, seek out a Genuine Teacher, find the essence of the mind, and base your practice on it. But at the time of taking the first step, you cannot be careless in investigating the road. At the time of your decision to go for enlightenment, you cannot be careless about selecting your teacher. Therefore you are taught to seek a Genuine Teacher, and not to plant yourself on heterodox paths, or within the Two Vehicles. A hair's-breadth difference at the beginning results in a thousand-*li* error later on. When you make the vow, there will be sudden release and the road of enlightenment will appear before your eyes. But full realization—this takes time, so you need to practice to reach it. Therefore he teaches practice depending upon the vow, which gradually severs all hindrances. When the hindrances are extirpated and the vow is fulfilled, then that which is beneath your feet is none other than the pure dharma-palace, to which you have naturally ascended. What is in front of your eyes is none other than the marvelously adorned realm, which you naturally witness.

There are three kinds of adornment. The first is the adornment of the natural world. The second is the adornment of sentiency. The third is the adornment of the wisdom of correct enlightenment.

Heaven covers and earth supports; mountains soar and rivers flow; the sun rises and the moon sets; the cold comes and the warmth departs; spring peaks and summer begins to bud; the flowers open and the flowers drop; the hills rise and holes sink; the pure and the polluted are wrapped in each other; one rests on the mountains and rides on the rivers; people and animals are mixed in one lot; the oceans and continents scatter and are submerged. Despite all kinds of confusion and disorder, the sagely and dull, the foolish and wise are clearly distinguished. In the space between Heaven and Earth, within the vast universe, all abide within; horizontally and vertically they are arranged in their order: this is the "adornment of the realm of the natural world."

On the outside [of the human body] there are seven openings; within, five viscera; the thirty-six components vertically and horizontally adorn. Yet within, the "mind-king" is master and the objects of the mind are attendants. The eighty-eight defilements come and go through the organs and their objects. Horizontally and vertically they dash about, busily creating all sorts of karma. Emotionally responding to a thousand differences they emerge and submerge in the four kinds of birth, rising and falling into the various destinies. This is the adornment of the realm of sentiency.

The essence of emptiness is great without location; the function of spiritual wisdom shines, penetrating within and without. The sun of wisdom shines brightly through every faculty; each object is empty of nature—just clear. The principle and wisdom merge together, equally containing the ten thousand forms, as the sun contains the sky and the lapis lazuli contains the moon. Sight, hearing, and all forms of awareness never miss their marvelous function. Color, odor, taste, and touch are all true marks. This is the adornment of correctly enlightened wisdom.

But correctly enlightened wisdom has never existed apart from the realms of adornment of the natural world and sentiency. This is why it is called the marvelously adorned realm. Separately seeking the marvelously adorned realm apart from the other two realms of adornment is like seeking the water apart from the waves, or seeking the gold apart from the vessel—to the end you will never apprehend the principle. Hence it is said: "The Buddha-dharma is contained in the world"; you cannot separate the world and enlightenment. Seeking *bodhi* apart from the world is like looking for horns on a rabbit. This, then, is the marvelous adorned realm of the wisdom of correct enlightenment. So, without changing a single aspect of the world, he opens the great gate of liberation. This message can be found in expressions such as: "on the tip of a hair he manifests the world of the jewel-king," and "sitting on a single dust-mote he turns the great wheel of the dharma."

The *Gāthā*

[Sutra (#60)] [*T* 842.17.916c14; *HPC* 7.147b19]

爾時世尊、欲重宣此義而説偈言：

<pre>
彌 勒 汝 當 知   一 切 諸 衆 生
不 得 大 解 脱   皆 由 貪 欲 故
墮 落 於 生 死   若 能 斷 憎 愛
及 與 貪 瞋 癡   不 因 差 別 性
皆 得 成 佛 道   二 障 永 銷 滅
求 師 得 正 悟   隨 順 菩 薩 願
依 止 大 涅 槃   十 方 諸 菩 薩
皆 以 大 悲 願   示 現 入 生 死
現 在 修 行 者   及 末 世 衆 生
勤 斷 諸 愛 見   便 歸 大 圓 覺
</pre>

Then the World-Honored One, wanting to restate the gist of this, spoke a verse; he said:

> Maitreya, you should know
> That the nonattainment of great liberation
> By all sentient beings
> Is only due to desire;
> Therefore they are drawn into life and death.
> If you can separate yourself from like and dislike,
> As well as desire, hatred, and ignorance
> You will all perfect the Buddha's Way

And permanently destroy the Two Hindrances,
Without needing any "distinctions in nature."
Seek a teacher who has the correct awakening,
Practice the vow to arouse the *bodhi*-mind,
Rely on Great Nirvana.
The bodhisattvas in the ten directions
All appear in the world of *saṃsāra*
Relying on the greatly compassionate vow.
Present practitioners
As well as sentient beings of the degenerate age
Should strive to eliminate all attached views
And directly return to Great Perfect Enlightenment.

[Kihwa] [*HPC* 7.147c3]

The only reason all sentient beings are not liberated is because of the Three Poisons.[8] If you eliminate the Three Poisons, then there is no such thing as greater and lesser capacity—all accomplish the Buddha-way. Therefore you must first find the right teacher and grasp his correct insights. Based on your vow, practice, severing hindrances, and proceed to realization. All the bodhisattvas of the ten directions, depending on their vow of compassion, appear in the world to save sentient beings. Present and future practitioners should strive to sever all hindrances and to directly return to Perfect Enlightenment.

6

Pure Wisdom
Bodhisattva

[Kihwa] [*HPC* 7.147c9]

Purity opposes filth; wisdom opposes ignorance. Ignorance, through the stain of its pollution, beclouds the clarity of the truth. Wisdom, by means of the effervescence of its purity, adorns the path of enlightenment. He is called "Pure Wisdom" because he uses his pure wisdom to dissolve the becloudment and stain of ignorance to reveal the clarity of the truth and bring about the completion of omniscience.

Why does Pure Wisdom follow up Maitreya with further questions? Maitreya raised his questions in reaction to the discussion in the chapter of Vajragarbha, which said "first severing the root of transmigration," in order to make the sentient beings convert their attached love into compassion. This bodhisattva in turn questions in reaction to the discussion in the chapter of Maitreya in regard to the "distinctions in level of practice and realization," and likewise induces the sentient beings to convert their ignorance into wisdom. The severing of anxiety at the level of faith, the severing of the "understanding-obstruction" at the level of worthy, and the nonabiding enlightenment at the level of sage, that includes the abilities of "neither arising nor cessation of thought," "no adding of knowledge," and "no discernment of reality": these are brought about through Pure Wisdom's inducement of the sentient beings to convert their ignorance into omniscience.

The meaning of such sayings as "wisdom and ignorance are both *prajñā*" is the completion of omniscience—the view that is not attached to duality. This is the relevance of the order of Maitreya's conversion of attached love into compassion and Pure Wisdom's conversion of ignorance into wisdom. My verse:

The single fount of purity having been revealed
He requests further explanation to clarify the stages.

Knowing that one does not gradually advance in skill and then
   ascend to perfection,
True and false are both forgotten, the sun rises in the sky.

Pure Wisdom's Question on
the Distinctions in Level of Practice

[Sutra (#61)] [*T* 842.17.916c26; *HPC* 7.148a4]

於是清淨慧菩薩在大衆中、即從座起。頂禮佛足右繞三匝
。長跪叉手而白佛言：大悲世尊。爲我等輩廣説如是不思
議事、本所不見本所不聞。我等今者蒙佛善誘、身心泰然
、得大饒益。願爲諸來一切法衆重宣法王圓滿覺性。一切
衆生及諸菩薩、如來世尊、所證所得云何差別？令末世衆
生聞此聖教、隨順開悟漸次能入。作是語已、五體投地。
如是三請終而復始。

The bodhisattva Pure Wisdom rose from his seat in the great assembly. He bowed his head to the Buddha's feet, and circumambulated
him three times to the right. He then knelt down with his hands
clasped and addressed the Buddha saying:

"Greatly Compassionate World-Honored One; you have magnan-
imously explained for all of our group this inconceivable matter,
which was originally not seen and originally not heard. We who
are presently here and have received your superb instruction have
gained composure of body and mind, and received great benefit. I
would like to request this: Would you re-explain the nature of the
Perfect Fulfilling Enlightenment of the King of the Dharma for
those who have come for your teaching? What differences are there
between that which is grasped and actualized by sentient beings,
bodhisattvas, and World-Honored Tathāgatas? Please let sentient
beings of the degenerate age hear this sagely teaching so that they
may conform to it, awaken through it and gradually become capable
of entering."

Having said this, he prostrated fully to the ground. He asked
this question three times in succession.

[Kihwa] [*HPC* 7.148a14]

Within noncyclic existence, they deludedly see cyclic existence; within
no practice-and-realization, he provisionally introduces practice-and-
realization—this is why it is called "inconceivable." Ignorance does not
permeate true suchness[1] yet there is permeation; when true suchness
undergoes permeation, it is not changed, yet there is a change. Hence
the existence of the three subtle and six coarse defilements.[2] This is

why arising is regarded as inconceivable. True suchness does not permeate ignorance, yet there is permeation; When ignorance undergoes permeation, it is not changed, yet there is change. Hence the existence of the Three Vehicles and the Single Vehicle. This is why practice and severing are regarded as inconceivable. Since these two kinds of inconceivability[3] are the topics that the members of this assembly have not yet heard about, they now avail themselves to the Buddha's extensive exposition [of the matter]. This is why the bodhisattva praises him as "greatly compassionate" and is "encouraged." Receiving the Buddha's instruction, they know that the situation can be changed, that the mind is to be reflected upon, and they may have total conviction in the reality of practice and realization. This is what is meant by "composure of body and mind," and "receiving great benefit."

The Buddha's prior discourse, while revealing the distinctions in the Five Natures, has not given the reasons for the distinctions. This is something that the ignorant have not yet been able to fathom on their own, and is also the reason why Pure Wisdom asks this question to the Buddha. Sentient beings of the degenerate age who have not yet received this teaching have no means through which to obtain this knowledge, so therefore the Buddha, relying on Pure Wisdom, explains it, fully enlightening their ignorance. This is why he says "sentient beings of the degenerate age hear this and awaken, and are gradually able to enter."

The Buddha's Answer

[Sutra (#62)] [*T* 842.17.917a6; *HPC* 7.148b8]

爾時世尊告清淨慧菩薩言：善哉、善哉。善男子、汝等乃
能爲末世衆生請問如來漸次差別。汝今諦聽、當爲汝説。
時清淨慧菩薩奉教歡喜、及諸大衆默然而聽。

Then the World-Honored One, addressing the bodhisattva Pure Wisdom, said:

"Excellent, excellent! Good son, you have asked well for the bodhisattvas and sentient beings of the degenerate age about the distinction that the Tathāgata makes [between] the levels [of attainment by practitioners]. Now listen well, and I shall explain these for you." The bodhisattva Pure Wisdom received this instruction with reverence and great joy. All the members of the great assembly became silent and listened.

[Kihwa] [*HPC* 7.148b13]

Sentient beings of the degenerate age who have not received the Buddha's instruction do not know about the distinctions in practice and realization, and thus cannot avoid the stain of ignorance. Now Pure Wisdom raises this question for the beings to undarken the path of cultivation of reality. This is why the Buddha readily approves of the question.

In Reality, There are No Stages

[Sutra (#63)] [*T* 842.17.917a10; *HPC* 7.148b17]

善男子、圓覺自性非性、性有循諸性起。無取無證。於實相中、實無菩薩及諸衆生。何以故？菩薩衆生皆是幻化、幻化滅故無取證者。譬如眼根不自見眼、性自平等無平等者。

Good sons, although the self-nature of Perfect Enlightenment is not a nature [like the previously described natures], nonetheless, a nature exists that is concomitant with the arising of all natures. But there is neither acquisition nor realization of it. From the point of view of reality, there are actually neither bodhisattvas nor sentient beings. Why? Bodhisattvas and sentient beings are nothing but illusory appearances, and since illusory appearances are erased, there is neither "acquirer" nor "realizer." It is like the eye not being able to see itself: in the nature's own equality, there is nothing that is "equal."

[Kihwa] [*HPC* 7.148b22]

The self-nature of Perfect Enlightenment is itself empty, and is originally divorced from names and marks. But there is also a nature that is not empty, which spiritually penetrates, senses and responds; following conditions it completes all individual dharmas. Yet this conditioned nature is itself empty—its essence does not really exist. Thus the same is true of practice and realization, which exist according to conditions, but lack inherent reality. Therefore he says that bodhisattvas and sentient beings are all illusion. The phrase "it is just like the eye . . ." shows that beginning and end are connected, and that the mind and the objects share the same reality—there is no separate thing. Since, in the development of subject and object, there is actually no subject or object, the nonexistence of subject and object is also nonexistent. Therefore he says "in the nature's own equality there is nothing that is equal."

[Sutra (#64)] [*T* 842.17.917a13; *HPC* 7.148c6]

衆生迷倒、未能除滅一切幻化。於滅未滅、妄功用中便顯差別。若得如來寂滅隨順、實無寂滅及寂滅者。

Sentient beings are thoroughly confused and are unable to rid themselves of all illusory appearances. Since they have not extinguished [the mark of] cessation in illusory activity, they automatically make discriminations. If they attain accordance with the extinction of the Tathāgata, there is really neither extinction nor person who brings extinction about.

[*Translator's note*: Here the text does not say "mark of" cessation. This is Kihwa's interpretation, which he explains below. The four marks that he refers to are the marks of arising, abiding, changing, and cessation, which he treats according to the framework of the *Awakening of Faith*. The meaning of these four marks as developed in the *Awakening of Faith* is that each thought, or thought-moment, has these four aspects. In terms of the exercise of gaining awareness of thought in meditation and eliminating its mistaken function, the most subtle (and difficult) point at which one can be aware is the point of arising of thought. The most coarse (and easiest) point at which one can cut off thought is at its point of cessation. For a comprehensive discussion of the four marks, see Wŏnhyo's *Kisillon so*, HPC 1.698-722; T 1844.44.202a-226a.

In his commentary to this passage, Tsung-mi also makes reference to the four marks of the *Awakening of Faith*, but does not discuss them to the extent that Kihwa does here. These four marks are to be distinguished from the Four Traces of self, person, sentient being, and life, which are the topic of discussion in chapter 9. Because of Kihwa's interpretation of this line, my translation of it is different from Luk's. In order to make the interpretation of this passage compliant with Kihwa's subsequent explanation, it is necessary to assign two different English terms "cessation" and "extinction" to the successive appearances of the logograph *mieh/myŏl* 滅.]

[Kihwa] [*HPC* 7.148c9]
Having already elucidated the character of the equality that lacks distinctions, he now wants to explain the distinctions in level, starting with an explanation of the rationale for the distinctions. The consequence of one instant of delusion in this mind is the Four Marks. The consequence of the Four Marks is cyclic existence. If you want to lay bare cyclic existence, you need to extinguish the Four Marks. Since these marks are originally empty, and take their substance based on falsity, they are called "illusory transformations." Since these marks are already illusory, and their extinction cannot be real, they are understood as having function but are still called "false."

The extinction of the Four Marks is not a sudden extinction; their elimination is gradual, proceeding from coarse to subtle. The coarseness and subtlety is as follows: the mark of arising is the subtle of the subtle; the mark of abiding is the coarse of the subtle; the mark of changing is the subtle of the coarse; the mark of ceasing is the coarse of the coarse. From the standpoint of arising, the sequence is from subtle to coarse:

arising, abiding, changing, and ceasing. From the standpoint of cultivation and severing, the sequence is from coarse to subtle: ceasing, changing, abiding, and arising. If you extinguish the mark of cessation, then you have for the first time attained the level of faith. If you extinguish the changing mark, then you are transformed to the level of worthy. If you extinguish the abiding mark, you are transformed to the level of sage. If you extinguish the arising mark, you have finished by accomplishing the level of fruition (Buddhahood). Thus, the person at the level of faith has extinguished the mark of ceasing, but has not yet extinguished the mark of changing. The person at the level of worthy has extinguished the mark of changing, but has not yet extinguished the mark of abiding. The person at the level of sage has extinguished the mark of abiding but has not yet extinguished the mark of arising. The person at the level of fruition has extinguished the mark of arising, and there is nothing further to be extinguished. This is the meaning of "severing delusion."

Outer worldlings have advanced to the level of faith but have not yet advanced to the level of worthy. Those of the level of faith have advanced to the level of worthy but have not yet advanced to the level of sage. Those of the level of worthy have advanced to the level of sage but have not yet advanced to the level of fruition. Those of the level of sage who have advanced to the level of fruition have no further level on which to advance. This is the meaning of "realizing reality." Hence, those who have "already ceased and advanced" finish earlier and those who have "not yet ceased and advanced" finish later. This means that those who are enlightened at the prior levels [i.e., levels of faith and worthy] should not receive the appellation of the later levels [levels of sage and fruition]. The earlier are inferior to the later and the later are superior to the earlier. Hence, within "neither superior nor inferior" there are superior and inferior, and within nondistinction there is distinction. Therefore the sutra says: "Since they have not extinguished the mark of cessation, in illusory activity they automatically make discriminations." When the Four Marks are completely extinguished, then there is not even a trace of cessation, and you return to original reality. Therefore he says "If they attain accordance with the extinction of the Tathāgata, there is really neither extinction nor person who brings it about." This section above shows how it is that the levels are distinguished and yet lack distinction.

The Worldling's Accordance with the Enlightened Nature

[Sutra (#65)] [*T* 842.17.917a16; *HPC* 7.149a18] ▼

善男子、一切眾生從無始來由妄想我及愛我者、曾不自知
念念生滅、故起憎愛、耽著五欲。若遇善友教令開悟淨圓

覺性。發明起滅即知此生性自勞慮。若復有人勞慮永斷得
法界淨、即彼淨解爲自障礙。故於圓覺而不自在。此名凡
夫隨順覺性。

Good sons, all sentient beings, because of a deludedly conceived "self" and attachment to that self, have beginninglessly never known moment-to-moment arising and cessation for themselves; therefore they give rise to attraction and aversion, and become addicted to the objects in the five sense fields. If they meet a Genuine Teacher he will awaken them to the essence of pure Perfect Enlightenment. Discovering arising and cessation, they will directly know that this life's very nature is that of anxiety. If there is a person who permanently severs that anxiety and experiences the purity of the reality-realm, but who allows his understanding of clarity in turn to become a hindrance, this person is tending toward Perfect Enlightenment but is not perfectly free. He is called a "worldling who is according with the nature of enlightenment."

[Kihwa] [HPC7.149b1]

The word "life (生)" in "this *life*'s very nature (此生性自)" should be "mind" (心). The text should say: "directly know that this *mind*'s very nature is that of anxiety (即知此心性自勞慮)." Whereas earlier the Buddha has explained the *reasons* for distinguishing the levels of attainment, here he precisely elucidates the *distinctions* themselves. Within the nature there are no *skandhas*, yet we deludedly give rise to the five *skandhas*. Within the *skandhas* there is no self, but we mistakenly give rise to the traces of a self. As a consequence of there being traces of self, we produce attached views and with moment-to-moment arising and cessation, we agitate our true nature. Unaware of our arising of discriminations and addiction to desires, we create karma and invite its rewards, and thus remain bound in the level of the unenlightened. If you can gain access to the guidance of a Genuine Teacher, he will disclose the enlightened nature that originally lacks arising and ceasing. Since you now realize how arising and ceasing disturb the true nature, you will now know that it is only because of mistaken discrimination that the nature itself has anxiety, and that the perfectly clear and pure essence is changed to a condition of pollution. The mind originally has no anxiety, and the nature is originally clear and composed. If, within this mind you can permanently sever anxiety, then the nature's pure essence will be manifested, and all things will be real and pure. If at this point you do not again produce views, you will attain liberation on the spot, and accomplishment of true accordance. Yet even if anxiety is severed and your pure understanding is manifested before you, if this pure understanding reverts into falsity, becoming itself an obstruction to the perfectly enlightened pure nature, then this is the case of an outer worldling who is on the verge of ascent to the level of faith, but who, obstructed by his understanding of purity, is not able to accomplish true accordance.

The Beginner Bodhisattva's Accordance with the Enlightened Nature

[Sutra (#66)] [*T* 842.17.917a21; *HPC* 7.149b18]

善男子、一切菩薩見解爲礙。雖斷解礙、猶住見覺。覺礙爲礙而不自在。此名菩薩未入地者隨順覺性。

Good sons, all bodhisattvas see their understanding as an obstruction. But even if they eliminate the "understanding-obstruction" they still abide in a view of enlightenment. This "enlightenment-obstruction" becomes a hindrance and they are not perfectly free. They are called bodhisattvas who have not yet entered the *bhūmis*[4] who are according with the nature of enlightenment.

[Kihwa] [*HPC* 7.149b21]

Once the understanding of purity has been manifested, it reverts to become an obstruction. Then you once again use expedient wisdom to reflect on this obstruction in order to do away with the understanding of purity. Even though the "understanding-obstruction" has been erased, the view of the reflection (on the obstruction) also reverts to become false, and then becomes an obstruction to the nature of pure enlightenment. This is the accordance with the enlightened nature carried out by the person at the stage of faith who is ascending to the level of worthy, but who has not yet entered the level of sage. Even though it is called "accordance," since he is obstructed by his view of enlightenment, he is still not able to accomplish the real accordance.

The Advanced Bodhisattva's Accordance with Perfect Enlightenment

[Sutra (#67)] [*T* 842.17.917a24; *HPC* 7.149c3]▼

善男子、有照有覺俱名障礙、是故菩薩常覺不住。照與照者同時寂滅。譬如有人自斷其首。首已斷故無能斷者。則以礙心自滅諸礙。礙已斷滅無滅礙者。修多羅教如標月指。若復見月、了知所標畢竟非月。一切如來種種言説開示菩薩亦復如是。此名菩薩已入地者隨順覺性。

Good sons, since the possession of illumination and enlightenment are termed together as "hindrance" and "obstruction," the bodhisattva is always enlightened without abiding. Illumination and illuminator simultaneously vanish. It is like the case of a person who cuts off his own head—when the head is cut off, there is no longer any "cutter." Hence the use of the obstructing mind to eliminate all obstructions: when obstructions have been eliminated, there is no one to eliminate obstructions. The teachings of the sutras are like the finger pointing to the moon. If you also look at the moon and completely understand, then that which is pointing is ultimately not the moon.[5] All the various words and explanations of the Tathāgata that are used to awaken bodhisattvas are also like this. They are called "bodhisattvas who have entered the *bhūmis* who are according with the nature of enlightenment."

[Kihwa] [*HPC* 7.149c11]

The "understanding of purity" of the prior passage is the same as "possession of illumination" here. The "view of enlightenment" of the prior passage is the same as "possession of enlightenment" here. Not only does the understanding of purity become an obstruction; the view of enlightenment is also called an obstruction. It is like when you use a medicine to treat a sickness, and the medicine itself ends up causing another side-effect. If you use a dream to awaken from a dream, then this awakening is also a dream. If you are aware that the pure understanding is an obstruction, and you also do not abide in enlightenment, then, together with the prior pure understanding, both obstructions are dissolved simultaneously. It is like a man cutting off his own head. Once the head is cut off, there is no longer any "cutter." To be regarded as a man, one must have both body and head. When one has both body and head, one can have life. Once the head is cut off, body and life are lost at the same time. When body and head have been severed, there is no longer anyone capable of cutting.

In the bodhisattva's use of expedient wisdom, when the pure understanding and the view of enlightenment are both dissolved, all the obstructions are erased, and there is no longer any dissolving wisdom. "Expedient wisdom" is also called "obstructing thought." If, when the obstructions are dissolved, you do not avoid the thought of a subjective dissolver, this makes an obstruction of the purity and the enlightenment—therefore it is called "obstructing thought." Yet if, following on the dissolution of all obstructions, you again dissolve, this is the accordance with the enlightened nature carried out at the level of the worthy who has ascended to the level of sage, but who has not yet ascended to the level of fruition. Even though it is called "accordance," since the person has not ascended to the final level, he has not accomplished real accordance.

The passage that goes from "the teachings of the sutras" up to "to awaken bodhisattvas are also like this (修多羅教如標月指。若復見月、了知所標畢竟非月。一切如來種種言説開示菩薩亦復如

是)" belongs right after the line in the chapter of Voice of Discernment Bodhisattva that says "these are called the twenty-five wheels of the bodhisattvas"[6] and has been mistakenly inserted here. In transmitting the theme, [this arrangement of the text] does not result in *jen*.

[*Translator's note*: Here Kihwa is using one of his favorite metaphors for the proper flow of the theme of the text *hyŏlmaek* (血脈), which literally means "blood circulation" and which is in turn, equivalent to his understanding of *jen* in its medical usage. The meaning of non-*jen* is explained in his *Hyŏn chŏng non*, where he cites the usage of the term *jen* (仁) in the ancient Chinese medical texts. As Kihwa explains it, the medical term non-*jen* refers to a condition of lack of flow in the nerves, which results in the symptoms of numbness or paralysis. When Kihwa says "non-*jen*" here, he means that the flow of the text has been obstructed by the presence of a phrase that is out of place. See the *Hyŏn chŏng non*, HPC 7.219b19–c13.]

The Tathāgata's Accordance with Perfect Enlightenment

[Sutra (#68)] [*T* 842.17.917b2; *HPC* 7.150a7]

善男子、一切障礙即究竟覺。得念失念無非解脱。成法破
法皆名涅槃。智慧愚癡通爲般若。菩薩外道所成就法同是
菩提。無明眞如無異境界。諸戒定慧及淫怒癡俱是梵行。
衆生國土同一法性。地獄天宮皆爲淨土。有性無性齊成佛
道。一切煩惱畢竟解脱。法界海慧照了諸相猶如虛空。此
名如來隨順覺性。

Good sons, all hindrances are none other than ultimate enlightenment. Whether you attain mindfulness or lose mindfulness, there is no nonliberation. Establishing the dharma and refuting the dharma are both called nirvana; wisdom and folly are equally *prajñā*; the method that is perfected by bodhisattvas and false teachers is the same *bodhi*; ignorance and suchness are not different realms; morality, concentration, and wisdom, as well as desire, hatred, and ignorance are all divine practices; sentient beings and lands share the same dharma nature; hell and heaven are both the Pure Land; those having Buddha-nature and those not having it equally accomplish the Buddha's enlightenment. All defilements are ultimately liberation. The reality-realm's oceanlike wisdom completely clarifies all marks to be just like empty space. This is called "the Tathāgata's accordance with the nature of enlightenment."

[Kihwa] [*HPC* 7.150a16]
These ten pairs of opposites show the insight of the Buddha. All those who have not yet ascended to the fruition level see duality within the

realm of reality. Those who have already ascended to the fruition level only perceive a single category. The passage from the words "all hindrances are none other than final enlightenment" up to "all defilements are ultimate liberation" reflect the meaning of "only knowing a single category" and "perceiving non-dualistically." "The reality-realm's oceanlike wisdom" refers to the vastness of the wisdom-gate [teaching] that operates throughout the reality-realm. "All marks" refers to such characteristics as nature and aspects, existence and nonexistence, illumination and obscuration, form and emptiness. The phrase, "the reality-realm's oceanlike wisdom completely clarifies all marks to be just like empty space," means that with the silently luminous, nondual vast limitless wisdom, one completely clarifies the middle way of nonduality between absolute and mundane, marks and no-marks. This is the accordance with the enlightened nature carried out by the person who has ascended to the level of fruition. At this level the principle has been fully actualized and discriminations fully annulled. There is nothing else beyond this. This is the first time it is "accordance" that can be said to be "with reality." This is the level the Buddha is speaking of when he says, "If you attain the Tathāgata's accordance of complete cessation, there is actually neither extinction nor person who brings about extinction."

Direct Accordance with the Nature of Enlightenment

[Sutra (#69)] [T 842.17.917b9; HPC 7.150b6]

善男子、但諸菩薩及末世衆生居一切時、不起妄念。於諸
妄心、亦不息滅。住妄想境、不加了知。於無了知、不辨
眞實。彼諸衆生聞是法門、信解受持不生驚畏、是則名爲
隨順覺性。善男子、汝等當知如是衆生已曾供養百千萬億
恒河沙諸佛及大菩薩、植衆德本。佛説是人名爲成就一切
種智。

Good sons, if all bodhisattvas and sentient beings of the degenerate age would just desist from giving rise to false thoughts at all times, and when in false states of mind, not strive for cessation; when abiding in false conceptual realms, not try to impose a complete understanding; while lacking complete understanding, not try to analyze true reality. If these sentient beings, hearing this teaching, believe, understand, assimilate, and remember it without being shocked or frightened by it, they are said to be "according with the nature of enlightenment."

Good sons, you should all be aware that these sentient beings have already made offerings to myriads of buddhas a quintillion times as numerous as the grains of sand in the Ganges River, and have cultivated their roots of virtue with as many great bodhisattvas. I call these people "fully developed in omniscience."

[Kihwa] [*HPC* 7.150b14]

Earlier he explained the distinctions in the progressive levels. Here he shows the sudden realization accomplished by those of sudden faculties who extinguish thought. What he means in this passage is that since the nature originally lacks thought, you need not give rise to thought. Even if you do arise thought, since thoughts are inherently empty, you need not extinguish them. Even if you are abiding in false conceptual realms, since the realms are originally this mind, you should not distinguish them. Without distinctions, you won't arise discriminations. Since people take these conditions to be reality, the Buddha teaches these four "should nots," showing how to abandon thought.

Since this expedient teaching transcends regular discrimination, some, when hearing it, will be doubtful. But if there are others who hear it and are readily convinced of its truth, and thus put it into practice exactly as it has been explained, then they will not slip off into distinctions and will accomplish the true accordance. Having done this, they will manifest complete *bodhi* without leaving this body. These people have in the past accumulated a deep store of virtue. Hence, when they reach this point, they are able to abandon their [discriminating] mind. Their meritorious virtue now complete, they are called "perfected in omniscience." This is the meaning of "sudden realization." From the line "the self-nature of enlightenment is not a nature, yet natures exist" up to "the Tathāgatas' accordance with the enlightened nature" expresses distinction from the standpoint of nondistinction. From the line "at all times" up to "perfected in omniscience" expresses nondistinction from the perspective of distinction. This is distinction within equality and equality within distinction, in order to show that the various levels are actually equal from beginning to end.

The *Gāthā*

[Sutra (#70)] [*T* 842.17.917b15; *HPC* 7.150c6]

爾時世尊、欲重宣此義而説偈言：

清淨慧當知   圓滿菩提性
無取亦無證   無菩薩衆生
覺與未覺時   漸次有差別
衆生爲解礙   菩薩未離覺
入地永寂滅   不住一切相
大覺悉圓滿   名爲徧隨順
末世諸衆生   心不生虛妄
佛説如是人   現世即菩薩

供養恒沙佛　功德已圓滿
雖有多方便　皆名隨順智

Then the World-Honored One, wanting to restate the gist of this, composed a verse. He said:

> Pure Wisdom, you should know
> The nature of perfect *bodhi*
> Has no acquisition, no realization
> Neither bodhisattva nor sentient being.
> Yet between the times of enlightenment and nonenlightenment
> There are differences in level.
> Sentient beings are obstructed by their understanding;
> Bodhisattvas are not free from enlightenment.
> Entering the *bhūmis* they are forever tranquil
> And do not abide in any mark.
> Great enlightenment fully includes everything
> And is called "pervasively according."
> Sentient beings of the degenerate age
> Whose minds do not give rise to falsity
> I call "Appearing in the world as bodhisattvas."
> They have made offerings to countless buddhas
> And are already replete with virtuous merit.
> Even though there are many expedient teaching methods
> As a sum, they are called "the wisdom that apprehends every-
>> thing."

[Kihwa] [*HPC* 7.150c14]

The nature of *bodhi* lacks acquisition and realization; it also lacks enlightenment and delusion. It is only in regard to awareness or nonawareness, elimination or nonelimination of the Four Marks that there are distinctions of level such as "worldling," "worthy," "sage," and "fruition." If you are only able to, in one thought-moment, forget the [discriminating] mind; then in the body of a worldling you are able to directly transcend the stage of worthy, pass over the rank of sage and consummate omniscience. These people who have already made offerings to all buddhas and are replete with virtuous merit, forget the notions of "worldling," "worthy," "sage," and "fruition" and experience sudden realization. Although there are distinctions in sudden and gradual, they are not categorized as deep and shallow—all are called "accordance." Therefore each stage is called "according with the nature of enlightenment."

7

Power and Virtue Unhindered Bodhisattva

[Kihwa] [*HPC* 7.150c23]

The pressure of a force on people, coupled with their awe of this force, is called "power." Blessings coming down to people, and their love and appreciation for these is called "virtue." Power is contrasted with virtue and is similar to anger. Virtue is contrasted with power, but is antithetical to anger. Virtue is the ability to gather and bring in. Power is the ability to subdue. This is why they are said to be in contrast with each other. Anger should not be touched; power is not to be transgressed: this is how they are similar. Anger is capable of bringing about anxiety and pain, while virtue can compassionately succor. This is how they differ from each other. The meaning of "power and virtue unhindered" is the simultaneous practice of power and compassion, to kill and give life according to the situation, to be unimpeded like a king.

[*Translator's note*: The term being translated here as "unhindered" is one of two in this chapter that are especially difficult to adequately render into English. The binome *tzu-tsai/chajae* 自在 had a considerable history in Taoist technical usage, as well as in common usage, before being utilized in Buddhism as a technical term. The Taoist connotation is close to that of the related term *chayŏn (tzu-jan)* 自然, meaning "self-so," "natural," "free and at ease." Even before Buddhism, the term had implications of the achievement of an enlightened state in which the human being was free from suffering and anxiety. But with the advent of Ch'an and Hua-yen Buddhism, *chajae* takes on even deeper connotations, many of which are indicated throughout the *SPE* in general, and this chapter in particular.

The major theoretical underpinnings of the Buddhist *chajae* can be understood through the concepts of mutual containment, nonobstruc-

166

tion, and interpenetration in Hua-yen, except that in the case of *chajae*, these are understood to be fully enacted in the personage of an enlightened being, such as the Buddha. Because the universe is interpenetrated and unobstructed, and since the Buddha is able to experience the universe as it actually is, his mind is able to penetrate all things and affairs: he is able to be aware of the sufferings of all beings and respond to them. The reason he is able to be so capable of awareness and response is because he has rid himself of all afflictions, anxieties, biases, and attachments, and so he never feels compelled to be trapped in dichotomies of good and evil, activity and quiescence, or subject and object. Hence the term *chajae* carries the meanings of liberation, nonobstruction, detachment, relaxedness, and omnipotence. Unfortunately, choosing any one of these terms forces us to leave out the other connotations. It is also difficult to find an equivalent term in English, that is not a negative form such as "unobstructed" or "unconstrained." The special characteristic of the bodhisattva in this chapter is that he is able to simultaneously blend within his person an authoritative sternness ("power") and gentle kindness ("virtue") without any conflict.]

[Kihwa]

Why does this bodhisattva raise another question following Pure Wisdom? Pure Wisdom based his questions on Maitreya's transformation of attached love into compassion, and then proceeded to make the sentient beings transform their ignorance into wisdom. Power and Virtue again raises a question following up on Pure Wisdom's transformation of ignorance into wisdom, and causes the people to transform their anger into power. Only when pity and wisdom guide each other, and kindness and power are practiced together can one be called "unhindered." Nonhindrance indicates the attainment of breadth in mind and ease in body and a certain pliancy in dealing with situations.

[*Translator's note*: *Pliancy* is a translation of the Sino-Korean logographic compound *ch'ing-an/kyŏng'an* 輕安 (in Sanskrit *praśrabdhi*), an important Buddhist technical term that is, like *chajae*, difficult to render with a single English word. Written with the ideographs *kyŏng* (輕 "light") and *an* (安 "peaceful"), the term refers to a condition of lightness in body and mind and effortlessness in action, and is very close in connotation with the term *chajae*. But it is quite a bit more than just lightness and flexibility; it is a state of blissful exhilaration that one experiences through deep meditation. In Indian Buddhist meditative traditions, *praśrabdhi* refers to a specific level of attainment. Charles Luk glosses *praśrabdhi* as "the fourth of the seven characteristics of bodhi, alleviation of all weight of body and mind causing the meditator to feel light, free

                    Sutra of Perfect Enlightenment

and at ease" (p. 229). Because of the multiple connotations of exhilaration and bliss, adaptability and skillfulness, translations such as "lightness," "flexibility" "bliss," and "pliancy" lack the multiplicity in meaning required to adequately render the term. Therefore, we hope that the reader may keep in mind the breadth of connotations being indicated here by the English word "pliancy."]

[Kihwa]

When facing difficulty one handles it calmly and without anxiety. The causes of people's not attaining pliancy and their inability to be free from anxiety are the Three Poisons.[1] But it is especially anger that causes trouble. Anger springs from contrary emotions—it is born in response to the environment. Not only does it agitate oneself, but others as well. Wounds to the spirit, damage of one's virtue, harm to creatures, and injury to life itself—there are none of these that do not spring from it. This is why anger errs with power and negates virtue. One can attain neither pliancy nor nonhindrance. The bodhisattvas fully realize the body and mind to be empty and negate the marks of self and other, and so they continually abide in the midst of agreeable and disagreeable environments without being agitated by the agreeable or disagreeable. They are able to cause demons and heretics to hear the Buddha's name and see his form,[2] such that their harmful intentions are destroyed and their spirits are vanquished. The bodhisattvas cause all beings to revere and admire the Buddha, such that they harmoniously follow and convert themselves. This is why the bodhisattva Power and Virtue Unhindered uses the prior discussions of the various natures and expedient means to set up his questions. His intention lies in causing all the people together to convert anger into power, simultaneously attaining pliancy and consummating nonhindrance.

The Buddha answers the questions by teaching the three meditations, saying in the teaching on each meditation that it will "arise pliancy from within" and concluding by saying that it is "something that self and other and body and mind cannot attain to." This is why he causes sentient beings to empty their minds and forget characteristics, so that they can themselves have the ability to transform anger into peace and consummate power and virtue. The order of the continuity of the discourse from Maitreya to Pure Wisdom and from Pure Wisdom to Power and Virtue Unhindered is like this. My verse:

> Generally, the expedient means of accordance are numberless,
> But quiescence, observation of the illusory and *dhyāna* are the
>   three main principles.
> Do not embrace these three as different kinds of paths:

Among a thousand ways, there are no roads that do not return to one's hometown.

Power and Virtue's Question on the Types of Meditation

[Sutra (#71)] [*T* 842.17.917b27; *HPC* 7.151b9]

於是威德自在菩薩在大眾中、即從座起。頂禮佛足、右繞
三匝。長跪叉手而白佛言：大悲世尊。廣爲我等分別如是
隨順覺性、令諸菩薩覺心光明、承佛圓音、不因修習而得
善利。世尊、譬如大城外有四門。隨方來者非止一路。一
切菩薩莊嚴佛國及成菩提非一方便。惟願世尊廣爲我等宣
説一切方便漸次。并修行人總有幾種？令此會菩薩及末世
衆生求大乘者速得開悟、遊戲如來大寂滅海。作是語已、
五體投地。如是三請終而復始。

Then the bodhisattva Power and Virtue Unhindered arose from his seat in the great assembly. He bowed to the feet of the Buddha and circumambulated him three times to the right. He then knelt down with his hands clasped and addressed the Buddha saying:

"Greatly Compassionate World-Honored One, you have analyzed for us at length this accordance with the enlightened nature, causing the enlightened minds of the bodhisattvas to effloresce and receive the Buddha's Perfect Voice, and causing them to receive excellent benefit that is not caused by religious practice.

"World-Honored One, it is like a great city that has four gates on its exterior—those who come from various directions are not limited to one path. Similarly, all bodhisattvas who adorn Buddha-lands and who perfect enlightened wisdom are not limited to a single expedient method. World-Honored One, my only wish is that you explain in detail for us the gradations of all the expedient methods. In general, how many kinds of religious practitioners are there? Please allow the bodhisattvas and sentient beings of the degenerate age who are seeking the great vehicle to quickly attain awakening and to sport about in the Tathāgata's great ocean of cessation-extinction."[3]

Having said this, he prostrated to the ground. He asked this question three times in succession.

[Kihwa] [*HPC* 7.151b21]

The enlightened nature is pure. It is afire with a spiritual luminescence, an efflorescence that penetrates within and without, an illumination that permeates countless eons. Therefore he says "enlightened minds . . . effloresce." When covered and obscured by the Four Marks, this illumination cannot appear. One must have extinguished the marks in order to attain the first manifestation of luminosity. Now the Buddha teaches them, allowing them to experience the unveiling of light. This is how it is that the multitude's "enlightened minds effloresce." When the marks are extinguished, the brightness appears.

This doctrine is recondite, and can only be apprehended through practice. But now, the audience, with but a single hearing of this teaching is able to attain the "emission of light." Because of this profound blessing he says they "receive excellent benefit." Even though the topics of the various natures of practitioners and the gradations in expedient methods have already been fully explained, those of duller faculties have not yet been able to understand, and so he offers a simile to clarify and help them to awaken. Sometimes the Buddha says "Great Ocean of Cessation-Extinction," and sometimes he says "Great Ocean of Perfect Enlightenment." The single fount from which Buddhas are born is called the Great Ocean of Perfect Enlightenment. Practice and ultimate realization is called the Great Ocean of Cessation-Extinction. The meaning of Great Perfect Enlightenment, is "no place where its essence does not permeate," and "no place where its function does not operate." The meaning of Great Cessation-Extinction is "no mark not erased" and "no delusion not extinguished."

[Sutra (#72)] [*T* 842.17.917c7; *HPC* 7.151c11]

爾時世尊告威德自在菩薩言：善哉、善哉。善男子、汝等乃能為諸菩薩及末世衆生問於如來如是方便。汝今諦聽、當為汝說。時威德自在菩薩奉教歡喜、及諸大衆默然而聽。

Then the World-Honored One, addressing the bodhisattva Power and Virtue Unhindered, said:

"Excellent, excellent! Good son, you have questioned well for the bodhisattvas and sentient beings of the degenerate age about these expedient methods of the Tathāgata. Listen well now, and I shall explain them for you." The bodhisattva Power and Virtue Unhindered received this teaching with awe and joy; all those in the great crowd became silent and listened.

[Kihwa] [*HPC* 7.151c16]

Since universally causing sentient beings to depend on meditation, accord with enlightenment, and arrive together in the state of non-hindrance is also the Buddha's original intention, he gladly approves of the question.

The Buddha's Answer:
There are Three Kinds of Expedients

[Sutra (#73)] [*T* 842.17.917c11; *HPC* 7.151c18]

善男子、無上妙覺徧諸十方。出生如來與一切法同體平等
。於諸修行實無有二。方便隨順其數無量。圓攝所歸、循
性差別當有三種。

Good sons, unsurpassed marvelous enlightenment pervades all the
ten directions. It gives birth to all tathāgatas, who share the same
equal essence with all dharmas. As far as the various practices are
concerned, there is in reality, no duality. Nonetheless, the expedient
methods that conform to Perfect Enlightenment are numberless.
Among these, there are three general types that all practitioners
rely on, according to the differences in their inclination.

[Kihwa] [*HPC* 7.151c22]

Wanting to clarify the three kinds of meditation as the expedient
methods for according with the nature of enlightenment, he first explains
the single practice as numberless, and then that the numberless can be
categorized into three. Enlightenment pervades all the ten directions,
and gives birth to buddhas and dharmas. These buddhas and dharmas
are equal in their essence. Therefore, even though there are many aspects
to practice, there is actually no duality among them. But even though
there is actually no duality, the methods are numberless. And even
though the methods are numberless, they can be summed up by three.

Śamatha

[Sutra (#74)] [*T* 842.17.917c14; *HPC* 7.152a3]

善男子、若諸菩薩悟淨圓覺、以淨覺心取靜爲行。由澄諸
念覺識煩動、靜慧發生。身心客塵從此永滅、便能內發寂
靜輕安。由寂靜故、十方世界諸如來心於中顯現、如鏡中
像。此方便者名奢摩他。

Good sons, some bodhisattvas awaken pure Perfect Enlightenment,
and using the mind of pure enlightenment take quiescence as their
practice. Then, by settling all thoughts they become aware of the
agitated motion of the consciousness, and thus produce quiescent
wisdom. From this, the mind, the body and external objects are
permanently extinguished and they directly generate quiescent
pliancy from within themselves. Because of this cessation and quiescence, the minds of all the tathāgatas in all the worlds in the ten

directions are made manifest, just like the images in a mirror. This expedient method is called *śamatha*.

[*Translator's note*: *Śamatha* is one of the most common forms of meditation practice, that is also found in other Indian meditation systems besides Buddhism. It refers to the retrieval of an agitated, scattered mind to a concentrated focus on a single object. In many meditative training systems it is the first form of meditation taught, since the ability to focus the mind is necessary for any form of advanced meditative practice. *Śamatha* is commonly translated into Chinese with the ideographs *chih* 止, which means literally, "to stop" and *ting* 定 , which literally means "to settle." In the *SPE*, it is translated most of the time with *ching* 靜, which means "still," "quiet," or "silent." The term *śamatha* has been previously translated into English with such various terms as "stopping," "calm abiding," "cessation," and so on. I render it here as "quiescence" because of the meaning of the ideograph *ching*, and because of other aspects of the context of the discussion that surrounds the word in this sutra.]

[Kihwa] [*HPC* 7.152a9]
Previously he explained the one as numberless, and the numberless as summed up in three. Here he begins his concrete exposition of the three kinds of meditation.

You have already awakened to Perfect Enlightenment, which is originally pure, lacking all kinds of scattered motion. You should then gather in your scatteredness, grasp hold of quiescence and make this your practice. If you don't, then your entire mind will be deluded, and unable to illuminate, thus enabling the stimulation of the deluded consciousness. By gathering in scatteredness and returning to quiescence, the true mind will be unified and clear. Since the agitated motion of the deluded consciousness can be clarified by the wisdom of awakening, the conscious mind is immobilized, and quiescent wisdom is aroused. From here, the body, mind and objective defilements are permanently extinguished and the pliancy of cessation and quiescence is directly manifested. The defilements vanish and luminosity is born, motion stops, and quiescence is manifest: hence, one attains Buddha-mind and manifests it in oneself. It is like a single dirty mirror facing a multitude of clear mirrors. Because of its dirt, the mirror cannot receive the reflection from the other mirrors. Once the dirt is completely removed, the reflection from this mirror can reflect in all the other mirrors, and the reflections from all the other mirrors can reflect in this one mirror. All the images reflect back and forth, perfectly interpenetrating without obstruction. This is the first meditation, called *śamatha*, which means "quiescence."

Samāpatti

[Sutra (#75)] [*T* 842.17.917c20; *HPC* 7.152a23]

善男子、若諸菩薩悟淨圓覺、以淨覺心、知覺心性及與根
塵皆因幻化。即起諸幻以除幻者。變化諸幻而開幻衆。由
起幻故便能内發大悲輕安。一切菩薩從此起行漸次增進。
彼觀幻者非同幻故、非同幻觀。皆是幻故幻相永離。是諸
菩薩所圓妙行如土長苗。此方便者名三摩鉢提。

Good sons, some bodhisattvas awaken pure Perfect Enlightenment,
then using the pure enlightened mind, completely realize that the
nature of mind as well as the faculties and objects are all based on
illusory transformations. Here they produce various illusions in
order to remove illusion. Creating (transforming)[4] all illusions, they
enlighten the illusory multitude. From the production of illusion
they are able to arouse great compassionate pliancy within. All
bodhisattvas who follow this "arising practice" gradually advance
in practice. Since the "observation of illusion" is not the same as
illusion, it is also not the same as "illusory observation." Since both
are [recognized as] illusory, illusory marks are permanently
removed. This marvelous practice that is perfected by bodhisattvas
is like a shoot growing out of the ground. This expedient method
is called *samāpatti*.

[*Translator's note*: *Samāpatti* is normally used as a term synonymous with
samādhi, referring generally to a deep state of meditative absorption.
In the *SPE* it is being used as a synonym for *vipaśyanā* (usually rendered
in Sino-Korean as *kuan/kwan* 觀), which means "analytical meditation"
or "observing meditation." Whereas the prior *śamatha* meditation has a
tendency to ignore the myriad phenomena, *vipaśyanā* meditation
accepts them, but sees them according to a correct doctrinal principle,
such as dependent origination. *Vipaśyanā* can be interpreted then, as a
"proper way of seeing the world while not closing oneself off to the
world." While *śamatha* is associated with the concentration aspect of
the Buddhist path, *vipaśyanā* is associated with the wisdom aspect. In
the *SPE*, *samāpatti* refers especially to the exercise of seeing the illusory
nature of existence, as taught in chapters two and three. Therefore the
term "as-illusion *samāpatti* (*samādhi*)." Since, in the practice of *samāpatti*,
one does not shut out the world, but extends oneself out to the world,
it is also the form of meditation that is associated with the practice of
compassion.]

[Kihwa] [*HPC* 7.152b7]

   Having awakened the pure, marvelous awareness of Perfect Enlightenment that originally lacks confusion, bodhisattvas now produce illusory

wisdom in order to remove deluded errors. Creating illusory expedients, they awaken the deluded followers. Having used illusory wisdom to remove their *own* delusions, they also use illusory expedients to awaken the multitudes from their delusion. Hence, great compassionate pliancy is directly manifested. Why do those who do this practice of production[5] gradually advance? If the "observation of illusion" were the same as the illusion, even though wanting to advance, one could never consummate the practice. It is because one is not the same as illusion that he is able to advance. Moreover, it is not only error and delusion that are illusory: since the observing wisdom is also ultimately illusion, when it is finally removed, the marvelous practice is perfected.

This marvelous practice of the bodhisattvas has already, depending on the quiescent meditation, removed illusion and attained quiescence. Now again, depending on the "as-illusory" observation, the marks of quiescence are also removed. This kind of gradual advancement is like a sprout of grain, growing in dependence upon the earth. This meditation is called *samāpatti*. *Samāpatti* means "creation through transformation." The above-discussed *śamatha* observes form to be the same as emptiness, removing falsity and returning to the real. *Samāpatti* observes emptiness to be the same as form, producing compassion to transform sentient beings. The sentence in the sutra that says "they completely realize that the nature of mind as well as the faculties and objects are all based on illusory transformations. Here they produce various illusions in order to remove illusion" actually relates to the sentence in the passage on *śamatha* that says "Then, by settling all thoughts they become aware of the agitated motion of the consciousness, and thus produce quiescent wisdom. From this, the mind, the body and external objects are permanently extinguished." Only the line that says "Creating [transforming] all illusions, they enlighten the illusory multitude" specifically applies to this meditation. The line that says "Since the 'observation on illusion' is not the same as illusion" is also related to the same sentence in the section on *śamatha*. "By settling all thoughts they become completely aware of the agitated motion of the consciousness, and thus produce quiescent wisdom." If you do not settle the thoughts, then since both body and mind are the same as illusory transformations, you cannot gain awareness over the agitated motion of the consciousness. Since the settling of all thoughts is not the same as illusory transformation, awareness can be gained over the agitated motion of the consciousness without following it. When it says below in the sutra "bodhisattvas do not become attached to transformations"[6] it is referring to this sentence. The phrase "it is also not the same as 'illusory observation.'. . . Since both are [recognized as] illusory, illusory marks are permanently removed" also applies to this meditation. This means that even though you observe the body and mind to be illusory transformations, and attain the consummation of quiescent meditation, since quiescent meditations are ultimately nothing but illusion, the marks of quiescence are also removed, whereupon you consummate the "as-illusion" observation. When the text says "illusory marks are permanently removed" it means that the marks of quiescence are also removed. When it says below "not attached to the marks of quiescence,"[7] it is referring exactly to this. Since the "as-illusion" observation is consummated based on quiescent meditation, the flow of the text is like this.

Dhyāna

[Sutra (#76)] [*T* 842.17.917c27; *HPC* 7.152c15]

善男子、若諸菩薩悟淨圓覺、以淨覺心不取幻化及諸靜相
、了知身心皆爲罣礙。無知覺明不依諸礙、永得超過礙無
礙境、受用世界及與身心、相在塵域。如器中鍠、聲出于
外。煩惱涅槃不相留礙。便能內發寂滅輕安。妙覺隨順寂
滅境界自他身心所不能及。衆生壽命皆爲浮想。此方便者
名爲禪那。
　善男子、此三法門皆是圓覺親近隨順。十方如來因此成
佛。十方菩薩種種方便一切同異皆依如是三種事業。若得
圓證即成圓覺。善男子、假使有人修於聖道教化成就百千
萬億阿羅漢辟支佛果。不如有人聞此圓覺無礙法門、一剎
那頃隨順修習。

Good sons, some bodhisattvas awaken pure Perfect Enlightenment, and using the pure enlightened mind, avoid attachment to illusory transformations and the marks of quiescence, fully realizing body and mind both to be obstructions. Without awareness of the illumination of enlightenment (of *śamatha*) and without depending on all sorts of obstructions (the illusions analyzed in *samāpatti*), they eternally transcend realms of obstruction and nonobstruction, receiving and using the world as well as body and mind, whose marks abide in the objective realm. It is comparable to the ringing sound in a bell that penetrates to the outside. Affliction and nirvana not hindering each other, the bodhisattvas are directly enabled to produce the pliancy of cessation-extinction from within. Accordance with marvelous enlightenment and the realm of cessation and extinction is something that self and other, body and mind are unable to reach. Sentient beings and life are all just floating concepts. This expedient method is called *dhyāna*.

[*Translator's note*: The term *dhyāna* in itself does not originally possess the distinctive connotations being assigned to it in this text. It is usually just one of the terms for meditation, or deep concentration, synonymous with such terms as *samāpatti* and *samādhi*. In the *SPE*, however, *dhyāna* is assigned a specific meaning as a form of meditation that simultaneously includes and transcends the prior two of *śamatha* and *samāpatti*: it is the "middle path" of the two other meditations. The Chinese ideographs with which *dhyāna* is written include the word *ch'an/sŏn* 禪, which will become the name for the movement in Buddhism with which the *SPE* is closely associated.]

[Sutra]

> Good sons, these three practices are all close accordance with Perfect Enlightenment; the tathāgatas in the ten directions achieve buddhahood depending upon these, and all the various and sundry expedient methods of the bodhisattvas of the ten directions, with all their similarities and differences are without exception derived from these three activities. If you perfectly actualize these, it is the same as perfectly actualizing enlightenment.
>
> Good sons, if there were a person who cultivated the sagely path and elevated a quadrillion people to the stage of *arhat* and *pratyeka-buddha*, he would not be equal to the person who heard this unobstructed teaching ("dharma-gate") of Perfect Enlightenment and practiced it for only an instant.

[Kihwa] [*HPC* 7.153a6]

Having realized that Perfect Enlightenment is neither empty nor provisional, and yet is both empty and provisional, they will neither become attached to nor cast away nature and marks, truth and falsity, and all other dichotomies. Since enlightenment is not provisional, they do not become attached to illusory transformation. Since enlightenment is not empty, they do not become attached to the marks of quiescence. Also, since enlightenment is not provisional, they thoroughly realize body and mind to be obstructions. Since enlightenment is empty, there is no awareness of the illumination of enlightenment. The phrase "fully realize body and mind both to be obstructions" means that one observes body and mind to be obstructions and penetrates to the emptiness of their nature. The phrase "without awareness of enlightenment" means that having clearly penetrated to their emptiness in nature, they do not abide in their awareness of emptiness. If this were not the case, then it would be like being able to see the moon but being unable to forget its brightness. The line "do not attach to illusory transformation" is related to the line from the earlier passage that says "remove illusion."

"Fully realize body and mind both to be obstructions" is related to the earlier line that says "they will completely realize that body and mind as well as the faculties and objects are all based on illusory transformations." "Without awareness of the illumination of enlightenment" refers to the earlier line that says "illusory marks are permanently removed."

The words "do not become attached to illusory transformation or the marks of quiescence" are indicative of advanced practice. The words "fully realize body and mind both to be obstructions" and "without awareness of the illumination of enlightenment" are indicative of advanced knowledge. In the earlier discussion the order was knowledge first and practice next. Therefore it says "they will completely realize that the nature of the enlightened mind as well as the faculties and objects are all based on illusory transformations. Here they produce various illusions in order to remove illusion." It also says "it is also not the same as the illusory-observation.' Since both are [recognized as] illusory, illusory marks are permanently removed." This is the order of advancement through practice.

But now the text says "do not become attached to illusory transformation or the marks of quiescence" and then after this "fully realize body and mind both to be obstructions." It also says "without awareness of the illumination of enlightenment." These lines all indicate an order of practice *preceding* knowledge. The latter is raised to refer to the former. But this should be understood as nothing other than a way of referring to the former. It is not an effort to lay strict claims about a difference in order. To understand that one first detaches from illusory transformations and the marks of quiescence, and then later fully realizes the body and mind to be obstructions, and that there is also no awareness of the illumination of enlightenment, would not make sense. As for the line that says "without depending on all sorts of obstructions": it is not simply the illusory transformations of body and mind that are obstructions. Since quiescent meditation and the view of emptiness are also obstructions, they are not to be depended upon. As for the line that says "they permanently transcend realms of obstruction and nonobstruction," the "obstructions" are the illusory transformations of body and mind. The "nonobstructions" are quiescent meditation and the view of emptiness. Hence, what is permanently transcended are the illusory transformations of body and mind and the realms of quiescent meditation and views of emptiness. The phrase "without depending on all obstructions" merely sums up the passage starting from "do not attach to illusory transformations," it has no other special significance.

Now since they fully realize that the enlightened nature is originally not provisional, they are not bound by the view of [the observation of] illusion, and they are able to consummate quiescent meditation. Since they fully realize that the enlightened nature is originally not empty, they are not bound by quiescent meditation and are able to consummate "as-illusion" observation. But also, since they fully realize that despite its emptiness, the nature of enlightenment is also provisional, unattached to quiescence, they simultaneously return to illusory transformation. This is the meaning of "receiving and using the world as well as body and mind, whose marks abide in the objective realm." Since they fully realize that despite its provisionality, the nature of enlightenment is emptiness, unattached to the observation of illusion, they simultaneously return to the marks of quiescence. This is what is referred to by "It is comparable to the ringing sound in a bell that penetrates to the outside."

"Receiving and using the world" applies to the earlier meditation "within illusion transforming all illusion." Only the words "it is comparable to the ringing sound in a bell that penetrates to the outside" properly apply to this contemplation. Since this third form of meditation is unattached to quiescence and simultaneously utilizes the as-illusory [observation], one is not obstructed by defilement. Since it is unattached to [the observation of] illusion and utilizes quiescence, one is not obstructed by nirvana. Since the defilements and nirvana do not hinder each other, the pliancy of cessation-extinction directly manifests itself.

"Cessation" is something that occurs within quiescence. "Extinction" refers to the extinction of illusion. Above we said "one consummates quiescence, yet is not attached to quiescence." Here we say "unattached to the marks of quiescence, one nonetheless returns to the marks of quiescence." Above we said "one extinguishes illusion yet returns to the illusory." Now we say "although one is identified with illusion, one nonetheless extinguishes illusion." This is why we have said that the "cessation" is none other than the cessation that occurs within quiescence, and that the "extinction" is none other than the extinction contained within the extinction of illusion.[8]

Why is it that each of the three meditations produces "pliancy"? If illusions are not extinguished, then when they are stimulated they will move; the body and mind become coarse and heavy and one cannot attain serenity. When illusions are permanently extinguished, there is complete stillness, body and mind are clear and light—then one has attained serenity. This is the meaning of the "pliancy of cessation-quiescence." But even if one has removed illusion and become stable, if he should become attached to quiescent meditation and not arouse the compassion to transform the suffering of others, then his awareness will be limited and his body and mind will not reach pliancy. But if he can remove illusion and become stable, and furthermore detach from his quiescence and arouse compassion to transform the suffering of others, then his awareness will become universal and his body and mind will attain pliancy. This is the meaning of "great compassionate pliancy." If he is unattached to quiescence but does not return to the marks of quiescence; or is he has returned to [contemplation of] illusion and does not also extinguish illusion, then his awareness will not attain nonhindrance and his body and mind will also not be pliant. If he is unattached to quiescence yet returns to the marks of quiescence; if he identifies with illusion and also extinguishes the marks of illusion, then his awareness will for the first time attain nonhindrance, and body and mind will attain pliancy. This is the realm of "cessation-extinction pliancy" and "accordance with marvelous enlightenment." In this realm there are no marks not annihilated and no delusions not extinguished. This kind of serene quiescence and marvelous profound perfect illumination are things that are unattainable through the body and mind of self and other, or the Four Traces of self, person, sentient being, and life.[9]

The view of the existence of self and other submerges into love and hatred. Then body and mind become coarse and heavy and cannot attain pliancy. This is why the text says that "the realm of cessation and extinction is something that self and other, body and mind are unable to reach." The position of the Four Traces within this realm is like that of the clouds in the vast sky, which coalesce with each other without distinction.

This is the *dhyāna* meditation, and *dhyāna* means "cessation-extinction." Among these three meditations, it can be said that the first two do not embrace the second two, yet the second two must embrace the first two. Since the first two do not embrace the second two, the teaching of the first meditation cannot explain the implications of the second. The teachings of the second meditation cannot explain the implications of the third. Since the second two must embrace the first two, the teaching of the second meditation first refers to the context of the first meditation, and then proceeds to elucidate its own implications. The text connected with the third meditation also first refers to the context of the two meditations of quiescence and illusion-observation, and then proceeds to elucidate its own implications.

These three dharma-gates are all methods of according with Perfect Enlightenment. The tathāgatas of the ten directions accomplish their Way on the basis of these. The bodhisattvas of the ten directions practice and actualize depending on these. If one attaches to the exclusive practice of only one of the three, then he will not accomplish the real accordance. One must practice unobstructedly and actualize unlimitedly—then it can for the first time be called "the real accordance." If you want to penetrate to the marvelous realm of Perfect Enlightenment, you must enter through these gates. If you enter through these, you will advance to that marvelous realm without obstruction. Therefore he says "unobstructed dharma-gate." If someone hears this teaching and is briefly able to practice it, his merit will surpass that of the accomplishments of a trillion sages of the Two Vehicles.

The *Gāthā*

[Sutra (#77)] [*T* 842.17.918a11; *HPC* 7.154a23]

爾時世尊、欲重宣此義而説偈言：

威德汝當知　　無上大覺心
本際無二相　　隨於諸方便
其數即無量　　如來總開示
便有三種類　　寂靜奢摩他
如鏡照諸像　　如幻三摩提
如苗漸增長　　禪那唯寂滅
如彼器中鍠　　三種妙法門
皆是覺隨順　　十方諸如來
及諸大菩薩　　因此得成道
三事圓證故　　名究竟涅槃

Then the World-Honored One, desiring to reiterate the gist of this, spoke a verse. He said:

Power-Virtue, you should know
Even though the unsurpassed mind of great enlightenment
Originally has not even two marks.
The expedient methods for according with it
Are numberless.
When I explain them according to general type,
There are three kinds:
Stable *śamatha*
Is like a mirror reflecting all images;
As-illusion *samādhi*
Is like a shoot growing out of the ground;
Dhyāna is only cessation-extinction
Like the sound in the bell.
These three kinds of marvelous dharma-practices
Are all accordance with enlightenment.
The tathāgatas in the ten directions
As well as all the great bodhisattvas
Are able to attain the Way based on these.
The full realization of these three activities
Is called "absolute nirvana."

[Kihwa] [*HPC* 7.154b7]

Enlightenment originally has no duality, yet expedients are count-less. The countless expedients are summarized in three. Quiescence is like a clear, bright mirror. Illusion-contemplation is like a shoot grow-ing out of the ground. *Dhyāna* is like the sound within the bell. Al-though these three dharma-gates have distinctions of deep and shal-low, in their relation to Perfect Enlightenment, they are all called "ac-cordance." The buddhas and bodhisattvas accomplish the Way based on these. The complete realization of the three is called Great Nirvana.

8

Voice of Discernment
Bodhisattva

[Kihwa] [*HPC* 7.154b13]

The wisdom-mirror is perfectly clear, and there is no confusion between "yes" and "no." This is called "discernment." Sound arises in the mind and vibrates out into the world. This is called "voice." "Voice of Discernment" means that the different teachings expounded by the Single Voice are directly understood in a single hearing and clearly discerned without confusion.

[*Translator's note*: "Single Voice" (also "Perfect Voice") is an important technical term in the development of Chinese doctrinal Buddhism, referring to the fact that from an absolute standpoint, the Buddha only gave a single teaching, even though this teaching would end up being interpreted variously. The credit for the establishment of this concept is given to Bodhiruci, who, when he came to Chang-an in 502 CE, explained that the existence of teachings of small/great vehicle and teachings of emptiness/existence is due to the variations in the predilections of people. The usage of this term is clearly related to the theme of this chapter, since here a multiplicity of teachings will be given for people of various dispositions. In the *Awakening of Faith*, see *T* 1666.32.575c10.]

[Kihwa]
Why does this bodhisattva follow Power and Virtue Unhindered with another question? This bodhisattva will transform mental agitation into subtle discernment. The meaning of "mental agitation" is that of the large wavelike formations of coarse apprehension and fine analysis[1] and the consciousness that depends on the discriminations of the faculties. When it abides in worldlings, it is inversion and illusion. When it abides in the sage, it is adept discrimination and subtle intelligence. The reason agitation is an "obscuration" is because it prevents the mind

from focusing as it clambers among the objects of the world. Agitation regards meditation as its enemy as it hides itself in the darkness, creating conflict; it goes in and out through the organs among the realms of objects, form, and mind; it plays carelessly between yes and no, good and evil. Enhancing the karmic consciousness of ignorance, it obstructs the person's natural spiritual luminosity. Since this bodhisattva uses meditational wisdom to illuminate and obliterate confusion, transforming it into adept discrimination and subtle intelligence, the differentiated teachings possessed by the Buddha are clearly distinguished without a doubt. Power and Virtue has already used the wisdom of meditation to cause the sentient beings to transform their anger into power. Now this bodhisattva wants to have the sentient beings again use these meditations to clarify their confusions, transforming these into adept discrimination and subtle intelligence. Therefore, he asks the Buddha to teach the various practices of expedient methods that lie within the area of meditation. Within the text are the twenty-five applications of simple, compound and perfect practices. It is by means of these that he will cause the sentient beings to transform mental agitation into subtle discernment.

Concerning the doctrine of the simple, compound and perfect: if one's faculties are not equal to that of Voice of Discernment, one cannot ask the question. If one's knowledge is not correct and universal, one cannot enlighten others. The teacher connects them directly to the Way, like an arrowhead fitting together with its shaft. Its gist is like this. From the chapter of Vajragarbha up to now, each one of the bodhisattvas has converted one of the Five Obscurations into the Five Virtues. And although the Five Obscurations and Five Virtues are not explicitly named in the text, they are expressed in the names of the individual bodhisattvas, and are also implicit in the questions and answers of the sutra.[2] The reader cannot but see this. My verse:

The three meditations provisionally establish the path of practice.
The simple, compound, and perfect are divided into twenty-five.
Trapped in the anxiety of a dream, the dawn has not yet arrived.
Awakening comes relying on the ancients—it is high noon.

Voice of Discernment's Question on the Application of the Three Meditations

[Sutra (#78)] [*T* 842.17.918a22; *HPC* 7.154c19]

於是辨音菩薩在大衆中、即從座起。頂禮佛足、右繞三匝
、長跪叉手而白佛言：大悲世尊。如是法門甚爲希有。世

尊、此諸方便一切菩薩於圓覺門有幾修習？願爲大衆及末
世衆生方便開示、令悟實相。作是語已、五體投地。如是
三請終而復始。

Then the bodhisattva Voice of Discernment rose from his seat in
the great assembly. He bowed to the feet of the Buddha and circumambulated him three times to the right. He then knelt down with
his hands clasped and addressed the Buddha saying:

"Greatly Compassionate World-Honored One, this teaching is
quite wondrous! World-Honored One, for all the bodhisattvas
engaged in the teaching and practice of Perfect Enlightenment,
how many different kinds of these expedient methods are there? I
beseech you to use expedient methods to teach those at this great
assembly and sentient beings of the degenerate age, and cause them
to awaken to the marks of reality."

Having said this, he prostrated to the ground. He asked this
question three times in succession.

[Kihwa] [*HPC* 7.155a3]

Sentient beings abandon enlightenment, and tethered by the bonds
of karma, are submerged in the sea of poison. How can they resurface?!
Returning to the origin is truly difficult. The Tathāgata, with his special
skills, reveals the three meditations, and encourages the beings to
depend on these to accord with the nature of enlightenment. This is
why the bodhisattva calls it "wondrous." Again, one being numberless,
and the numberless being grouped into three—this is difficult to conceive.
Each one is complete in its accordance with enlightenment, and when
all three are perfectly actualized, it is also called "complete." This is
truly "wondrous," and this is why he praises it saying: "this teaching is
quite wondrous." This bodhisattva praised the teaching because he realizes just how wondrous it actually is. That is why he is said to possess
discernment. Concerning the time of the practice of the three meditations and the doctrine of simple, compound and perfect: the wisdom-
penetration of those of superior capacity exists *a priori* to linguistic
expression. Since those of middling and inferior capacity have not yet
been awakened, and have not yet attained knowledge, he asks the questions about the number of kinds of practice.

[Sutra (#79)] [*T* 842.17.918a28; *HPC* 7.155a14]

爾時世尊、告辨音菩薩言：善哉、善哉。善男子、汝等乃
能爲諸大衆及末世衆生問於如來如是修習。汝今諦聽、當
爲汝説。時辨音菩薩奉教歡喜、及諸大衆默然而聽。

Then the World-Honored One, addressing the bodhisattva Voice
of Discernment, said: "Excellent, excellent! Good son; you have

questioned well for the bodhisattvas and sentient beings of the degenerate age about the various practices of the Tathāgata. Now listen well, and I shall explain for you." The bodhisattva Voice of Discernment received this teaching with reverence and joy. All those in the great crowd became silent and listened.

[Kihwa] [*HPC* 7.155a19]

The Buddha has already taught the three meditations. Now he wants to teach their various applications and thus gather in all types of sentient beings. Since the bodhisattva's request matches this aim, the Buddha praises the question.

The Buddha's Answer:
The Twenty-Five Applications

[Sutra (#80)] [*T* 842.17.918b3; *HPC* 7.155a21]

善男子、一切如來圓覺清淨本無修習及修習者。一切菩薩及末世眾生依於未覺幻力修習。爾時便有二十五種清淨定輪。

Good sons, the Perfect Enlightenment of all tathāgatas is pure, originally having neither practice nor practitioner. When they practice, all bodhisattvas and sentient beings of the degenerate age depend upon the power of unenlightened illusion. At that time (the time of practice dependent upon illusion) there are twenty-five kinds of pure meditation applications.[3]

[Kihwa] [*HPC* 7.155b1]

Since enlightenment is originally divorced from thought, it is not applicable to practice. It is only because of nonenlightenment that there is the false existence of the Four Marks[4] that obstruct the spiritual luminosity. It is in order to eliminate the Four Marks that he establishes the three meditations. The "enlightenment" of "nonenlightenment" is the lack of enlightenment that exists prior to enlightenment. Subsequent enlightenment implies freedom from thought and the abandonment of discriminations. If each one of the Four Marks is abandoned, then you can be said to be "enlightened." If you cling to the marks through transmigration, you cannot be called enlightened. If you want to abandon discriminations, you must use meditation practice. Since meditation practice has differences according to the disposition of the practitioner, twenty-five variations are taught. This is called "practice within no-practice" and "variation within non-variation."

The Three Single Applications

[Sutra (#81)] [*T* 842.17.918b6; *HPC* 7.155b10] ▼

若諸菩薩唯取極靜、由靜力故永斷煩惱究竟成就、不起于
座便入涅槃。此菩薩者名單修奢摩他。

　若諸菩薩唯觀如幻、以佛力故變化世界種種作用、備行
菩薩清淨妙行、於陀羅尼不失寂念及諸靜慧。此菩薩者名
單修三摩鉢提。

　若諸菩薩唯滅諸幻不取作用獨斷煩惱、煩惱斷盡便證實
相。此菩薩者名單修禪那。

Some bodhisattvas exclusively grasp ultimate quiescence, and
through the power of quiescence permanently sever affliction absolutely and perfectly, and directly enter nirvana without rising from
their seats. These bodhisattvas are called practitioners of *śamatha*
only.

Some bodhisattvas exclusively observe all-as-illusion, and by
means of Buddha-power transform the world and carry out various
activities, thoroughly putting into operation all the marvelous pure
bodhisattva practices. In all continuous concentrations they do not
fail in cessation of thought and quiescent wisdom. These bodhisattvas are called practitioners of *samāpatti* only.

Some bodhisattvas exclusively extinguish all illusions, and without activity in the world individually sever affliction. Affliction
completely severed, they directly actualize the marks of reality.
These bodhisattvas are called practitioners of *dhyāna* only.

Applications Initiated with Śamatha

若諸菩薩先取至靜、以靜慧心照諸幻者、便於是中起菩薩
行。此菩薩者名先修奢摩他後修三摩鉢提。

　若諸菩薩以靜慧故證至靜性、便斷煩惱永出生死。此菩
薩者名先修奢摩他後修禪那。

　若諸菩薩以寂靜慧復現幻力種種變化度諸眾生、後斷煩
惱而入寂滅。此菩薩者名先修奢摩他中修三摩鉢提後修禪
那。

　若諸菩薩以至靜力斷煩惱已、後起菩薩清淨妙行度諸眾
生。此菩薩者名先修奢摩他中修禪那後修三摩鉢提。

　若諸菩薩以至靜力心斷煩惱、後度眾生建立境界。此菩
薩者名先修奢摩他齊修三摩鉢提禪那。

　若諸菩薩以至靜力資發變化後斷煩惱。此菩薩者名齊修
奢摩他三摩鉢提後修禪那。

　若諸菩薩以至靜力用資寂滅後起作用變化世界。此菩薩
者名齊修奢摩他禪那後修三摩鉢提。

Some bodhisattvas first attain perfect quiescence, and through the mind of quiescent wisdom shed light on all illusions and directly within these illusions arise the bodhisattva practices. These bodhisattvas are called practitioners of *samatha* first and *samāpatti* next.

Some bodhisattvas actualize the perfectly quiescent nature through quiescent wisdom, and then directly sever affliction and permanently escape from life and death. These bodhisattvas are called practitioners of *samatha* first and *dhyāna* next.

Some bodhisattvas use cessation-quiescent wisdom to remanifest illusion-power and establish all kinds of transformations to save sentient beings. Subsequently they sever affliction and enter cessation-extinction. These bodhisattvas are called practitioners of *samatha* first, *samāpatti* next, and *dhyāna* last.

Some bodhisattvas use the power of perfect quiescence to sever all affliction. They then produce the pure, marvelous practices of the bodhisattvas and save all sentient beings. These bodhisattvas are called practitioners of *samatha* first, *dhyāna* next and *samāpatti* last.

Some bodhisattvas use the mind empowered by perfect quiescence to sever affliction and then save sentient beings and establish objective realms. These bodhisattvas are called practitioners of *samatha* first and subsequent simultaneous *samāpatti* and *dhyāna*.

Some bodhisattvas use the power of perfect quiescence to aid in the initiation of transformations, then subsequently sever afflictions. These bodhisattvas are called practitioners of simultaneous *samatha* and *samāpatti*, followed by the practice of *dhyāna*.

Some bodhisattvas use perfect quiescence to aid in extinction, and subsequently carry out activities to transform the world. These bodhisattvas are called practitioners of simultaneous *samatha* and *dhyāna*, who subsequently practice *samāpatti*.

Applications Initiated with Samāpatti

若諸菩薩以變化力種種隨順而取至靜、此菩薩者名先修三摩鉢提後修奢摩他。

若諸菩薩以變化力種種境界而取寂滅、此菩薩者名先修三摩鉢提後修禪那。

若諸菩薩以變化力而作佛事安住寂靜而斷煩惱、此菩薩者名先修三摩鉢提中修奢摩他後修禪那。

若諸菩薩以變化力無礙作用斷煩惱故安住至靜、此菩薩者名先修三摩鉢提中修禪那後修奢摩他。

若諸菩薩以變化力方便作用至靜寂滅二俱隨順、此菩薩者名先修三摩鉢提齊修奢摩他禪那。

若諸菩薩以變化力種種起用資於至靜後斷煩惱、此菩薩
者名齊修三摩鉢提奢摩他後修禪那。

　若諸菩薩以變化力資於寂滅後住清淨無作靜慮、此菩薩
者名齊修三摩鉢提禪那後修奢摩他。

Some bodhisattvas use transformation power to make various kinds of accordance, and thereby attain perfect quiescence. These bodhisattvas are called practitioners of *samāpatti* first and *śamatha* next.

Some bodhisattvas use transformation power to create various realms, and thereby attain cessation-extinction. These bodhisattvas are called practitioners of *samāpatti* first and *dhyāna* next.

Some bodhisattvas use transformation power to carry out Buddha-works. Then, abiding in cessation-quiescence, they sever affliction. These bodhisattvas are called practitioners of *samāpatti* first, *śamatha* next, and *dhyāna* last.

Some bodhisattvas use transformation power's unhindered function to sever affliction, and are therefore able to abide in perfect quiescence. These bodhisattvas are called practitioners of *samāpatti* first, *dhyāna* next, and *śamatha* last.

Some bodhisattvas use transformation power for the activity of expedient teaching and then practice within both perfect quiescence and extinction together. These bodhisattvas are called practitioners of *samāpatti* first, followed by simultaneous *śamatha* and *dhyāna*.

Some bodhisattvas use the various generative functions of transformation power to aid in the attainment of perfect quiescence and subsequently sever affliction. These bodhisattvas are called practitioners of simultaneous *samāpatti* and *śamatha*, followed by *dhyāna*.

Some bodhisattvas use transformation power to aid in extinction, and subsequently abide in pure uncreated quiescence of thought. These bodhisattvas are called practitioners of simultaneous *samāpatti* and *dhyāna* followed by *śamatha*.

Applications Initiated with Dhyāna

若諸菩薩以寂滅力而起至靜住於清淨、此菩薩者名先修禪
那後修奢摩他。

　若諸菩薩以寂滅力而起作用於一切境，寂用隨順、此菩
薩者名先修禪那後修三摩鉢提。

　若諸菩薩以寂滅力種種自性安於靜慮而起變化、此菩薩
者名先修禪那中修奢摩他後修三摩鉢提。

　若諸菩薩以寂滅力無作自性起於作用清淨境界歸於靜慮
、此菩薩者名先修禪那中修三摩鉢提後修奢摩他。

若諸菩薩以寂滅力種種清淨而住靜慮起於變化、此菩薩
者名先修禪那齊修奢摩他三摩鉢提。

若諸菩薩以寂滅力資於至靜而起變化、此菩薩者名齊修
禪那奢摩他後修三摩鉢提。

若諸菩薩以寂滅力資於變化而起至靜清明境慧、此菩薩
者名齊修禪那三摩鉢提後修奢摩他。

Some bodhisattvas use the power of extinction to arise perfect quiescence and abide in purity. These bodhisattvas are called practitioners of *dhyāna* first and *śamatha* next.

Some bodhisattvas use the power of extinction, yet enter activity, and this negating function is practiced within all realms. These bodhisattvas are called practitioners of *dhyāna* first and *samāpatti* next.

Some bodhisattvas use the various self natures of extinction power, and abiding in mental quiescence, produce transformations. These bodhisattvas are called practitioners of *dhyāna* first, *śamatha* next, and *samāpatti* last.

Some bodhisattvas use the inactive self-nature of extinction power to engage in activity, then purify the objective realm and return to quiescence. These bodhisattvas are called practitioners of *dhyāna* first, *samāpatti* next, and *śamatha* last.

Some bodhisattvas use the various purity of extinction power, then, abiding in mental equipoise, produce transformations. These bodhisattvas are called practitioners of *dhyāna* first, followed by simultaneous *śamatha* and *samāpatti*.

Some bodhisattvas use extinction power to aid in the attainment of quiescence, and then give rise to transformations. These bodhisattvas are called practitioners of simultaneous *dhyāna* and *śamatha*, followed by *samāpatti*.

Some bodhisattvas use extinction power to aid in transformation, produce perfect quiescent purity and illuminate objective wisdom. These bodhisattvas are called simultaneous practitioners of *dhyāna* and *samāpatti*, followed by *śamatha*.

Simultaneous Consummation of All Three

若諸菩薩以圓覺慧、圓合一切於諸性相無離覺性。此菩薩
者名為圓修三種自性清淨隨順。善男子、是名菩薩二十五
輪、一切菩薩修行如是。

Some bodhisattvas, using the wisdom of Perfect Enlightenment, harmoniously blend all of these, and in connection with all natures and characteristics, never separate from the enlightened nature.

These bodhisattvas are called "practitioners of the three kinds of accordance with the purity of the self-nature." Good sons, these are called 'the twenty-five applications' of the bodhisattvas, and all bodhisattvas practice like this.

[Kihwa] [*HPC* 7.156b8]

The passage in the chapter of Pure Wisdom Bodhisattva that says "The teachings of the sutras are like the finger pointing to the moon"[5] belongs here after the line just above which says "Good sons, these are called 'the twenty-five applications' (是名菩薩二十五輪)" but is mistakenly placed there (in the chapter of Pure Wisdom). This mistaken placement occurs despite the fact that the theme of the finger-moon simile does not fit to the text just above it that says "when obstructions have been eliminated"[6] and it does not fit the theme of the line below it that discusses the meaning of accordance with the nature of enlightenment.[7] That portion of the text says "They are called bodhisattvas who have entered the *bhūmis* who are according with the nature of enlightenment (此名菩薩已入地者隨順覺性)." Here, it says "These bodhisattvas are called 'practitioners of the three kinds of accordance with the purity of the self-nature.'" Because of the similarity of the language with such words as "accordance" and "These bodhisattvas" [someone] probably ended up confusing the two passages. Also, the concluding sentence here says "Good sons, these are called 'the twenty-five applications'" In the other chapters the words "Good sons" have come *after* this kind of concluding remark. Why? After treating the twenty-five applications in this chapter, he concludes by saying that "these are the twenty-five applications." [Based on an observation of the other chapters] we would expect him to make one more statement starting with "Good sons...". For example, in the chapter of Maitreya, after finishing his treatment of the Five Natures, he concludes that discussion by saying "This is the 'distinction of the five natures' of sentient beings."[8] After this conclusion he initiates a further discussion, saying "Good sons..." as we can verify for ourselves. If we place that passage here, the text is smooth and the meaning matches the context. It should say:

此菩薩者名爲圓修三種自性清淨隨順。是名菩薩二十五輪。善男子、修多羅教如標月指。若復見月了知所標畢竟非月。一切如來種種言說開示菩薩亦復如是。一切菩薩修行如是。

These bodhisattvas are called practitioners of the three kinds of accordance with the purity of the self-nature, and these are called the bodhisattvas' twenty-five applications. Good sons, the teaching of the sutras is like the finger pointing to the moon. If you also look at the moon, you will fully realize that that which is pointing is ultimately not the moon. All the various words and explanations of the Tathāgata that are used to awaken bodhisattvas are also like this. All bodhisattvas practice like this.

The finger is a metaphor for the content of the sutra instruction, and is also a metaphor for the content of contemplation practice, which is none other than the twenty-five applications. The twenty-five applications are also various kinds of revelation, just like the finger pointing to the moon. The moon is a metaphor for the aim of sutra instruction and is also a metaphor for the aim of meditation practice, which is none other than the so-called "nature of pure Perfect Enlightenment" and the "marvelous mind of nirvana." This is expounded in the sutras and actualized in meditation. It is like using one's finger to point to the moon and then, relying on the finger, seeing the moon. This is why he teaches this kind of practice to the bodhisattvas. One who has not yet seen the moon needs to depend on the finger to see it. Once the moon is seen, the finger can be forgotten. One who has not yet actualized enlightenment must practice meditation in order to attain realization. Once one has attained realization, he can discard the meditation. The metaphor of using a raft to cross the river, but once the river is crossed, discarding the raft, is the same as this. Therefore we can be sure that the three sentences in the chapter of Pure Wisdom starting with "the teachings of the sutras"[9] belong here, after "twenty-five applications" and have been mistakenly placed in the middle of the sentence that says "according with the nature of Perfect Enlightenment." When this passage is placed there, it fits like a tumor on the body. When it is placed here, it fits like two pieces of a *fu-chieh*.[10] Since the Buddha has taught the twenty-five applications, he is afraid that the people will attach to this teaching as "reality," and attach to the meditation as "realization"— therefore he makes this explanation. How, then, is one to proceed? The twenty-five applications are all expedient methods for entering the Way. To provisionally use these methods to enter the Way is fine. But to hold rigidly to expedients and not be prepared to release them will not do.

Furthermore, in the *gāthā* it says "There are none among the tathāgatas of the ten directions/And the practitioners of the three worlds/Who do not rely upon these methods/In their attainment of perfection of *bodhi.*" But in the main text it only says "all bodhisattvas," leaving out the words "all tathāgatas," which are found in the *gāthā*. How can it be that the main text lacks something that appears only in the *gāthā*? Thus we can see that the words "all tathāgatas" are definitely omitted from here and mistakenly placed there. Also, if in that part of the text there is no phrase "extinction of obstructions," then it fits together with this passage "they are called bodhisattvas." Then the text and the theme accord with each other, and the meaning can flow like blood circulating through the body. It is like a person's recovery after a tumor is removed.

The Method of Choosing an Appropriate Application

[Sutra (#82)] [*T* 842.17.919a15; *HPC* 7.157a9]

若諸菩薩及末世眾生依此輪者、當持梵行寂靜思惟 . . .

If you bodhisattvas and sentient beings of the degenerate age want to utilize these applications, you must maintain practices of purity, quiescence, contemplation . . .

[Kihwa] [*HPC* 7.157a11]

"Practices of purity" is *śīla.* "Quiescence" is *samādhi.* "Contemplation" is *prajñā.* These are all taught at the outset of practice. Why are they taught? The dharmas of *śīla, samādhi,* and *prajñā* are the means by which the student of Buddhism starts and finishes his practice. Therefore "strict maintenance of practices of purity, quiescence, and contemplation" can be understood as the point of departure. It is like the passage in Universal Vision that says "first relying on the Tathāgata's practice of *śamatha* . . . and living in harmony with like-minded students, then practicing silent sitting in a quiet room, they should . . . make the following analysis."[11] "Depending on meditation to consummate *bodhi* and actualize nirvana"—this is why these three are called the full gamut of practice. This meaning is reflected by such sayings as "only the Buddha himself kept the pure precepts" the "ocean-seal *samādhi*" and the "oceanlike wisdom of the reality-realm." Another example is "The Tathāgata put on his robes and carrying his bowl, entered the city to beg for food. Finished eating, he laid out his mat and sat in meditation. After this he arose from meditation and expounded the dharma."[12] Within all of the stages of practice and realization, there are none who do not use these to adorn the path of enlightenment. That is why I say that they are both the beginning and completion of practice. Minister P'ei said "that which is expounded by the Tripitaka is *śīla, samādhi,* and *prajñā*—nothing more."[13] Isn't it the truth?

[Sutra (#83)] [*T* 842.17.919a16; *HPC* 7.157b2]

 . . . 求哀懺悔。經三七日、於二十五輪各安標記。至心求哀、隨手結取。依結開示便知頓漸。一念疑悔即不成就。

 . . . and sincerely repent. Then passing through three weeks, settle upon whichever of the twenty-five applications is indicated on your lot.[14] With your whole mind and a repentant spirit, immediately choose one. Depending on what is indicated on the chosen lot, you will immediately know whether you are to practice the sudden or gradual. If there is one moment of doubt you will not be able to accomplish your assigned application.

[Kihwa] [*HPC* 7.157b5]

Through three weeks, repent diligently and sincerely pray for the Buddha's secret response, and then choose one of the lots. Whether the indication on the lot is for sudden or gradual practice, it is the secret guidance from the Buddha. Depending on this you will know whether you should practice the sudden or gradual. Even if the expedient indicated is far from what you have been expecting, this is the Buddha's grant, which you should neither doubt nor regret. If you doubt or regret it, then the meditation cannot be accomplished.

The *Gāthā*

[Sutra (#84)] [*T* 842.17.919a18; *HPC* 7.157b11]

爾時世尊、欲重宣此義而說偈言：

辨音汝當知　　一切諸菩薩
無礙清淨慧　　皆依禪定生
所謂奢摩他　　三摩提禪那
三法頓漸修　　有二十五種
十方諸如來　　三世修行者
無不因此法　　而得成菩提
唯除頓覺人　　并法不隨順

Then the World-Honored One, desiring to reiterate the gist of this, spoke a verse. He said:

Voice of Discernment, you should know,
All bodhisattvas'
Unobstructed pure wisdom
Is without exception, produced from meditation.
The so-called *śamatha*, *samāpatti*, and *dhyāna*—
The three methods of sudden and gradual practice—
Have twenty-five applications.
There are none among the tathāgatas of the ten directions
And the practitioners of the three worlds
Who do not rely upon these methods
In their attainment of perfection of *bodhi*—
Except for suddenly enlightened people
And those who have nothing to do with the dharma.

[Kihwa] [*HPC* 7.157b17]

The twenty-five applications are methods of cultivation. Suddenly enlightened people do not depend upon cultivation, but in a single leap directly enter the stage of the Tathāgata. "Those who have nothing to do with the dharma" are *icchantikas* who have severed the roots of goodness. Not valuing religious cultivation they harm themselves and abandon themselves. The suddenly enlightened see these expedient methods as worn-out "straw dogs." *Icchantikas* look upon these expedient means the same way they would view a donkey dancing in the branches of a mulberry tree. Even though the wise and foolish are not the same, they are the same in their not valuing religious cultivation. This is why the sutra says "Except for immediately enlightened people/ And those who have nothing to do with the dharma."

[Sutra (#85)] [*T* 842.17.919a27; *HPC* 7.157c1]

> 一切諸菩薩　　及末世衆生
> 常當持此輪　　隨順勤修習
> 依佛大悲力　　不久證涅槃

All bodhisattvas
And sentient beings of the degenerate age,
Should always embrace these applications,
Following them, endeavoring to practice them.
Relying on the power of the Buddha's great compassion,
Before long they will actualize nirvana.

[Kihwa] [*HPC* 7.157c3]

Above, it was said "[There are none] who do not rely upon these methods/In their attainment of perfection of *bodhi*." Here it says "Relying on the power of the Buddha's great compassion/Before long they will actualize nirvana." *Bodhi* and nirvana are the two unsurpassed fruits of all Buddhist practitioners. Within the "purity of the Perfect Enlightenment of all tathāgatas"[15] the Buddha has revealed the twenty-five applications. He finishes by mentioning the two unsurpassed fruits of *bodhi* and nirvana. The reader should pay close attention to this.

Explication of the Twenty-Five Applications: The Parable of the Castle

In the realm of reality and purity there is no principle of disorder. The True Man of No Status also does not come and go.[16] Within the first movement of the True Man lies the origin of calamity. Once the womb of calamity has been created, then arising and ceasing show themselves.

Once arising and ceasing show themselves, the wise and the foolish become distanced from each other. Since the wise and foolish tread different paths, above and below are distinguished, ruler and subject are determined. The wise are above and are that which the foolish lean upon. The foolish are below and are that which the wise gather together. Since those existing below are the foolish and the small-minded men, their world cannot but be in disorder. Since the ones existing above are the wise and superior men, there cannot but be skillful management of disorder. But when it comes time to for them to deal with rebellion, and to distribute the halberds and shields, they need to test the worth of the men and assign them to the appropriate posts.

In the handling of men's abilities there are many approaches, and in the quelling of rebellion there is not just one method. Establishing the teaching according to the capacities of beings [in Buddhism] is like properly using people's abilities [in governing the state]. Adjusting the remedy according to the disease is like the measures for quelling rebellion. "Quiescence (*śamatha*)" is like the job of bringing order to the vassals of the realm. "Contemplation of as-illusion (*samāpatti*)" is like the task of fending off outside armies. "Cessation (*dhyāna*)" is like the matter of handling affairs within the emperor's private domain.[17] Following the directives of the king of enlightenment, at the break of day the wise general does not allow the thieves of consciousness to arise, and extinguishes objective defilement, quieting the faculties and observing the objective realm with detachment. These are the characteristics of quiescence. The wise minister and clever general carefully survey inner and outer and arouse the power of illusory transformation, creating various functions. These are the characteristics of "as-illusion contemplation." Following the master of the castle, who gathers and prepares the infantry, they listen for the commands of the prince, and within the domain there is silence; the sky is vast and clear. These are the characteristics of cessation meditation.

As for the distribution into twenty-five applications: There are some people who can do the job of keeping order inside the larger realm, but who cannot fend off outsiders or handle the affairs of the emperor's central domain. There are some who can assume the role of defending against outside attacks, but are unable to keep order within the realm, or handle the affairs of the central domain. There are some who can handle the affairs of the central domain, but who can neither fend off outside attack, nor keep order within the larger realm. These are comparable to the simple practice of the three meditations. Those who can first do the job of keeping order inside the realm, and next fend off external attack are like those who practice *śamatha* first and *samāpatti* next. Those who can first keep order inside the realm and then after handle the affairs of the central domain are like those who do *śamatha* first and *dhyāna* next. Those who can first keep order within the realm, next fend off external attacks, and then finally handle the affairs of the central domain are like those who practice *śamatha* first, *samāpatti* next, and *dhyāna* last. Those who can first keep order within the realm, next handle the affairs of the central domain, and finally fend off external attacks are like those who practice *śamatha* first followed by *dhyāna* and then *samāpatti*. Those who can first keep order within the realm and then next simultaneously defend the borders and handle the central affairs are like those who practice *śamatha* first followed by simultaneous *samāpatti* and *dhyāna*. Those who can first simultaneously keep order within the realm and fend off attack, and subsequently handle the affairs of the central domain are like those who practice simultaneous *śamatha* and *samāpatti* first, followed by *dhyāna*. Those who can first simultaneously keep order within the realm and handle the affairs of the central domain and then fend off outside attacks are like those who practice simultaneous *śamatha* and *dhyāna* followed by *samāpatti*. These represent the first seven of the applications.

The subsequent fourteen can be understood in the same way. It is just that in the first seven, *śamatha* takes precedence over *samāpatti* and *dhyāna*. Then some come before, some after and some simultaneously. In the next seven, *samāpatti* has precedence and *śamatha* and *dhyāna* either come before each other, after each other, or simultaneously. In the final seven, *dhyāna* has precedence, and *śamatha* and *samāpatti* either come before or after each other, or simultaneously, as with the others. If there is a person who can move from generalship to ministership, handling both without obstruction, stabilizing movement and silencing speech, never missing in *samādhi*, then this is comparable to the perfect practice of all three meditations. If you utilize people in this way, then there will be no such thing as a "neglected Worthy"[18] in your country. If disorder is quelled in this way, then there will be no disorder not quelled. The Buddha's "no sentient being not responded to" and "no disease not treated" are the same as this. This is the same as "straightening the crooked without remainder."[19] The skillful handling of expedient means can be seen in this. If you lack the wisdom eye, the characteristics of the twenty-five applications are somewhat difficult to clearly distinguish. But if they are arranged like this, does not the meaning become clear?

Now even though the principle only has a single taste, the teaching has a thousand variations. Setting up the teaching with many paths, they all return to a single destination. It is the same with the capacities of sentient beings. Although the gates they enter are various, the realm to which they arrive is the same. When you finally ascend the road of great enlightenment and you turn back to observe what you have done up to this point, then it will seem just like a dream. The saying "coming and going and observing the world is just like the affairs of a dream" is the same as this. The Buddha says "the teaching of the sutras is just like the finger pointing to the moon. If you also look at the moon, you will fully realize that the pointing finger is ultimately not the moon."[20] Can we really call this an error? It is like bringing order to the country— once the realm is at peace then ruler and subject form a single body, inner and outer merge as one, and halls of litigation are turned into places for quiet contemplation. Halberds and shields are returned for use in digging the earth and cutting trees. At this time the name of unpraised goodness is exalted. How can there ever again exist the job of quelling disorder? This is truly the "governance of the six states"[21] where there is already no disorder.

> One man moves on the base of great peace
> And knowing the Way, the Way is greatened.
> Without transmission of the orders from the Son of Heaven,
> The times are calm and bountiful,
> And the song of Great Peace is sung.

9

Purifier of All Karmic Hindrances Bodhisattva

[*Translator's note*: The middle portion of this chapter, which contains a discussion of the Four Traces of "self," "person," "sentient being," and "life" is one of the most difficult sections to follow. It is not that its sentences embody the deepest doctrinal profundities of the sutra—the first three chapters contain the most profound Buddhist discourse. The difficulty lies in the fact that it is not easy to grasp the intent of the discussion and its frame of reference. Furthermore, if we can trust the judgment of Kihwa concerning the correctness of the sentence structure, this portion of the text has the highest concentration of copyist errors.

The central portion of this chapter consists of an explanation of the subtle action of mental karma, where "karmicity" is defined as "trace" or "remainder" from a prior cognitive activity. Karma will be defined by Kihwa in his prefatory remarks as "already-ness" (*i-jan/iyŏn* 已然), meaning, "something has happened" or "it is past." Each one of the Four Traces is the "remainder" or "mark" of a normal action of mental awareness, either objective or self-reflexive, that remains in the mind, or "reifies" such that the person identifies with it. The term being translated here as "trace" is *hsiang/sang* (相), which I have translated elsewhere in the text as "mark," and sometimes as "attribute" and "characteristic." Since we already have "Four Marks" in an earlier chapter (arising, abiding, changing, and ceasing), we should avoid confusion by using a different term. And since the four *hsiang* being discussed here have distinctly "residual" connotations, I have used the word "trace."

The author of the sutra will label each one of the traces with a special term to distinguish its functional awareness from the others. All four of these are words that are normally used to describe an aspect of enlightenment, which is of some significance in that they are here being used with negative connotations. This distinct and separate naming of each of the four can be seen as a means of helping to distinguish one level of activity from the next. I will introduce them here so that some confusion can be avoided. To the trace of self, he has attached the word *cheng/chŭng* (證 translated elsewhere in this text as "realize"), which I have translated here as "witness." To the trace of person, he has attached the word *wu/o* (悟) translated here as "cognize." To the trace of "sentient being" he has attached the word *liao/ryo* (了), which I have rendered as "realize," and to the trace of "life" he has attached *chüeh/kak* (覺), which I have rendered as "be aware." It is significant that each one of these "awareness-words" normally has connotations of enlightenment in one context or another, and indeed, in this chapter, they are referred to as "wisdoms." But by the fact of their lingering as karmic traces, each one of them transforms into a hindrance, unless the practitioner, by perfect illumination, is able to dissolve all remainder, the way hot water melts an ice cube. For the purpose of understanding the particular passage that elucidates the Four Traces, Kihwa's commentary is probably more indispensable than it has been anywhere in the sutra.]

[Kihwa] [*HPC* 7.159c7]

Nondefilement is purity, "already-ness (已然)" is karma. "Already-ness" is the opposite of the "not-yet (未然)." When a single thought does not arise, there is merely brightness, only illumination. This is the origin of the "not-yet." Once a single thought has arisen and all the faculties unleash consciousness, this is the "already-ness" of karma. When this mind is "already" and has become karmic, then the three subtle and six coarse defilements[1] struggle with each other in their activity; they hinder and conceal the luminosity of the spirit. Because of this, brightness is refracted as ignorance, and purity is transformed into defilement. The meaning of "purifying all karmic hindrances" is gradually eliminating all karmic hindrances from the gross to the subtle until there are none left to eliminate. Purity, then, means "completely undefiled."

Why is a question asked after the chapter of Voice of Discernment? From the chapter of Vajragarbha up to the chapter of Voice of Discernment there has been a continuous discussion of the Five Obscurations, which are the afflictions that pollute the true nature. Yet there has not yet been a clarification of how the afflictions come into being. Therefore this bodhisattva completely goes to the source of the matter and asks this question, and the Tathāgata teaches the "Four Traces" to be the cause of the troubles. The question says: "If this enlightened mind is originally pure, what defilements make all sentient beings suffer in delusion and be unable to enter?" This points to the Five Obscurations as that from whence come the afflictions that defile the true nature. The answer says: "[You] discern these four delusions to be an actual self-essence, and because of this readily create the two states of hatred and love." "Hatred and love" are the same as the "anger and desire" from among the Five Obscurations. Of course, included along with desire and anger are agitation, dullness, and doubt. But this is like the case of the Four Traces, when sometimes only the "self-trace" is mentioned, intended to exemplify all the others. This shows that the Five Obscurations, which are the afflictions that pollute the true nature, have their effect due to the Four Traces. Thus, when the Five Obscurations are cleared away, and you are rid of the Four Traces, then the coarse and subtle hindrances are extirpated. There is purity without remainder and enlightenment is naturally apparent everywhere. Purifier of Karma Bodhisattva's taking up from the prior chapter and asking this question is based on this. My verse:

> First, because of nonenlightenment one rejects the true eternal.
> Then, giving rise to self and person, people encounter great
>   suffering.
> The clouds of the Four Traces are opened, the single reality is
>   disclosed;
> The depth of the ocean and the clarity of the sky reflect the
>   myriad forms.

[Sutra (#86)] [*T* 842.17.919b1; *HPC* 7.160a9

於是淨諸業障菩薩在大衆中、即從座起。頂禮佛足右繞三
匝、長跪叉手而白佛言：大悲世尊。爲我等輩廣説如是不
思議事、一切如來因地行相、令諸大衆得未曾有。覩見調
御歷恒沙劫勤苦境界一切功用猶如一念。我等菩薩深自慶
慰。

The bodhisattva Purifier of All Karmic Hindrances arose from his seat in the great assembly. He bowed to the Buddha's feet, and circumambulated him three times to the right. He then knelt down with his hands clasped and addressed the Buddha, saying:

"Greatly Compassionate World-Honored One, you have explained at length for all of us this inconceivable matter of the aspects of the practice of the causal stage of all Tathāgatas, enabling all in the great assembly to gain that which they have never had. Having had this chance to see the Tamer,[2] all of their passage through realms of suffering for countless *kalpas* seems as if it were but an instant of thought. We bodhisattvas have been greatly encouraged."

[Kihwa] [*HPC* 7.160a16]
Within the single taste[3] of noncultivation he taught three meditative practices. Since these were difficult to comprehend, he again revealed the [twenty-five] applications. These completely embrace all kinds of

sentient beings, who, although they may not be able to fully master these applications, can comprehend them. "All the effective activities" then, refers to the twenty-five applications, and these are used "passing through realms of suffering in countless *kalpas*." Depending on the Buddha's instruction, they have come to know all this directly in a single thought-moment. Therefore they have been "greatly encouraged."

The Question of Purifier of Karmic Hindrances: The Removal of Obstructions

[Sutra (#87)] [*T* 842.17.919b6; *HPC* 7.160a21] ▼

世尊、若此覺心本性清淨、因何染污使諸眾生迷悶不入？ 唯願如來廣爲我等開悟法性、令此大眾及末世眾生作將來 眼。說是語已、五體投地。如是三請終而復始。

World-Honored One, if this enlightened mind is originally pure, what kind of defilements cause sentient beings to suffer in delusion and not enter? My only request is that you thoroughly awaken to the nature of existence, and cause those in this great assembly and sentient beings of the degenerate age to create the "future eye." After finishing this speech, he prostrated himself to the ground. He asked this three times in succession.

[Kihwa] [*HPC* 7.160b2]

[The intransitive verb] *kai-wu* (開悟 "to awaken") should be [transitive verb] *kai-shih* (開示 "awaken others," "disclose," "reveal"), since with the word *kai-wu*, the sentence does not flow properly.

[*Translator's note*: If we follow Kihwa's assertion, the line can be translated as "My only request is that you thoroughly reveal the nature of reality, and cause those in this great assembly and sentient beings of the degenerate age to create the 'future eye.'"]

[Kihwa]

The next, "create the future eye" should be understood to mean "awaken" (*kai-wu*). "Nature of enlightenment" and "nature of existence" are terms that refer to essence and function. "Nature of enlightenment" is the unmanifest source of dependent origination, the time when practice and realization have not been activated. "Nature of existence" refers to all of dependent origination that allows for the distinction between delusion and enlightenment and for the carrying out of practice and realization. Now he is asking about the reasons for delusion and suffering, and the method of practice and realization. Therefore he says "reveal to us the nature of existence." If he said "nature of enlightenment," that would mean that it has already been revealed to them—they have already experienced awakening. Since he says "nature of existence," then they have not yet experienced enlightenment; therefore there is the present request to be awakened. If they do not receive the awakening teaching, then they will not be able to awaken, and will be unable to "create the future eye."

[Sutra (#88)] [*T* 842.17.919b10; *HPC* 7.160b12]

爾時世尊告淨諸業障菩薩言：善哉、善哉。善男子、汝等乃能爲諸大衆及末世衆生諮問如來如是方便。汝今諦聽、當爲汝説。時淨諸業障菩薩奉教歡喜、及諸大衆默然而聽。

Then the World-Honored One, addressing the bodhisattva Purifier of All Karmic Hindrances, said: "Excellent, excellent! Good son, you have asked well for sentient beings of the degenerate age about the expedient methods of the Tathāgata. Listen well, and I shall explain for you." The bodhisattva Purifier of All Karmic Hindrances reverently and joyfully received this teaching; those in the great assembly became silent and listened.

[Kihwa] [*HPC* 7.160b17]

Since the removal of gross hindrances and subtle afflictions is also the Buddha's basic intention, he gladly approves of the question.

The Buddha's Answer: The Four Traces

[Sutra (#89)] [*T* 842.17.919b14; *HPC* 7.160b19]

善男子、一切衆生從無始來、妄想執有我人衆生及與壽命、認四顛倒爲實我體。由此便生憎愛二境。於虛妄體重執虛妄。二妄相依生妄業道。有妄業故妄見流轉。厭流轉者妄見涅槃。由此不能入清淨覺。非覺違拒諸能入者。有諸能入非覺入故。是故動念及與息念皆歸迷悶。何以故？由有無始本起無明爲己主宰、一切衆生生無慧目。身心等性皆是無明。譬如有人不自斷命。是故當知有愛我者。我與隨順非隨順者、便生憎怨。爲憎愛心養無明故、相續求道、皆不成就。

Good sons, from beginningless time all sentient beings deludedly conceive and attach to the existence of "self," "person," "sentient being," and "life"[4]—they discern these four distortions to be a real self-essence. From this they directly give rise to the two states of attraction and aversion. In this false essence, they again become attached to falsehood. These two delusions interact to produce the path of deluded karma ("activity"), and since there is deluded karma, they deludedly perceive transmigration. Those who come to dislike *saṃsāra* deludedly perceive nirvana, and because of this are unable to enter pure enlightenment. It is not that enlightenment rejects those who are capable of entry—rather, it is because those capable of entry do not awaken and enter. Therefore whether one's thoughts are jumping around or silenced—both conditions ultimately revert to deluded anxiety. Why? Because there is beginningless originally arisen ignorance that becomes the subjective ego; thus all sentient beings produce the eye of ignorance. The various natures of body, mind, and so on, are nothing but ignorance. Take for example the person who does not want to end his own life. Therefore, you should know there is enjoyment of "selfhood" when things go well. When things don't go as one likes, then hatred and anger arise. Since this mind of attraction/aversion nourishes ignorance, those who strive to cultivate the Way never attain it.

[Kihwa] [*HPC* 7.160c8]

A single thought includes all the myriad dharmas of the three realms. Without deluded conceptualization, all the myriad dharmas vanish together. Since the nature originally lacks a self, imagination [of a self] in the midst of its absence is called "deluded conceptualization." No-self conceiving a self—this is indeed falsehood! Depending on this self we further arise the two views of attraction and aversion; therefore he says "again attach to falsehood." These two false views work with each other to produce karma and bring suffering; we pass through the Four Kinds of Birth and are imprisoned in the Five Destinies.[5] Yet even if we get sick of suffering and cut off its origination, cultivate the way of realization and cessation, we are still stuck in the unconditioned. Not trying to transcend this, we remain [trapped] with the myriads of beings in *saṃsāra*. Even though rising and falling are not the same, and purity and defilement are different, in terms of nonentry into enlightenment, all are the same. Sentient beings are stuck in the conditioned (*saṃskṛta*)[6] and the practitioners of the Two Vehicles are stuck in the unconditioned (*asaṃskṛta*). In the pure ocean of enlightenment, essence and attributes both are submerged together. This is because both *saṃskṛta* and *asaṃskṛta* go too far. It is like avoiding drowning by jumping into the fire or escaping the peaks by falling into the ravines—neither extreme can avoid suffering.

How is it so? The nature is originally perfectly clear, lacking any discursive thought. As soon as discursive thought moves even slightly, this perfect clarity is obscured and there is the appearance of ignorance.

Even though the practitioners of the Two Vehicles have already severed affliction and are already free from *saṃsāra*, they have still not forgotten their "subjectivity." Therefore they both return to deluded affliction and do not enter the ocean of enlightenment. It is like when the thief has not yet been removed from the household, or a country that is not yet at peace. The sentient being's original arising of ignorance is like the fetus in the womb. Even though it lacks eyes, its inherent *ch'i* takes shape and initiates the movement of thought. These are all characteristics of ignorance. It is like human beings and the life faculty. People live by being joined with life. To cut off one's life is truly difficult; to desire to remove ignorance—is this not also difficult? Because the chieftain has not yet been expelled, his followers, though subdued, immediately re-arise. Since the roots and trunk still remain, the branches and leaves, though gone, immediately grow again. Since primary and secondary delusions exacerbate each other and have not been permanently severed, even though we pass through many *kalpas* continually seeking enlightenment, we do not attain it.

The word "continually" refers to "moment-to-moment continuation" without any interval. It is not the "pervasive function of the seeds [in the *ālayavijñāna*]."[7] The meaning of "continuing without interval" is as a later line says: "Sentient beings of the degenerate age do not perceive their self-natures. Although they struggle through many *kalpas* of difficult practice in cultivating the Way, it is merely called *saṃskṛta*. They are ultimately incapable of consummating the fruits of sagehood."[8] It also says: "Even though they struggle with great effort, they merely exacerbate their various afflictions, and therefore are unable to enter pure enlightenment."[9] The meanings of "struggle through difficult practice" and "diligently endeavor" are equivalent to "continuously seek the way."

[*Translator's note*: Kihwa is stressing the fact that it is extremely difficult to remove delusion because what is termed as "ignorance" begins with the most subtle actions of the human consciousness, which are difficult to be aware of. As long as these subtle actions of the human consciousness continue to take place, then no matter what strenuous effort one makes in practice, ignorance will continue to re-arise. The four kinds of subtle karmic mental activity will now be introduced.]

The Explanation of the Four Traces

[Sutra (#90)] [*T* 842.17.919b25; *HPC* 7.161a15] ▼

善男子、云何我相？謂諸眾生心所證者。善男子、譬如有
人百骸調適忽忘我身。四支弦緩、攝養乖方微加針艾、則

知有我。是故證取方現我體。善男子、其心乃至證於如來
畢竟了知清淨涅槃皆是我相。

Good sons, what is the "trace of self"?[10] It is that which is witnessed[11] by the mind of sentient beings. Good sons, when you are in good health, you naturally forget about your body. But when the body becomes sick, and you make an effort correct the infirmity, with the slightest application of moxibustion and acupuncture you are immediately aware of your existence as a self. Thus, it is only in reference to this "witnessing" that you perceive and grasp to an apparent self-essence. Good sons, every kind of witnessing from this level up to the Tathāgata's perfect perception of pure nirvana, is all the "trace of self."

善男子、云何人相？謂諸眾生心悟證者。善男子、悟有我
者不復認我。所悟非我悟亦如是。悟已超過一切證者悉爲
人相。善男子、其心乃至圓悟涅槃俱是我者心存少悟備殫
證理皆名人相。

Good sons, what is the "trace of person"? It is the cognition by sentient beings of the prior "witnessing." Good sons, once the self is cognized it is not again recognized in the same way.[12] It is the same in the case where that which is cognized is nonself. This "cognition," which has gone beyond every kind of "witnessing," is the "trace of person." Good sons, if, from this level of basic recognition of self up to the perfect recognition of nirvana as self, there remains in the mind even the smallest remainder of cognition that completely includes the witnessing of principle, all are called the "trace of person."

善男子、云何眾生相？謂諸眾生心自證悟所不及者。善男
子、譬如有人作如是言：我是眾生。則知彼人說眾生者非
我非彼。云何非我？我是眾生、則非是我。云何非彼？我
是眾生、非彼我故。善男子、但諸眾生了證了悟皆爲我人
而我人相所不及者存有所了名眾生相。

Good sons, what is the "trace of sentient being"? It is that which is beyond the self-witnessing and cognition of the minds of all sentient beings. Good sons, take for example the person who says "I am a sentient being." What this person has called "sentient being," is neither self nor other.[13] Why is it not self? Since self is "sentient being," it is not self. Why is it not "other?" Since "self" is sentient being, it cannot be another self. Good sons, what sentient beings realize in witnessing and realize in cognition is nothing more than the traces of self and person. That which does not reach the traces of self and sentient being, yet which remains as realized, is the trace of sentient being.

善男子、云何壽命相？謂諸衆生心照清淨覺所了者。一切業智所不自見猶如命根。善男子、若心照見一切覺者皆爲塵垢。覺所覺者不離塵故如湯銷氷。無別有氷知氷銷者。存我覺我亦復如是。

Good sons, what is the "trace of life"? It is that which sentient beings realize through the mind's pure illuminating awareness.[14] The inability of all of the prior karmic wisdoms to reflect on themselves is just like the life-faculty. Good sons, when one sees with the mind's illumination, all awarenesses are nothing but defilement. Since that of which the awarenesses are aware is not free from defilement, it is like hot water melting ice: there is neither discrimination of the existence of ice nor knowledge of the ice's melting. The remaining existence of a self and the awareness of a self are just like this.

[Kihwa] [*HPC* 7.161b15]

In the discussion of the Four Traces there are four sections. Each of these passages has three parts. The beginning of each part is indicated by the phrase "Good sons." Each also has a conclusion. If you understand the line of thought, the theme is penetrated by a single thread. Although it seems extremely complex and convoluted, once you perceive the flow of the text, it becomes clear that the problem is that in the three sections of the text that treat "person," "sentient being," and "life" there are errors of omission. There are also places where entire phrases are out of their proper order. Therefore the meaning of one line does not follow with the next, and the theme does not flow. For example, the two phrases "there remains in the mind even the smallest remainder of cognition (心存少悟)" and "which completely includes the witnessing of principle (備殫證理)" are probably reversed. It should say: "from this level of basic recognition of self up to the perfect recognition of nirvana as self, completely including the witnessing of principle, there remains in the mind even the smallest remainder of cognition, all are called the 'trace of person' (其心乃至圓悟涅槃俱是我者備殫證理心存少悟皆名人相)" Also where it says "why is it not other? Since the self is sentient being, it is not another self (云何非彼？我是衆生非彼我故)," above "not other (非彼)," the text is probably missing the word "therefore (則)." Also, the "self (我)" of "that self (彼我)" is probably mistakenly inserted. It should read: "Why is it not other? Since the self is sentient being, therefore it is not other (云何非彼？我是衆生則非彼故)." Again, right below "realize through the mind's pure illuminating awareness (清淨覺所了者)," the text is probably missing the phrase "Good sons (善男子)." And below, the sentence "since that of which the awarenesses are aware is not free from defilement (覺所覺者不離塵故)" should probably say "is called the trace of life (名壽命相)." The sections that discuss the other three traces have this kind of structure. Also in the line "remainder of self and awareness of self are also like this (存我覺我亦復如是)" the word "remaining existence (存)" in "remaining existence of self (存我)" should probably be "nonexistence (無)" instead. It should say "the nonexistence of self and awareness of self are also like this (無我覺我亦復如是)." If it is done this way, then it fits to the simile, which says "there is no discrimination of the existence of ice or knowledge of the ice's melting." Also, the lines from "It is like hot water melting ice (如湯銷氷)" up to "are just like this (亦復如是)," should be placed after "just like the life-faculty (猶如命根)." The sentence from "Good sons, when one sees with the mind's illumination (善男子、若心照見)" up to "therefore it is not free from defilement (不離塵故)" should be moved further back to the position of conclusion. It needs to come after "also like this (亦復如是)." The beginning part should be in front. Thus the text should read:

善男子、云何壽命相？謂諸眾生心照清淨覺所了者。善男子、一切業智所不自見猶如命根。如湯銷氷無別有氷知氷銷者。無我覺我亦復如是。善男子、若心照見一切覺者皆爲塵垢。覺所覺者不離塵故名壽命相。

Good sons, what is the "trace of life"? This refers to that which sentient beings realize through the mind's illuminating pure awareness. Good sons, that which is not perceivable by the totality of karmic wisdom is just like the life-faculty. It is like hot water melting ice: there is no discrimination of the existence of ice or knowledge of the ice's melting. The nonexistence of a self and the awareness of a self are just like this. Good sons, when one sees with the mind's illumination, all these awarenesses are nothing but defilement. Since that of which the awarenesses are aware is not separate from defilement, it is called the "trace of life."

From "Good sons, what is the 'trace of self'?" up to here, he explains the Four Traces, and according to the "trace," a term for the specific type of awareness is attached. After this, he says: "Good sons, sentient beings of the degenerate age do not perceive the Four Traces, and though they may struggle through many *kalpas* of difficult practice while cultivating the Way, it is still nothing but conditioned existence. They are ultimately incapable of consummating the fruits of sagehood." In this case, the meanings of the sentences agree with each other, and the theme is clear; the reader will understand very well.

In the sentence that says "it refers to that which is perceived by the mind of sentient beings," "sentient being" is a synonym for "worldling." In the case of "worldling" there are "inner worldlings" and "outer worldlings,"[15] which is just like saying "people" and having a difference between wise people and foolish people. The "sentient beings" mentioned here are those who are above the level of the Two Vehicles and below the level of Equal Enlightenment. Therefore the hindrances that are to be removed are the subtle delusions, to be distinguished from the gross delusions that bind the "outer worldlings."

Although these Four Traces have the same name as the Four Marks that are taught in the *Diamond Sutra*, their meaning is different. The Four Traces in this text are taught in connection with the subtle delusions that appear in cultivation and realization. Those [in the *Diamond Sutra*] are those possessed by sentient beings in general. The mind's possession of something to witness, and the witnessing mind's inability to forget this, is called the "Trace of Self." Even including [such exalted states as] witnessing the Tathāgata and nirvana, if one does not let go of what is witnessed, it is called the "trace of self." Not letting go of what has been witnessed, one immediately cognizes this mistake. The not-letting go of this cognizing mind is called "the trace of person." The cognizance that [all such good things as] even perceiving the Tathāgata and nirvana are nothing but "self," are all cognizance of this mistake. Even when the witnessing mind is completely exhausted, if the cognizing mind still remains, then it is also called "trace of person."

Cognizing "witnessing" as a mistake and that the "self" cannot be justified; knowing "cognition" is a mistake, and that "person" cannot be justified, the "realizing mind" still remains, and is called the "trace of sentient being." The mind, luminous and pure, is aware of this "realization" as a mistake but is not able to let go of the awareness. This is called the "trace of life." As for the phrase "all karma and wisdom": "karma" is the opposite of "nature" and "wisdom" is the opposite of "delusion." The traces of what has already happened are called "karma"; not being confused about the correct and incorrect is called "wisdom."

The mind has an experience of witnessing something and the witnessing mind is not let go of; there is cognition of the witnessing as a mistake, and realization that the cognition is also a mistake, and these stretch out without being let go of. These are [what I have called] "the traces of already-ness." Once you "let go," then everything heretofore is erased and you accord with the nature of enlightenment. Not letting go, you are confused and act haphazardly; "alreadiness" comes to fruition, and this is called "karma." Once not-letting go of witnessing is cognized as a mistake, and not-letting go of cognition and not-letting go of realization are in turn known as mistakes, then the correct and incorrect are not confused; therefore it is called "wisdom."

When it says "all," [the three] mistakes of witnessing, cognition, and realizing are the same, and yet [in terms of] karma and wisdom there are differences. The phrase "that which is not perceivable [by the totality of karmic] wisdom is just like the life-faculty," means that the mind illuminates purity and becomes aware of knowing as a mistake. All karmic wisdoms undergo enlightenment and are suddenly fused. They disappear from view, self-erased. There is no longer a subjectively knowing mind capable of reflection on the traces of self-erasure, or subjective erasing awareness. Only this enlightened mind exists, completely alone, just like the life-faculty, which does not have an "other." It is like ice being melted in hot water: there is no separate ice such that one could know the ice is melted. Only the hot water remains by itself: there is no "other thing." The awareness that selfhood is a mistake, and that there is no separate self to be known as a "self," is the same sort of case.

From here to the conclusion of the discussion of the Four Traces, even though the text only mentions this fact in regards to the trace of self, the other traces should be considered as included. If you want to make the discussion complete, it should say: "When you are aware that selfhood is a mistake, there is no separate self that can be known as self; when you are aware that 'person' is a mistake, there is no separate person that can be known as person. When you are aware that 'sentient being' is a mistake, there is no separate sentient being that can be known as sentient being. Only the mind that is aware of something like a life-faculty singularly remains." This meaning is the same as the above text.

Above, the terms "witnessing," "cognition," and "realization" are applied respectively to "self," "person," and "sentient being." It is only when we get to this point that it says "awareness/enlightenment."[16] This is because all the karmic wisdoms of witnessing, cognition, and realization are suddenly fused on the experience of enlightenment. It has already been determined that witnessing, cognition, and realization are mistakes, so in the concluding sentences they are called "traces," and depending upon the mind of enlightenment they can be extinguished. The Buddha would also like to categorize the mind of enlightenment as a mistake, and so in the conclusion it is also called a "trace." The text says: "Good sons, if the mind illuminates all awarenesses, then all are defilement. Since that which is known by awareness is not separate from defilement, it is called 'trace of life.'" "All awarenesses" refers to all the karmic wisdoms of witnessing, cognition, and realization. As for "that which is known by awareness," awareness (*chiao/kak*, "enlightenment" 覺) is "illumination." "That which is known" are "all the awarenesses." This means that even though one is aware that all the awarenesses of witnessing, cognition, and realization are defilement, since this mind of awareness is also defilement, it is called "trace of life."

Self, person, sentient being and life are also called "traces," are also called "karma" and are also called "wisdom." "Wisdom" is a synonym for "nature." "Karma" is a synonym for "trace." The relationship between "trace" and "karma" and between "wisdom" and "nature" is just like that between the words *yen* and *mu* (眼 and 目; synonymous logographs that mean "eye"). When nature arises, it is "trace," when it is "already" it is called "karma." The "already-ness" of karma is none other than the "trace" of the arising of nature. "Luminous stillness" is nature, "perfect clarity" is wisdom. The "perfect clarity" that is "wisdom" is none other than the "luminous stillness" that is nature. In terms of self the author says "witness"; in terms of "person" he says "cognize"; in terms of sentient being he says "realize"; and in terms of life he says "awareness." In terms of witnessing, cognition, realization, and awareness, we can know the mistakes one after the other, but still be unable to let go of our discriminations and sever our bonds. Therefore they are called "karma" and "trace." If, one by one, we let go of our discriminations and sever our bonds, then the so-called witnessing, cognition, realization, and awareness will be perfectly clear in their essence. Severing expectation and dependence is only called wisdom; it is not called "karma." It is only called nature; it is not called "trace."

The Errors that Result from Not Perceiving the Action of the Four Traces

[Sutra (#91)] [*T* 842.17.919c17; *HPC* 7.162c16] ▼

善男子、末世衆生不了四相、雖經多劫勤苦修道、但名有
爲。終不能成一切聖果。是故名爲正法末世。

Good sons, sentient beings of the degenerate age do not perceive the Four Traces, and though they may struggle through many *kalpas* of difficult practice while cultivating the Way, it is still nothing but conditioned existence. They are ultimately incapable of consummating the fruits of sagehood. Therefore it is called the age of degeneration of the true dharma.

[*Translator's note*: If we translate this line in this context, it should be rendered as it is: "age of the degeneration of the true dharma." As Kihwa will explain in his commentary just below, he thinks this line is out of place here. Later on, he will also explain why he understands it to mean something like "the true dharma in the degenerate age." In his amended version of the text, Kihwa has moved this line down to sutra passage #95.]

[Kihwa] [*HPC* 7.162c19]

The last sentence, which starts with "Therefore (是故 . . .)," should come later in the text, after "not fall into mistaken views (不墮邪見)."[17] If it is taken out, then the sentence "they are finally incapable of consummating the fruits of sagehood (終不能成一切聖果)" can be linked together with the next sentence that says "Why? Since they regard these traces of self to be nirvana (何以故？認一切我爲涅槃)."

The Subtlety of the Traces

[Sutra (#92)] [*T* 842.17.919c19; *HPC* 7.162c21]

何以故？認一切我爲涅槃故、有證有悟名成就故。譬如有
人認賊爲子。其家財寶終不成就。何以故？有我愛者亦愛
涅槃、我愛根爲涅槃相。有憎我者亦憎生死、不知愛者眞
生死故別憎生死。名不解脫。

Why? Because they regard these traces of self to be nirvana, and they regard their witnessing and cognition to be consummation [of enlightenment]. It is like a man who mistakes a thief for his son. His family's holdings can never be secure. Why? Because the lover of self also loves nirvana, and takes the suppression of the root of self-love as the characteristic of nirvana. The hater of self also hates *saṃsāra*, and not knowing that it is the attached love itself that is actually *saṃsāra*, he discriminates *saṃsāra* and hates it. This is called "non-liberation."

[*Translator's note*: Within the structure of the original Chinese, it would be quite possible to render this last line as "he singles out *saṃsāra* for disdain, calling it 'nonliberation,'" with the implication that the hater of *saṃsāra* is disparaging *saṃsāra* in particular. But in Kihwa's subsequent commentary, he takes the phrase "nonliberation" as a kind of summary description of both the love of nirvana and the hate of *saṃsāra* that are described in this passage. I am not sure if I agree with Kihwa's interpretation here, but in order to have his commentary make sense, I have translated it the way that he sees it, and have also punctuated the Chinese sentence according to this interpretation.]

[Kihwa] [*HPC* 7.163c4]

The words "hater of self" in this context are used in contrast to the above "lover of self." As for the words "nonliberation:" there is firm attachment to trace of self inside, and the complementary manifestation of love and hatred outside. The internal and external [delusions] exacerbate each other and they bring about nonliberation. We do not even need to discuss true and false, good and evil, sacred and profane, suffering and pleasure. The mere sentiments of attraction and aversion and selecting and rejecting, are nothing but the pair of love and hatred. It is this pair that is permeated by ignorance, embraced by the trace of self, and that results in the inability for self-liberation.

[Sutra (#93)] [*T* 842.17.919c23; *HPC* 7.163a10]

云 何 當 知 法 不 解 脱 ？ 善 男 子 、 彼 末 世 衆 生 習 菩 提 者 以 己 微
證 爲 自 清 淨 。 由 未 能 盡 我 相 根 本 。 若 復 有 人 讚 歎 彼 法 即 生
歡 喜 便 欲 濟 度 。 若 復 誹 謗 彼 所 得 者 、 便 生 瞋 恨 。 則 知 我 相
堅 固 執 持 潜 伏 藏 識 。 遊 戲 諸 根 、 曾 不 間 斷 。 善 男 子 、 彼 修
道 者 不 除 我 相 、 是 故 不 能 入 清 淨 覺 。 善 男 子 、 若 知 我 空 無
毀 我 者 。 有 我 説 法 我 未 斷 故 、 衆 生 壽 命 亦 復 如 是 。

How can you know this dharma as "nonliberation?"[18] Good sons, these sentient beings of the degenerate age who are practicing *bodhi* regard the ego's infinitesimal perception as their own purity, and are therefore unable to penetrate to the root of the self-trace. If someone praises their [mistaken] dharma, then they will be over-joyed and immediately try to save him. But if someone criticizes their attainments, they will be filled with anger and resentment. Hence, you can know that the trace of self is being firmly held to; it is concealed in the store consciousness and is playing freely throughout the faculties without interruption. Good sons, if these practioners of the Way do not remove the trace of self, they will be unable to enter pure enlightenment. Good sons, if the emptiness of self is known, there can be no "eliminator of self." If, holding to self, you expound this dharma, it is because you have not yet elimi-nated self. It is the same with "sentient being" and "life."

[Kihwa] [*HPC* 7.163a19]
These two separate sentences have been placed together: "If the empti-ness of self is known, there can be no eliminator of self. If, holding to self, you expound this dharma, it is because you have not yet elimi-nated self." If we filled in the whole passage, it should say: "If the emp-tiness of self is known, there can be no eliminator of self. If there is someone who would eliminate self, it is because the self is not yet empty. If you eliminate the trace of self, there is no self to teach the dharma. If there is a self to teach the dharma, it means that the self has not been eliminated." Now, the first part has been put up to the beginning but also left at the end. The last has been moved to the end but also left at the beginning. In the matching of the two phrases together in this way, we can see the author's skill in making a point concise.

Delusion in Regard to One's Own Attainment

[Sutra (#94)] [*T* 842.17.920a2; *HPC* 7.163b2]

善男子、末世眾生說病爲法。是故名爲可憐愍者。雖勤精
進增益諸病、是故不能入清淨覺。善男子、末世眾生不了
四相、以如來解及所行處爲自修行、終不成就。或有眾生
未得謂得、未證謂證、見勝進者心生嫉妒。由彼眾生未斷
我愛、是故不能入清淨覺。

Good sons, sentient beings of the degenerate age [mistakenly] understand these afflictions to be the dharma. Therefore they are called "the pitiable." Even though they struggle with great effort, they merely exacerbate their various afflictions, and therefore are unable to enter pure enlightenment. Good sons, sentient beings of the degenerate age do not discern the Four Traces, and erroneously taking the understanding and practice of the Tathāgata to be their own practice, they ultimately do not accomplish enlightenment. Thus there are sentient beings who understand nonattainment to be attainment and regard nonrealization as realization. When they see an adept practitioner, they are filled with jealousy. It is exactly because these sentient beings do not sever their love of self that they are unable to enter pure enlightenment.

[Kihwa] [*HPC* 7.163b9]

From the beginning of this chapter up until this point, the author has explained in depth the defilement of the view of self. He has repeatedly discussed it as the hindrance to enlightenment. In the section below, he explains the marvelous method of completely eliminating the hindrances of delusion.

Overcoming These Hindrances and Finding a Teacher

[Sutra (#95)] [*T* 842.17.920a8; *HPC* 7.163b12]▼

善男子、末世眾生希望成道無令求悟。惟益多聞增長我見
。但當精勤降伏煩惱起大勇猛。未得令得未斷令斷。貪瞋
愛慢諂曲嫉妒對境不生、彼我恩愛一切寂滅。佛說是人漸
次成就。求善知識不墮邪見。

Good sons, sentient beings of the degenerate age hope for buddhahood but do not exert themselves to achieve awakening; they merely extend their intellectual knowledge, further enhancing the view of self. What they *should* do is just endeavor to subdue the afflictions and arouse great courage: attain what they have not attained, sever what they have not severed. Not allowing the

greed, anger, love, pride, flattery, perversion, jealousy, and envy
that are directed at the objective realm to arise, and extinguishing
all love and attachment to self and other—I call these people "gradually consummated." Finding a Genuine Teacher,[19] you will not fall
into mistaken views.

[Kihwa] [*HPC* 7.163b18]
The sentence mentioned earlier, "Therefore it is called the age of the
degeneration of the true dharma (是故名爲正法末世),"[20] which came
after "they will finally be incapable of perfecting all sagely fruits (終不
能成一切聖果)," should be placed here directly after "not fall into
mistaken views (不墮邪見)." It has been mistakenly placed in that earlier location. When the words "age of the degeneration of the true
dharma (正法末世)" are located there, it is like having sawdust in your
eye. When they are placed here, it is like adding a flower to a silk bro-
cade. The text should say: "Finding a genuine teacher, you will not fall
into mistaken views, therefore it is called the true dharma [in the] degenerate age (求善知識不墮邪見是故名爲正法末世)."

What then, is the meaning of "true dharma"? This is the time when
the true dharma is proliferated. "Degenerate age" is the time when
wrong teachings flourish. Yet, even if this were the age of the true
dharma, if you fall into mistaken views, then it is called "the degenerate
age of the true dharma." And even if this is the degenerate age, if you
do not fall into mistaken views, then it is called "the true dharma in the
degenerate age." Sentient beings of the degenerate age do not seek enlightenment, they only seek to extend their knowledge, which further
develops the view of self—namely, "falling into mistaken views."

Get rid of pride and insolence and seek a genuine teacher. If you depend
upon what he sets up for you and struggle courageously, desire and
repugnance will not come to life; love and attachment will vanish. This
is what is meant by "not falling into mistaken views." Therefore it is
called the "true dharma in the degenerate age." This is how one may
"gradually accomplish enlightenment."

[Sutra (#96)] [*T* 842.17.920a12; *HPC* 7.163c9]

若於所求別生憎愛、則不能入清淨覺海。

But if you discriminate, and have a special feeling of attraction or
aversion regarding the [teacher] you are seeking, you will be unable
to enter the ocean of pure enlightenment.

[Kihwa] [*HPC* 7.163c11]
If you seek a genuine teacher and struggle courageously, then you
are already free from the mistakes of excessive intellectuality and
heightened ego. Yet if you discriminate and distinguish attraction and

aversion while you are looking for the genuine teacher, then you will not be able to avoid the hindrances that come from the view of self, and you will be unable to enter enlightenment. From earlier in the text where it says "not able to enter," "not able to accomplish," "not able to consummate," and "not able to be liberated," down to here, the word "not" (不) appears nine times, while "gradually consummated (漸次 成就)" appears once. To the bodhisattva's single question about delusion, affliction, and not entering, the Buddha explains over and over like this about the traces of self, hindrances to enlightenment, and mistaken thinking. When he says "consummated," he only says it once, and also says "gradually." From this we can see that the traces of self, hindrances to enlightenment and wrong thinking are tenacious and difficult to remove. As for the "ocean of enlightenment," if you do not struggle courageously to completely eliminate the traces of self, you will be unable to enter.

The *Gāthā*

[Sutra (#97)] [*T* 842.17.920a13; *HPC* 7.163c22]

爾時世尊、欲重宣此義而説偈言：

淨業汝當知　一切諸衆生
皆由執我愛　無始妄流轉
未除四種相　不得成菩提
愛憎生於心　諂曲存諸念
是故多迷悶　不能入覺城
若能歸悟刹　先去貪瞋癡
法愛不存心　漸次可成就
我身本不有　憎愛何由生
此人求善友　終不墮邪見
所求別生心　究竟非成就

Then the World-Honored One, desiring to reiterate the gist of this, spoke a verse. He said:

Purifier of Karma, you should know
That because of attachment to and love of self
All sentient beings
Deludedly transmigrate without beginning.
Not removing four kinds of traces
They cannot accomplish *bodhi*.
Since love and hatred arise in the mind
And flattery and perversion remain in all thoughts
There is much delusion and grief;

You are unable to enter the citadel of enlightenment.
If you are able to return to the enlightened realm,
First leave all desire, hatred, and ignorance.
When the dharma of attraction does not remain in the mind
You can gradually accomplish enlightenment.
The self and body originally do not exist:
How can attraction and aversion arise?
If this person seeks a Genuine Teacher
He will never fall into evil views.
But if "something separate to be sought" arises in his mind
There will ultimately be no consummation of enlightenment.

[Kihwa] [*HPC* 7.164a7]

It is due to attachment to the trace of self that we are deluded and unable to enter enlightenment. If you realize there is no single thing to love, you can gradually accomplish enlightenment. If you do not arise sentiments in regards to the teacher, then you are able to reach Peerless Correct Equal Enlightenment.

10

Universal Enlightenment Bodhisattva

[Kihwa] [*HPC* 7.164a12]

When light is great and illuminating everywhere it is called "universal." Having been awakened and shining universally is called "enlightenment." Thus "Universal Enlightenment" implies the lustrous shining of the moon of wisdom, and the radiant opening of the flower of compassion, which illumines dark byways and awakens the deluded masses. Why does this bodhisattva follow up Purifier of Hindrances with another question? From Vajragarbha down to Voice of Discernment the discussions have worked one by one toward the dissolution of the coarse hindrances that are the Five Obscurations. The chapter of Purifier of Karma fully exhausts the source of affliction, severing completely the subtle delusions that constitute the Four Traces. Once the coarse and subtle defilements are eliminated, the great wisdom of Perfect Enlightenment shines brightly, such that it is able to arouse great compassion in order to universally enlighten the deluded multitude.

This bodhisattva teaches the sentient beings of the degenerate age by asking about the methods for guiding others. The Tathāgata has them seek someone with correct insight so that they do not fall into mistaken views, and this will be the method for guiding the beings of the degenerate age. The earlier bodhisattvas have all raised questions for the whole assembly inquiring about the methods of advancement through practice. But now Universal Enlightenment only asks to have the consciousnesses of the bodhisattvas evanesce and attain great tranquillity, and does not ask about the methods for advancement through practice. He only asks for the sake of the sentient beings regarding the method by which they should be guided. The attainment of "great tranquillity" is through the extinction of hindrances and the manifestation of enlightenment. He questions about the methods for awakening beings in

order to universally enlighten the deluded multitude. This is why he
follows Purifier of Karma with another question. My verse:

> The Right View seeks to be created as well as to create,
> The equalization of enmity and affection, neither "yes"
>   nor "no."
> At the place of the arousal of the Four Minds, the light of
>   wisdom is renewed;
> The blind masses of the Great Earth, together have the
>   veils removed.

The Question of Universal Enlightenment:
The Curing of Maladies

[Sutra (#98)] [*T* 842.17.920a25; *HPC* 7.164b6]

於是普覺菩薩在大衆中、即從座起。頂禮佛足、右繞三匝
。長跪叉手而白佛言：大悲世尊。快說禪病令諸菩薩得未
曾有。心意蕩然獲大安隱。

Then the bodhisattva Universal Enlightenment arose from his seat
in the great assembly. He bowed to the Buddha's feet and circumambulated three times to the right. He then knelt down with his
hands clasped and addressed the Buddha, saying: "Greatly Compassionate World-Honored One. You have clearly explained the
meditation maladies, allowing the bodhisattvas to attain that which
they had not yet experienced. Their consciousnesses have been completely stilled and they have attained great tranquillity."

[Kihwa] [*HPC* 7.164b10]

The Buddha is like the king of doctors, and the sentient beings are
like sick children. The children take their medicine, but it causes a bad
reaction. Their minds are still congested and their energies are still
unstable. The king devises numerous methods that he applies according
to the situation. The sicknesses now removed, they experience release.
Their minds are opened wide and their bodies are settled. They can for
the first time be called "great men" and handle their part of the family
business. From Vajragarbha on down, all the bodhisattvas have addressed
the Buddha with words of praise. But nonetheless their speech has borne
with it an element of doubt, since each of them has had something
regarding which he was not satisfied. But here, Universal Enlightenment uses praising words only. This is because all of the bodhisattva's
doubts have been completely removed and they have entered enlightenment. They will not again conjecture in a doubtful way.

[Sutra (#99)] [T 842.17.920a28; HPC 7.164b17]

世尊、末世眾生去佛漸遠賢聖隱伏、邪法增熾。使諸眾生
求何等人？依何等法？行何等行？除去何病？云何發心令
彼羣盲不墮邪見？作是語已、五體投地。如是三請終而復
始。

"World-Honored One, as the sentient beings of the degenerate age
become increasingly removed from the Buddha, the sages and
worthies conceal themselves, while the mistaken dharma grows
and spreads. What kind of person should the sentient beings seek?
On what kind of teachings should they rely? What kind of practice
should they carry out? What kind of maladies should we remove,
and what kind of resolution should we make, so as to prevent the
blind multitude from falling into mistaken views?" Having said
this, he prostrated himself to the ground. He asked this question
three times in succession.

[Kihwa] [HPC 7.164b22]
Having remedied one sickness, they will now treat another sickness.
While the doctor-king is still in the world, he can use the methods that
he has well-tested in application to other illnesses. But when the doctor-
king is gone, mistaken teachings grow and spread, and the diseases of
the beings transform and multiply. One cannot treat all of them with a
single remedy. Therefore he must teach multiple methods for treatment, and so the bodhisattva asks this question for the sentient beings
of the degenerate age.

[Sutra (#100)] [T 842.17.920b4; HPC 7.164c3]

爾時世尊告普覺菩薩言：善哉、善哉。善男子、汝等乃能
諮問如來如是修行、能施末世一切眾生無畏道眼、令彼眾
生得成聖道。汝今諦聽、當為汝説。時普覺菩薩奉教歡喜
、及諸大眾默然而聽。

Then the World-Honored One, addressing the bodhisattva Universal Enlightenment, said: "Excellent, excellent! Good Son, you have
been able to question the Tathāgata on this kind practice that is
able to impart to all sentient beings the fearless Eye of the Way and
cause them to attain the sagely Path. Now listen well, and I shall
teach you." The bodhisattva Universal Enlightenment received this
teaching with great joy. Those in the great assembly became silent
and listened.

[Kihwa] [HPC 7.164c9]
Since the further clarification of expedient means for the sentient
beings of the degenerated age is also the Buddha's original intent, he
praises this question.

Finding a Genuine Teacher

[Sutra (#101)] [*T* 842.17.920b9; *HPC* 7.164c11]

善男子、末世眾生將發大心、求善知識。欲修行者、當求
一切正知見人、心不住相、不著聲聞緣覺境界、雖現塵勞
心恒清淨。示有諸過、讚歎梵行、不令眾生入不律儀。求
如是人即得成就阿耨多羅三藐三菩提。

Good sons, sentient beings of the degenerate age must arouse "great mind" and seek Genuine Teachers. Those who want to practice should seek out only someone with correct insight, whose thoughts do not abide in characteristics, who is not attached to the realms of the *arhat*s and *pratyekabuddhas*, and whose mind is constantly pure even while manifesting the world's afflictions. Even while pointing out your various faults, he praises your *brahmacarya*,[1] and prevents you from breaking the precepts. If you find this kind of person, you can attain *anuttarā-samyak-saṃbodhi*.

[Kihwa] [*HPC* 7.164c17]

To cleave to the Way and cultivate the real you must first establish your will. You must vow to attain great enlightenment and to save all sentient beings. The arousal of this kind of resolution is called "great mind." One who practices himself and teaches others, who is skillful at knowing what to encourage and what to admonish, and who has no confusion about what is the right or wrong course, is called a "Genuine Teacher." When doubts are completely cleared away, the eye of right transmission is clear and bright. This kind of insight that does not slip into nihilism or eternalism is called "correct insight." When the various dharmas of conditioned and unconditioned, worldling and sage, are contained together without attachment, it is called "not abiding in characteristics." Not abiding in the unconditioned, one does not slip into the view of nihilism. Not abiding in the conditioned, one does not slip into the view of eternalism. This is why it is called "correct insight." If you seek this kind of person and engage in this kind of practice, then you will not stray onto other paths, and you will accord with the nature of enlightenment. Thus, you will accomplish *bodhi*.

[Sutra (#102)] [*T* 842.17.920b13; *HPC* 7.165a4] ▼

末世眾生見如是人、應當供養不惜身命。彼善知識四威儀
中常現清淨乃至示現種種過患、心無憍慢。況復摶財妻子
眷屬。若善男子於彼善友不起惡念、即能究竟成就正覺。
心華發明照十方刹。

Sentient beings of the degenerate age who meet this kind of person, should make offerings to him, not sparing body or life. This Genuine Teacher constantly manifests purity throughout the four postures.[2] Although he shows you your various errors and afflictions, his mind lacks pride, even as far as holding on to property, wife, children and retainers.[3] Good Sons, if you do not arouse any negative feelings toward this Good Friend, you will ultimately be able to accomplish Correct Enlightenment. Your mind-flower will blossom, illuminating the worlds of the ten directions.

[Kihwa] [*HPC* 7.165a10]

The part of the sentence starting with "even as far as (況復)" should be located right after the line "not sparing body or life (不惜身命)." The passage from "this Genuine Teacher (彼善知識)" up to "his mind lacks pride (心無憍慢)" naturally fits to the passage "Goods Sons, if . . . (若善男子)."

[*Translator's note*: Therefore, the passage should read as follows:

末世眾生見如是人、應當供養不惜身命、況復搏財妻子眷屬。彼善知識四威儀中常現清淨乃至示現種種過患、心無憍慢。若善男子於彼善友不起惡念、即能究竟成就正覺。心華發明照十方刹。

Sentient beings of the degenerate age who meet this kind of person, should make offerings to him, not sparing body or life, even as far as holding on to property, wife, children, and retainers. This Genuine Teacher constantly manifests purity throughout the four postures. Although he shows you your various errors and afflictions, his mind lacks pride. Good sons, if you do not arouse any negative feelings toward this Good Friend, you will ultimately be able to accomplish correct enlightenment. Your mind-flower will blossom, illuminating the worlds of the ten directions.]

[Kihwa]

Since there is no place where the sagely nature does not penetrate, he fully knows all the expedient means, both the pleasant and the unpleasant ones that worldly discrimination cannot fathom. That is why he has no reason to be proud. The seeds of *bodhi* take root in the mind-ground. Nourished by the rain of the dharma, they bear forth flower and fruit, whose fragrance permeates numberless realms and whose radiance illuminates the ten directions. Hence he says "Your mind-flower will blossom, illuminating the worlds of the ten directions." This answers the first question.

The Four Maladies

[Sutra (#103)] [*T* 842.17.920b19; *HPC* 7.165a17]

The Contrivance Malady

善男子、彼善知識所證妙法應離四病。云何四病？一者作
病。若復有人作如是言、我於本心作種種行、欲求圓覺。
彼圓覺性非作得故説名爲病。

Good Sons, the subtle dharma that is actualized by this Genuine
Teacher should be free from the Four Maladies. What are the Four
Maladies? The first is the malady of "contrivance." Say, for example,
there is someone who says "based on my original mind I shall carry
out various practices" and wants to achieve Perfect Enlightenment.
Since the nature of Perfect Enlightenment is not something that
can be attained by contrivance, it is called a "malady."

[*Translator's note*: "Contrivance" constitutes my rendering of *tso/chak*
作 in the present context. Other possible renderings might be "creation"
or "production," but Kihwa specifically defines the meaning below as
"doing with intention." It is in order to include the "intentional" aspect
of the meaning that I have chosen "contrivance." Someone thinks that
by his own special abilities and efforts (study, meditation, ritual, special
techniques, associating with spiritual people, doing good deeds, etc.)
that he can attain enlightenment. While a person's efforts cannot be
said to be meaningless, one should not expect that any arbitrary program of practice will necessarily lead to enlightenment. Luk translates
as "the illness of action."]

The Naturalist Malady

[Sutra (#104)]

二者任病。若復有人作如是言。我等今者不斷生死不求涅
槃。涅槃生死無起滅念。任彼一切隨諸法性、欲求圓覺。
彼圓覺性非任有故、説名爲病。

The second is the "naturalist" malady. Say, for example, there is
someone who says, "We should presently neither cut off *saṃsāra*
nor seek nirvana. *Saṃsāra* and nirvana actually lack any conception
of arising and ceasing. We should just naturally go along with the
various natures of reality," and wants to achieve Perfect Enlightenment. Since the nature of Perfect Enlightenment does not come about
through "accepting things as they are," this is called a "malady."

[*Translator's note*: I translate *jen/im* (任) as "naturalism" but only after strongly considering the usage of the term "acceptance" as it is interpreted in many modern/Western mental therapy and twelve-step programs to imply "accepting life on life's terms" or "accepting things as they are." This approach can be compared to a caricaturized "Taoist" view of Lao-tzu or Chuang-tzu. Being natural, just going along with things as they are, not trying to manipulate events—*wu-wei*. The cultivation of such an attitude could certainly be seen as a praiseworthy level of spiritual attainment. But the Buddha says that his enlightenment is not to be met in this way. Luk translates as "the illness of letting alone."]

The Stopping Malady

[Sutra (#105)]

三者止病。若復有人作如是言。我今自心永息諸念得一切
性寂然平等、欲求圓覺。彼圓覺性非止合故、説名爲病。

The third is the "stopping" malady. Say, for example, there is someone who says "from my present thought, I shall permanently stop all thought and thus apprehend the cessation and equanimity of all natures" and wants to achieve Perfect Enlightenment. Since the nature of Perfect Enlightenment is not met through the stopping of thoughts, it is called a "malady."

The Annihilation Malady

[Sutra (#106)]

四者滅病。若復有人作如是言。我今永斷一切煩惱、身心
畢竟空無所有、何況根塵虛妄境界一切永寂、欲求圓覺。
彼圓覺性非寂相故、説名爲病。離四病者則知清淨。作是
觀者名爲正觀。若他觀者名爲邪觀。

The fourth is the "annihilation" malady. Say, for example, there is someone who says "I will now permanently annihilate all defilements. Body and mind are ultimately empty, lacking anything. How much more should all the false realms of the sense organs and their objects be permanently erased?" and seeks Perfect Enlightenment. Since the characteristic of the nature of Perfect Enlightenment is not annihilation, it is called a "malady." When you are free from the Four Maladies, you will be aware of purity. The making of this observation is called "correct understanding." Any other observation is called "mistaken understanding."

[*Translator's note*: The annihilation malady is representative of a common tendency in Buddhism, especially Zen Buddhism. One might also call it the "emptiness" sickness. Holding inappropriately to an attitude of nonexistence of self and world can result in a dangerous nihilistic attitude. Luk translates as "the illness of elimination."]

[Kihwa] [*HPC* 7.165b10]

"Contrivance" means "doing with intention" and implies the creation of all good dharmas. "Stopping" means "stopping of thought" and implies the cessation of all mistaken thoughts. "Naturalism" means "letting things follow their course" and implies going along with all that the mind creates, without grasping to "contrivance" or "stopping." "Annihilation" means "extinction" and implies the destruction of defilements through the two emptinesses of mind and objects. Contrivance, stopping, naturalism, and annihilation are attitudes in which the practitioner should not get stuck. As soon as there is something to which the mind gets attached, then there is an obstruction to enlightenment, and so it is called a malady.

Now the word "should" of "should be free from . . ."[4] is a term indicating uncertain expectation. The insights of the Genuine Teacher, already being correct, *should* be free from the Four Maladies. But if he still has some attachment to one of the four views, he cannot be completely relied upon. Therefore the text says "should." The words near the end of this passage that say "when you are free of the Four Maladies you will be aware of purity" also carry the nuance that there are some who are not yet free.

Within the nature of Perfect Enlightenment there are no traces whatsoever of the Four Maladies. Once there is attachment to even one of them, purity is denied. One method can be trusted, but the other cannot. The ability to clearly discern what is acceptable and what is not, is called "correct insight." If it is not, then it is "mistaken." This answers the second question.

Interacting with the Genuine Teacher

[Sutra (#107)] [*T* 842.17.920c4; *HPC* 7.165b24]

善男子、末世衆生欲修行者應當盡命供養善友事善知識。彼善知識欲來親近應斷憍慢。若復遠離應斷瞋恨。現逆順境猶如虛空。了知身心畢竟平等、與諸衆生同體無異。如此修行方入圓覺。

Good sons, sentient beings of the degenerate age should exhaust their life energies in making offerings to Good Friends and serving Genuine Teachers. If the Genuine Teacher becomes close and familiar with you, you should not be proud. If he is distant, you should not be resentful. The states of unpleasantness and pleasantness are just like the empty sky. Fully realize that body and mind are ultimately equalized and that you share the same essence with all sentient beings without difference. If you practice in this way you will enter Perfect Enlightenment.

[Kihwa] [*HPC* 7.165c6]

When the mind has attachment and aversion, it cannot harmonize with enlightenment. If you want to experience this enlightenment, then you must discard these sentiments. Sometimes agreeable, sometimes disagreeable, a mind without attraction or aversion apprehends self and other to be of the same body without difference. If you practice like this then you will enter Perfect Enlightenment. This answers the third question.

[Sutra (#108)] [*T* 842.17.920c8; *HPC* 7.165c10]

善男子、末世衆生不得成道由有無始自他憎愛一切種子、故未解脱。若復有人觀彼怨家如己父母、心無有二即除諸病。於諸法中自他憎愛亦復如是。

Good sons, when sentient beings of the degenerate age are unable to accomplish the Way, it is because of the presence of beginningless seeds of self and other, attraction and aversion. Therefore they are not liberated. If there is someone who looks upon his enemy as the same as his father and mother—whose mind completely lacks duality, then he will eliminate all maladies. Then within all dharmas, self and other, attraction and aversion will also be eliminated in the same way.

[Kihwa] [*HPC* 7.165c15]

All maladies originate in views such as those of attraction and aversion, affection and resentment. When self and other are both forgotten and the mind lacks duality, then the maladies are removed. This answers the fourth question.

[Sutra (#109)] [*T* 842.17.920c11; *HPC* 7.165c17]

善男子、末世衆生欲求圓覺應當發心作如是言。盡於虛空一切衆生我皆令入究竟圓覺。於圓覺中無取覺者、除彼我人一切諸相。如是發心不墮邪見。

Good sons, all sentient beings of the degenerate age who want to seek Perfect Enlightenment should make their resolution, saying the following: "I vow to cause every sentient being throughout the universe to enter the ultimate Perfect Enlightenment." Within that Perfect Enlightenment there is no attachment to "enlightenment" nor are there any of the traces of self, person, and so on. If you make this kind of resolve, you will not fall into mistaken views.

[Kihwa] [*HPC* 7.165c21]

Saving all beings is called "vast, great mind." Causing them to enter enlightenment is called "foremost mind." Not attaching to enlightenment is called "constant mind." Removing the traces of self, and so on, is called "normal ('not-inverted') mind." When they begin to make their resolve, their minds are uncertain, and if they do not encounter the Tathāgata's path of correct cultivation, they cannot avoid falling into the pit of mistaken views. They should transcend the four minds and thus avoid slipping into mistaken views. This answers the fifth question.

The *Gāthā*

[Sutra (#110)] [*T* 842.17.920c15; *HPC* 7.166a2]

爾時世尊、欲重宣此義而說偈言：

普覺汝當知　末世諸眾生
欲求善知識　應當求正見
心遠二乘者　法中除四病
謂作止任滅　親近無憍慢
遠離無瞋恨　見種種境界
心當生希有　還如佛出世
不犯非律儀　戒根永清淨
度一切眾生　究竟入圓覺
無彼我人相　常依止智慧
便得超邪見　證覺般涅槃

Then the World-Honored One, wanting to restate the gist of this, delivered a verse, saying:

Universal Enlightenment, you should know
That sentient beings of the degenerate age
Who desire to find a Genuine Teacher
Must look for one with the Right View
Whose mind is far removed from the Two Vehicles
And in regard to the Dharma has removed the Four Maladies,
Which are called contrivance, stopping, naturalism, and annihi-
　　lation.
If he becomes intimate with you, don't be proud
And if he is distant, don't be resentful.
Observing various realms, your mind will then produce the
　　miraculous.

And if you leave home like the Buddha
Do not do what is contrary to the precepts.
With the root of the precepts constantly pure,
You save all sentient beings
So that they ultimately enter Perfect Enlightenment.
Free from the traces such as "self" and "person"
You constantly rest in wisdom.
You are naturally able to transcend of mistaken views
Actualizing enlightenment and *parinirvāṇa*.

[Kihwa] [*HPC* 7.166a10] ▼

The two phrases starting from "Do not do (不犯)" are originally connected in the main text as part of the answer to the first question.[5] But here in the *gāthā* they are attached to the part that constitutes the answer regarding the removal of the maladies, and thus do not fit. They should be placed right after the line which says "whose mind is far removed from the Two Vehicles (心遠二乘者)." Thus the *gāthā* should read:

應當求正見心遠二乘者
不犯非律儀戒根永清淨

Must look for one with the Right View
Whose mind is far removed from the Two Vehicles
Who does not break the precepts
And whose root of the precepts is constantly pure.

This seems right if we check it against the main text, which says: "and who is not attached to the realms of the *arhat*s and *pratyekabuddha*s, and whose mind is constantly pure even while manifesting the world's afflictions. Even while pointing out your various faults, he praises your *brahmacarya*, and prevents you from breaking the precepts."

The phrases "whose minds is far removed from the Two Vehicles," "does not break the precepts," and "precepts pure, removing sickness" describe one who has the Right View. "Making the resolve" means that one should seek this kind of teacher who possesses the Right View, submit to him, and practice as he instructs. Just look at yourself and see whether or not you are sincere. Serve that Good Friend whether it be in the condition of intimacy or distance. If he keeps his distance, do not get angry. If he is cordial, do not be overjoyed. When your mind lacks "agreeable" and "disagreeable," both come as surprises. Arousing Buddha-like thoughts, practice like this, saving sentient beings. With your mind removed from "self" and "person," constantly resting in wisdom, you easily leap over mistaken views and actualize nirvana.

11

Perfect Enlightenment Bodhisattva

[Kihwa] [*HPC* 7.166b1]
The condition of virtue being replete and transformation being carried out virtually everywhere is called "Perfect." Knowledge illuminating virtually everything and virtually every dharma being realized is called "Enlightenment." "Perfect Enlightenment" means that the enlightenment of self and other are completed such that they are identical with innate enlightenment—that there is no place that enlightenment has not fully permeated. Why does this bodhisattva ask another question after Universal Enlightenment Bodhisattva? Even though the questions asked by Universal Enlightenment have resulted in the transformation of beings, this transformation has not been pervasive. Since the transformation has not been pervasive, we know that their realization has also not been complete. Therefore, the bodhisattva asks again for the sake of the sentient beings about the methods of transformation. The Tathāgata responds with a special teaching of expedient means, introducing the three retreat periods in order to finally bring all of the beings back together to Perfect Enlightenment. After this, there will be no realization not completed and no transformation that is not pervasive. Actualization and transformation both reach their fullest extent, with no place where they are not completed. This is why Universal Enlightenment has followed with another question. My verse:

> When the wind stops, the waves are stilled: the meditation has
> been consummated.
> The retreat is completed: then and there the person is naturally
> at peace.
> The specific and the universal[1] are practiced together, and
> although they are different paths,
> When the Buddha-state is manifested, there are not two kinds.

[Sutra (#111)] [*T* 842.17.920c27; *HPC* 7.166b15]

於是圓覺菩薩在大眾中、即從座起。頂禮佛足、右繞三匝
。長跪叉手而白佛言：大悲世尊。爲我等輩廣説淨覺種種
方便、令末世衆生有大增益。

The bodhisattva Perfect Enlightenment arose from his seat in the
great assembly, bowed his head to the Buddha's feet, and circumambulated him three times to the right. He knelt down with his
hands clasped, and addressed the Buddha, saying: "Greatly Compassionate World-Honored One, you have extensively explained
pure enlightenment for us, as well as various expedient methods.
You have allowed sentient beings of the degenerate age to prosper
greatly in their practice."

[Kihwa] [*HPC* 7.166b19]

In saying "various expedient methods" he is referring to the three
meditations and their various implementations, as well as the five questions and answers pursued in the chapter of Universal Enlightenment,
practicing by means of which one will not slip into mistaken views. It
is because there has been an enhancement of wisdom and life,[2] that he
says "prosper greatly."

Perfect Enlightenment's Question
for Those Having Difficulty in According

[Sutra (#112)] [*T* 842.17.921a1; *HPC* 7.166b23]

世尊、我等今者已得開悟。若佛滅後末世衆生未得悟者、
云何安居，修此圓覺清淨境界？此圓覺中三種淨觀以何爲
首？惟願大悲爲諸大衆及末世衆生施大饒益。作是語已、
五體投地。如是三請、終而復始。

"World-Honored One, those of us present here have already awakened. But if, after your passing away, sentient beings of the degenerate age have not yet been able to awaken, how should they
conduct meditation retreats to cultivate this pure realm of Perfect
Enlightenment? And in the practice of the three kinds of pure
meditation within Perfect Enlightenment, what are the initial
steps? I only beg for your great compassion so that you will confer
great benefit on the members of this great assembly and the
sentient beings of the degenerate age." After saying this, he prostrated fully to the ground. He asked this question three times in
succession.

[Kihwa] [*HPC* 7.166c5]

He starts off by saying, "Those of us present here have already awakened." They are resting on the ocean of enlightenment with nothing to fear. These words constitute, full, unarguable self-approval. Because the bodhisattvas are already enlightened, he does not question any further about the matter of advancement through cultivation for those at the assembly. He only asks about the methods for awakening the sentient beings of the degenerate age. This is the same as the question asked just before by Universal Enlightenment, except that he goes a bit further. The words "confer great benefit" mean he asks the Buddha to explain to those at the great assembly the means of saving sentient beings, and thus they are greatly benefited. His not asking for methods of advancement through cultivation for the members of the great assembly, is, again, because those at the assembly have already been awakened; "they have completely stilled their consciousnesses and attained great tranquillity."[3] That is why there is no question about cultivation and advancement for those in the assembly—there is only the question for the sentient beings of the degenerate age. But since the words "confer great benefit" actually imply a request to explain methods of gradual advancement for the degenerate age, the phrase "great benefit" contains two meanings.

The Buddha's Answer: Further Expedients

[Sutra (#113)] [*T* 842.17.921a6; *HPC* 7.166c16]

爾時世尊告圓覺菩薩言：善哉、善哉。善男子、汝等乃能
問於如來如是方便、以大饒益、施諸衆生。汝今諦聽、當
爲汝說。時圓覺菩薩奉教歡喜、及諸大衆默然而聽。

Then the World-Honored One, addressing the bodhisattva Perfect Enlightenment, said: "Excellent! Excellent! Good Son, you have questioned well to the Tathāgata about these kind of expedient means in order to confer great benefit on the sentient beings. Now listen well, and I shall explain for you." The bodhisattva Perfect Enlightenment received this teaching with great joy. All those in the great assembly became silent and listened.

[Kihwa] [*HPC* 7.166c21]

Going further now for those of inferior capacity, the bodhisattva requests an explanation of the preparatory practices for the site of enlightenment. Since this is also the Buddha's original intention, he is more than happy to teach.

Retreats, Ritual and Repentance

[Sutra (#114)] [*T* 842.17.921a10; *HPC* 7.166c23] ▼

善男子、一切衆生若佛住世、若佛滅後、若法末時、有諸
衆生具大乘性、信佛秘密大圓覺心、欲修行者。若在伽藍
安處徒衆有緣事故、隨分思察如我已説。若復無有他事因
緣、即建道場當立期限。若立長限、百二十日。中期百日
。下期八十日、安置淨居。若佛現在當正思惟。若佛滅後
施設形像、心存目想、生正憶念、還同如來常住之日。懸
諸幡華、經三七日、稽首十方諸佛名字、求哀懺悔。遇善
境界得心輕安、過三七日一向攝念。若經夏首三月安居、
當爲清淨菩薩止住、心離聲聞、不假徒衆。至安居日即於
佛前作如是言：我比丘比丘尼優婆塞優婆夷某甲踞菩薩乘
、修寂滅行、同入清淨實相住持。以大圓覺爲我伽藍、身
心安居平等性智。涅槃自性無繫屬故、今我敬請不依聲聞
。當於十方如來及大菩薩三月安居。爲修菩薩無上妙覺大
因緣故、不繫徒衆。善男子、此名菩薩示現安居過三期日
、隨往無礙。

Good Sons, among all sentient beings, whether it is when the Buddha
is alive, or after he has passed away, or even during the period of
the degeneration of the dharma, there are a number who have the
aptitude for Mahāyāna and who have faith in the Buddha's mysterious mind of great Perfect Enlightenment, and who want to practice it. If they are living in the temple with many other followers,
then they have numerous commitments[4] and so they should just
analyze according to the situation, as I have already taught.

On the other hand, if they are not bound by commitments then
they should erect a site of enlightenment and institute an intensive
retreat. A long-term retreat should be 120 days. A medium-length
retreat should be 100 days. A short one, 80 days, sitting quietly in a
pure environment. If the Buddha is present, then you can directly
correct your thoughts. If he has already passed away, then set up
an image of him, and letting your mind abide in the mental picture
of this image, you can bring about correct mindfulness, just the
same as when he was here. After hanging up the banners and
flowers,[5] go through a period of three weeks, making obeisance to
the names of all the Buddhas in the ten directions, repenting and
confessing all of your sins. Encountering excellent states of consciousness, your mind attains pliancy and you pass through three
weeks with your thoughts focused.

If you pass through to the beginning of the retreat, then for three
months you will abide in stillness, and carry out the pure quiet

sitting of the bodhisattvas, with your mind free from the designs of the *śrāvakas* and from involvements with other practitioners.[6] When you come to the day of the retreat, in front of the Buddha, say this: "I, *bhikṣu/bhikṣuṇī/upāsaka/upāsikā*[7] so-and-so, would board the vehicle of the bodhisattvas, cultivate their practices of cessation-extinction, and enter with them into their abiding in the pure marks of the real. I take great Perfect Enlightenment as my temple, with body and mind dwelling peacefully in the wisdom of the equality of the nature. Since the self-nature of nirvana is not restricted in any way, I now respectfully pray that I may not abide in the views of the *śrāvakas*. And I will abide for three months of quiet retreat with the tathāgatas and great bodhisattvas of the ten directions. Since I will be cultivating the bodhisattva's great causes and conditions of unsurpassed marvelous enlightenment, I will not be constrained by the limitations of the other practitioners."[8]

Good Sons, this is called "the bodhisattvas' exemplifying silent retreat." After passing through the three terms, you can practice anywhere without obstruction.

[Kihwa] [*HPC* 7.167a21]
The passage that says "you pass through three weeks with your thoughts focused (過三七日一向攝念)" should come immediately after "confessing sins (懺悔)." Trying to focus one's thoughts *after* attaining pliancy just doesn't make sense. If those "who want to practice" are presently committed to the work of teaching and enlightening those people who come to the monastery, then they should just keep up the meditations taught earlier, utilizing them according to their situation. But if you are not presently engaged in some such commitment, you should inaugurate a meditation retreat in order to cultivate these contemplations. For the first three weeks you should pay obeisance to the buddhas and practice penance. After this, fully concentrate your mind and practice like this until you encounter the excellent states of consciousness and attain pliancy of mind. If you practice without repentance, then defilement will be conditioned into your meditation. If you try to practice like this, it is difficult to attain pliancy.

It is comparable to a person dyeing clothes: if he washes the clothes thoroughly and then adds the dye, then the color will come out pure. But if he doesn't wash them the color will not be pure. So in the case of encountering excellent states of consciousness and attaining pliancy of mind, the power to strive for these is based in the three weeks of repentance. It does not come from concentrating the mind in *śamatha*. The meaning of the sentence "pass through three weeks with your thoughts focused" is that one goes for three weeks in a focused state of self-reflection and repentance. After three weeks of concentrated repentance, you abide in correct mindfulness. You should not think that you attain pliancy of mind, then concentrate your mind and abide in correct mindfulness. It should now be clear that the passage that says "you pass through three weeks with your thoughts focused" should be after "confessing sins."

Below, in the elucidation of the three kinds of meditation, each one concludes with the line that says "if it is really not one of the states of mind about which you were previously instructed, then afterwards you should not attach to it." You should understand the "excellent states of mind" just mentioned above to be the same as these later-mentioned "states of mind." In the chapter of the bodhisattva Power and Virtue Unhindered, in the passages where he taught the three kinds of meditation, he concluded each by saying "generate pliancy from within." The "pliancy of mind" taught in this chapter is the same as that "pliancy generated from within." "Pliancy" is the same as "excellent states of mind." There is nothing else new being expressed here. The "state of cessation-extinction" expressed in chapter 7 in the lines that say "they are directly enabled to produce the pliancy of cessation-extinction from within"[9] and the connected line "accordance with marvelous enlightenment and the realm of cessation and extinction" are both the same as the "excellent states" mentioned here.

"If you pass through to the beginning of the retreat" but you are not satisfied with your condition, then even though the start of the retreat is at hand, you should not just enter the retreat along with the crowd. What is required is just that each of the would-be entrants states his name and freely expresses what is in his mind, opening up the truth about his condition. If I have already "taken Perfect Enlightenment as my temple" then any place I choose to go is a "site of enlightenment." Why should it be necessary to follow the schedule of the other practitioners in order to have it considered a valid retreat? After all, the body of Perfect Enlightenment is vast, boundless without exterior, such that *yin* and *yang* still cannot embrace it. How could even all of space contain it? This being the case, then South, North, East, and West are all sites of enlightenment. Through the highways and through the byways, where can it not go? This is called the bodhisattvas' exemplification of the meditation retreat. Once your retreat is completed, then even if the summer term is not over,[10] you can go anywhere without obstruction.

Expedients for Entry into Śamatha

[Sutra (#115)] [*T* 842.17.921a28; *HPC* 7.167c7]

善男子、若彼末世修行眾生求菩薩道入三期者、非彼所聞
一切境界、終不可取。

Good Sons, if, when these practicing sentient beings of the degenerate age who seek the Way of the bodhisattvas enter the three
meditation terms, they experience meditative states that are different from those outlined [in this sutra], they should not become
attached to them.

[Kihwa] [*HPC* 7.167c10]
In the short phrase "enter the three terms" he is inferring "as I instructed you, for the first three weeks pay obeisance to the buddhas
and do penance. Having passed through three weeks with your
thoughts concentrated, you will meet with excellent mental states, and
attain pliancy" then, "if they experience meditative states that are different from those outlined in this sutra, they should not attach to them."
It seems obvious that between the phrases "enter the three terms" and
"if they experience different meditative states" he intends to imply all
the other teachings he suggested above. At this point he is just making
a general reference. He gives specific examples below.

[Sutra (#116)] [*T* 842.17.921b2; *HPC* 7.167c16]

善男子、若諸衆生修奢摩他、先取至靜不起思念。靜極便
覺。如是初靜、從於一身至一世界覺亦如是。善男子、若
覺遍滿一世界者、一世界中有一衆生起一念者、皆悉能知
。百千世界亦復如是。非彼所聞一切境界、終不可取。

Good sons, those sentient beings who will practice *śamatha* must
first grasp perfect quiescence, not allowing any cogitation to arise.
Quiescence taken to its furthest limit results directly in enlightenment. If you can have this kind of initial quiescence, then proceeding from one body, enlightenment will extend like this throughout
a whole world. Good sons, when enlightenment fully pervades a
whole world, if there is one sentient being within that world who
allows a single thought to arise, all, without exception, will know
it. The same is true in the case of a hundred thousand worlds. If it
is not one of the meditative states about which you were previously
instructed, you should not be attached to it.

[Kihwa] [*HPC* 7.167c23]
From beginning to end, the work is never separate from the two
concepts of quiescence and purity. When quiescence is brought to its
absolute, then there is purity. When purity is brought to its absolute,
one's luminosity penetrates everywhere. In this case, the meaning of
"enlightenment" is the wisdom that is free from thoughts. We say
"luminosity" because wisdom is like a clear mirror, and thoughts are
like filth. If the mirror has filth, then no matter how close you come to

it, it won't reflect anything. But if the mirror lacks filth, it reflects anything, whether it be far or near. When wisdom is not separated from
thought, you run into a wall with everything you attempt. When wisdom *is* separated from thought, the myriad dharmas illuminate each
other, and the body is the lamp of wisdom, as are countries and lands.
This is because when wisdom is purified, and clearly reflecting, there is
no obstruction between individual phenomena. The function of *śamatha*
meditation lies in the internal production of cessation-quiescent pliancy.
If the state that you experience is not this one, you should not become
attached to it.

Expedients for Entry into Samāpatti

[Sutra (#117)] [*T* 842.17.921b8; *HPC* 7.168a8]

善男子、若諸眾生修三摩鉢提、先當憶想十方如來十方世
界一切菩薩。依種種門漸次修行勤苦三昧廣發大願自熏成
種。非彼諸聞一切境界終不可取。

Good sons, those sentient beings who want to practice *samāpatti*
should first become mindful of all the tathāgatas of the ten directions and all the bodhisattvas of all the worlds in the ten directions.
Depending on their various methods they should grow by degrees
though practice, struggling against suffering towards *samādhi*,
broadly manifesting the great vow [to save sentient beings], which
in turn infuses [the store consciousness] resulting in [the production of] seeds. But if it is not one of the states about which you
were previously instructed, you should not become attached to it.

[Kihwa] [*HPC* 7.168a13]

"Various methods" is a reference to "correcting oneself and then transforming others." More precisely "various methods of practice." "Struggling against suffering toward *samādhi*" means that the reliance on the
two general aspects of self-and-then-other-improvement to apply
oneself toward the overcoming of suffering and delusion is how one
attains *samādhi*. The practitioner of the contemplation of illusion,
remembering that the buddhas and bodhisattvas have practiced like
this in their own attainment of *samādhi*, should make his vow, saying "I
will also practice like them in order to consummate *samādhi*." This kind
of mindfulness will infuse [the store consciousness] and become seeds.
The function of the contemplation of illusion is the internal generation
of great compassionate pliancy. If this is not the state that you have
attained to, you should not attach to it.

Expedients for Entry into Dhyāna

[Sutra (#118)] [*T* 842.17.921b12; *HPC* 7.168a20]

善男子、若諸衆生修於禪那先取數門、心中了知生住滅念
。分齊頭數、如是周徧四威儀中。分別念數無不了知、漸
次增進乃至得知百千世界一滴之雨。猶如目觀所受用物。
非彼所聞一切境界終不可取。

Good Sons, if these sentient beings want to practice *dhyāna*, they
must first utilize the technique of breath observance, and in the
depths of their mind become fully aware of the arising, abiding,
and cessation of each thought. They must be clear in their discrimination of the breath count and practice it pervasively during each
of the four postures. There is no limit to how far this mindfulness
of the discrimination of breaths can penetrate, as one can gradually
advance to the point where he can be aware, within the space of
one hundred thousand worlds, of the falling of a single drop of
rain, as if it were an object presented directly to him. But if it is
really not one of the states of mind about which you were previously instructed, then afterwards you should not be attached to it.

[Kihwa] [*HPC* 7.168b2]

The mind is originally perfectly bright; its radiance pervades the reality-
realm. But obstructed by conceptualization, it cannot function the way
it should. If, even when practicing quiescent mediation, the concept of
quiescence still remains, and even when practicing the contemplation
of illusion, the illusory is also not forgotten, then you must rely on
cessation meditation in order to extinguish these conceptions. It is like
the sun in the sky: there is no darkness that it does not illuminate; no
distance to which it does not shine. It is also like a wise king who has
not only subdued the outlaws of the land, but who also knows the lair
of their chieftain. Since the chieftain cannot remain in hiding, he can
no longer lay his plans for lawlessness. He is even converted into a
loyal retainer, and serves intimately at court. The country becomes a
place of tranquillity, and the people are forever after without anxiety.
In the interior and exterior, from far and near, all follow one man. The
various matters of the country are all known to this ruler.

Cessation-meditation is the same. As the merit of its practice takes
effect, the observing wisdom clearly discerns. The faculties, the body,
and the container world together become the realm of wisdom. The
coarse and subtle marks of thought have nothing that they do not fully
realize. Discriminations of the myriad dharmas all attain knowledge.
The function of cessation meditation consists in internally producing

cessation-extinction pliancy. If this is not the realm that you have attained, you should not be attached to it.

[Sutra (#119)] [*T* 842.17.921b16; *HPC* 7.168b15]

是 名 三 觀 初 首 方 便 。

These are called the introductory expedients of the three meditations.

[Kihwa] [*HPC* 7.168b16]
Even though the three meditations were taught earlier, the explanation here has gone further in order to further instruct those of middling and inferior capacities. Even if one is a fool, but he listens carefully to a detailed explanation, he too can understand. But if he doesn't make the effort, he'll never get it.

[Sutra (#120)] [*T* 842.17.921b17; *HPC* 7.168b19]

若 諸 眾 生 徧 修 三 種 勤 行 精 進 、 即 名 如 來 出 現 于 世 。

If sentient beings pervasively practice these three kinds of meditation, and keep working diligently to advance, they will be called "tathāgatas appearing in the world."

[Kihwa] [*HPC* 7.168b21]
With the three meditations fully cultivated, omniscient wisdom is matured, and a myriad virtues are embodied. This is called "Buddha appearing."

The Case of Further Inability to Practice

[Sutra (#121)] [*T* 842.17.921b18; *HPC* 7.168b23]

若 後 末 世 鈍 根 眾 生 心 欲 求 道 不 得 成 就 、 由 昔 業 障 。 當 勤 懺 悔 常 起 希 望 。 先 斷 憎 愛 嫉 妬 諂 曲 、 求 勝 上 心 。 三 種 淨 觀 隨 學 一 事 、 此 觀 不 得 復 習 彼 觀 。 心 不 放 捨 漸 次 求 證 。

If subsequent sentient beings of the degenerate age of dull faculties desire in their hearts to attain the Way, but somehow always fall short of their goal, it is because of karmic hindrances from the past. They must strive for repentance and confession and continuously re-arouse their hopes. They must first sever love and hatred, jealousy, envy, flattery, and calumny and strive for the unsurpassed state of mind. Since the three types of meditation are all the investigation of the same single matter, if one meditation doesn't work, try again with one of the others. Don't let your mind dissipate, and gradually strive for realization.

[Kihwa] [*HPC* 7.168c4]

If those of dull faculties do not strive diligently, their merit will not suffice for consummation. They must first repent of their faults and cut off their hindrances and then they can apply their strength toward practice, striving energetically without laziness, in order to actualize entry.

The *Gāthā*

[Sutra (#122)] [*T* 842.17.921b22; *HPC* 7.168c7]

爾時世尊、欲重宣此義而說偈言：

圓覺汝當知　一切諸衆生
欲求無上道　先當結三期
懺悔無始業　經於三七日
然後正思惟　非彼所聞境
畢竟不可取　奢摩他至靜
三摩正憶持　禪那明數門
是名三淨觀　若能勤修習
是名佛出世　鈍根未成者
常當勤心懺　無始一切罪
諸障若消滅　佛境便現前

Then the World-Honored One, wanting to restate the gist of this, spoke a verse. He said:

Perfect Enlightenment, you should know
That all sentient beings
Who want to seek the unsurpassed
Must, at the outset of the three retreats,
Repent of and admit their beginningless actions
For a period of three weeks.
Thereupon they will have correct thought.
But if they do not experience the states as they have been taught
They should not grasp them.
In *śamatha* perfect quiescence;
In *samāpatti* correct mindfulness;
In *dhyāna* clear observance of the breath.
These are called "the three purifying meditations."
Those who diligently practice
Are called "Buddhas appearing in the world."
Those of dull faculties who cannot bring this into effect
Must continuously strive at repentance

Of their beginningless crimes.
When all hindrances are extinguished
The Buddha-state appears before your eyes.

[Kihwa] [*HPC* 7.168c15]

Since single-minded concentration of the will results directly in the attainment of your goals, you must strive to do the retreat, repenting of your acts and rectifying your thoughts. Repenting of your karma, the karma is extinguished; with thoughts rectified and discriminations severed, you attain pliancy in each meditation. But if this state is not equal to the one you heard about in the chapter of Power and Virtue Unhindered, you should not become attached to it. The three kinds of pliancy are the state of the Buddha. If you are able to intimately experience this kind of state, then since there is no hindrance not extinguished, and no virtue not manifested, you are called an "appearing Buddha." Each person originally shares in the exact same Buddha-realm, but because of karmic hindrances they cannot attain to [the Buddha's] level. If the mountain of hindrances is toppled, the Buddha-state is directly manifested. The Buddha has explained the coordinated practice of the three meditations separately and pervasively for those of superior, middling, and inferior capacities. His vast compassion and universal effort at salvation "straightening the crooked without remainder" is evident here.

12

Most Excellent of Worthies Bodhisattva

[Kihwa] [*HPC* 7.169a1]

One whose extraordinary endowments allow him to handle any responsibility is called a "Worthy."[1] The ability to clearly distinguish right and wrong and to crush evil and disclose the correct is called "excellence." The name "most excellent of worthies" is applied to one who has become a true "vessel of the dharma"[2] and is ready for Buddhahood. He is one who has attained the True Eye, has conquered demons, and has turned the wheel of the dharma. Being the leader in the production of all kinds of goodness, he is regarded by all of the other worthies as the best. Why does he raise a question following Perfect Enlightenment Bodhisattva? The chapter by chapter elucidation of the gist of the teaching from Mañjuśrī down to Perfect Enlightenment has been completely executed—the Correct Doctrine is complete. Since it is now fit to be handed down to future generations and awaken their understanding, this bodhisattva requests the Buddha to assign the sutra a name by which it can be pervasively transmitted. This is why Excellent of the Worthies is call "Most" excellent, and this is why he asks this question following Perfect Enlightenment Bodhisattva.

Most Excellent of Worthies' asking the question following Perfect Enlightenment is like Samantabhadra's questioning after Mañjuśrī. Mañjuśrī and Perfect Enlightenment are the same in rank. Samantabhadra and Most Excellent of Worthies possess the same virtue. Possessing the same rank and the same virtue, they begin and end the sutra in similar ways. Mañjuśrī has produced faith in the world of *hwaŏm*,[3] and dealt with the stage of realization.[4] The chapters from Samantabhadra to Perfect Enlightenment dealt with the initiation of practices depending on awakening, and concerning this, all deal with continuous practice after enlightenment. The treatment by Perfect Enlightenment of "total realization" and his being followed up by Most Excellent of Worthies can be understood in the same way.

240

Concerning the structure of the sutra: the presentation of the teacher and his audience at the sermon is called the "Introduction." "Awakening-practice-realization-transformation" together constitute the "Correct Doctrine." This last chapter is distinguished as the "Dissemination" section. Having reached this point, the body of the sutra is complete. The excellent work of all buddhas is consummated. My verse:

> Depending on its name, the teaching is received, believed and
>   put into practice.
> According to the situation it is elucidated to the people to
>   remove their blindness.
> Their seeds infused [by the teaching], myriad beings attain to
>   the level of realization.
> This is why supernatural beings endeavor to protect it.

The Questions of Most Excellent of Worthies: Transmission of the Teaching

[Sutra (#123)] [*T* 842.17.921c4; *HPC* 7.169b1] ▼

於是賢善首菩薩在大眾中、即從座起。頂禮佛足、右繞三匝。長跪叉手而白佛言：大悲世尊。廣爲我等及末世眾生開悟如是不思議事。世尊、此大眾教名字何等？云何奉持？眾生修習得何功德？云何使我護持經人流布此教？至於何地？作是語已、五體投地。如是三請、終而復始。

The bodhisattva Most Excellent of Worthies arose from his seat in the great assembly. He bowed his head to the feet of the Buddha and circumambulated him three times to the right. He then knelt down with his hands clasped and addressed the Buddha, saying:

"Greatly Compassionate World-Honored One. You have enlightened extensively for we [bodhisattvas] and the sentient beings of the degenerate age about this inconceivable matter.[5] World-Honored One: What names are applied to this Mahāyāna teaching? How should it be cleaved to and practiced? What kinds of merits will be obtained by sentient beings who practice according to it? How shall those who cleave to and practice it be protected? And to what lands should this teaching be propagated?"

Having said this, he prostrated fully to the ground. He repeated this question three times in succession.

[Kihwa] [*HPC* 7.169b9]

The phrase "You have enlightened (開悟)" should be "you have revealed (開示)." Since he has said "extensively for us," how can [the intransitive verb] "enlighten" make sense in this sentence? What he has "revealed" from the beginning of the sutra up to this point are the dharma-practices of the causal stage of the Tathāgata, the realm of the most intimate realization of enlightenment, the virtuous functions hidden in the secret store, and the dharma-instruction that has never yet been heard. Since these are all things that are outside the reach of the ordinary conceptualizing consciousness, this matter is called "inconceivable."

The Buddha's Answer: Guidelines and Names

[Sutra (#124)] [*T* 842.17.921c11; *HPC* 7.169b15]

爾 時 世 尊 告 賢 善 首 菩 薩 言 ： 善 哉 、 善 哉 。 善 男 子 、 汝 等 乃
能 爲 諸 菩 薩 及 末 世 衆 生 問 於 如 來 如 是 經 教 功 德 名 字 。 汝 今
諦 聽 、 當 爲 汝 説 。 時 賢 善 首 菩 薩 奉 教 歡 喜 。 及 諸 大 衆 默 然
而 聽 。

Then the World-Honored One, addressing the bodhisattva Most Excellent of Worthies, said: "Excellent! Excellent! Good Son, you have asked well for the bodhisattvas and sentient beings of the degenerate age about the merits and names of this sutra teaching. Now listen well, and I shall explain for you." The bodhisattva Most Excellent of Worthies received this instruction with great joy. Those in the great assembly became silent and listened.

[Kihwa] [*HPC* 7.169b20]

Since the installation of the sutra's names, the disclosure of its virtues, the encouragement of its practice and its continued transmission are all the Buddha's original intention, he acknowledges the question with praise.

The Names of the Sutra

[Sutra (#125)] [*T* 842.17.921c16; *HPC* 7.169b22]

善 男 子 、 是 經 百 千 萬 億 恒 河 沙 諸 佛 所 説 。 三 世 如 來 之 所 守
護 。 十 方 菩 薩 之 所 歸 依 。 十 二 部 經 清 淨 眼 目 。 是 經 名 大 方
廣 圓 覺 陀 羅 尼 。 亦 名 修 多 羅 了 義 。 亦 名 秘 密 王 三 昧 。 亦 名
如 來 決 定 境 界 。 亦 名 如 來 藏 自 性 差 別 。 汝 當 奉 持 。 善 男 子
、 是 經 唯 顯 如 來 境 界 。 唯 佛 如 來 能 盡 宣 説 。 若 諸 菩 薩 及 末
世 衆 生 依 此 修 行 漸 次 增 進 、 至 於 佛 地 。

Good sons, this scripture is that which is taught by billions upon billions of countless buddhas; it is that which is protected by the tathāgatas of the three times; it is that which is relied upon by the bodhisattvas of the ten directions; it is the pure eye of the twelve divisions of the scriptures. This scripture is called The Great Curative Extensive Perfect Enlightenment *Dhāraṇī*; it is also called The Sutra of the Fully Revealed Meaning; it is also called The Mysterious Royal *Samādhi*; it is also called the Tathāgata's Realm of Full Decisiveness; it is also called The Distinction of the Self-Nature of the Tathāgatagarbha. You should cleave to it and practice according to it.

Good Sons, this scripture expresses nothing but the state of the tathāgatas, and only the buddha-tathāgatas are able to fully explain it. If the bodhisattvas and sentient beings of the degenerate age practice according to this sutra, they will gradually advance to Buddhahood.

Purview of the Sutra

善男子、是經名爲頓教大乘、頓機衆生從此開悟。亦攝漸修一切羣品。譬如大海不讓小流。乃至蚊虻及阿修羅飲其水者、皆得充滿。

Good Sons, this scripture is called the Sudden Teaching of the Mahāyāna, and sentient beings with the capacity for the sudden will awaken through it. But it also embraces the gradual practice of all sentient beings. It is like a great ocean that does not deny the entrance of any small stream; and mosquitoes and horseflies, as well as Asuras, may drink its water and take their fill.

Merits of Studying and Practicing the Sutra

善男子、假使有人純以七寶積滿三千大千世界以用布施。不如有人聞此經名及一句義。善男子、假使有人教百恒河沙衆生得阿羅漢果。不如有人宣說此經、分別半偈。善男子、若復有人聞此經名信心不惑。當知是人非於一佛二佛種諸福慧、如是乃至盡恒河沙一切佛所種諸善根、聞此經教。汝善男子、當護末世是修行者、無令惡魔及諸外道惱其身心令生退屈。

Good Sons, say for instance there were a man who, with the purest of motivations, gathered the seven jewels in a quantity sufficient to fill a trichiliocosm (a billion worlds), and then gave them all away for charity. This man's merit would not be equal to that of a man who heard the name of this scripture and understood the meaning of a single passage.

Good Sons, say for example there was a man who taught sentient beings as many as a hundred times the amount of the grains of sand in the Ganges River such that they all attained the level of *arhat*. This man's merit would not be equal to someone who explicated a half of a *gāthā* of this scripture. If there is any person who hears the name of this sutra and believes in it fully without a shadow of a doubt, then you can know that this person has not only sown the seeds of blessings and wisdom with one buddha or two buddhas, but has cultivated his roots of goodness with countless myriads of buddhas, listening to this sutra-teaching.

Good Sons, you should protect sentient beings of the degenerate age who are practicing this, and not let evil spirits and heretics upset their thoughts or cause them to lose heart.

The *Gāthā*

爾時世尊、欲重宣此義而説偈言:

賢 善 首 當 知　　是 經 諸 佛 説
如 來 善 護 持　　十 二 部 眼 目
名 爲 大 方 廣　　圓 覺 陀 羅 尼
現 如 來 境 界　　依 此 修 行 者
增 進 至 佛 地　　如 海 納 百 川
飲 者 皆 充 滿　　假 使 施 七 寶
積 滿 三 千 界　　不 如 聞 此 經
若 化 河 沙 衆　　皆 得 阿 羅 漢
不 如 宣 半 偈　　汝 等 於 來 世
護 是 宣 持 者　　無 令 生 退 屈

Then the World-Honored One, wanting to restate the gist of this, spoke a verse. He said:

> Most Excellent of Worthies, you should know
> This scripture is that which all buddhas teach
> And that which all tathāgatas well protect
> It is the eye of the twelve divisions.
> It is called
> The Great Curative Extensive Perfect Enlightenment *Dhāraṇī*.
> It is the expression of the realm of the Tathāgata.
> Those who practice according to it

Gradually advance to Buddhahood.
It is like an ocean that accepts all rivers
And gives all of the thirsty their fill.
If there were a person who donated the seven jewels
Enough to fill a trichiliocosm
It would not be equal to hearing this sutra.
If someone transformed countless beings
Such that they all reached arhatship
It would not be equal to the explication of half a *gāthā*.
You must all, for the later generations,
Protect those who give and receive this teaching
And not allow them to backslide.

Guarantees of Protection by Supernatural Beings

爾時會中有火首金剛、摧碎金剛、尼藍婆金剛等八萬金剛
并其眷屬即從座起。頂禮佛足右繞三匝而白佛言：世尊。
若後末世一切衆生有能持此決定大乘、我當守護如護眼目
、乃至道場所修行處。我等金剛自領徒衆晨夕守護、令不
退轉。其家乃至永無災障疫病銷滅。財寶豐足常不乏少。
爾時大梵王、二十八天王、并須彌山王、護國天王等即從
座起。頂禮佛足右繞三匝而白佛言：世尊。我亦守護是持
經者。常令安隱心不退轉。爾時有大力鬼王名吉槃茶與十
萬鬼王即從座起。頂禮佛足右繞三匝而白佛言：我亦守護
是持經人朝夕侍衛、令不退屈。其人所居一由旬内若有鬼
神侵其境界我當使其碎如微塵。佛説此經已一切菩薩天龍
鬼神八部眷屬及説天王梵王等一切大衆、聞佛所説皆大歡
喜信受奉行。

Then, from the midst of the great assembly, there arose Fiery-haired
Vajra-warriors, Pulverizing Vajra-warriors, Blue Vajra-warriors—
altogether eighty thousand Vajra-warriors with their retinues.
They got up from their seats, bowed their heads to the feet of the
Buddha, and circumambulated him three times to the right. Then
they addressed the Buddha, saying "World-Honored One, if sentient beings of the degenerate age are able to cleave to this Scripture
of Mahāyāna Decisiveness, we shall protect them as if protecting
our own eyes, and we shall also protect the places where they carry
out their practices. We Vajra-warriors shall guide these people,
protecting them morning and night, such that they do not retrogress. Their households shall never suffer from calamity; sickness

shall be eradicated; their material possessions shall be abundant; and they shall never suffer from poverty.

Then the Great Brahma Kings, the Kings of the Twenty-Eight Heavens, together with the Kings of Mt. Sumeru and the Nation-Protecting Kings, arose from their seats. They bowed their heads to the Buddha's feet, circumambulated him to the right, and addressed him, saying: "World-Honored One, we shall also protect those who cleave to this scripture. We shall bring them tranquillity and not allow them to retrogress."

Then a Great Mighty Demon King, whose name was Kumbhāṇḍa, together with a hundred thousand Demon Kings, arose from his seat. He bowed his head to the Buddha's feet and circumambulated him three times to the right. He addressed the Buddha, saying: "I shall also protect those who cleave to this scripture by guarding them morning and night and not letting them retrogress. If an evil spirit should dare to approach within the area of one *yojana*[6] to the place of the practitioner's abode, I shall smash him into atoms."

The Buddha having finished his preaching of this scripture, the bodhisattvas, the *devas*, *nāgas*, *yakṣās* and the rest of the eight kinds of spiritual beings[7] along with their retinues, as well as the Heavenly Kings, Brahma Kings, and the rest of the great assembly, having heard what the Buddha taught, were all filled with great joy. They believed, embodied, and practiced this teaching.

Appendix:

Re-Translation of the
Sutra of Perfect Enlightenment
According to the Amendments
by Kihwa

Preface

Thus I have heard. One time, the Bhagavan entered the supramundane great radiant bright *garbha*, in the exactly attained *samādhi*, where all tathāgatas abide in radiant splendor. This is the ground of pure enlightenment of sentient beings, the equal original reality where body and mind are completely erased. He completely filled the ten directions with the accordance with nonduality, and in this nondual state manifested all pure lands.

He was with one hundred thousand great bodhisattva-mahāsattvas. Those who served as leaders of the assembly were: Mañjuśrī Bodhisattva, Samantabhadra Bodhisattva, Universal Vision Bodhisattva, Vajragarbha Bodhisattva, Maitreya Bodhisattva, Pure Wisdom Bodhisattva, Power and Virtue Unhindered Bodhisattva, Voice of Discernment Bodhisattva, Purifier of All Karmic Hindrances Bodhisattva, Universal Enlightenment Bodhisattva, Perfect Enlightenment Bodhisattva, and Most Excellent of Worthies Bodhisattva. With their retinues, all entered into the same *samādhi* as the Tathāgata at this assembly of the equal dharma.

1. Mañjuśrī Bodhisattva

Mañjuśrī Bodhisattva arose from his seat in the great assembly. He bowed his head to the Buddha's feet and circumambulated him three times to the right. He then knelt down with his hands clasped and addressed the Buddha, saying:

"Greatly Compassionate World-Honored One. Please, for all members of this assembly who have come for your dharma, teach us about the dharma-practice of the Tathāgata's originally arisen pure causal stage. Also, please teach the bodhisattvas to arouse pure mind in the great vehicle and become distantly removed from all afflictions, such that they can prevent the future sentient beings of the degenerate age who seek the great vehicle from falling into mistaken views." Having said this, he prostrated to the ground. He asked this question three times in succession.

Then the World-Honored One, speaking to Mañjuśrī Bodhisattva, said: "Excellent! Excellent! Good son, you have been able to ask for the bodhisattvas about the dharma-practice of the causal stage of the Tathāgata, and have caused all the bodhisattvas to arouse the pure mind in the great vehicle. You have also caused all sentient beings of the degenerate age who seek the great vehicle to gain correct abiding such that they do not fall into erroneous views. Now listen well, and I shall explain for you." Mañjuśrī Bodhisattva received the teaching with reverence and joy; all those in the great assembly became silent and listened.

"Good sons, the unsurpassed King of the Dharma possesses the great *dhāraṇī*-entrance. It is called 'Perfect Enlightenment.' From it is manifested all purity: suchness, *bodhi*, nirvana, and the *pāramitās* with which he teaches bodhisattvas. All Tathāgatas in their originally arisen causal stage rely on the perfect illumination of the attributes of pure enlightenment to permanently sever ignorance and directly accomplish the Buddha-Way.

"What is ignorance? Good sons, all sentient beings fall into various inverted views without beginning. Just like a disoriented person who confuses the four directions, they mistakenly take the Four Elements as the attributes of their bodies and the conditioned shadows of the Six Objects as the attributes of their mind. It is just like when our eyes are diseased and we see flowers in the sky, or a second moon.

"Good sons, the sky actually has no flowers—they are the false attachment of the diseased person. And because of this false attachment, not only are we confused about the self-nature of the sky; we are also mixed up about the place where real flowers come from. From this there is the falsely existent transmigration through life and death. Therefore it is called 'ignorance.'

"Good sons, this 'ignorance' actually lacks substance. It is like a man who is dreaming. At the time of the dream, there is no nonexistence, until he awakens and finds that there is nothing for him to hold on to. Similarly, when the sky-flowers disappear from the sky, you cannot say that there is a definite point of their disappearance. Why? Because there is no point at which they arise. All sentient beings falsely perceive arising and ceasing within this condition of non-arising. Therefore they say that there is 'transmigration through life-and-death.'

"Good sons, the practice of Perfect Enlightenment in the causal stage of the Tathāgata is to know that these are 'sky-flowers,' which is the same as knowing that there is no transmigration, and that there is no body/mind to undergo life-and-death. But they are not caused to be nonexistent. It is because they lack original nature.

"Now, this [prior] awareness is just like empty space. Yet since the knowledge that it is like empty space is none other than the appearance of sky-flowers, you also cannot say that there is no nature of awareness. When existence and nonexistence are both dispelled, it is called 'according with pure enlightenment.'

"Why? Because its nature is completely empty; because it is eternally changeless; because there is neither arising nor ceasing within the Matrix of the Tathāgata, and because there are no fixed points of view. Like the nature of the reality-realm, it is totally complete and perfect, pervading the ten directions. Therefore it is called the 'dharma-practice of the causal stage.' Bodhisattvas, relying upon it, arouse their pure mind within the Mahāyāna. Sentient beings of the degenerate age who practice relying on this will not fall into erroneous views."

Then, the World-Honored One, wanting to restate the gist of this, spoke a verse. He said:

> Mañjuśrī, you should know
> All Tathāgatas
> From their originally arisen causal stage
> Penetrate ignorance
> With enlightened wisdom.
> Knowing it to be like sky-flowers
> They are able to escape transmigration.
> It is like the man in the dream
> Who has nothing to grasp upon awakening.
> Awareness is like space
> Equal, changeless.
> Enlightenment pervading the worlds of the ten directions
> Is none other than the attainment of the Buddha-way.
> All illusions cease at no-place
> And in accomplishing the Way there is nothing attained.
> That's because the original nature is complete, perfect.
> In it, bodhisattvas
> Are able to produce *bodhicitta*.
> All sentient beings of the degenerate age
> Practicing this, will avoid erroneous views.

2. Samantabhadra Bodhisattva

Then Samantabhadra Bodhisattva rose from his seat in the great assembly. He bowed to the Buddha's feet and circumambulated him three times to the right. He knelt down with his hands clasped, and said to the Buddha:

"Greatly Compassionate World-Honored One. I would like to ask for all the Bodhisattvas at this assembly and for the sentient beings of the degenerate age who are practicing Mahāyāna: Please reveal the expedient stages of practice and let them hear of this pure realm of perfect enlightenment. How should we practice?

"World-Honored One, if these sentient beings know about 'illusion,' and that body and mind are also illusion, how can they remedy illusion using illusion? If all illusory natures are completely annihilated, then there is no mind. Who is going to carry out the practice? Moreover, based on this, how can you teach the practice of 'illusion'? If all sentient beings originally do not practice, then they will remain forever trapped within the illusion of life and death. Not having penetrated the realm of the illusory, how will they liberate the mind that is trapped in false conceptualization?" Having said this, he prostrated fully to the ground. He asked this question three times in succession.

Then the World-Honored One, speaking to Samantabhadra Bodhisattva, said: "Excellent, excellent! Good son, you have well asked the Tathāgata on behalf of the bodhisattvas and the sentient beings of the degenerate age about the expedient stages of the practice of the bodhisattva's 'as-illusion-*samādhi*.' This practice enables all the sentient beings to gain freedom from illusion. Now listen well, and I shall explain it for you." Samantabhadra received this teaching with great joy and reverence; all in the great assembly became silent and listened.

"Good sons, all sentient beings' various illusions are born from the perfectly enlightened marvelous mind of the Tathāgata, just like the sky-flowers come to exist in the sky. Even though the illusory flowers vanish, the nature of the sky is indestructible. The illusory mind of sentient beings also vanishes based on illusion, and while all illusions are utterly erased, the enlightened mind is unchanged. The use of illusion to speak of enlightenment is also called illusion. If you say there is enlightenment, you are not yet free from illusion. If you say there is no enlightenment, this is the same thing. Therefore, the cessation of illusion is called 'unchanging.'

"Good sons, all bodhisattvas and sentient beings of the degenerate age should separate from all illusory and false realms. By firmly abiding in separation from thought, you also separate from the thought of 'illusion.' As this separation becomes illusion, you again separate from it. You again separate from this separation from separation from illusion, until you reach 'nothing to be separated from,' which is the removal of all illusion. It is like making a fire with two sticks. The fire blazes and the wood is consumed; the ashes fly away and the smoke vanishes. Using illusion to remedy illusion is exactly like this. Yet even though all illusions are extinguished, you do not enter into nothingness.

"Good sons, when you know illusion, you are immediately free, without devising expedient means. Freedom from illusion is in itself enlightenment, and there are no stages. All bodhisattvas and sentient beings of the degenerate age who depend upon this practice will accordingly be able to free themselves from all illusion."

Then the World-Honored One, wanting to restate the gist of this, spoke a verse. He said:

> Samantabhadra, you should know
> The beginningless illusory ignorance
> Of all sentient beings
> Is all created from
> The perfectly enlightened mind of all Tathāgatas.
> It is just like the sky-flowers
> Which have their appearance in relation to the sky;
> Though the sky-flowers vanish
> The sky has never changed.
> Illusion is born from enlightenment;
> In the cessation of illusion, enlightenment remains perfectly
>   complete.
> This is because the enlightened mind is changeless.
> If these bodhisattvas
> And sentient beings of the degenerate age
> Always appropriately separate from illusion,
> They will completely free themselves from it.
> Like the flame that springs from wood:
> The wood is consumed and the flame again disappears.
> If you are enlightened, then there are no stages of practice
> Nor is there such a thing as expedient means.

3. Universal Vision Bodhisattva

Then the bodhisattva Universal Vision arose from his seat in the great assembly. He bowed to the Buddha's feet and circumambulated him three times to the right. He then knelt down with his hands clasped and addressed the Buddha, saying: "Greatly Compassionate World-Honored One, I beg of you on behalf of the bodhisattvas of this assembly and the sentient beings of the degenerate age, to expound on the bodhisattvas' stages and practice. How should they think? How should they abide? For sentient beings who have not yet awakened, what kinds of expedient means should be devised to cause them all to awaken?

World-Honored One, if these sentient beings lack the correct expedients and correct thought, then, when they hear you explain this *samādhi*, confusion will arise in their minds and they will be unable to awaken and enter. Please arouse your compassion for us and for the sentient beings of the degenerate age, and provisionally explain these expedient methods." Having said this, he prostrated himself to the ground. He made this request three times in succession.

Then the World-Honored One, addressing the bodhisattva Universal Vision, said: "Excellent, excellent! Good son, you have asked well for the bodhisattvas and sentient beings of the degenerate age about the stages of the Tathāgata's practice; about his thought and abiding, and about the explanation of all the various expedient means. Now listen well, and I shall explain for you." Universal Vision Bodhisattva received this instruction with great joy. The great assembly became silent and listened.

"Good sons, these newly awakened bodhisattvas and sentient beings of the degenerate age who yearn for the pure enlightened mind of the Tathāgata must correct their thoughts and rid themselves of all illusions, first relying on the Tathāgata's practice of *śamatha*. Firmly established in moral discipline and living in harmony with like-minded students, then practicing silent sitting in a quiet room, they should uninterruptedly be mindful of the following:

"This present body is a synthesis of the Four Elements. Hair, nails, teeth, skin, flesh, bones, marrow, brains, and pigment all return to Earth. Saliva, mucus, pus, blood, sputum, scum, phlegm, tears, semen, urine, and feces all return to Water. Heat returns to Fire, and movement returns to Wind. When the Four Elements have been separated, where can the false body exist? Now you know that this body ultimately has no substance. As a synthesis it appears, but in reality it is like an illusion conjured by a magician. When these four factors temporarily combine, the Six Faculties falsely appear; through the internal and external matching of the Six Faculties and Four Elements, there is the deluded apprehension of conditioned energy. Within this conglomeration, there seem to be marks of this conditioned energy, which is provisionally called 'mind.'

"Good sons, if this false mind does not have its Six Objects, it cannot exist. If the Four Elements are separated, there are no objects to be experienced. At this point, the cognized objects each disperse and vanish, and ultimately there is no dependently arisen mind to be seen.

"Good sons, since the illusory body of this sentient being vanishes, the illusory mind also vanishes. Since the illusory mind vanishes, illusory objects also vanish. Since illusory objects vanish, illusory vanishing also vanishes. Since illusory vanishing vanishes, nonillusion does not vanish. It is like polishing a mirror: when the filth is gone, its brightness naturally appears.

"Good sons, you should understand both body and mind to be illusory filth. When the defiled aspects are permanently extinguished, the entire universe becomes pure."

"Good sons, it is like a pure *maṇi*-pearl that reflects the five colors, depending upon its surroundings. The foolish see that pearl as really having these colors.

"Good sons, it is the same with the pure nature of Perfect Enlightenment: it appears in people's bodies and minds, according to their individual type. Yet these fools say that pure Perfect Enlightenment really has body and mind. It is only because these people are unable to free themselves from illusory appearances that I call body and mind 'illusory filth.' The one who opposes and removes illusory filth is called the 'bodhisattva.' When filth is gone, its opposition is removed; then there is no opposition, no filth, nor anything to be named.

"Good sons, because these bodhisattvas and sentient beings of the degenerate age fully realize [the nature of] all illusion and dispel all [illusory] images, they directly experience limitless purity.

"Good sons, Enlightenment reveals limitless space. Since enlightenment is perfectly clear, the manifest mind is pure. Since the mind is pure, the objects of vision are pure. Since vision is pure, the eye faculty is pure. Since the eye faculty is pure, the visual consciousness is pure. Since this consciousness is pure, hearing is pure. Since hearing is pure, the ear faculty is pure. Since the faculty is pure, the auditory consciousness is pure. Since the consciousness is pure, all perception is pure, and so it is true for smell, taste, touch, and conceptualization as well.

"Good sons, since the eye faculty is pure, the color spectrum is pure. Since color is pure, the field of sound is also pure. The same is true of the fields of smell, taste, touch, and conceptualization.

"Good sons, since the Six Objects are pure, the Earth element is pure. Since Earth is pure, Water is pure, and so are Fire and Wind.

"Good sons, since the Four Elements are pure, the Twelve Loci, the Eighteen Realms, and the Twenty-Five Kinds of Existence are pure. Since these are pure, the Ten Powers, the Four Kinds of Fearlessness, the Four Types of Unobstructed Wisdom, the Buddha's Eighteen Distinctive Characteristics, and the Thirty-Seven Aids to Enlightenment are pure, and so on up to the eighty-four thousand *dhāraṇī*-entrances, everything is pure.

"Good sons, since all true marks are pure in their nature, one body is pure. Since one body is pure, many bodies are pure. Since many bodies are pure the same is true of all sentient beings in the ten directions, who are perfectly enlightened and pure.

"Good sons, since one world is pure, many worlds are pure. Since many worlds are pure, we can see that throughout all of space, completely including the three times, all things are equal, pure, and changeless.

"Good sons, since space is equal and changeless, you should know that the nature of enlightenment is equal and changeless. Since the Four Elements are changeless, you should know that the nature of enlightenment is equal and changeless. The same holds true all the way up through the eighty-four thousand *dhāraṇī*-entrances that are equal and changeless. Therefore you should know that the nature of enlightenment is equal and changeless.

"Good sons, the unchanging purity of the nature of enlightenment completely pervades—it includes everything without restriction. Therefore you should know that the six faculties completely pervade the reality-realm. Since the faculties completely pervade, you should know that the six sensory fields completely pervade the reality-realm. Since the sensory fields completely pervade, you should know that the Four Elements completely pervade the reality-realm. It is the same way with all things, including the *dhāraṇī*-entrances, which completely pervade the reality-realm.

"Good sons, since this marvelous nature of enlightenment completely pervades, there is neither conflict nor confusion between the natures of the faculties and their objects. Since the faculties and objects have no conflict, it is like this through all of existence, including in the *dhāraṇī*-entrances, which have neither conflict nor confusion. It is like one hundred thousand lamps shining in one room. Their light completely pervades without conflict or confusion.

"Good sons, since their enlightenment is fully perfected, you should know that bodhisattvas are not attached to dharmas, and do not seek liberation from dharmas. They do not hate *saṃsāra* and do not love nirvana. They do not venerate one for keeping the precepts, nor despise the person who breaks them. They are not in awe of the adept practitioner and do not look down on the beginner. Why? Because they are all enlightened. It is like vision seeing an object. The vision completely pervades without experiencing attraction or aversion. Why? Vision, in essence, has no duality, therefore it has neither attraction nor aversion.

"Good sons, these bodhisattvas and sentient beings of the degenerate age who cultivate this mind and are able to fully consummate it, have neither cultivation nor consummation. Their Perfect Enlightenment illuminates everywhere, and is perfectly still, without duality. Here, Buddha-worlds a quintillion times as many as the incalculable amount of grains of sand in the Ganges River haphazardly arise and cease like flowers in the sky. There is neither sameness nor difference, neither bondage nor freedom. Now you know for the first time that all sentient beings are originally perfect buddhas; that *saṃsāra* and nirvana are like last night's dream.

"Good sons, since they are like last night's dream, you should know that *saṃsāra* and nirvana have neither arising nor ceasing, neither coming nor going. In the realization of this there is neither gain nor loss, neither selecting nor rejecting. In the one who realizes, there is no 'contrivance,' 'stopping,' 'naturalism,' or 'annihilation.' In this realization there is neither subject nor object, and ultimately neither realization nor realized one. The nature of all dharmas is equal and indestructible.

"Good sons, these bodhisattvas use this kind of practice, gradually advance like this, think in this way, abide in this way, use these kinds of expedient means, and awaken in this way. If you seek this kind of dharma, you will not again be vexed."

Then the World-Honored One, wanting to restate the gist of this, spoke a verse. He said:

> Universal Vision, you should know
> The bodies and minds of all sentient beings
> Are only illusion.
> The body is composed of the Four Elements;
> The mind depends upon the Six Objects.
> When the Four Elements disperse,
> Who will be there as a synthesis?
> In this kind of gradual practice
> All is completely pure,
> Unchanging, pervading the reality-realm.
> Without contrivance, stopping, naturalism or annihilation
> And also without any subjective "realizer,"
> All Buddha-worlds are
> Just like sky-flowers.
> The three times are all the same
> Ultimately without coming or going.
> Bodhisattvas who have recently arisen their minds
> And sentient beings of the degenerate age
> Who want to enter the Buddha Way
> Should practice like this.

4. Vajragarbha Bodhisattva

The bodhisattva Vajragarbha rose from his seat in the great assembly and bowed his head to the Buddha's feet. He circumambulated him three times to the right, and then he knelt down with his hands clasped and said to the Buddha:

"Greatly Compassionate World-Honored One, you have lectured superbly for all these bodhisattvas about the purity of Perfect Enlightenment, the great *dhāraṇī*, the reality-practice of the causal stage and gradual practices according to provisional explanations. You have cleared away the sentient beings' clouds of darkness; all those at this dharma assembly, having received your compassionate instruction, have clarified their optical illusions and purified their wisdom eye.

"World-Honored One; if all sentient beings are originally perfect buddhas, then how can they also possess ignorance? If sentient beings are originally ignorant, how can you say that they have always been perfect buddhas? If all the worldlings in the ten directions are originally perfectly enlightened, but later give rise to ignorance, at what point do all these Tathāgatas regenerate these afflictions? My only request is that you not discard your limitless great compassion and that you reveal the concealed treasure to the bodhisattvas and sentient beings of the degenerate age. This will cause bodhisattvas to gain unshakable faith, and allow all sentient beings of the degenerate age to gain access to this teaching, which is a sutra instruction of the complete doctrine, such that they can permanently sever doubt and regret." Having said this, he prostrated himself to the ground. He asked this question three times in succession.

Then the World-Honored One, speaking to the bodhisattva Vajra-garbha, said: "Excellent, excellent! Good son, you have asked well for the bodhisattvas and sentient beings of the degenerate age about the Tathāgata's extremely deep and recondite final expedient means. This is the highest teaching given by the bodhisattvas, the fully revealed doctrine of the Great Vehicle, which is able to cause the enlightening bodhisattvas of the ten directions, as well as the sentient beings of the degenerate age to gain unshakable faith and permanently sever doubt and remorse. Now listen well, and I shall explain this for you." Vajragarbha Bodhisattva received this instruction with reverence and great joy and those in the great assembly became silent and listened.

"Good sons, all worlds begin and end, are born and die, having prior and after. They exist and do not exist, gather and scatter, arise and cease. This cyclical motion of going and returning without a moment's lapse, variously being selected and rejected, is all cyclic existence. The nature of the Perfect Enlightenment that is discerned without having left cyclic existence is simply samsaric. If you think you can escape cyclic existence in this way, you are completely off the mark. It is comparable to the way in which shaking the eyes can make still water appear to move, or the way that a transfixed gaze can enable the appearance of a fire-wheel. In the same way, clouds flying past the moon make it seem to move, and when you are in a moving boat, the shore appears to move.

"Good sons, all these things are in motion without cease, and even though the objects are already still, you can't get a fix on them. How can you possibly expect to get a glimpse of the Buddha's Perfect Enlighten-ment with the transmigratory, samsaric, stained mind that has never been clear? Because of this, you are prone to give rise to these three doubts.

"Good sons, it is like an illusory eye-disease falsely engendering a vision of sky-flowers. If the illusory eye-disease is removed, you cannot ask: 'Now that this eye-disease is cleared away, when will other eye-diseases reappear?' Why? Because these two things—flowers and eye-disease, are not interdependent. It is also like when the sky-flowers vanish from the sky. You can't ask, 'When will the sky again produce sky-flowers?' Why? Since the sky originally has no flowers, they do not arise and cease. *Saṃsāra* and nirvana are the same as arising and ceasing; marvelous enlightenment illuminates perfectly, and is free from flowers or eye-disease.

"Good sons, you should know that the sky does not exist for an instant nor does it not exist for an instant. How much more so it is in the Tathāgata's closely according with Perfect Enlightenment and becoming the sky's equal original nature.

"Good sons, it is like smelting gold ore. The gold does not come into being because of smelting; once it is perfected, it will never again become ore. Even though it passes through endless time, the nature of the gold is never corrupted. It is wrong to say that it is not originally perfect. The Perfect Enlightenment of the Tathāgata is also like this.

"Good sons, the marvelous perfectly enlightened mind of the Tathāgatas originally has neither *bodhi* nor nirvana; it has neither accomplishment of buddhahood nor non-accomplishment of buddhahood; no false cyclic existence and no noncyclic existence.

"Good sons, in the final stage of the *śrāvaka* path, there is complete severance of the karmic activities of word, thought, and action. Yet *śrāvakas* are still incapable of attaining their own actualized and manifest nirvana. How can you possibly expect to fathom the Tathāgata's state of Perfect Enlightenment using discursive thought? It is like trying to burn Mt. Sumeru with the fire from a firefly—it is impossible! Using the cyclic mind, you produce cyclic views and you will never be able to enter the Tathāgata's ocean of perfect tranquillity. Therefore, I say that all bodhisattvas and sentient beings of the degenerate age should first sever the beginningless root of cyclic existence.

"Good sons, habituated discursive thought arises from the conditioned mind. The six data-fields, false conceptualization, and conditioned energies are not the true essence of mind—indeed, they are like sky-flowers. But using discursive thought to discern the Buddha-state is like the sky-flowers' further producing 'sky-fruits.' Circular false thoughts are useless here.

"Good sons, false, floating thoughts and numerous clever views are incapable of perfecting the expedient means of Perfect Enlightenment.

Using this kind of discrimination, you cannot even formulate a proper question."

Then the World-Honored One, desiring to restate the gist of this, spoke a verse, saying:

> Vajragarbha, you should know
> The Tathāgata's perfectly tranquil nature
> Has never had a beginning or end.
> If you use the cyclic mind
> Discursive thought just revolves,
> At most, reaching the limits of cyclic existence,
> And you are unable to enter the Buddha-ocean.
> It is like smelting gold ore:
> The gold does not exist because of smelting,
> Yet crude gold, from smelting
> Once subsequently perfected,
> Never returns to the state of ore.
> *Saṃsāra* and nirvana,
> Worldlings and Buddhas
> Like sky-flowers, are appearances.
> Discursive thought is just an illusory phenomenon:
> How can it penetrate falsity?
> Only after you fully know this mind
> Can you seek Perfect Enlightenment.

5. Maitreya Bodhisattva

The bodhisattva Maitreya arose from his seat in the great assembly and bowed his head to the Buddha's feet. He circumambulated him three times to the right, and then knelt down with his hands clasped. He addressed the Buddha, saying:

"Greatly Compassionate World-Honored One, you have opened wide the secret treasure for the bodhisattvas and have made all in the great assembly deeply awaken to transmigration and distinguish between the correct and mistaken. You have been able to impart the Fearless Eye of the Way and unshakable faith in Great Nirvana to the sentient beings of the degenerate age; they will not again chase after cyclic existence or give rise to cyclic views.

"World-Honored One; if the bodhisattvas and sentient beings of the degenerate age aspire to float on the Tathāgata's great tranquil ocean, how should they sever the root of cyclic existence? In the various kinds of cyclic existence, how many types of beings are there? How many differences are there in types of practice of the Buddha's *bodhi*? When we reenter the dirty and difficult world, what kinds of teaching devices should we establish to save all sentient beings? I implore you not to relax in your world-saving great compassion and that you clarify the wisdom eye of all practicing bodhisattvas and sentient beings of the degenerate age, illuminate their mind-mirror, and completely awaken them to the Tathāgata's unsurpassed insight." After saying this, he prostrated fully to the ground. He asked this question three times in succession.

Then the World-Honored One, addressing the bodhisattva Maitreya, said: "Excellent, excellent! Good son, you have questioned well on behalf of the bodhisattvas and sentient beings of the degenerate age about the Tathāgata's mysterious, secret, subtle doctrine. You have enabled the bodhisattvas to purify their wisdom eye, and allowed all sentient beings of the degenerate age to permanently sever themselves from cyclic existence. Their minds will awaken to their true characteristic and they will possess the equipoise that comes with the awareness of the non-arising characteristic of existence. Now listen well, and I shall explain this for you." Maitreya received this instruction with joy and great reverence. All those in the great assembly became silent and listened.

"Good sons, all sentient beings are in cyclical existence because of their possession, from beginningless time, of affection, attached love, craving, and desire. Since all the different types of beings—those born from eggs, those born from wombs, those born from moisture, and those born by transformation—all receive their birth and life from sexual desire, you should realize that cyclic existence has attached love as its basis. This tendency to be gripped by attached love is abetted by the existence of all desires, and therefore it is able to empower the continuity of *saṃsāra*. Desire arises depending upon attached love; life power exists depending upon desire. Furthermore, the attached love and life of sentient beings have desire as their root. Attached love and desire are causes; attached love and life are results.

"It is in reference to the objects of desire that you produce all varieties of comfort and discomfort. When the object is contrary to the attached mind, you give rise to aversion and jealousy and go around creating all sorts of karma. It is because of this that you are reborn as a hell-being or a hungry ghost. But then, knowing that desire should be abandoned and adhering to the path of abandonment of karmic activity, you cast off evil and enjoy goodness; hence, you are reborn as a god or man. Again, knowing that you should dislike all forms of attachment, you let go of attachment and enjoy detachment. This greatly nourishes the root of attachment and you automatically produce conditionally enhanced positive states. But since all of this is cyclic existence you still do not attain to the sagely Way. Therefore, sentient beings who desire to be free from life and death and want to escape cyclic existence, first have to sever desire and rid themselves of attached love.

"Good sons, when bodhisattvas appear in the world to teach, it is not based on attachment. It is only because of their compassionate intention to have the sentient beings discard attachment that they provisionally take on all kinds of desire and enter life-and-death. If all sentient beings of the degenerate age can cast off their desires and remove love and hate, they will permanently end their cyclic existence. Seeking the perfectly enlightened state of the Tathāgata in their pure minds, they will directly attain awakening.

"Good sons, due to their inherent desire, sentient beings generate ignorance and manifest the distinctions and inequalities of the Five Natures. Due to the Two Hindrances they manifest deep and shallow [afflictions]. What are the Two Hindrances? The first is the noetic hindrance, which obstructs correct awareness; the second is the phenomenal hindrance, which enables the continuation of *saṃsāra*.

"What are the 'Five Natures'? Good sons, if sentient beings have not yet been able to destroy the Two Hindrances, this is called "nonconsummation of one's Buddhahood." If sentient beings permanently discard desire, then they have succeeded in removing the phenomenal hindrance, but have not yet severed the noetic hindrance. They are able to awaken in the way of *śrāvakas* and *pratyekabuddhas* but are not able to manifest and dwell in the state of the bodhisattva.

"Good sons, if all sentient beings of the degenerate age desire to float on the great ocean of the Tathāgata's Perfect Enlightenment, they should first arouse the determination to do away with the Two Hindrances. Once the Two Hindrances are subdued, one can awaken and enter the state of the bodhisattva. After permanently destroying the noetic and phenomenal hindrances, one is able to enter the sublime Perfect Enlightenment of the Tathāgata, and able to fully accomplish *bodhi* and great nirvana.

"Good sons, all sentient beings without exception actualize Perfect Enlightenment. When you meet a Genuine Teacher, rely on the dharma-practice of the causal stage that he sets up for you. When you follow this practice, both sudden and gradual will be contained. If you come upon the correct path of practice of the unsurpassed *bodhi* of the Tathāgatas, then there are no 'superior' or 'inferior' abilities of people: all accomplish buddhahood.

"If, while seeking a Genuine Teacher, sentient beings meet one with mistaken views, they will not gain the correct awakening. Although this is called the 'heterodox nature,' the fault lies with the teacher, not with the sentient beings. This is the 'distinction of the Five Natures' of sentient beings.

"Good sons, it is only through their Greatly Compassionate expedient means that bodhisattvas enter the secular world, awakening the unenlightened, manifesting various forms and shapes, functioning in agreeable and disagreeable circumstances. It is only relying on the beginningless pure power of their vow to save all beings that they physically work together with these people and cause them to accomplish buddhahood. Any sentient being of the degenerate age who would arouse the mind intensified toward great Perfect Enlightenment must arouse the pure great determination of the bodhisattvas. He should say, 'I hereby vow to dwell in the Perfect Enlightenment of the Buddha, to seek Genuine Teachers and not to plant roots with heterodox paths or practitioners of the Two Vehicles.' Practicing based on this vow, you sever the hindrances one by one. When the hindrances are gone, the vow is fulfilled. You will automatically ascend to the Pure Dharma Palace of Liberation, and actualize the marvelously adorned realm of Great Perfect Enlightenment."

Then the World-Honored One, wanting to restate the gist of this, spoke a verse; he said:

> Maitreya, you should know
> That the nonattainment of great liberation
> By all sentient beings
> Is only due to desire;
> Therefore they are drawn into life and death.
> If you can separate yourself from like and dislike,
> As well as desire, hatred, and ignorance
> You will all perfect the Buddha's way
> And permanently destroy the Two Hindrances,
> Without needing any "distinctions in nature."
> Seek a teacher who has the correct awakening,
> Practice the vow to arouse the *bodhi*-mind
> Rely on Great Nirvana.
> The bodhisattvas in the ten directions
> All appear in the world of *saṃsāra*
> Relying on the Greatly Compassionate vow.
> Present practitioners
> As well as sentient beings of the degenerate age
> Should strive to eliminate all attached views
> And directly return to Great Perfect Enlightenment.

6. Pure Wisdom Bodhisattva

The bodhisattva Pure Wisdom rose from his seat in the great assembly. He bowed his head to the Buddha's feet, and circumambulated him three times to the right. He then knelt down with his hands clasped and addressed the Buddha saying:

"Greatly Compassionate World-Honored One; you have magnani-mously explained for all of our group this inconceivable matter, which was originally not seen and originally not heard. We who are presently here and have received your superb instruction have gained compo-sure of body and mind, and received great benefit. I would like to re-quest this:

Would you re-explain the nature of the Perfect Fulfilling Enlighten-ment of the King of the Dharma for those who have come for your teaching? What differences are there between that which is grasped and actualized by sentient beings, bodhisattvas, and World-Honored Tathāgatas? Please let sentient beings of the degenerate age hear this sagely teaching so that they may conform to it, awaken through it, and gradually become capable of entering." Having said this, he prostrated fully to the ground. He asked this question three times in succession.

Then the World-Honored One, addressing the bodhisattva Pure Wis-dom, said: "Excellent, excellent! Good son, you have asked well for the bodhisattvas and sentient beings of the degenerate age about the distinc-tions that the Tathāgata makes [between] the levels [of attainment by practioners]. Now listen well, and I shall explain these for you." The bodhisattva Pure Wisdom received this instruction with reverence and great joy. All the members of the great assembly became silent and listened.

"Good sons, although the self-nature of Perfect Enlightenment is not a nature [like the previously described natures], nonetheless, a nature exists that is concomitant with the arising of all natures. But there is neither acquisition nor realization of it. From the point of view of real-ity, there are actually neither bodhisattvas nor sentient beings. Why? Bodhisattvas and sentient beings are nothing but illusory appearances, and since illusory appearances are erased, there is neither 'acquirer' nor 'realizer.' It is like the eye not being able to see itself: in the nature's own equality, there is nothing that is 'equal.' Sentient beings are thor-oughly confused and are unable to rid themselves of all illusory ap-pearances. Since they have not extinguished [the mark of] cessation in illusory activity, they automatically make discriminations. If they at-tain accordance with the extinction of the Tathāgata, there is really nei-ther extinction nor person who brings extinction about.

"Good sons, all sentient beings, because of a deludedly conceived 'self' and attachment to that self, have beginninglessly never known mo-ment-to-moment arising and cessation for themselves; therefore they give rise to attraction and aversion, and become addicted to the objects in the five sense fields. If they meet a Genuine Teacher he will awaken them to the essence of pure Perfect Enlightenment. Discovering aris-ing and cessation, they will directly know that this mind's very nature is that of anxiety. If there is a person who permanently severs that anxiety and experiences the purity of the reality-realm, but who allows his understanding of clarity in turn to become a hindrance, this person is tending toward Perfect Enlightenment but is not perfectly free. He is called a 'worldling who is according with the nature of enlightenment.'

"Good sons, all bodhisattvas see their understanding as an obstruction. But even if they eliminate the 'understanding-obstruction' they still abide in a view of enlightenment. This 'enlightenment-obstruction' becomes a hindrance and they are not perfectly free. They are called 'bodhisattvas who have not yet entered the *bhūmis* who are according with the nature of enlightenment.'

"Good sons, since the possession of illumination and enlightenment are termed together as 'hindrance' and 'obstruction,' the bodhisattva is always enlightened without abiding. Illumination and illuminator simultaneously vanish. It is like the case of a person who cuts off his own head—when the head is cut off, there is no longer any 'cutter.' Hence the use of the obstructing mind to eliminate all obstructions: when obstructions have been eliminated, there is no one to eliminate obstructions. They are called 'bodhisattvas who have entered the *bhūmis* and who are according with the nature of enlightenment.'

"Good sons, all hindrances are none other than ultimate enlightenment. Whether you attain mindfulness or lose mindfulness, there is no nonliberation. Establishing the dharma and refuting the dharma are both called nirvana; wisdom and folly are equally *prajñā*; the method that is perfected by bodhisattvas and false teachers is the same *bodhi*; ignorance and suchness are not different realms; morality, concentration, and wisdom, as well as desire, hatred, and ignorance, are all divine practices; sentient beings and lands share the same dharma nature; hell and heaven are both the Pure Land; those having Buddha-nature and those not having it equally accomplish the Buddha's enlightenment. All defilements are ultimately liberation. The reality-realms's oceanlike wisdom completely illumines all marks to be just like empty space. This is called 'the Tathāgata's accordance with the nature of enlightenment.'

"Good sons, if all bodhisattvas and sentient beings of the degenerate age would merely do this: at all times, not give rise to false thoughts; in false states of mind, not strive for cessation; when abiding in false conceptual realms, not try to impose a complete understanding; while lacking complete understanding, not try to analyze true reality. If these sentient beings, hearing this teaching, believe, understand, assimilate, and remember it without being shocked or frightened by it, they are said to be 'according with the nature of enlightenment.'"

"Good sons, you should all be aware that these sentient beings have already made offerings to myriads of Buddhas a quintillion times as numerous as the grains of sand in the Ganges River, and have culti-vated their roots of virtue with as many great bodhisattvas. I call these people 'fully developed in omniscience.'"

Then the World-Honored One, wanting to restate the gist of this, composed a verse. He said:

> Pure Wisdom, you should know
> The nature of perfect *bodhi*
> Has no acquisition, no realization
> Neither bodhisattva nor sentient being.
> Yet between the times of enlightenment and
>   nonenlightenment
> There are differences in level.
> Sentient beings are obstructed by their understanding;
> Bodhisattvas are not free from enlightenment.
> Entering the *bhūmis* they are forever tranquil
> And do not abide in any mark.
> Great enlightenment fully includes everything
> And is called "pervasively according."
> Sentient beings of the degenerate age
> Whose minds do not give rise to falsity
> I call "appearing in the world as bodhisattvas."
> They have made offerings to countless buddhas
> And are already replete with virtuous merit.
> Even though there are many expedient teaching methods
> As a sum, they are called "the wisdom that apprehends
>   everything."

7. Power and Virtue Unhindered Bodhisattva

Then the bodhisattva Power and Virtue Unhindered arose from his seat in the great assembly. He bowed to the feet of the Buddha and circumambulated him three times to the right. He then knelt down with his hands clasped and addressed the Buddha saying:

"Greatly Compassionate World-Honored One, you have analyzed for us at length this accordance with the enlightened nature, causing the enlightened minds of the bodhisattvas to effloresce and receive the Buddha's Perfect Voice, and causing them to receive excellent benefit that is not caused by religious practice.

"World-Honored One, it is like a great city that has four gates on its exterior: those who come from various directions are not limited to one path. Similarly, all bodhisattvas who adorn Buddha-lands and who perfect enlightened wisdom are not limited to a single expedient method. World-Honored One, my only wish is that you explain in detail for us the gradations of all the expedient methods. In general, how many kinds of religious practitioners are there? Please allow the bodhisattvas and sentient beings of the degenerate age who are seeking the great vehicle to quickly attain awakening and to sport about in the Tathāgata's great ocean of cessation-extinction." Having said this, he prostrated to the ground. He asked this question three times in succession.

Then the World-Honored One, addressing the bodhisattva Power and Virtue Unhindered, said: "Excellent, excellent! Good son, you have questioned well for the bodhisattvas and sentient beings of the degenerate age about these expedient methods of the Tathāgata. Listen well now, and I shall explain them for you." The bodhisattva Power and Virtue Unhindered received this teaching with awe and joy; all those in the great crowd became silent and listened.

"Good sons, unsurpassed marvelous enlightenment pervades all the ten directions. It gives birth to all Tathāgatas, who share the same equal essence with all dharmas. Thus, as far as the various practices are concerned, there is in reality, no duality. Nonetheless, the expedient methods that conform to Perfect Enlightenment are numberless. Among these, there are three general types that all practitioners rely on, according to the differences in their inclination.

"Good sons, some bodhisattvas awaken pure Perfect Enlightenment, and using the mind of pure enlightenment take quiescence as their practice. Then, by settling all thoughts they become aware of the agitated motion of the consciousness, and thus produce quiescent wisdom. From this, the mind, the body, and external objects are permanently extinguished and they directly generate quiescent pliancy from within themselves. Because of this cessation and quiescence, the minds of all the Tathāgatas in all the worlds in the ten directions are made manifest, just like the images in a mirror. This expedient method is called *śamatha*.

"Good sons, some bodhisattvas awaken pure Perfect Enlightenment, then using the pure enlightened mind, completely realize that the nature of mind as well as the faculties and objects are all based on illusory transformations. Then here they produce various illusions in order to remove illusion. Creating all illusions, they enlighten the illusory multitude. From the production of illusion they are able to arouse great compassionate pliancy within. All bodhisattvas who follow this 'arising practice' gradually advance in practice. Since the 'observation of illusion' is not the same as illusion, it is also not the same as 'illusory observation.' Since both are [recognized as] illusory, illusory marks are permanently removed. This marvelous practice that is perfected by bodhisattvas is like a shoot growing out of the ground. This expedient method is called *samāpatti*.

"Good sons, some bodhisattvas awaken pure Perfect Enlightenment, and using the pure enlightened mind, avoid attachment to illusory transformations and the marks of quiescence, fully realizing body and mind both to be obstructions. Without awareness of the illumination of enlightenment (of *śamatha*) and without depending on all sorts of obstructions (the illusions analyzed in *samāpatti*), they eternally transcend realms of obstruction and nonobstruction, receiving and using the world as well as body and mind, whose marks abide in the objective realm. It is comparable to the ringing sound in a bell that penetrates to the outside. Affliction and nirvana not hindering each other, the bodhisattvas are directly enabled to produce the pliancy of cessation-extinction from within. Accordance with marvelous enlightenment and the realm of cessation and extinction is something that self and other, body and mind are unable to reach. Sentient beings and life are all just floating concepts. This expedient method is called *dhyāna*.

"Good sons, these three practices are all close accordance with Perfect Enlightenment; the Tathāgatas in the ten directions achieve buddhahood depending upon these, and all the various and sundry expedient methods of the bodhisattvas of the ten directions, with all their similarities and differences are without exception derived from these three activities. If you perfectly actualize these, it is the same as perfectly actualizing enlightenment.

"Good sons, if there were a person who cultivated the sagely path and elevated a quadrillion people to the stage of *arhat* and *pratyekabuddha*, he would not be equal to the person who heard this unobstructed teaching of Perfect Enlightenment and practiced it for only an instant."

Then the World-Honored One, desiring to reiterate the gist of this, spoke a verse. He said:

> Power-Virtue, you should know
> Even though the unsurpassed mind of great enlightenment
> Originally has not even two marks.
> The expedient methods for according with it
> Are numberless.
> When I explain them according to general type,
> There are three kinds:
> Stable *śamatha*
> Is like a mirror reflecting all images;
> *Samādhi*
> Is like a shoot growing out of the ground;
> *Dhyāna* is only cessation-extinction
> Like the sound in the bell.

These three kinds of marvelous dharma-practices
Are all accordance with enlightenment.
The Tathāgatas in the ten directions
As well as all the great bodhisattvas
Are able to attain the Way based on these.
The full realization of these three activities
Is called "absolute nirvana."

8. Voice of Discernment Bodhisattva

Then the bodhisattva Voice of Discernment rose from his seat in the great assembly. He bowed to the feet of the Buddha and circumambulated him three times to the right. He then knelt down with his hands clasped and addressed the Buddha saying:

"Greatly Compassionate World-Honored One, this teaching is quite wondrous! World-Honored One, for all the bodhisattvas engaged in the teaching and practice of Perfect Enlightenment, how many different kinds of these expedient methods are there? I beseech you to use expedient methods to teach those at this great assembly and sentient beings of the degenerate age, and cause them to awaken to the marks of reality." Having said this, he prostrated to the ground. He asked this question three times in succession.

Then the World-Honored One, addressing the bodhisattva Voice of Discernment, said: "Excellent, excellent! Good son, you have questioned well for the bodhisattvas and sentient beings of the degenerate age about the various practices of the Tathāgata. Now listen well, and I shall explain for you." The bodhisattva Voice of Discernment received this teaching with reverence and joy. All those in the great crowd became silent and listened.

"Good sons, the Perfect Enlightenment of all tathāgatas is pure, originally having neither practice nor practitioner. When they practice, all bodhisattvas and sentient beings of the degenerate age depend upon the power of unenlightened illusion. At that time (the time of practice dependent upon illusion) there are twenty-five kinds of pure meditation applications.

"Some bodhisattvas exclusively grasp ultimate quiescence, and through the power of quiescence permanently sever affliction absolutely and perfectly, and directly enter nirvana without rising from their seats. These bodhisattvas are called practitioners of *śamatha* only.

"Some bodhisattvas exclusively contemplate all-as-illusion, and by means of Buddha-power transform the world and carry out various activities, thoroughly putting into operation all the marvelous pure bodhisattva practices. In all continuous concentrations they do not fail in cessation of thought and quiescent wisdom. These bodhisattvas are called practitioners of *samāpatti* only.

"Some bodhisattvas exclusively extinguish all illusions, and without activity in the world individually sever affliction. Affliction completely severed, they directly actualize the marks of reality. These bodhisattvas are called practitioners of *dhyāna* only.

"Some bodhisattvas first attain perfect quiescence, and through the mind of quiescent wisdom shed light on all illusions and directly within these illusions produce the bodhisattva practices. These bodhisattvas are called practitioners of *śamatha* first and *samāpatti* next.

"Some bodhisattvas actualize the perfectly quiescent nature through quiescent wisdom, and then directly sever affliction and permanently escape from life and death. These bodhisattvas are called practitioners of *śamatha* first and *dhyāna* next.

"Some bodhisattvas use cessation-quiescent wisdom to remanifest illusion-power and establish all kinds of transformations to save sentient beings. Subsequently they sever affliction and enter cessation-extinction. These bodhisattvas are called practitioners of *śamatha* first, *samā-patti* next, and *dhyāna* last.

"Some bodhisattvas use the power of perfect quiescence to sever all affliction. They then produce the pure, marvelous practices of the bodhi-sattvas and save all sentient beings. These bodhisattvas are called practitioners of *śamatha* first, *dhyāna* next, and *samāpatti* last.

"Some bodhisattvas use the mind empowered by perfect quiescence to sever affliction and then save sentient beings and establish objective realms. These bodhisattvas are called practitioners of *śamatha* first and subsequent simultaneous *samāpatti* and *dhyāna*.

"Some bodhisattvas use the power of perfect quiescence to aid in the initiation of transformations, then subsequently sever afflictions. These bodhisattvas are called practitioners of simultaneous *śamatha* and *samā-patti*, followed by the practice of *dhyāna*.

"Some bodhisattvas use perfect quiescence to aid in extinction, and subsequently carry out activities to transform the world. These bodhi-sattvas are called practitioners of simultaneous *śamatha* and *dhyāna*, who subsequently practice *samāpatti*.

"Some bodhisattvas use transformation power to make various kinds of accordance, and thereby attain perfect quiescence. These bodhisattvas are called practitioners of *samāpatti* first and *śamatha* next.

"Some bodhisattvas use transformation power to create various realms, and thereby attain cessation-extinction. These bodhisattvas are called practitioners of *samāpatti* first and *dhyāna* next.

"Some bodhisattvas use transformation power to carry out Buddha-works. Then, abiding in cessation-quiescence, they sever affliction. These bodhisattvas are called practitioners of *samāpatti* first, *śamatha* next, and *dhyāna* last.

"Some bodhisattvas use transformation power's unhindered function to sever affliction, and are therefore able to abide in perfect quiescence. These bodhisattvas are called practitioners of *samāpatti* first, *dhyāna* next, and *śamatha* last.

"Some bodhisattvas use transformation power for the activity of expedient teaching and then practice within both perfect quiescence and extinction together. These bodhisattvas are called practitioners of *samāpatti* first, followed by simultaneous *śamatha* and *dhyāna*.

"Some bodhisattvas use the various generative functions of transformation power to aid in the attainment of perfect quiescence and subsequently sever affliction. These bodhisattvas are called practitioners of simultaneous *samāpatti* and *śamatha*, followed by *dhyāna*.

"Some bodhisattvas use transformation power to aid in extinction, and subsequently abide in pure uncreated quiescence of thought. These bodhisattvas are called practitioners of simultaneous *samāpatti* and *dhyāna* followed by *śamatha*.

"Some bodhisattvas use the power of extinction to produce perfect quiescence and abide in purity. These bodhisattvas are called practitioners of *dhyāna* first and *śamatha* next.

"Some bodhisattvas use the power of extinction, yet enter activity, and this negating function is practiced within all realms. These bodhisattvas are called practitioners of *dhyāna* first and *samāpatti* next.

"Some bodhisattvas use the various self-natures of extinction power, and abiding in mental quiescence, produce transformations. These bodhisattvas are called practitioners of *dhyāna* first, *śamatha* next, and *samāpatti* last.

"Some bodhisattvas use the inactive self-nature of extinction power to engage in activity, then purify the objective realm and return to quiescence. These bodhisattvas are called practitioners of *dhyāna* first, *samāpatti* next, and *śamatha* last.

"Some bodhisattvas use the various purity of extinction power, then, abiding in mental equipoise, produce transformations. These bodhisattvas are called practitioners of *dhyāna* first, followed by simultaneous *śamatha* and *samāpatti*.

"Some bodhisattvas use extinction power to aid in the attainment of quiescence, and then give rise to transformations. These bodhisattvas are called practitioners of simultaneous *dhyāna* and *śamatha*, followed by *samāpatti*.

"Some bodhisattvas use extinction power to aid in transformation, produce perfect quiescent purity and illuminate objective wisdom. These bodhisattvas are called simultaneous practitioners of *dhyāna* and *samāpatti*, followed by *śamatha*.

"Some bodhisattvas, using the wisdom of Perfect Enlightenment, harmoniously combine all of these, and in connection with all natures and characteristics, never separate from the enlightened nature. These bodhisattvas are called 'practitioners of the three kinds of accordance with the purity of the self-nature,' and these are called the bodhisattvas' twenty-five applications.

"Good sons, the teaching of the sutras is like the finger pointing to the moon. If you also look at the moon, you will fully realize that that which is pointing is ultimately not the moon. All the various words and explanations of the Tathāgata that are used to awaken bodhisattvas are also like this. All bodhisattvas practice like this.

"If you bodhisattvas and sentient beings of the degenerate age want to utilize these applications, you must maintain practices of purity, quiescence, contemplation, and sincerely repent. Then passing through three weeks, settle upon whichever of the twenty-five applications is indicated on your lot. With your whole mind and a repentant spirit, immediately choose one. Depending on what is indicated on the chosen lot, you will immediately know whether you are to practice the sudden or gradual. If there is one moment of doubt you will not be able to accomplish your assigned application."

Then the World-Honored One, desiring to reiterate the gist of this, spoke a verse. He said:

> Voice of Discernment, you should know,
> All bodhisattvas'
> Unobstructed pure wisdom
> Is without exception, produced from meditation.
> The so-called *śamatha*, *samāpatti* and *dhyāna*—
> The three methods of sudden and gradual practice—
> Have twenty-five applications.
> There are none among the tathāgatas of the ten
>   directions
> And the practitioners of the three worlds
> Who do not rely upon these methods
> In their attainment of perfection of *bodhi*—
> Except for suddenly enlightened people
> And those who have nothing to do with the dharma.
> All bodhisattvas
> And sentient beings of the degenerate age,
> Should always embrace these applications,
> Following them, endeavoring to practice them.
> Relying on the power of the Buddha's great compassion,
> Before long they will actualize nirvana.

9. Purifier of All Karmic Hindrances Bodhisattva

The bodhisattva Purifier of All Karmic Hindrances arose from his seat in the great assembly. He bowed to the Buddha's feet, and circumambulated him three times to the right. He then knelt down with his hands clasped and addressed the Buddha, saying:

"Greatly Compassionate World-Honored One, you have explained at length for all of us this inconceivable matter of the aspects of the practice of the causal stage of all tathāgatas, enabling all in the great assembly to gain that which they have never had. Having had this chance to see the Tamer, all of their passage through realms of suffering for countless *kalpas* seems as if it were but an instant of thought. We bodhisattvas have been greatly encouraged.

"World-Honored One, if this enlightened mind is originally pure, what kind of defilements cause sentient beings to suffer in delusion and not enter? My only request is that you thoroughly reveal to us the nature of existence, and cause those in this great assembly and sentient beings of the degenerate age to create the 'future eye.'" After finishing this speech, he prostrated himself to the ground. He asked this three times in succession.

Then the World-Honored One, addressing the bodhisattva Purifier of All Karmic Hindrances, said: "Excellent, excellent! Good son, you have asked well for sentient beings of the degenerate age about the expedient methods of the Tathāgata. Listen well, and I shall explain for you." The bodhisattva Purifier of All Karmic Hindrances reverently and joyfully received this teaching; those in the great assembly became silent and listened.

"Good sons, from beginningless time all sentient beings deludedly conceive and attach to the existence of 'self,' 'person,' 'sentient being,' and 'life.' They discern these four distortions to be a real self-essence. From this they directly give rise to the two states of attraction and aversion. In this false essence, they again become attached to falsehood. These two delusions interact to produce the path of deluded karma, and since there is deluded karma, they deludedly perceive transmigration. Those who come to dislike *saṃsāra* deludedly perceive nirvana, and because of this are unable to enter pure enlightenment. It is not that enlightenment rejects those who are capable of entry—rather, it is because those capable of entry do not awaken and enter. Therefore, whether one's thoughts are jumping around or silenced, both conditions ultimately revert to deluded anxiety. Why? Because there is beginningless originally arisen ignorance that becomes the subjective ego. Thus all sentient beings produce the eye of ignorance. The various natures of body, mind, and so on, are nothing but ignorance. Take for example the person who does not want to end his own life. Therefore, you should know there is enjoyment of 'selfhood' when things go well. When things don't go as one likes, then hatred and anger arise. Since this mind of attraction/aversion nourishes ignorance, those who strive to cultivate the Way never attain it.

"Good sons, what is the 'trace of self?' It is that which is witnessed by the mind of sentient beings. Good sons, when you are in good health you naturally forget about your body. But when the body becomes sick, and you make an effort correct the infirmity, with the slightest application of moxibustion and acupuncture you immediately become aware of your existence as a self. Thus, it is only in reference to this 'witnessing' that you perceive and grasp to an apparent self-essence. Good sons, every kind of witnessing from this level up to the Tathāgata's perfect perception of pure nirvana, is all the 'trace of self.'

"Good sons, what is the 'trace of person'? It is the cognition by sentient beings of the prior 'witnessing.' Good sons, once the self is cognized it is not again recognized in the same way. It is the same in the case where that which is cognized is nonself. This 'cognition,' which has gone beyond every kind of 'witnessing,' is the 'trace of person.' Good sons, if, from this level of basic recognition of self up to the perfect recognition of nirvana as self, completely including the witnessing of principle, there remains in the mind even the smallest remainder of cognition, all are called the 'trace of person.'

"Good sons, what is the 'trace of sentient being'? It is that which is beyond the self-witnessing and cognition of the minds of all sentient beings. Good sons, take for example the person who says 'I am a sentient being.' What this person has called 'sentient being,' is neither self nor other. Why is it not self? Since self is 'sentient being,' it is not self. Why is it not other? Since the self is sentient being, therefore it is not other. Good sons, what sentient beings realize in witnessing and realize in cognition is nothing more than the traces of self and person. That which does not reach the traces of self and sentient being, yet which remains as realized, is the trace of sentient being.

"Good sons, what is the 'trace of life'? This refers to that which sentient beings realize through the mind's illuminating pure awareness. Good sons, that which is not perceivable by the totality of karmic wisdom is just like the life-faculty. It is like hot water melting ice: there is no discrimination of the existence of ice or knowledge of the ice's melting. The nonexistence of a self and the awareness of a self are just like this. Good sons, when one sees with the mind's illumination, all these awarenesses are nothing but defilement. Since that of which the awarenesses are aware is not separate from defilement, it is called the 'trace of life.'

"Good sons, sentient beings of the degenerate age do not perceive the Four Traces, and though they may struggle through many *kalpas* of difficult practice while cultivating the Way, it is still nothing but conditioned existence. They are ultimately incapable of consummating the fruits of sagehood. Why? Because they regard these traces of self to be nirvana, and they regard their witnessing and cognition to be consummation [of enlightenment]. It is like a man who mistakes a thief for his son. His family's holdings can never be secure. Why? Because the lover of self also loves nirvana, and takes the suppression of the root of self-love as the characteristic of nirvana. The hater of self also hates *saṃsāra*, and not knowing that it is the attached love itself that is actually *saṃsāra*, he singles out *saṃsāra* for disdain, calling it 'non-liberation.'

"How can you know this dharma as 'nonliberation'? Good sons, these sentient beings of the degenerate age who are practicing *bodhi* regard the ego's infinitesimal perception as their own purity, and are therefore unable to penetrate to the root of the self-trace. If someone praises their [mistaken] dharma, then they will be overjoyed and immediately try to save him. But if someone criticizes their attainments, they will be filled with anger and resentment. Hence, you can know that the trace of self is being firmly held to; it is concealed in the store consciousness and is playing freely throughout the faculties without interruption.

"Good sons, if these practioners of the Way do not remove the trace of self, they will be unable to enter pure enlightenment. Good sons, if the emptiness of self is known, there can be no 'eliminator of self.' If, holding to self, you expound this dharma, it is because you have not yet eliminated self. It is the same with 'sentient being' and 'life.'

"Good sons, sentient beings of the degenerate age [mistakenly] understand these afflictions to be the dharma. Therefore they are called 'the pitiable.' Even though they struggle with great effort, they merely exacerbate their various afflictions, and therefore are unable to enter pure enlightenment.

"Good sons, sentient beings of the degenerate age do not discern the Four Traces, and erroneously taking the understanding and practice of the Tathāgata to be their own practice, they ultimately do not accomplish enlightenment. Thus there are sentient beings who understand non-attainment to be attainment and regard nonrealization as realization. When they see an adept practitioner, they are filled with jealousy. It is exactly because these sentient beings do not sever their love of self that they are unable to enter pure enlightenment.

"Good sons, sentient beings of the degenerate age hope for buddhahood but do not exert themselves to achieve awakening; they merely extend their intellectual knowledge, further enhancing the view of self. What they *should* do is just endeavor to subdue the afflictions and arouse great courage: attain what they have not attained, sever what they have not severed. Not allowing the greed, anger, love, pride, flattery, perversion, jealousy, and envy that are directed at the objective realm to arise, and extinguishing all love and attachment to self and other—I call these people 'gradually consummated.' Finding a Genuine Teacher, you will not fall into mistaken views. Therefore it is called the true dharma in the degenerate age. But if you discriminate, and have a special feeling of attraction or aversion regarding the [teacher] you are seeking, you will be unable to enter the ocean of pure enlightenment."

Then the World-Honored One, desiring to reiterate the gist of this, spoke a verse. He said:

> Purifier of Karma, you should know
> That because of attachment to and love of self
> All sentient beings
> Deludedly transmigrate without beginning.
> Not removing four kinds of traces
> They cannot accomplish *bodhi*.
> Since love and hatred arise in the mind
> And flattery and perversion remain in all thoughts
> There is much delusion and grief;
> You are unable to enter the citadel of enlightenment.
> If you are able to return to the enlightened realm,
> First leave all desire, hatred, and ignorance.
> When the dharma of attraction does not remain in the mind
> You can gradually accomplish enlightenment.
> The self and body originally do not exist:
> How can attraction and aversion arise?
> If this person seeks a Genuine Teacher
> He will never fall into evil views.
> But if 'something separate to be sought' arises in his mind
> There will ultimately be no consummation of enlightenment.

10. Universal Enlightenment Bodhisattva

Then the bodhisattva Universal Enlightenment arose from his seat in the great assembly. He bowed to the Buddha's feet and circumambulated three times to the right. He then knelt down with hands clasped and addressed the Buddha, saying:

"Greatly Compassionate World-Honored One. You have clearly explained the meditation maladies, allowing the bodhisattvas to attain that which they had not yet experienced. Their consciousnesses have been completely stilled and they have attained great tranquillity.

"World-Honored One, as the sentient beings of the degenerate age become increasingly removed from the Buddha, the sages and worthies conceal themselves, while the mistaken dharma grows and spreads. What kind of person should the sentient beings seek? On what kind of teachings should they rely? What kind of practice should they carry out? What kind of maladies should we remove, and what kind of resolution should we make, so as to prevent the blind multitude from falling into mistaken views?" Having said this, he prostrated himself to the ground. He asked this question three times in succession.

Then the World-Honored One, addressing the bodhisattva Universal Enlightenment, said: "Excellent, excellent! Good son, you have been able to question the Tathāgata on this kind practice that is able to impart to all sentient beings the fearless Eye of the Way and cause them to attain the sagely Way. Now listen well, and I shall teach you." The bodhisattva Universal Enlightenment received this teaching with great joy. Those in the great assembly became silent and listened.

"Good sons, sentient beings of the degenerate age must arouse 'great mind' and seek Genuine Teachers. Those who want to practice should seek out only someone with correct insight, whose thoughts do not abide in characteristics, who is not attached to the realms of the *arhats* and *pratyekabuddhas*, and whose mind is constantly pure even while manifesting the world's afflictions. Even while pointing out your various faults, he praises your *brahmacarya*, and prevents you from breaking the precepts. If you find this kind of person, you can attain *anuttarā-samyak-saṃbodhi*.

"Sentient beings of the degenerate age who meet this kind of person, should make offerings to him, not sparing body or life, or even holding on to property, wife, children and retainers. This Genuine Teacher constantly manifests purity throughout the four postures. Although he shows you your various errors and afflictions, his mind lacks pride.

"Good sons, if you do not arouse any negative feelings toward this Good Friend, you will ultimately be able to accomplish correct enlightenment. Your mind-flower will blossom, illuminating the worlds of the ten directions.

"Good sons, the subtle dharma that is actualized by this Genuine Teacher should be free from the Four Maladies. What are the Four Maladies? The first is the malady of 'contrivance.' Say, for example, there is someone who says 'based on my original mind I shall carry out various practices' and wants to achieve Perfect Enlightenment. Since the nature of Perfect Enlightenment is not something that can be attained by contrivance, it is called a 'malady.'

"The second is the 'naturalist' malady. Say, for example there is someone who says, 'We should presently neither cut off *saṃsāra* nor seek nirvana. *Saṃsāra* and nirvana actually lack any conception of arising and ceasing. We should just naturally go along with the various natures of reality' and wants to achieve Perfect Enlightenment. Since the nature of Perfect Enlightenment does not come about through accepting things as they are, this is called a 'malady.'

"The third is the 'stopping' malady. Say, for example, there is someone who says 'from my present thought, I shall permanently stop all thought and thus apprehend the cessation and equanimity of all natures' and wants to achieve Perfect Enlightenment. Since the nature of Perfect Enlightenment is not met through the stopping of thoughts, it is called a 'malady.'

"The fourth is the 'annihilation' malady. Say, for example, there is someone who says 'I will now permanently annihilate all defilements. Body and mind are ultimately empty, lacking anything. How much more should all the false realms of the sense organs and their objects be permanently erased,' and seeks Perfect Enlightenment. Since the characteristic of the nature of Perfect Enlightenment is not annihilation, it is called a 'malady.'

"When you are free from the Four Maladies you will be aware of purity. The making of this observation is called 'correct insight.' Any other insight is called 'mistaken insight.'

"Good sons, sentient beings of the degenerate age should exhaust their life energies in making offerings to Good Friends and serving Genuine Teachers. If the Genuine Teacher becomes close and familiar with you, you should not be proud. If he is distant, you should not be resentful. The states of unpleasantness and pleasantness are just like the empty sky. Fully realize that body and mind are ultimately equalized and that you share the same essence with all sentient beings without difference. If you practice in this way you will enter Perfect Enlightenment.

"Good sons, when sentient beings of the degenerate age are unable to accomplish the Way, it is because of the presence of beginningless seeds of self and other, attraction and aversion. Therefore they are not liberated. If there is someone who looks upon his enemy as the same as his father and mother—whose mind completely lacks duality, then he will eliminate all maladies. Then within all dharmas, self and other, attraction and aversion will also be eliminated in the same way.

"Good sons, all sentient beings of the degenerate age who want to seek Perfect Enlightenment should make their resolution, saying the following: 'I vow to cause every sentient being throughout the universe to enter the ultimate Perfect Enlightenment.' Within that Perfect Enlightenment there is no attachment to 'enlightenment' nor are there any of the traces of self, person etc. If you make this kind of resolve, you will not fall into mistaken views."

Then the World-Honored One, wanting to restate the gist of this, delivered a verse, saying:

> Universal Enlightenment, you should know
> That sentient beings of the degenerate age
> Who desire to find a Genuine Teacher
> Must look for one with the Right View
> Whose mind is far removed from the Two Vehicles
> Who does not break the precepts
> And whose root of the precepts is constantly pure.
> Who in regard to the Dharma has removed the Four Maladies,
> Which are called contrivance, stopping, naturalism, and
>   annihilation.
> If he becomes intimate with you, don't be proud
> And if he is distant, don't be resentful.
> Observing various realms, your mind will then produce the
>   miraculous.
> And if you leave home like the Buddha,
> You save all sentient beings
> So that they ultimately enter Perfect Enlightenment.
> Free from the traces such as "self" and "person,"
> You constantly rest in wisdom
> You naturally attain transcendence of mistaken views
> Actualizing enlightenment and *parinirvāṇa*.

11. Perfect Enlightenment Bodhisattva

The bodhisattva Perfect Enlightenment arose from his seat in the great assembly, bowed his head to the Buddha's feet, and circumambulated him three times to the right. He knelt down with his hands clasped, and addressed the Buddha, saying:

"Greatly Compassionate World-Honored One, you have extensively explained pure enlightenment for us, as well as various expedient methods. You have allowed sentient beings of the degenerate age to prosper greatly in their practice.

"World-Honored One, those of us present here have already awakened. But if, after your passing away, sentient beings of the degenerate age have not yet been able to awaken, how should they conduct meditation retreats to cultivate this pure realm of Perfect Enlightenment? And in the practice of the three kinds of pure meditation within Perfect Enlightenment, what are the initial steps? I only beg for your great compassion so that you will confer great benefit on the members of this great assembly and the sentient beings of the degenerate age." After saying this, he prostrated fully to the ground. He asked this question three times in succession.

Then the World-Honored One, addressing the bodhisattva Perfect Enlightenment, said: "Excellent! Excellent! Good son, you have questioned well to the Tathāgata about these kinds of expedient means in order to confer great benefit on sentient beings. Now listen well, and I shall explain for you." The bodhisattva Perfect Enlightenment received this teaching with great joy. All those in the great assembly became silent and listened.

"Good sons, among all sentient beings, whether it is when the Buddha is alive, or after he has passed away, or even during the period of the degeneration of the dharma, there are a number who have the aptitude for Mahāyāna and who have faith in the Buddha's mysterious mind of great Perfect Enlightenment, and who want to practice it. If they are living in the temple with many other followers, then they have numerous commitments and so they should just analyze according to the situation, as I have already taught.

"On the other hand, if they are not bound by commitments then they should erect a site of enlightenment and institute an intensive retreat. A long-term retreat should be 120 days. A medium-length retreat should be 100 days. A short one, 80 days, sitting quietly in a pure environment. If the Buddha is present, then you can directly correct your thoughts. If he has already passed away, then set up an image of him, and letting your mind abide in the mental picture of this image, you can bring about correct mindfulness, just the same as when he was here. After hanging up the banners and flowers, go through a period of three weeks, making obeisance to the names of all the Buddhas in the ten directions. Repenting and confessing all of your sins, you pass through three weeks with your thoughts focused. Encountering excellent states of consciousness, your mind attains pliancy.

"If you pass through to the beginning of the retreat, then for three months you will abide in stillness, and carry out the pure quiet sitting of the bodhisattvas, with your mind free from the designs of the *śrāvakas* and from involvements with other practitioners. When you come to the day of the retreat, in front of the Buddha, say this: "I, *bhikṣu/bhikṣunī/ upāsaka/upāsikā* so-and-so, would board the vehicle of the bodhisattvas, cultivate their practices of cessation-extinction, and enter with them into their abiding in the pure marks of the real. I take great Perfect Enlightenment as my temple, with body and mind dwelling peacefully in the wisdom of the equality of the nature. Since the self-nature of nirvana is not restricted in any way, I now respectfully pray that I may not abide in the views of the *śrāvakas*. I will abide for three months of quiet retreat with the Tathāgatas and great bodhisattvas of the ten directions. Since I will be cultivating the bodhisattva's great causes and conditions of unsurpassed marvelous enlightenment, I will not be constrained by the limitations of the other practitioners.

"Good sons, this is called 'the bodhisattvas' exemplifying silent retreat.' After passing through the three terms, you can practice anywhere without obstruction.

"Good sons, if, when these practicing sentient beings of the degenerate age who seek the Way of the bodhisattvas enter the three meditation terms, they experience meditative states that are different from those outlined in this sutra, they should not become attached to them.

"Good sons, those sentient beings who will practice *śamatha* must first grasp perfect quiescence, not allowing any cogitation to arise. Quiescence taken to its furthest limit results directly in enlightenment. If you can have this kind of initial quiescence, then proceeding from one body, enlightenment will extend like this throughout a whole world.

"Good sons, when enlightenment fully pervades a whole world, if there is one sentient being within that world who allows a single thought to arise, all, without exception, will know it. The same is true in the case of a hundred thousand worlds. If it is not one of the meditative states about which you were previously instructed, you should not be attached to it.

"Good sons, those sentient beings who want to practice *samāpatti* should first become mindful of all the Tathāgatas of the ten directions and all the bodhisattvas of all the worlds in the ten directions. Depending on their various methods they should grow by degrees though practice, struggling against suffering towards *samādhi*, broadly manifesting the great vow [to save sentient beings], which in turn infuses [the store consciousness] resulting in [the production of] seeds. But if it is not one of the states about which you were previously instructed, you should not become attached to it.

"Good sons, if these sentient beings want to practice *dhyāna*, they must first utilize the technique of breath observance, and in the depths of their mind become fully aware of the arising, abiding, and cessation of each thought. They must be clear in their discrimination of the breath count and practice it pervasively during each of the four postures. There is no limit to how far this mindfulness of the discrimination of breaths can penetrate, as one can gradually advance to the point where he can be aware, within the space of one hundred thousand worlds, of the falling of a single drop of rain, as if it were an object presented directly to him. But if it is really not one of the states of mind about which you were previously instructed, then afterwards you should not be attached to it. These are called the introductory expedients of the three meditations.

"If sentient beings pervasively practice these three kinds of meditation, and keep working diligently to advance, they will be called 'tathāgatas appearing in the world.' If subsequent sentient beings of the degenerate age of dull faculties desire in their hearts to attain the Way, but somehow always fall short of their goal, it is because of karmic hindrances from the past. They must strive for penance and confession and continuously re-arouse their hopes. They must first sever love and hatred, jealousy, envy, flattery, and calumny and strive for the unsurpassed state of mind. Since the three types of meditation are all the investigation of the same single matter, if one meditation doesn't work, try again with one of the others. Don't let your mind dissipate, and gradually strive for realization."

Then the World-Honored One, wanting to restate the gist of this doctrine, spoke a verse. He said:

> Perfect Enlightenment, you should know
> That all sentient beings
> Who want to seek the unsurpassed
> Must, at the outset of the three retreats,
> Repent of and admit their beginningless actions
> For a period of three weeks.
> Thereupon they will have correct thought.
> But if they do not experience the states as they have been taught
> They should not grasp them.
> In *śamatha* perfect quiescence;
> In *samāpatti* correct mindfulness;
> In *dhyāna* clear observance of the breath.
> These are called "the three purifying meditations."
> Those who diligently practice
> Are called "Buddhas appearing in the world."
> Those of dull faculties who cannot bring this into effect
> Must continuously strive at repentance
> Of their beginningless crimes.
> When all hindrances are extinguished
> The Buddha-state appears before your eyes.

12. Most Excellent of Worthies Bodhisattva

The bodhisattva Most Excellent of Worthies arose from his seat in the great assembly. He bowed his head to the feet of the Buddha and circumambulated him three times to the right. He then knelt down with his hands clasped and addressed the Buddha, saying:

"Greatly Compassionate World-Honored One. You have extensively revealed this inconceivable matter for [we bodhisattvas] and the sentient beings of the degenerate age. World-Honored One: What names are applied to this Mahāyāna teaching? How should it be cleaved to and practiced? What kinds of merits will be obtained by sentient beings who practice according to it? How shall those who cleave to and practice it be protected? And to what lands should this teaching be propagated?" Having said this, he prostrated fully to the ground. He repeated this question three times in succession.

Then the World-Honored One, addressing the bodhisattva Most Excellent of Worthies said: "Excellent! Excellent! Good son, you have asked well for the bodhisattvas and sentient beings of the degenerate age about the merits and names of this sutra teaching. Now listen well, and I shall explain for you." The bodhisattva Most Excellent of Worthies received this instruction with great joy. Those in the great assembly became silent and listened.

"Good Sons, this scripture is that which is taught by billions upon billions of countless buddhas; it is that which is protected by the Tathāgatas of the three times; it is that which is relied upon by the bodhisattvas of the ten directions; it is the pure eye of the twelve divisions of the scriptures. This scripture is called The Great Curative Extensive Perfect Enlightenment *Dhāraṇī*; it is also called The Sutra of the Fully Revealed Meaning; it is also called The Mysterious Royal *Samādhi*; it is also called the Tathāgata's Realm of Full Decisiveness; it is also called The Distinction of the Self-Nature of the Tathāgatagarbha. You should cleave to it and practice according to it.

"Good sons, this scripture expresses nothing but the state of the tathāgatas, and only the buddha-tathāgatas are able to fully explain it. If the bodhisattvas and sentient beings of the degenerate age practice according to this sutra, they will gradually advance to Buddhahood.

"Good Sons, this scripture is called the Sudden Teaching of the Mahāyāna, and sentient beings with the capacity for the sudden will awaken through it. But it also embraces the gradual practice of all sentient beings. It is like a great ocean that does not deny the entrance of any small stream; and mosquitoes and horseflies, as well as Asuras, may drink its water and take their fill.

"Good sons, say for instance there were a man who, with the purest of motivations, gathered the seven jewels in a quantity sufficient to fill a trichiliocosm, and then gave them all away for charity. This man's merit would not be equal to that of a man who heard the name of this scripture and understood the meaning of a single passage.

"Good sons, say for example there was a man who taught sentient beings as many as a hundred times the amount of the grains of sand in the Ganges River such that they all attained the level of *arhat*. This man's merit would not be equal to someone who explicated a half of a *gāthā* of this scripture. If there is any person who hears the name of this sutra and believes in it fully without a shadow of a doubt, then you can know that this person has not only sown the seeds of blessings and wisdom with one buddha or two buddhas, but has cultivated his roots of goodness with countless myriads of buddhas, listening to this sutra-teaching.

"Good sons, you should protect sentient beings of the degenerate age who are practicing this, and not let evil spirits and heretics upset their thoughts or cause them to lose heart."

Then the World-Honored One, wanting to restate the gist of this, spoke a verse. He said:

> Most Excellent of Worthies, you should know
> This scripture is that which all buddhas teach
> And that which all Tathāgatas well protect.
> It is the eye of the twelve divisions.
> It is called
> The Great Curative Extensive Perfect Enlightenment *Dhāraṇī*
> It is the expression of the realm of the Tathāgata.
> Those who practice according to it
> Gradually advance to Buddhahood.
> It is like an ocean that accepts all rivers
> And gives all of the thirsty their fill.
> If there were a person who donated the seven jewels
> Enough to fill a trichiliocosm
> It would not be equal to hearing this sutra.
> If someone transformed countless beings
> Such that they all reached arhatship
> It would not be equal to the explication of half a *gāthā*.
> You must all, for the later generations
> Protect those who give and receive this teaching
> And not allow them to backslide.

Then, from the midst of the great assembly, arose Fiery-haired Vajra-warriors, Pulverizing Vajra-warriors, Blue Vajra-warriors—altogether eighty thousand Vajra-warriors with their retinues. They got up from their seats, bowed their heads to the feet of the Buddha, and circumambulated him three times to the right. Then they addressed the Buddha, saying:

"World-Honored One, if sentient beings of the degenerate age are able to cleave to this Scripture of Mahāyāna Decisiveness, we shall protect them, as if protecting our own eyes, and we shall also protect the places where they carry out their practices. We Vajra-warriors shall guide these people, protecting them morning and night, such that they do not retrogress. Their households shall never suffer from calamity; sickness shall be eradicated; their material possessions shall be abundant and they shall never suffer from poverty.

Then the Great Brahma Kings, the Kings of the Twenty-Eight Heavens, together with the Kings of Mt. Sumeru and the Nation-Protecting Kings, arose from their seats. They bowed their heads to the Buddha's feet, circumambulated him to the right, and addressed him, saying:

"World-Honored One, we shall also protect those who cleave to this scripture. We shall bring them tranquillity and not allow them to retrogress."

Then a Great Mighty Demon King, whose name was Kumbhāṇḍa, together with a hundred thousand Demon Kings, arose from his seat. He bowed his head to the Buddha's feet and circumambulated him three times to the right. He addressed the Buddha, saying:

"I shall also protect those who cleave to this scripture by guarding them morning and night and not letting them retrogress. If an evil spirit should dare to approach within the area of one *yojana* to the place of the practitioner's abode, I shall smash him into atoms."

The Buddha having finished his preaching of this scripture, the bodhisattvas, the *devas, nāgas, yakṣās* and the rest of the eight kinds of spiritual beings along with their retinues, as well as the Heavenly Kings, Brahma Kings, and the rest of the great assembly, having heard what the Buddha taught, were all filled with great joy. They believed, embodied, and practiced this teaching.

Notes

Introduction

1. The full Chinese title of the text is *Ta-fang-kuang yüan-chüeh hsiu-to-lo liao-i ching* (大方廣圓覺修多羅了義經 *Complete Explanation Sutra of Great Corrective Extensive Perfect Enlightenment*).

2. The Ch'eng brothers are the two Sung Neo-Confucian thinkers Ch'eng-i (程頤 1033–1107) and Ch'eng-hao (程顥 1032–85). These writings of these two, along with Chu Hsi (朱熹 1130–1200), laid much of the groundwork for what ended up becoming orthodox Neo-Confucianism, which in turn became predominant in Chosŏn dynasty Korea.

3. Modern historical-philological research has yielded the conclusion that the *Platform Sutra* is most likely an eighth-century text, and thus could not have been written by Hui-neng.

4. In the strictest meaning of original usage in Abrahamic scholarly traditions, the *apocrypha* are the fourteen books of scriptural style and of late composition that were excluded from the canon of the Old Testament. For a complete treatment of the phenomenon of Abrahamic apocrypha, see Willis Barnestone's *The Other Bible: Ancient Esoteric Texts*. Also see Robert Buswell's discussion of the term on pages 3–7 of his introduction to *Chinese Buddhist Apocrypha*.

5. Robert Buswell, in his introductory essay to the volume *Chinese Buddhist Apocrypha*, gives a concise explanation of the interplay of the multiplicity of factors that played a part in the attainment of canonicity by a text. Other articles in the same volume also treat the same question in detail from a variety of perspectives. For a perspicacious literary-critical analysis of the various factors involved in the attainment or nonattainment of canonicity by a text, see Barbara Herrnstein Smith's essay "Contingencies of Value." Smith clarifies the dynamics of the interplay of the wide range of "value judgments" involved in canon formation. Although her analysis is directly concerned with the formation of the modern/Western literary canon, her observations can well be applied to the formation of other canons, including that of East Asian Buddhism.

6. Well-defined positions expressing a belief in the fundamental purity or goodness of the human mind can be discerned in Chinese philosophical writings

as early as the *I Ching, Li Chi,* and *Lun yü*. Mencius, who strongly supported the same conviction, was motivated to articulate his reasons with force in the face of opposition expressed by some of his contemporaries. The core of Mencius' argument on this position can be found in book 6A, sections 1–6 of the *Mencius*, where he disputes the position taken by his colleague Kao-tzu 告子, who argued that the mind is neither originally evil nor originally good. Mencius' position was severely criticized later by Hsün-tzu 荀子 (third century BCE), who argued in his writings (collected under the same name—the *Hsün-tzu*) that the human nature is originally evil, and therefore human beings need training and discipline in order to form societies. Despite the rational clarity of Hsün-tzu's argument, his views regarding the originally evil character of the human mind did not receive strong acknowledgment from the subsequent East Asian philosophical tradition.

7. For a revealing exposition of the problem of the coexistence of the positions of original enlightenment (or purity) and original ignorance (or defilement), see Peter Gregory's article, "The Problem of Theodicy in the *Awakening of Faith*."

8. The most thorough discussion of the implications of the sudden/gradual problematic as they concern the religious practitioner is contained in the book by Sung Bae Park, *Buddhist Faith and Sudden Enlightenment*.

9. *T'i* originally means body or substance, and refers to the more internal, more essential, hidden, important aspects of a thing. *Yung* refers to the more external, superficial, obvious, functional aspects of something. Through the *t'i-yung* view, any aspect of existence can be seen as having both dimensions. But the construction is always relative in its usage, and should not be equated with such reified Western opposites as spirit/matter, signified/signifier, and so on. For a more complete explanation of the meaning and usage of this framework, see my articles entitled "The Composition of Self-Transformation Thought in Classical East Asian Philosophy and Religion" and "East Asia's Unexplored Pivot of Metaphysics and Hermeneutics: Essence-Function/Interpenetration."

10. A vital point to be grasped concerning the essence-function model of the human being is that although these two aspects are called "inner" and "outer," or "fundamental" and "superficial," the person is never to be conceived as being divided into separate parts. These are two ways of looking at the singular human being—they are expedient tools that serve for an effective, but eternally fluid analysis. Inner/outer, fundamental/superficial are one, and are defined in terms of mutual interpenetration. It is this aspect of the essence-function relationship that distinguishes it from possible Western analogs such as spirit/matter, creator/creature, signified/signifier, and so on.

11. The meaning of this term is explained in my article "East Asia's Unexplored Pivot of Metaphysics and Hermeneutics: Essence-Function/Interpenetration."

12. The first usage of the *t'i-yung* construction is traditionally attributed to Wang-pi, in his commentary to the *Tao Te Ching*, especially to chapter 38. There is no clear evidence, however, to prove that he was the first to utilize this concept.

13. Robert Buswell offers an excellent summary explaining how East Asian Buddhist scholars were compelled to give special treatment to the conflicting

theories of *ālayavijñāna* and *tathāgatagarbha*, corresponding to the concepts of innate enlightenment and original ignorance that they received in the Indian texts. See *Formation of Ch'an Ideology*, pp. 78–104.

14. The first listing of the *SPE* in a catalog of Buddhist scriptures is found in Chih-sheng's *Kai-yüan shih-chiao-lu*, which was published in 726.

15. The first three patriarchs of the Hua-yen school, Tu-shun (杜順 557–640), Chih-yen (智嚴 602–668), and Fa-tsang (法藏 643–712) all lived prior to the time of the probable writing of the *SPE*.

16. In the *Awakening of Faith*, see *T* 1666.32.577a.26. In the *Sūtra of Perfect Enlightenment*, see *T* 842.17.915a.20–21.

17. *T* 842.17.915b.15–18.

18. *T* 1666.32.578b.25–26; trans. Sung Bae Park, *Wŏnhyo's Commentaries*.

19. *T* 842.17.913b22–28.

20. *T* 1666.32.576b27–c1

21. *T* 1666.32.576c.10

22. *T* 842.17.914a.10–12.

23. The *CYC* also received commentarial treatment from Kihwa: the *Sŏn chong yŏnggajip kwaju sŏrŭi* (Annotated Redaction of the Text and Commentaries to the *Compilation of Yung-chia of the Ch'an School*) *HPC* 7.170–216.

24. In the *CYC* he outlines the course of practice in ten chapters in terms of increasing depth and subtlety. The content of these chapters is arranged in a rational order for the guidance of practitioners, the aim being to explain clearly to the practitioner the proper way to prepare for the combined practice of *śamatha* and *vipaśyanā*; how to develop them, consummate them and then transmit them to others. The content, style, and language of the *SPE* and *CYC* are so close that one might even be given to wonder if the two authors were not in some way personally associated (or even the same person?). A good deal of historical and textual analysis would be necessary to develop a viable argument, but given the time period in which he lived, the circles in which he traveled, and the greatly similar content and style of his two known works with the *SPE*, if I were to begin looking for the author of the *SPE*, I would start with someone like Yung-chia.

25. *T* 2154.55.565a1–4. Buddhatrāta is not listed as the translator of any other text, nor is any biographical information available.

26. These works, which are no longer extant, are those by Wei-ch'üeh, Wu-shih, Chien-chih, and Tao-ch'üan. Tsung-mi discusses the commentaries by his four predecessors in his preface to the Great Commentary. See *Z* 243.9.335a.

27. The pivotal role played by Tsung-mi in the transformation of Buddhism in East Asian is elaborated masterfully by Peter Gregory in his book *Tsung-mi and the Sinification of Buddhism*.

28. In the appendix to his *Tsung-mi*, Peter Gregory lists seven extant and non-extant works in approximately seventy-eight fascicles by Tsung-mi related to the *SPE*. See *Tsung-mi*, pp. 320–25.

29. Translation by Peter Gregory, *Tsung-mi and the Sinification of Buddhism*, p. 54.

30. Hsiao-tsung wrote the *Yü chu yüan chüeh ching* (The Imperial Commentary to the *Sutra of Perfect Enlightenment*). Z 251.10.151–66.

31. Te-ch'ing wrote the *Yüan chüeh ching chih chieh* (Direct Explanation of the *Sutra of Perfect Enlightenment*). Z 258.10.480–509. Translated into English by Charles Luk together with his rendition of the sutra.

32. Besides Tsung-mi's work, there are about sixteen extant Chinese premodern commentaries on the *SPE* contained in volumes 9 and 10 of the *Zokuzōkyō*. As one reads through these, their reliance on Tsung-mi's initial work is quite noticeable.

33. Wŏnhyo composed eighty-six works in over two hundred fascicles. Of these twenty-one are extant. Information regarding Wŏnhyo and progress on a large-scale effort to translate his works into English is available on the WWW at http://www.human.toyogakuen-u.ac.jp/~acmuller/budkor/wonhyotranslation.htm.

34. See *Formation of Ch'an Ideology*, pp. 123–25.

35. For English translations of excerpts from the treatises of these two figures, see *The Korean Approach to Zen*, pp. 12–14.

36. The fact that I have located mention of the *SPE* first in Ŭich'ŏn does not mean that the text was not present in Korea at an earlier date. Nonetheless, its lack of citation in other materials does indicate a lack of widespread currency.

37. To date, three reliable full-length studies on Chinul have been published in English: Hee-Sung Keel's *Chinul: The Founder of the Korean Sŏn Tradition*; Robert Buswell's *The Korean Approach to Zen* (reprinted as *Tracing Back the Radiance*) and Jae Ryong Shim's Ph.D. dissertation, "The Philosophical Foundation of Korean Zen Buddhism: The Integration of Sŏn and Kyo by Chinul (1158–1210)."

38. In the development of Chinul's main positions, other scriptures that played an important role included the *AMF, HYC,* and *Platform Sutra,* while other important mentors included Ta-hui (大慧 1089–1163), and Li T'ung-hsüan (李通玄 635–730).

39. The *Hsin hua-yen ching lun* is an influential commentary on the *Hua-yen ching* written by the T'ang scholar Li T'ung-hsüan. Chinul's longest work is a subcommentary to this work, entitled *Hwaŏm non chŏryo*. HPC 4.767–869.

40. The sutra passage is from *T* 842.17.914c6. Chinul's citation in the *Chinsim chiksŏl* is at *HPC* 4.718a2–7. See sutra passage #29 in the subsequent translation.

41. *HPC* 4.718a17–20. Citation from *SPE* is at *T* 842.17.914c2–6

42. *HPC* 4.720b16–23. This citation spans two sections in the *SPE, T* 842.17. 913b22–24 and *T* 842.17.913b28–c2.

43. The number of quotes from the *SPE* in Chinul's writings are about the same as those from the *AMF,* with the two of these forming the largest single segment of his scriptural citations.

44. This is a massive collection of ancient precedents from Ch'an and pre-Ch'an Buddhist literature that comprises the entire fifth volume of the *HPC*.

45. The *Chogye chingak kuksa ŏrok*.

46. For these similes in Hyesim's teaching record, see, for example, *HPC* 6.20a, 6.31a, 6.32b, 6.33b, and so on.

47. *HPC* 6.57c.

48. *HPC* 6.67–68.

49. The *Paeg'un hwasang ŏrok, HPC* 6.637a–668c.

50. *HPC* 6.696a21–25. The citation of the *SPE* is not exact, being derived from the passage at *T* 842.17.914a12–14.

51. A reference to Chou kung-tan 周公旦 and Shao-kung 召公, two worthies who cooperated together in the establishment of the Chou dynasty. This translation is from the *Hamhŏ tang tŭkt'ong hwasang haengjang, HPC* 7.250c6–11.

52. While the *Haengjang* does not specify the exact amount of time that Kihwa spent with Muhak prior to his travels, it does indicate that the combined length of study and travel was seven years.

53. "Dropping the wash bucket" is a common Ch'an metaphor for a sudden and unexpected awakening to reality and a concomitant release of all kinds of self-imposed anxieties.

54. *HPC* 7.251a.4–9.

55. The material resulting from these lectures would later be published as the *Kŭmgang panyaparamilgyŏng o ka hae sŏrŭi*.

56. The title of the first chapter of the *Chuang Tzu*.

57. *HPC* 7.251a.18–22.

58. *HPC* 7.251b.1–5.

59. A line from the *Sutra of Perfect Enlightenment*. See *T* 842.17.913c.4–5; chapter 1, sutra passage #11 in this translation.

60. For more detail on the *Hyŏn chŏng non*, see chapter 7 of my Ph.D. dissertation, or my article "The Buddhist-Confucian Conflict in the Early Chosŏn and Kihwa's Syncretic Response: The *Hyŏn chŏng non*."

61. Li wrote a famous commentary to the *Hua-yen ching* entitled *Hsin Hua-yen ching lun*.

62. *HPC* 4.768a.

63. This issue is treated by Chinul most explicitly in his *Chinsim chiksŏl* (Straight Talk on the True Mind) and the *Wŏndon sŏngpullon* (The Perfect and Sudden Attainment of Buddhahood).

64. The general influence of Chinul's Sŏn-Kyo thought can be seen in the nature of the work of his most important disciple Hyesim, who compiled the largest anthology of scriptural and Sŏn writings collections in Korean Buddhism,—the *Sŏnmun yŏmsongjip* (Compilation of Examinations of and Verses on Ancient Precedents), which occupies the entire fifth volume of the *HPC*. Nonetheless, Hyesim did not directly address the Sŏn/Kyo problem in the confrontational manner of his teacher.

65. Kihwa's discussion in the *O ka hae* of the relationship of the worded and wordless teaching, which is introduced in the present context, is examined in further depth in my article "Kihwa's Analysis of the Relationship between the Worded and Wordless Teachings: The *O ka hae sŏrŭi*."

66. "Ts'ao-chi of Huang-mei" is more commonly known as Hui-neng, the Sixth Patriarch. Thus Kihwa is referring to the content of the *Platform Sutra of the Sixth Patriarch*.

67. *HPC* 7.12.c5–10.

68. The length of Śākyamuni's teaching career.

69. In the above two sentences Kihwa is alluding to the famous dictum from the *Heart Sutra*, "form is emptiness, emptiness is form."

70. *HPC* 7.42c21–43a5.

71. That is, a logic that is based on an understanding of emptiness, which often produces semantic relationships that are opposite from ordinary logic.

72. *HPC* 7.13b3–8.

73. *HPC* 7.13b11–12.

74. *HPC* 7.13b16–17

75. *HPC* 7.13c16–24.

76. These amendments are carefully explained in the course of the following translation. I have also done a full retranslation of the *SPE* according to the amendments of Kihwa that is included as an appendix to the present work.

77. There is one exception to this rule. Kihwa, once during his commentary to the *SPE* cites a passage directly from the *Śūraṅgama-sūtra.*

78. The first five characters of the full title of the *SPE* are 大方廣圓覺, which I translate in the main text, in accord with Kihwa's explanation, as "Great Curative Extensive Perfect Enlightenment."

79. The first four characters of the full title of the *Hua-yen ching* are 大方廣佛, which, according to Kihwa's interpretation, can be translated as "Great Curative Extensive Buddha."

80. *HPC* 7.126a18–24.

81. Although Kihwa's writings are much more extensive than those of Hyujŏng, Hyujŏng seems to have had greater personal impact in terms of number of disciples. His role as leader of the monk's militia that was instrumental in the expulsion of the invading Japanese army has served to make him a national folk hero.

82. *T* 842.17.914a19–20.

83. *HPC* 7.639a2–9.

84. See, for example, *HPC* 7.685b, 710b, 714a.

85. *HPC* 8.191c.

86. See Buswell, *The Zen Monastic Experience*, pp. 96–97.

87. *HPC* 10.49.

88. See *Kankoku bussho kaidai jiten*, pp. 195–96.

89. For a description of this modern curriculum, see Buswell, *The Zen Monastic Experience*, pp. 98–99, and Keel, *Chinul*, pp. 175–78.

90. The places in which my translation differs from Luk's are often due to the influences of the two different commentators we are following. Also related to the influence of the two different commentators are mine and Luk's divergent perspectives in the comparison of the *SPE* with related scriptures. Luk, following the commentary of Te-ch'ing, tends to cite the *Śūraṅgama-sūtra* when trying to connect doctrinal themes to other sutras. My translation, taking into account the usage of *AMF* hermeneutics and imagery by Kihwa, tends to cite the *Awakening of Faith.*

91. Yanagida, *Engakukyō*, p. 283.

92. Most prominent in this regard are the passages on the "dharma-prac-

tice" (sutra passages #11 and #12 below); the "separation from illusion" (sutra passage #22); and the long guided meditation in the chapter of Universal Vision (sutra passages #27–35).

Kihwa's Introduction to His Commentary

1. In opening up his introduction to the *SPE* by placing it in the framework of the Three Greatnesses of Essence, Attributes, and Function, Kihwa is making a strong allusion to the *Awakening of Faith*, the text in which these three concepts are developed.

2. See the chapter of Mañjuśrī, sutra passage #13.

3. *Dharma* 法 is a term that is used extensively by Kihwa (as it is in Buddhist literature in general) to include a broad scope of meanings. In this sentence its meaning of "quality," "essence," or "element" is implied. When the term *dharma* is used to refer to the qualities or basic constituents (*guṇa*) of existence, it often has objective (as opposed to subjective) connotations, especially in the case where Mahāyāna Buddhists talk about "the emptiness of self (subject) and dharmas (objects)." In the earlier Indian philosophical environment in which the term developed, *dharma* was a synonym for the Vedic term *ṛta*, which implied the ordering of the universe, not dissimilar from the emerging Chinese concept of *li* 理 (principle). Thus *dharma* was initially assimilated into early Indian Buddhism with the connotations of "the order of the universe," "law," "principle," and "reality." With these implications, *dharma* came to refer to the Buddha's teaching itself. It is precisely its inclusion of this broad range of meanings that makes it so attractive for use by Buddhist writers such as Kihwa. In translation, we can render it as "element," "objective situation," "reality," "principle," or "teaching," according to the situation (as I sometimes do) but anytime we render the term in this way, we eliminate the simultaneous implication of all the other meanings. Therefore I often leave it untranslated.

4. Chapter of Mañjuśrī, sutra passage #7; *T* 842.17.913b.19.

5. Chapter of Mañjuśrī, sutra passage #7; *T* 842.17.913b.20–21.

6. Chapter of Samantabhadra, sutra passage #21; *T* 842.17.914a.10–11.

7. I have chosen "curative" as my translation for *pang* based on Kihwa's interpretation of its meaning in this introduction. Another possibility would be "remedial" as an adjective derived from "remedy," but in colloquial usage the term "remedial" has inappropriate negative connotations.

8. Chapter of Mañjuśrī, sutra passage #6.

9. Chapter of Samantabhadra, sutra passage #22.

10. The term "forget" (*wang/mang* 忘) is used throughout Kihwa's commentary in a positive sense of "being free from."

11. Chapter of Universal Vision, sutra passage #36.

12. In Buddhism it is understood that there are certain situations where the practitioner must be forced to break the precepts.

13. The term "self-improvement and improvement of others" 自利利他 is discussed in the *Awakening of Faith* at *T* 1666.32.581c13 ff.

14. For example, chapter of Mañjuśrī, sutra passage #5.

15. This refers to a general theme in the sutra; this phrase is not found in the actual text.

16. A summary of sutra passage #31 in the chapter of Samantabhadra. See *T* 842.17.914c.16–19.

17. That is, from the standpoint of emptiness.

18. Chapter of Universal Vision, sutra passage #35; *T* 842.17.915a12.

19. Three capacities of sentient beings (三根) are superior capacity 上根 ("sharp faculties" 銳根), middling capacity 中根, and small capacity 下根 (also called "dull faculties" 鈍根). In Kihwa's treatment of this text, those of superior capacity are also categorized as being of "sudden" capacity 頓根. This recognition of the differences between people in terms of level of religious sensitivity is an important component of Mahāyāna Buddhist doctrine, and is directly related to the concept of expedient means. Kihwa will, throughout this commentary, specify which portions of the text are applicable to which levels of capacity.

20. Innate (original) enlightenment 本覺 is an important concept in such East Asian texts as the *SPE* and *AMF*. It refers to the fact that the original nature of the human mind is enlightenment, and that the realization of enlightenment is none other than the revelation of the person's fundamental nature. Initial, or "actualized" enlightenment (*shih-chiao/sigak* 始覺) is the first phenomenal experience of enlightenment that appears in contrast to habituated ignorance. For the explanation of these two in the *Awakening of Faith*, see *T* 1666.32.576b15 ff. and Hakeda, pp. 37–40.

21. As in the case of the above three quotes, Kihwa is fond of citing passages derived from his extensive familiarity with East Asian philosophical literature, Buddhist, Confucian, and Taoist, without naming his sources. I have located some of these, but unfortunately many must be left unidentified.

22. *I Ching, Hsi tz'u chuan*, section 1.

23. See Legge, *I Ching*, p. 420.

24. *I Ching, Hsi tz'u chuan*, section 1.

25. "Apprehension and discarding" refers to the exercise of appropriating the virtues that one currently lacks, while at the same time finding one's mistakes and eliminating them.

26. *I Ching, Hsi tz'u chuan*, section 1.

27. The line "penetrated by one thread from beginning to end (始終而一貫)" is one that we find repeated throughout Kihwa's writings. The *locus classicus* is *Analects* 4.15, where Confucius says "my Tao is penetrated by a single thread" (子曰、參乎、吾道一以貫之哉).

28. These citations from the *I Ching* are all from the same discussion contained in section 1 of the *Hsi tz'u chuan*. In this section "great" (which is associated with heaven) has a vertical connotation referring to the "height" of one's own wisdom. "Extensive" (associated with the earth) has a horizontal connotation and refers to the practice of compassion in reaching out to others.

29. *Hsi tz'u chuan*, section 1.

30. A "worldling" (*fan-fu/pŏmbu* 凡夫) is an unenlightened, ordinary person. The terms "worthy" and "sage" are originally of Confucian origin. The worthy (*hsien/hyŏn* 賢) is a person who has a significant degree of religious attainment—in the *SPE*, an *arhat* or *pratyekabuddha*. The sage (*sheng/sŏng* 聖) in the *SPE* is a practitioner of the highest stage prior to Buddhahood—a bodhisattva.

31. Chapter of Pure Wisdom, sutra passage #69; *T* 842.17.917b2; *HPC* 7.150a7.

32. I have not been able to locate this passage in the Confucian corpus.

33. *Hsi tz'u chuan*, section 1. In this section, heaven (nondelimitation) is now associated with "perfect" and earth (delimitation) is associated with the "cure."

34. The three powers (*san tsai/samjae* 三才) are heaven, man, and earth.

35. *I Ching, Hsi tz'u chuan*, section 1.

36. Each of the chapters of the *Sutra of Perfect Enlightenment* are named after the particular bodhisattva who acts as interlocutor for the Buddha in that chapter.

37. That is, chapters 2 through 9. There are twelve chapters altogether.

38. *T* 842.17.913b.19–20. Chapter of Mañjuśrī, sutra passage #7.

39. *T* 842.17.913b.21; *HPC* 7.129a2. Chapter of Mañjuśri, sutra passage #8.

40. Chapter of Universal Enlightenment, sutra passage #100; *T* 842.17.920a.29–b.1.

41. Chapter of Perfect Enlightenment, sutra passage #113; *T* 842.17.921a1.

42. This is not an actual phrase from that chapter.

43. Sutra passage #22; *T* 842.17.914a.21.

44. Sutra passage #28; *T* 842.17.914c.4; *HPC* 7.135c23..

45. *T* 842.17.915a23–24. Chapter of Universal Vision, sutra passage #36. Contrivance, stopping, naturalism, and annihilation (*tso/chak, chih/chi, jen/im, mieh/myŏl* 作止任滅). In chapter 10 of the sutra each of these four attitudes toward religious practice is shown to be counterproductive when taken to be a path in and of itself. Thus they are called "the Four Maladies." The position of the two words "contrivance 作" and "naturalism 任" is reversed here as compared to the line cited in sutra passage #36, but accords with the order in which the four are treated in chapter 10.

46. (*cheng-tsung/chŏngjong* 正宗), that is, the main expository body of the sutra.

47. (*liu t'ung fen/yut'ongbun* 流通分), which traditionally closes sutras and *śāstras*.

48. *Śūraṃgama-sutra, T* 945.19.130a21. Kihwa also cites this line in his commentary to sutra passage #22 in the chapter of Samantabhadra.

49. *T* 842.17.913b.19. Sutra passage #7 of the chapter of Mañjuśrī.

50. *T* 842.17.917c.12; *HPC* 7.151c18. Sutra passage #74 in the chapter of Power and Virtue Unhindered.

51. "Cultivation" here is a translation of *hsiu* 修, which I will also translate as "practice" in other places in the text. Here, I more specifically translate as "cultivation" to distinguish from *hsing* 行, the ideograph used in place of *hsiu* when this phrase is repeated just below, in the last line of the paragraph. Most of the time in this sutra the two terms are interchangeable, especially in the context similar to this, where "cultivation" or "practice" is being referred to in contrast to "faith" 信, "understanding" 解, "awakening" 悟, "realization" 證, and "transformation" 化.

52. The first four words of the title of the *Hwaŏmgyŏng* are "Great Curative Extensive Buddha." (Kor.: *tae-pang-kwang-pul* 大方廣佛). See the title pages of *T* 278 and 279 in *Taishō* vols. 9 and 10.

53. *Hwaŏm* (Ch. *hua-yen* 華嚴) literally means "adorned by flowers."

54. From Ŭisang's *Ocean Seal Samādhi*. See *Han'guk pulgyo chŏnsŏ*, vol. 2, p. 1. *Hwaŏm ilsŭng pŏpkye to* (華嚴一乘法界圖; Chart of the Dharma-world of the Single Vehicle of the Hua-yen), *T* 1887A.45.711a–716a.

55. A "fully revealed" (了義) doctrine scripture in East Asian Mahāyāna Buddhism is understood to be a text that does not attach itself to one aspect of the Buddhadharma. That is, it is not merely a simple, elementary doctrine, relying primarily on the relative truth, and neither is it a strictly "sudden" text, apprehensible only to those practitioners who are already in possession of the most profound religious insights. The *Sutra of Perfect Enlightenment*, though relatively short, embraces a variety of Buddhist perspectives, ranging from the most elementary to the most advanced.

56. Kihwa is here referring to a point about the etymology of the term *sūtra*, which has an etymology similar to that of the English term "text,"—is related in meaning to "textile."

57. For the explanation of the meaning of this technical term, see Kihwa's opening statement to the chapter of Mañjuśrī.

58. Doubting oneself, doubting the teacher, and doubting the dharma.

59. In the "Reception of Prediction by the Five Hundred Disciples" chapter of the *Lotus Sutra*, Ānanda and Rahula beg the Buddha to give predictions for them, since he has given predictions of Buddhahood for others. The Buddha responds by telling Ānanda that he will definitely become a Buddha in a future age, with the name "Tathāgata-King Mountain Sea Wisdom Omnipotent Penetration." See Leon Hurvitz' translation of the *Sutra of the Lotus Blossom of the Fine Dharma*, p. 166, and *T* 262.9.29b21–c15.

60. *Bhagavan*, a term commonly used to refer to Śākyamuni Buddha, was used in ancient Indian religion used to name sages. According to Tsung-mi, the term contains six meanings: authority (*aiśvarya*); correct meaning (*dharma*); freedom from worldly desires (*vairāgya*); auspiciousness (*śrī*); excellent reputation (*yaśas*), and liberation (*mokṣa*). The *Prajñāpāramitā-śāstra* attributes four kinds of qualities to the *bhagavan*: possession of virtue; possession of discrimination; praiseworthiness; and the ability to eradicate defilements. Other texts give other sets of meanings. See *Bukkyōgo daijiten*, p. 1091a.

1. Mañjuśrī

1. Below, sutra passage #13, last line.

2. The Sanskrit term *dhāraṇī* is most commonly used to refer to a long mantra that contains occult power as the essence of the Buddhist teachings. It is also translated into Chinese as "total retention," that is, memory—keeping the teaching in the mind without forgetting. It also indicates the retention of manifold virtues.

3. For the usage of this simile of disorientation in the *Awakening of Faith*, see

T 1666.38.577a3 ff. and 579c23. In the *Sutra of the Heroic March Samādhi*, see *T* 945.19.120b21–23.

4. That is, they are illusory.

5. The term "counteractive awareness" used here is similar to the concepts of "corrective" and "curative" defined in Kihwa's introduction.

2. Samantabhadra

1. Above, chapter of Mañjuśrī sutra passage #12.

2. That is, they are illusory.

3. Above, chapter of Mañjuśrī sutra passage #11.

4. In this passage, the addition of these four words changes the grammatical structure of the question, making it read much more smoothly. The general point remains the same.

5. Ignorance, desire, and hatred.

6. The Ten Fetters are: desire, hatred, ignorance, pride, doubt, view of self, extreme view, evil view, view of attachment to views, view of morality. The first five hinder those of lesser spiritual development while the second five hinder those of greater spiritual development.

7. The simile of water and waves is one of the more prominent utilized in the *Awakening of Faith*. See *T* 1666.32.578a7–12 and Hakeda, pp. 41 and 45.

8. Here, the ideograph *li* 離 and compound *yüan-li* 遠離 could both be rendered into English as noun and verb as "separating/separation" or "becoming free/freedom." *Separation* is the basic meaning of the term, but in Buddhist texts, 離 takes on strong connotations of "freedom" (from defilement, delusion, etc.). At first I attempted to translate the term consistently in one way, and then the other. But in both cases I felt the English to be too unnatural. Therefore, in this final version, I have used both "free" and "separate." In the earlier part of this passage, I have used "separate" to translate the compound *yüan-li* with a progressive verbal nuance, and at the end of the passage, have rendered the single ideograph *li* as "being free" with a resultant, "state-of-being" connotation.

9. *T* 945.19.130a21.

10. *T* 945.19.117c26.

3. Universal Vision

1. Most of the time I have translated *ju-huan san-mei/yŏhwansammae* (如幻三昧) as "as-illusion *samādhi*," which means to perceive the illusory nature of existence in a state of heightened consciousness. This term will be used throughout the rest of the sutra. But as Kihwa will point out in this chapter, the *samādhi* itself is also illusory, and thus I occasionally render it as "illusory *samādhi*," according to the context.

2. From the *Tao Te Ching*, chapter 64.

3. The six sensory faculties associated with the six organs of sight, smell, taste, hearing, touch, and the symbolic function of conceptualization.

4. The three practices are: moral discipline or "precepts" (*śīla*, 戒), concentration (*samādhi*, 定), and wisdom (*prajñā* 慧).

5. *HPC* 7.157a9. Sutra passage #83.

6. My rendering of this passage follows Robert Buswell's earlier translation of it in *The Korean Approach to Zen*, p. 169.

7. Five Colors is a classical Chinese term equivalent to "the whole spectrum," and thus means "all colors" or "any color."

8. The *Twelve Loci* and the *Eighteen Realms* are closely related concepts developed in Buddhist epistemology. The Twelve Loci are the six sense organs and their objects. The Eighteen Realms are the six sense faculties, their six objects, and the six consciousnesses that link the faculties and the objects.

9. The *Twenty-Five Kinds of Existence* are a subdivision of the three realms that sentient beings transmigrate through into twenty-five further specific states of being. There are fourteen of these existences in the Desire realm, seven in the Form realm, and four in the Formless realm. These are grouped into: the Four Evil Destinies, the Four Continents, the Six Heavens of Desire, the Four Meditation Heavens, the Heavens of the Five Pure Abodes, and the Four Spheres of the Formless Realm.

10. The *Ten Powers* are ten kinds of powers of awareness specially possessed by the Buddha, which are perfect knowledge of the following: (1) distinguishing right and wrong; (2) knowing the karmas of all sentient beings of the past, present, and future; (3) knowledge of all forms of meditation; (4) knowledge of the relative capacities of sentient beings; (5) knowledge of what sentient beings desire and think; (6) knowledge of the different levels of their existence; (7) knowledge of the results of various methods of practice; (8) knowledge of the transmigratory states of all sentient beings and the courses of karma they will follow; (9) knowledge of the past lives of all sentient beings and the nirvanic state of nondefilement; (10) knowledge of the methods of destroying all evil passions.

11. The *Four Kinds of Fearlessness*, or utter conviction in preaching the dharma, that are possessed by a buddha are: (1) fearlessness in asserting that he has attained Perfect Enlightenment; (2) fearlessness in asserting that he has destroyed all defilements; (3) fearlessness in showing people those elements that hinder the realization of the dharma, and (4) fearlessness in expounding the method of liberation.

12. The *Four Types of Unobstructed Wisdom* are: (1) no mistake in teaching; (2) no lack in regard to understanding the internal meaning of the teaching; (3) "unhindered speech," that is, the understanding of all languages; and (4) "unhindered ease in explanation," which is the free use of the above three in the effort of saving all sentient beings.

13. The *Eighteen Distinctive Characteristics* of the Buddha in East Asian Buddhism are (1–3) unmistaken thought, word, and deed; (4) mind of equality toward all beings; (5) stable mind in meditation; (6) all-embracing mind that rejects nothing; (7–11) the power of not-backsliding in terms of the aspiration,

diligence, mindfulness, concentration, and wisdom toward the salvation of all beings; (12) the power of not falling back from freedom into bondage; (13–15) the manifestation of wisdom power in thought, word, and deed for the purpose of saving all beings; (16–18) immediate total knowledge of all affairs of past, present, and future.

14. The *Thirty-seven Aids to Enlightenment* are thirty-seven kinds of practices for the attainment of enlightenment. They are: the Four Bases of Mindfulness, the Four Right Efforts, the Four Occult Powers, the Five Roots of Goodness, the Five Powers, the Seven Factors of Enlightenment, and the Eightfold Holy Path.

15. The *84,000 Dhāraṇī-Entrances,* means "all the Buddhist teachings." Eighty-four thousand should be understood to mean an infinitely large amount, due to the limitless possibilities of explanation of reality to sentient beings.

16. Or "natural world."

17. The *mano*-consciousness is the sixth of the eight layers of consciousness according to the framework developed by the school of Consciousness-only. Its function is in symbol-formation and conceptualization, and it is the locus for discriminative and rational thought. It also serves as the ruler of the five sensory consciousnesses, as it gathers and organizes their perceptions.

18. These four reifications of tendencies in religious practice are the main topic of discussion in chapter 10, starting from sutra passage #104.

4. Vajragarbha

1. Mentioned in sutra passage #2.
2. Sutra passage #8.
3. Sutra passage #24.
4. Sutra passage #36.
5. "信爲道源功德母、長養一切諸善法。" This is a well-known line that is cited regularly throughout Korean Buddhist writings, from the early unified Silla to the late Chosŏn. It originally comes from Buddhabhadra's translation of the *Ta fang kuang fo hua-yen ching,* fascicle 6 (T 278.9.433b6–7). Its frequent citation in Korean works is probably due to its appearance in Wŏnhyo's *Commentary on the Awakening of Faith (Kisillon so)* T 1844.44.203a28–29.

6. Imagine an evening campfire when someone pulls a burning rope out of the fire that now has a glowing tip. When your friend whirls the rope, and your gaze remains fixed, it looks like a spinning wheel.

7. A contemporary version of this metaphor is the feeling one gets when sitting in a stopped train with another train on the adjacent track. When one of the trains begins to move, it is sometimes difficult to tell which one is actually moving.

8. The classical Chinese term for "world" (世界) is comprised of the two Chinese ideographs *shih/se* (世) and *chieh/kye* (界). Kihwa treats the term by breaking into its two component parts and analyzing each for its philosophical connotations.

9. The simile of purifying gold will be told below in passage #45.

10. Kihwa has replaced "closely according" after the words "Perfect Enlightenment" with "marvelous mind."

11. The present rendering of this line represents a gradualistic, goal-oriented interpretation. It could also be translated as "The gold does not come into being because of smelting; it is already perfect gold, and will never again become ore," which would reflect a suddenistic understanding.

12. The four sages are the *śrāvaka, pratyekabuddha,* bodhisattva, and buddha.

13. Although the term "love" (*ai* 愛) usually has strong positive connotations, in this text it has negative connotations of clinging and attachment.

14. Above, sutra passage #41.

15. The Five Obscurations [*wu-kai/ogae* 五蓋] are five kinds of defilements that hamper the function of the true mind. As interpreted by Kihwa, they are: doubt, attached love, ignorance, anger, and agitation.

5. Maitreya

1. Sutra passage #36.

2. Sutra passage #47.

3. "Being" and "becoming" are also the tenth and eleventh of the twelve limbs of dependent origination.

4. Animal, hell-being, and hungry ghost.

5. Luk translates this line as "complete enlightenment is attainable by all sentient beings." See his translation, p. 211.

6. 九皋禽之翹足 . From the "Crying Crane" (鶴鳴) section of the *Shih ching* (*Book of Odes*). This metaphor refers to a situation where despite something being hidden in a far-away place, it is known to everyone. Thus, a metaphor for the interpenetrated nature of existence.

7. See the *Tao Te Ching*, chapter 64.

8. Ignorance, attraction, and revulsion.

6. Pure Wisdom

1. The doctrine of the mutual permeation of suchness and ignorance is developed in the *Awakening of Faith*. See *T* 1666.32.578a18–b25, and Hakeda, p. 56ff.

2. The *locus classicus* of the doctrine of the six coarse defilements and three subtle defilements is in the *Awakening of Faith*. See *T* 1666.32.577c26–578a3 and Hakeda, pp. 51–52.

3. That is, of arising of cyclic existence within noncyclic existence and of practice and actualization within nonpractice and actualization.

4. The *bhūmis* are the forty-first through fiftieth stages in the bodhisattva's course of practice.

5. The grammatical structure of this line would also allow for it to be rendered

in English as "But if you look again at the moon and completely understand, then what is being pointed to is ultimately not the moon." This interpretation goes one level deeper than the current translation and is worth considering. The present translation, however, accords with the interpretation given to this line by Kihwa in the chapter of Voice of Discernment below (sutra passage #81).

6. The end of sutra passage #81 in chapter 8. Kihwa will discuss the reasons for this textual correction in detail when he gets to that point in the text.

7. Power and Virtue Unhindered

1. Desire, anger, and ignorance.

2. The guarantee of sentient beings eventually becoming able "to hear the Buddha's name and see his form" is one of the vows of Amitābha Buddha.

3. The binome *chi-mieh/chŏngmyŏl* 寂滅 could normally be rendered into English with a single word such as "quiescence," "cessation," "extinction," "annihilation," or "erasure." But since in this commentary, and especially in chapters 7 and 8, Kihwa deliberately breaks the compound into its two component parts, we are forced to render the two words separately. Therefore "cessation-extinction."

4. The term *pien-hua/pyŏnhwa* 變化, rendered here as "creation" literally means "transformation." There is (from the standpoint of English) an overlap in meaning that is reflective of the Buddhist ontology, wherein there is no such thing as creation out of "nothing"—everything that appears in the world is nothing other than a transformation of what existed in the prior moment, through dependent origination. This being so, whenever the reader meets the term "illusory transformations" he/she may be aware that the author is referring to nothing other than the "created phenomena" of existence.

5. As contrasted to a "ceasing" practice, such as *śamatha*.

6. *HPC* 7.152c16; next sutra passage.

7. See the next sutra passage below.

8. Therefore, Kihwa is saying that each of the two logographic components of the binome *chi-mieh/chŏngmyŏl* 寂滅 refers back to one of the earlier meditations.

9. The Four Traces are discussed below, in chapter 9.

8. Voice of Discernment

1. "Coarse apprehension and fine analysis" is a translation of the Chinese *chüeh-kuan* (覺觀), which is in turn the earlier Chinese rendering of the Sanskrit *vitarka* and *vicāra*, which was later rendered as *hsin-tz'u* (尋伺). *Vitarka* is the coarse mental function of making a supposition or inference, while *vicāra* is the function of fine analysis. In the Ch'an school both are ultimately considered to be hindrances to meditation.

2. Vajragarbha has converted doubt into faith; Maitreya has converted attached love into compassion; Pure Wisdom has converted ignorance into wisdom; Power and Virtue Unhindered has converted anger into power; and Voice of Discernment will now convert agitation into correct discrimination or "discernment." What Kihwa is calling the Five Virtues are more commonly termed the Five Roots of Goodness.

3. The Chinese term translated here as "application" is *lun* (輪), meaning "wheel" or "ring."

4. An intralinear note here says "arising, abiding, changing, and cessation" to make it clear that it is these Four Marks that are being referred to here, rather than the Four Traces of self, person, sentient being, and life that are the topic of the next chapter.

5. 修多羅教如標月指。若復見月、了知所標畢竟非月。一切如來種種言説開示菩薩亦復如是. Pure Wisdom, sutra passage #67.

6. Sutra passage #67.

7. Sutra passage #67.

8. The last line of sutra passage #57 in the chapter of Maitreya.

9. Sutra passage #67. Instead of "three sentences" the original text says "the thirty-six words" (Chinese characters).

10. 符節. Two matching slips of wood on which a message or contract was written. Since the two were originally one piece until they were broken apart from each other, when fitted together they would match perfectly. This was a customary method for keeping agreements and contracts, with each of the two parties keeping one of the slips of wood.

11. Chapter of Universal Vision, sutra passage #27.

12. This is the opening passage from the *Diamond Sutra*. See *T* 235.8.748c21–23.

13. "Minister P'ei" is P'ei-hsiu (裴休; 797–870), a high official in the T'ang government. He was a devout practitioner of Buddhism, who developed close relationships with such major Buddhist figures as Tsung-mi and Huang-po. He is also intimately connected with the early dissemination of the *Sutra of Perfect Enlightenment*, having written a preface to Tsung-mi's major commentary on the sutra. This quote is a paraphrase of *Z* 243.9.323b21–22.

14. Here the practitioners are following a system by which they draw lots on which are written the instructions for the type of meditation they are to pursue during a meditation retreat.

15. The first line of the Buddha's teaching in this chapter.

16. The True Man of No Status (*wu-i shen-jen* 無位眞人) was one of Lin-chi's creations. In the *Lin-chi lu* we read: "Beyond the red-flesh group there is one True Man of No Status who constantly goes in and out of the front gates (sense organs) of all of you people." *T* 1985.47.496c9–10.

17. A distinction is being made here in a feudal-like system where the realm at large consists of two main parts: the domains of the emperor's own family, and the surrounding lands that are controlled by vassals.

18. In Confucian political thought, it is a poor reflection on the government if there is a person of outstanding abilities among the populace who is, for some

reason or other, not working in some capacity for the administration of the realm. This is a "neglected Worthy."

19. 曲成無遺. See the *I Ching*, Hsi-tz'u chuan, section 1. Ŭich'ŏn uses the same phrase in his essay on the *SPE*. See *HPC* 4.532a10.

20. Here Kihwa has given his interpretation of this passage by altering its form somewhat from the way it appears in the sutra.

21. The "six states" are the six competing kingdoms of the Chinese "warring states" period (403–221 BCE): the Han 韓, Wei 魏, Chao 趙, Yen 燕, Ch'i 齋, and Ch'u 楚.

9. Purifier of All Karmic Hindrances

1. The doctrine of the subtle and coarse marks is developed in the *Awakening of Faith*. See *T* 1666.32.577c26 ff.

2. "Tamer" is one of the ten epithets of the Buddha.

3. That is, within nonduality.

4. The doctrine of these "four traces (四相)" predates the *Sutra of Perfect Enlightenment*, being a prominent component of the discourse of the *Diamond Sutra*. Despite the fact that in his commentary, Kihwa states that the Four Traces of the *SPE* have a different connotation from those of the *Diamond Sutra*, some basic introduction to the concepts in the context of the *Diamond Sutra* is still helpful in following this discussion. In providing this background, I quote a lucid and concise portion of the commentary done on the *Diamond Sutra* by the contemporary Vietnamese Zen master Thich Nhat Hanh (*The Diamond That Cuts Through Illusion*, pp. 38–40), which reads as follows:

> "Self (我)" refers to a permanent, changeless identity, but since, according to Buddhism, nothing is permanent and what we normally call a self is made entirely of non-self elements, there is really no such entity as a self. Our concept of self arises when we have concepts about things that are not-self. . . . The concept of "person (人)" like the concept of self, is made only of nonperson elements—sun, clouds, wheat, space, and so on. Thanks to these elements, there is something we call a person. But erecting a barrier between the idea of person and the idea of nonperson is erroneous. . . . The concept of "living being (衆生)," *sattva* in Sanskrit, arises the moment we separate living from nonliving beings . . . but what we call nonliving makes what we call living beings possible. If we destroy the nonliving, we destroy the living. . . . We usually think of "life-span (壽命)" as the length of our life, beginning the moment we are born and ending when we die. We believe that we are alive during that period, no before or after. And while we are alive, we think that everything in us is life, not death.

5. The five *gati*: the hells, hungry ghosts, animals, human beings, devas.

6. *Saṃskṛta* (有爲) is translated into English as "conditioned," "compounded," or "created." Its two root components are *sam-*, which means

together, compounded, gathered (as in *saṃsāra, samutpāda, saṃgha,* etc.), and *kṛ,* which means "creation" (as in *karma*). Thus it refers to all of existence that is continually recreated through the joining of causes and conditions. *Asaṃskṛta* (無爲) or "unconditioned" is its antonym, created by the addition of an *a-* privative, meaning "un-" or "non-."

7. Kihwa makes this point because the Buddhist technical term *hsiang-hsü* 相續 has a special technical connotation in Fa-hsiang (Consciousness-only) discourse, that should not be read into the present discussion. Here the term refers merely to the unbroken continuity of struggle through *saṃsāra.*

8. Sutra passage #91.

9. Sutra passage #94.

10. Here, Luk translates *wu* (我 "self") as "ego."

11. At this point Luk translates *cheng/chŭng* 證 as "experience" where I have translated it as "witness." In some respects, his translation is smooth, and reflects clearly and simply the gist of the passage. The problem that I see in his translation, however, is that he does not render the term consistently, and instead of maintaining a uniform translation of *cheng* as "experience," switches back and forth to such terms as "realize" and "evidencing" within the same section, which makes it difficult for the reader to understand the structure of the discourse. He is also inconsistent in the same way with his translation of the other four terms. My somewhat rigid usage of "witness" is done in order to clearly distinguish *cheng* as a technical term in this chapter. I will also hold strcitly to a single rendering of the cognitive operations associated with the other traces in similar fashion.

12. That is, does not repeat the same mental function of witnessing "selfhood."

13. The cognition of "self" and "other" is the cognition of the prior "trace of person."

14. Here I follow Kihwa's reading of the passage, which links the phrase *chiao suo liao che* 覺所了者 to the passage before it. Luk and Yanagida link this phrase to the subsequent passage.

15. The meanings of "inner worldling" and "outer worldling" are discussed in the commentary to sutra passage #21 in the chapter of Samantabhadra.

16. Here, the word being translated as "awareness" is *chüeh* 覺, which has been rendered in the rest of the text as "enlightenment." I have rendered it differently in this section of this chapter to reflect a different usage. But here, both meanings are being merged into one, and thus, from this point, the meaning of "enlightenment" is also included.

17. Below, last line of sutra passage #95.

18. In Yanagida Seizan's translation of the *Engakukyō* (p. 195), this sentence is kept together with the prior paragraph, serving as its concluding passage—a rhetorical question which decries the impossibility of considering any dharma as "nonliberation." This means that he has also understood the structure of the prior line to be as I have mentioned in note 14, rather than as Kihwa sees it.

19. Genuine Teacher is a translation of *shan-chih-shih/sŏnjisik* (善智識 literally "good consciousness"), which is in turn the Chinese translation of the Sanskrit

kalyāṇa-mitra. This person is a reliable teacher with the correct insight who can properly help one along the Buddhist path.

20. Sutra passage #91 above.

10. Universal Enlightenment

1. "Practices of purity." A perfectly pure morality: literally, "the practices of Brahma."

2. Walking, standing, sitting, and lying down.

3. This last line reads a bit strangely. If it were not the case that Kihwa directly treats this odd structure below, I would rework the translation to make it smooth. But since Kihwa treats this line just below, I have translated the Chinese directly as it appears.

4. The first line in the above sutra passage.

5. Above, sutra passage #101.

11. Perfect Enlightenment

1. The "specific" (*pieh/pyŏl* 別) and "universal" (*pien/p'yŏn* 徧) can be understood as the discriminated teaching, or relative truth and the nondiscriminated teaching, or absolute truth. The "specific" can also refer to a teaching for people of specific capacities, with "universal" referring to a teaching that is appropriate for all beings.

2. "Wisdom" (*hye/hui* 慧) and "life" (*ming/myŏng* 命) are considered the essences of mind and body, respectively.

3. 心意蕩然獲大安隱。 From the prior chapter, last line of sutra passage #91.

4. Most importantly teaching and guiding other monks, nuns, and lay believers.

5. Banners and flowers are used to decorate the monastery during special events.

6. The meaning of the phrase *pu chia t'u chung* 不假徒衆, which I have translated as "free . . . from involvements with other practitioners" is not explained in detail by Kihwa. Tsung-mi understands it as involvements with one's fellow practitioners. Yanagida renders it "don't take any followers"; Luk says, "avoid being served by followers of Hīnayāna."

7. These are the Sanskrit terms for monk, nun, male lay practitioner, and female lay practitioner.

8. Tsung-mi identifies the "other practitioners" as those constrained by the customs of the Hīnayāna retreat.

9. From chapter 7, sutra passage #76.

10. It seems that Kihwa is following the interpretation of Tsung-mi here, in that there are apparently another group of (Hīnayāna?) practitioners following

a standardized schedule of a full summer retreat. Once one has completed his own retreat according to the guidelines given in this sutra, he is free to do as he pleases.

12. Most Excellent of Worthies

1. The term *hsien* 賢, translated here as "Worthy," has a long history in Confucian tradition, referring to a man of superior intellectual and moral qualities who would be eminently capable of handling a position of heavy responsibility in government. The Worthy was considered to be a category below that of sage (*sheng-jen* 聖人), a term usually reserved for founders of entire thought-systems: men such as Confucius, or legendary cultural heroes such as Yao and Shun.

2. One who is fully capable of understanding and trusting in the Buddhist teachings.

3. In Chinese, *hua-yen* 華嚴. *Hwaŏm* is the world "adorned by multifarious flowers, the world of perfect interpenetration" (*sa-sa-mu-ae* 事事無礙).

4. The highest stage in the Hwaŏm scheme, which Kihwa mentions in his introduction.

5. The awkward wording of this sutra passage is treated by Kihwa in his commentary directly below.

6. A *yojana* is an ancient Indian measure of distance. Depending upon the source, either seven or nine miles, the distance appropriate for one day's travel for an emperor.

7. Eight kinds of beings from Indian mythology. Formerly they were evil, but now having been converted by the Buddha, they protect his dharma. They are: (1) *devas* [gods] , (2) *nāgas* [snake kings], (3) *yakṣas* [spirits of the dead who fly about in the night], (4) *gandharvas* [half-ghost music masters], (5) *asuras* [demi-gods of evil disposition], (6) *garuḍas* [golden-winged birds that eat dragons] (7) *kiṃnaras* [neither human nor not human], and (8) *mahoragas* [snake spirits].

Works Cited

Kihwa's Works
(In the *Han'guk pulgyo chŏnsŏ* 韓國佛教全書)

Kŭmgang panyaparamilgyŏng o ka hae sŏrŭi 金剛般若波羅蜜經五家解説
誼 (Annotation to the Redaction of Five Commentaries on the *Diamond
Sutra*). *HPC* 7.10–107.

Kŭmgang panyaparamilgyŏng yun kwan 金剛般若波羅蜜經綸貫 (The
Penetrating Thread of the *Diamond Sutra*). *HPC* 7.116–21.

Taebanggwang wŏn'gak sutara youi kyŏng sŏrŭi 大方廣圓覺修多羅了義
經説誼 (Commentary on the *Sutra of Perfect Enlightenment*). *HPC*
7.122–69.

Sŏnjong yŏnggajip kwaju sŏrŭi 禪宗永嘉集科註説誼 (Annotated Redaction of the Text and Commentaries to the Compilation of Yung-
chia of the Ch'an School). *HPC* 7.170–216.

Hyŏn chŏng non 顯正論 (Exposition of the Correct). *HPC* 7.217–25.

Hamhŏ tang tŭkt'ong hwasang ŏrok 涵虛堂得通和尚語録 (The Record
of the Teachings of the Reverend Hamhŏ Tŭkt'ong). *HPC* 7.226–50.

Hamhŏ tang tŭkt'ong hwasang haengjang 涵虛堂得通和尚行状 (The Life
of Reverend Hamhŏ Tŭkt'ong, by his student Yabu). *HPC* 7.250–52.

Classical East Asian Buddhist Texts:
Chinese Titles (excluding *SPE*-related works)

Ch'an-tsung Yung-chia chi 禪宗永嘉集. By Yung-chia Hsüan-chüeh 永
嘉玄覺. *T* 2013. 48.387b–395c.

Ch'eng-tao k'o 證道歌 (Song of Enlightenment). By Yung-chia Hsüan-
chüeh 永嘉玄覺; *T* 2014.48.395c–396c.

Chin-kang ching chieh-i 金剛經解義 (Explanation of the Meaning of the
Diamond Sutra). By Hui-neng 慧能. *Z* 459.24.517–35.

Chin-kang ching shu-lun tsuan-yao 金剛經疏論纂要 (Collected Essentials of the *Diamond Sutra*). By Tsung-mi 宗密. *T* 1701.33.154–69

Chin-kang po-jo po-lo-mi ching 金剛般若波羅蜜經 (Diamond Sutra). *T* 235.8.748c–752c.

Chin-kang san-mei ching 金剛三昧經 (Vajrasamādhi-sūtra). *T* 273.9.365c–374b.

Ching-te chuan-teng lu 景德傳燈録 (Ching-te Record of the Transmission of the Lamp). By Tao-yüan 道原. *T* 2076.51.196–468.

Hsin Hua-yen ching lun 新華嚴經論 (Treatise on the New Translation of the *Flower Ornament Scripture*), 40 fasc. By Li T'ung-hsüan 李通玄. *T* 1739.36.721–1007.

Hua-yen ching. See *Ta-fang-kuang fo hua-yen ching*.

Ju leng chia ching 入楞伽經 (Laṅkāvatāra-sūtra). Trans. Śikṣānanda 實叉難陀. *T* 671.16. 514–86.

K'ai-yüan shih-chiao lu 開元釋教録 (The K'ai-yüan Catalog of Buddhist Texts). By Chih-sheng 智昇. *T* 2154.55.477–723.

Leng-chia a-pa-to-lo pao-ching 楞伽阿跋多羅實經 (Laṅkāvatāra-sūtra). trans. Gunabhadra. *T* 670.16.480a–514b.

Liu-tsu t'an ching 六祖壇經 (Platform Sutra of the Sixth Patriarch). *T* 2008.48.346a–362b.

Miao-fa lien-hua ching 妙法蓮華經 (Lotus Sutra). *T* 262.9.1a–63.

Ta chih-tu lun 大智度論 (Mahāprajñā-pāramitā-śāstra). Attributed to Nāgārjuna, trans. by Kumārajīva. *T* 1509.25.57c–756b.

Ta-sheng ch'i-hsin lun 大乘起信論 (Treatise on Awakening of Mahāyāna Faith). Attributed to Aśvaghoṣa. *T* 1665.32.575b–583b.

Ta-fang-kuang fo hua-yen ching 大方廣佛華嚴經 (Avataṃsaka-sūtra) [Flower Ornament Scripture], 60 fasc. Trans. by Buddhabhadra 佛馱跋陀. *T* 278.9.395a–788b.

Ta-fang-kuang fo hua-yen ching 大方廣佛華嚴經 (Avataṃsaka-sūtra) [Flower Ornament Scripture] 80 fasc. Trans. by Śikṣānanda 實叉難陀. *T* 279.10.1b–444c.

Tsung-ching lu 宗鏡録 (Record of the Source Mirror). By Yen-shou 延壽. *T* 2016.48.415–956.

Yung-chia chi 永嘉集. See *Ch'an-tsung Yung-chia chi*.

Classical East Asian Buddhist Texts
(not commentaries on *SPE*): Korean Titles

Chegyŏng hoeyo 諸經會要 (Diagrammatic Essentials of the Scriptures). By Ch'oenul 最吶. *HPC* 10.26–59.

Chinsim chiksŏl 眞心直説 (Straight Talk on the True Mind). By Chinul 知訥. *HPC* 4.715a–723c.

Chogye chin'gak kuksa ŏrok 曹溪眞覺國師語録 (The Teaching Record of the National Teacher Chin'gak). By Hyesim 慧諶. *HPC* 6.1–49.

Ijang ŭi 二障義 (Doctrine of the Two Hindrances). By Wŏnhyo 元曉. *HPC* 1.789–814.

Hwaŏm ilsŭng pŏpkye to 華嚴一乘法界圖 (Chart of the Single Vehicle Hua-yen Dharmadhātu). By Ŭisang 義湘. *T* 1887A.45.711a–716a.

Hwaŏm non chŏryo 華嚴論節要 (Essentials of the *Hua-yen lun*). By Chinul. *HPC* 4.767–869.

Kisillon so 起信論疏 (Commentary on the *Awakening of Faith*). By Wŏnhyo. *HPC* 1.698–722; *T* 1844.44.202a–226a.

Kŭmgang sammaegyŏng non 金剛三昧經論 (Treatise on the *Sutra of Adamantine Absorption*). By Wŏnhyo. *T* 1730.34.961a–1008a.

Naong hwasang ŏrok 懶翁和尚語録 (The Teaching Record of the Reverend Naong). *HPC* 6.702b–729c.

Paeg'un hwasang ŏrok 白雲和尚語録 (The Teaching Record of the Reverend Paeg'un). By Kyŏnghan 景閑. *HPC* 6.637a–668c.

Pŏpjip pyŏrhaeng nok chŏryo pyŏng'ip sagi 法集別行録節要并入私記 (Excerpts from the Dharma Collection and Special Practice Record with Personal Notes). By Chinul. *HPC* 7.740a–767b.

Samga kwigam 三家龜鑑 (Teaching Precedents from the Masters of the Three Traditions). By Hyujŏng 休靜. *HPC* 7.626a–634b.

Simmun hwajaeng non 十門和諍論 (Reconciliation of Disputes in Ten Aspects). By Wŏnhyo. *HPC* 1.838–841. [Fragments].

Sŏnmun yŏmsongjip 禪門拈頌集 (Compilation of Examinations of and Verses on Ancient Precedents). By Hyesim. *HPC* 5.1–925.

Sŏn'ga kwigam 禪家龜鑑 (Teaching Precedents from the Sŏn School). By Hyujŏng. *HPC* 7.634c–646a.

Soyodangjip 逍遙堂集 (Collected Works of Master Soyo). By T'ae-nŭng 太能. *HPC* 185a–200b.

Taegak kuksa munjip 大覺國師文集 (The Collected Writings of Ŭich'ŏn). *HPC* 4.528–567.

Taesŭng kisillon pyŏlgi 大乘起信論別記 (Expository Notes on the *Awakening of Faith*). By Wŏnhyo. *HPC* 1.677–697; *T* 1845.44.226a–240c.

Taesŭng kisillon so pyŏlgi hoebon 大乘起信論疏別記會本 (Combined Version of Wŏnhyo's Commentary and Expository Notes on the *Awakening of Faith*). *HPC* 1.733–88.

Wŏndon sŏngpullon 圓頓成佛論 (The Perfect and Sudden Attainment of Buddhahood). By Chinul. *HPC* 4.724a–732b.

Yŏlban chong'yo 涅槃宗要 (Essentials of the *Nirvāṇa Sutra*). By Wŏnhyo. *T* 1769.38.239a–255c.

Yŏngwŏldang taesa munjip 詠月堂大師文集 (The Collected Works of Yŏngwŏl). By Ch'ŏnghak 清學. *HPC* 8.221c–236c

The *Yüan chüeh ching* and
Its Chinese and Korean Commentaries

Yüan chüeh ching 圓覺經 (Sutra of Perfect Enlightenment). *T* 842.17.913a–922a.

Chinese Commentaries Contained in Buddhist Canonical Collections

Yüan chüeh ching ta shu 圓覺經大疏 (Great Commentary on the *Sutra of Perfect Enlightenment*). Tsung-mi. Z 243.9.324a–418b

Yüan chüeh ching ta shu 圓覺經大疏 (Great Commentary on the *Sutra of Perfect Enlightenment*), 12 fasc. Tsung-mi. Z 243.9.324a–418b.

Yüan chüeh ching ta shu ch'ao 圓覺經大疏鈔 (Subcommentary to the Great Commentary on the *Sutra of Perfect Enlightenment*), 26 fasc. Tsung-mi. Z 245.9.460–757.

Yüan chüeh ching ta shu ch'ao k'o 圓覺經大疏鈔科 (Outline to the Subcommentary of the *Sutra of Perfect Enlightenment*), 3 fasc. (first two fascicles missing). Tsung-mi. Z 244.9.419–459

Yüan chüeh ching lüeh shu 圓覺經略疏 (Abridged Commentary to the *Sutra of Perfect Enlightenment*). Tsung-mi. *T* 1795.39.523b–576b; Z 247.9.789–821.

Yüan chüeh ching lüeh shu k'o 圓覺經略疏科 (Outline of the Abridged Commentary). Tsung-mi. Z 246.9.758–88.

Yüan chüeh ching lüeh shu ch'ao 圓覺經略疏鈔 (Abridged Subcommentary to the *Sutra of Perfect Enlightenment*). Tsung-mi. Z 248.9.821–959.

Yüan chüeh ching tao-ch'ang hsiu-cheng i 圓覺經道場修證儀 (Manual of Procedures for the Cultivation of Realization of Ritual Practice According to the *Sutra of Perfect* Enlightenment), 18 fasc. Tsung-mi. Z 1475.74.375–512.

Yüan chüeh ching tao-ch'ang lüeh pen hsiu-cheng i 圓覺經道場略本修證儀 (An Abridged Commentary to 'Manual of Procedures for the Cultivation of Realization of Ritual Practice According to the *Sutra of Perfect Enlightenment*'), 1 fasc. Ching-yüan 淨源. Z 1476.74.512–17.

Yüan chüeh ching ch'ao pien i wu 圓覺經疏鈔辯疑誤 (Treating Doubts and Errors in the Subcommentary to the *Sutra of Perfect Enlightenment*), 2 fasc. Kuan-fu 觀復. Z 249.10.1–11.

Yüan chüeh ching lui chieh 圓覺經類解 (Various Understandings of the *Sutra of Perfect Enlightenment*), 8 fasc. Hsing-t'ing 行霆. Z 252.10.167–237.

Yüan chüeh ching shu ch'ao sui wen yao chieh 圓覺經疏鈔隨文要解 (Explanations of Pivotal Passages of the Text of Tsung-mi's Subcommentary), 12 fasc. Ch'ing-yüan 清遠. Z 250.10.12–151.

Yü chu yüan chüeh ching 御注圓覺經 (The Imperial Commentary to the *Sutra of Perfect Enlightenment*), Hsiao-tsung 孝宗. Z 251.10.151–66.

Yüan chüeh ching chi chu 圓覺經集註 (Collected Notes on the *Sutra of Perfect Enlightenment*), 2 fasc. Chü-chien, Yüan-ts'ui 元粹, Tsung-mi. Z 257.10.437–79.

Yüan chüeh ching hsü chu 圓覺經序註 (Notes on the Preface to the *Sutra of Perfect Enlightenment*), 1 fasc. Ju-shan 如山. Z 255.10.433–35.

Yüan chüeh ching lüeh shu hsü chu 圓覺經略疏序註 (Notes on the Preface to Tsung-mi's Abridged Commentary to the *Sutra of Perfect Enlightenment*), 1 fasc. Ju-shan. Z 256.10.435–38.

Yüan chüeh ching hsin ching 圓覺經心鏡 (The Mind-Mirror of the *Sutra of Perfect Enlightenment*), 6 fasc. Chi-ts'ung 智聰. Z 254.10.378–432.

Yüan chüeh ching chia sung chi chiang-i 圓覺經夾頌集講義 (Collected Lectures of Chiao on the *Sutra of Perfect Enlightenment*), 12 fasc. Chou-ch'i 周琪. Z 253.10.238–377.

Yüan chüeh ching chin shih 圓覺經近釋 (A Close Exegesis of the *Sutra of Perfect Enlightenment*), 6 fasc. T'ung-jun 通潤. Z 259.10.510–42.

Yüan chüeh ching chih chieh 圓覺經直解 (Direct Explanation of the *Sutra of Perfect Enlightenment*), 2 fasc. Te-ch'ing 德清. Z 258.10.480–509. Translated into English by Lu K'uan Yü together with his translation of the sutra.

Yüan chüeh ching yao chieh 圓覺經要解 (Explanation of the Essentials of the *Sutra of Perfect Enlightenment*), 2 fasc. Chi-cheng 寂正. Z 260.10 .543–73.

Yüan chüeh ching ching chieh hsü lin 圓覺經精解評林 (Seminal Explanations on the *Sutra of Perfect Enlightenment*), 2 fasc. (first fascicle only extant). Chiao-k'uang 琪竑. Z 261.10.573–99.

Yüan chüeh ching chu shih cheng pai 圓覺經句釋正白 (Correct Explanation of the Text of the *Sutra of Perfect Enlightenment*), Hung-li 弘麗. Z 262.10.599–693.

Yüan chüeh ching che i shu 圓覺經折義疏 (Discerning the Meaning of the Commentary to the *Sutra of Perfect Enlightenment*), 4 fasc. T'ung-li 通理. Z 263.10.694–770.

Classical Korean Commentaries

Kang wŏn'gak kyŏng palsa 講圓覺經發辭 (Some Words Regarding the Exposition of the *Sutra of Perfect Enlightenment*). Ŭich'ŏn 義天. In *Taegak kuksa munjip* 大覺國師文集. HPC 4.531–32.

Taebangkwang wŏn'gak sutara ryo ŭi kŏng sŏrui 大方廣圓覺了義經説誼 (Commentary on the *Sutra of Perfect Enlightenment*), 3 fasc. Hamhŏ Tŭkt'ong (Kihwa) 涵虛得通 (己和). HPC 7.122–69.

Wŏn'gakkyŏng kyŏngch'an so 圓覺經慶讚疏. By Hyujŏng. HPC 7.714a.

Ŏ chŏng ku kyŏlbŏn sŏk taebanggwang wŏn'gak sutara ryo ŭi kyŏng. 御定口訣 翻譯大方廣圓覺修多羅了義經 10 fasc. Se Cho-ŏ 世祖御. Chŏnju Anshim-sa Changpan 全州安心寺蔵板.

Wŏn'gakkyŏng sagi 圓覺經私記 (Personal Notes on the *Sutra of Perfect Enlightenment*), 1 fasc. Ŭich'ŏm 義沾. Dongguk University Photocopy Edition.

Modern Works

An, Kyehyŏn. *Han'guk pulgyo sasang sa yŏngu* (Studies in the History of Korean Buddhist Thought). Seoul: Dongguk University Press, 1982.

Barnestone, Willis. *The Other Bible: Ancient Esoteric Texts*. San Francisco: HarperCollins, 1984.

Buswell, Robert E. *The Korean Approach to Zen: The Collected Works of Chinul*. Honolulu: University of Hawaii Press, 1983.

———, ed. *Chinese Buddhist Apocrypha*. Honolulu: University of Hawaii Press, 1989.

———. *The Formation of Ch'an Ideology in China and Korea*. Princeton: Princeton University Press, 1989.

———. *Tracing Back the Radiance: Chinul's Korean Way of Zen*. Honolulu: University of Hawaii Press, 1991.

———. *The Zen Monastic Experience*. Princeton: Princeton University Press, 1992.

Ch'en, Kenneth. *Buddhism in China: A Historical Survey*. Princeton: Princeton University Press, 1964.

Cho Myŏnggi, ed. *Han'guk pulgyo sasang sa* (The Pak Kiljin Festschrift). Seoul, 1975.

Chong Pyong-cho. *Han'guk chonggyo sasangsa* (A History of Korean Religious Thought). Seoul: Yonsei University Press, 1991.

Chung Oh Shin. *Seisan daishi no zenke kikan kenkyū* (西山大師の禅家亀鑑研究). Tokyo: Sankibo busshorin, 1991.

Forte, Antonino. "The Relativity of the Concept of Orthodoxy in Chinese Buddhism: Chih-sheng's Indictment of Shih-li and the *Proscription of the Dharma Mirror Sutra*." In Buswell, *Chinese Buddhist Apocrypha*.

Goulde, John Isaac. "Anti-Buddhist Polemic in Fourteenth and Fifteenth Century Korea: The Emergence of Confucian Exclusivism." Ph.D. dissertation, Harvard University, 1985.

Gregory, Peter N. "The Problem of Theodicy in the *Awakening of Faith*." *Religious Studies* 22 (1986): 63–78.

———. *Tsung-mi and the Sinification of Buddhism*. Princeton: Princeton University Press, 1991.

Hakeda Yoshitō, trans. *The Awakening of Faith*. New York: Columbia University Press, 1967.

Hanh, Thich Nhat. *The Diamond That Cuts Through Illusion: Commentaries on the Prajñaparamita Diamond Sutra*. Berkeley, Calif.: Parallax Press, 1992.

Heo, Heung-sik. *Han'guk chungse pulgyosa yŏn'gu* (A Study of the History of Medieval Korean Buddhism). Seoul: Ilchogak, 1994.

Hirakawa, Akira. *Daijōkishinron*. Tokyo: Daizō shuppan, 1973.

Kamata, Shigeo. *Chūgoku Kegon shisōshi no kenkyū*. Tokyo, 1965.

———. *Shūmitsu kyōgaku no shisōshiteki kenkyū*. Tokyo, 1975.

———. *Chōsen bukkyōshi*. Tokyo: Tokyo University Press, 1987.

Keel, Hee-Sung. *Chinul: The Founder of the Korean Sŏn Tradition*. Berkeley Buddhist Studies Series. Seoul: Po Chin Chai, 1984.

Kodera, Takashi James. *Dōgen's Formative Years in China: An Historical Study and Annotated Translation of the Hōkyōki*. Boulder, Colo.: Prajna Press, 1980.

Kwŏn, Kijong. "Chosŏn chŏngi ŭi sŏngyo kwan" ("The Sŏn-Kyo Standpoint of the Early Chosŏn"). In Yi, ed., *Han'guk sŏn sasang yŏngu* (245–82).

Lancaster, Lewis and Sung Bae Park. *The Korean Buddhist Canon: A Descriptive Catalog*. Berkeley: University of California Press, 1979.

Lee, Kibaik. *A New History of Korea*. Trans. Edward W. Wagner. Cambridge: Harvard University Press, 1984.

Lee, Peter H, ed. *Sourcebook of Korean Civilization*. Vol. 1. New York: Columbia University Press, 1993.

Legge, James. *Analects, Great Learning and Doctrine of the Mean*. New York: Dover Publications, 1971

Lu, K'uan Yü (Charles Luk). *Ch'an and Zen Teaching*. Berkeley, Calif.: Shambhala Publications, 1962.

Mizuno, Kogen. *Buddhist Sūtras: Origin, Development, Transmission.* Tokyo: Kosei Publishing, 1980.

Mochizuki Shinkō. *Bukkyō kyōten seiritsushi ron.* Kyoto: Hōzōkan, 1946.

Muller, A. Charles. "Hamhŏ Kihwa: A Study of His Major Works." Ph.D. diss. SUNY Stony Brook, 1993.

———. "The Composition of Self-Transformation Thought in Classical East Asian Philosophy and Religion." *Bulletin of Toyo Gakuen University* 4 (March 1996): 141–52.

———. "East Asia's Unexplored Pivot of Metaphysics and Hermeneutics: Essence-Function/Interpenetration." WWWeb document: http://www. human.toyogakuen-u.ac.jp/~acmuller/articles/indigenoushermeneutics. htm. 1997.

———. "The Buddhist-Confucian Conflict in the Early Chosŏn and Kihwa's Syncretic Response: The *Hyŏn chŏng non.*" Paper delivered at the Annual Meeting of the American Academy of Religion, Chicago, November 18–22, 1994. WWWeb document: http://www.human .toyogakuen-u.ac.jp/~acmuller/budkor/aar-hcn.htm.

———. "Kihwa's Analysis of the Relationship between the Worded and Wordless Teachings: The *O ka hae sŏrŭi.*" *Journal of Korean Thought* 1 (forthcoming).

Nakamura Hajime. *Bukkyōgo daijiten.* Tokyo, 1975.

Ono Gemmyō. *Bussho kaisetsu daijiten.* 13 vols. Tokyo: Daitō shuppansha, 1933.

Park, Chong Hong. *Han'guk sasang sa: Pulgyo sasang p'yŏn.* Seoul, 1976.

Park, Sung Bae. *Buddhist Faith and Sudden Enlightenment.* Albany: State University of New York Press Press, 1983.

———. *Wŏnhyo's Commentaries on the Awakening of Mahāyāna Faith.* State University of New York Press Press, forthcoming

Price, A. F. *The Diamond Sutra and the Sutra of Hui-neng.* Boston: Shambhala Publications, 1969.

Rhi, Kiyong. *Han'guk pulgyo yŏn'gu* (Studies in Korean Buddhism). Seoul: Han'guk pulgyo yon'guwŏn, 1982.

Sakaino Kōyō. *Engakukyō* (Japanese translation of the *Yüan chüeh ching*). *Kokuyaku issai kyō.* Tokyo: Daitō shuppanshu, 1988. Kyōshū (Sutra Collection), vol. 5, pp. 309–41.

Shim, Jae Ryong. "The Philosophical Foundation of Korean Zen Buddhism: The Integration of *Sŏn* and *Kyo* by Chinul (1158–1210)." Ph.D. dissertation, University of Hawaii, 1979.

Smith, Barbara Herrnstein. "Contingencies of Value." In von Hallberg, ed., *Canons,* (pp. 5–39).

Song Ch'ŏnŭn. "Kihwa ŭi sasang" ("Kihwa's Thought"). In Cho Myŏnggi, ed., *Han'guk pulgyo sasang sa* (Pak Kiljin Festschrift)

Song, Hwan-gi. "Hamhŏ tŭkt'ong hwasang yŏn'gu" (A Study of The Reverend Hamhŏ Tŭkt'ong). Master's thesis, Dongguk University, 1974.

Tongguk Taehakkyo Pulgyo Munhwa Yŏnguso, ed. *Kankoku bussho kaidai jiten*. Tokyo, Kokusho kankōkai, 1972.

Wilhelm, Richard. *The I-Ching*. Princeton: Princeton University Press, 1973.

von Hallberg, Robert, ed. *Canons*. Chicago: Chicago University Press, 1984.

Wu, Joung-Sang. *Chosŏn chŏngi pulgyo sasang sa yŏn'gu* (Studies of the Buddhist Thought of the Early Chosŏn). Seoul: Dongguk University Press, 1966.

Yampolsky, Philip, trans. *The Platform Sutra of the Sixth Patriarch*. New York: Columbia University Press, 1967

Yanagida, Seizan. *Engakukyō* (Japanese translation of the *Yüan chüeh ching*). *Chūgoku senjutsu kyōten*, no. 1. Tokyo: Chikuma shobō, 1987.

Yi, Jae-ch'ang, ed. *Han'guk sŏn sasang yŏngu* (Studies in Korean Sŏn Thought). Seoul: Dongguk University Press, 1984.

Index

abiding, correct. → correct abiding

abiding mark, 157, 158

accordance with enlightened nature, at the stage of faith, 160; by advanced bodhisattvas, 160; by beginner bodhisattvas, 160; by the Tathāgata, 162; by worldlings, 158; direct, 163

actualized enlightenment, defined, 294

acupuncture, 205

adornment, of correctly enlightened wisdom, 151; of the natural world, 150; of the realm of sentiency, 150

affection, as a cause of transmigration, 141

age of the degeneration of the true dharma, 210

agitation, 182, 200

ākāśa, 108, 129

ālayavijñāna see also store consciousness, 8, 14, 144, 204, 212

as-illusion *samādhi*, 90, 91, 175

altruism, 28

AMF, in the later Chosŏn, 37, *SPE* and, 19; Wŏnhyo and, 17

Analects, 10, 11, 34, 288

Ānanda, 65, 66, 296

anāsrava, 70

anger, 166, 167, 168, 183, 200, 203; in contrast to virtue and power, 166

annihilation, 46; malady of, 116, 117, 223, 224

anuttarā-samyak-saṃbodhi, achievable

through the help of Genuine Teacher, 220; meaning of, 56

apocrypha, 7, 8, 38; Abrahamic, 7, 287

arhat, 176; not qualified as Genuine Teacher, 220

arising mark, 157, 158

arousal of pure mind (bodhicitta), 73, 74

Asaṅga, 144

asaṃskṛta, 203

as-illusion meditation, practiced singly, 186

āsrava, 70

attached love, 44, 136, 140, 141; as basis of *saṃsāra*, 136, 141; conversion into compassion, 153; distinguished from compassion, 143; removal of, 142; transformed into kindness, 137

attachment, 147, 225; as impure, 110; severing, 140

attraction, 225; not in the nature of vision, 114

Avataṃsaka-sūtra see Hua-yen ching

aversion, 225; not in the nature of vision, 114

Awakening of Faith, 3, 5, 8, 9, 12, 13, 15, 20, 23, 34–38, 288, 289, 290–294, 297, 300, 303; cited, 289; essence-function in, 46; four marks and, 157; in Korea, 17; Single Voice doctrine in, 182; *SPE* and, 13, 14, 34; Wŏnhyo and, 18